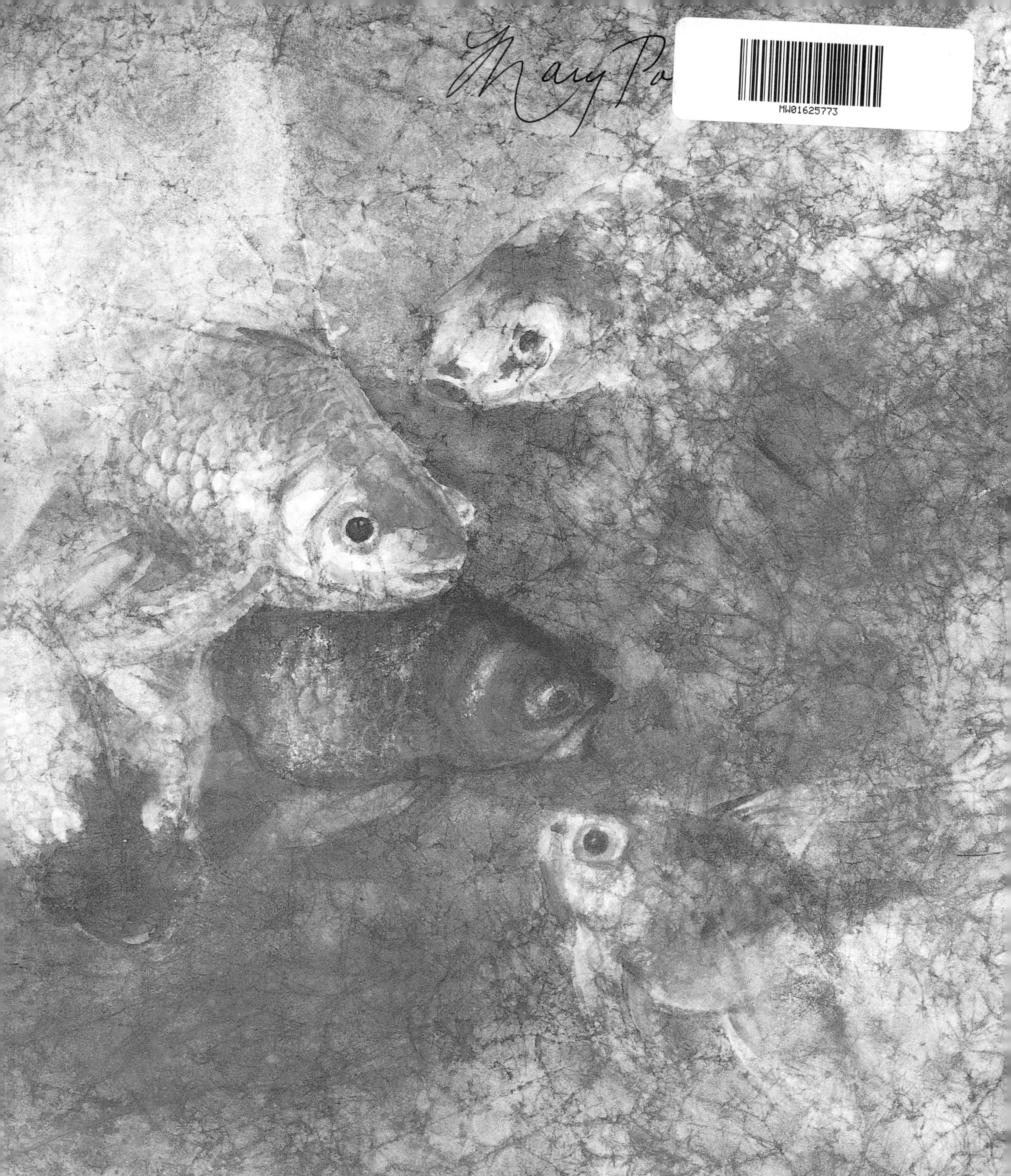
MW01625773

The Watercolor World of Cheng-Khee Chee

徐請沂水彩畫輯

陸儼少題

To
Mary Pat
With appreciation for
your friendship
Cheng-Khee Chee
AWS DF
9/23/2002

徐請沂

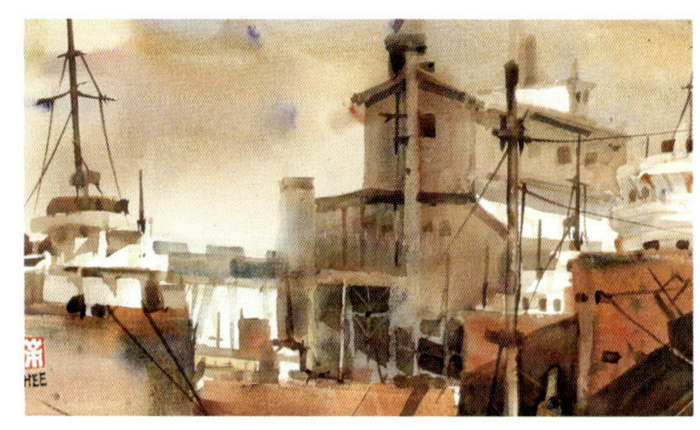

The Watercolor World of Cheng-Khee Chee

This publication is made possible by the generous support of the Potlatch Corporation, USA, in conjunction with Cheng-Khee Chee's One-Man Exhibition organized by the Singapore Art Museum, February 13 – March 3, 1997

First published in the United States of America in 1997
by Chee Studio
1508 Vermilion Road
Duluth, Minnesota 55812
Fax: (218)724-6153

Design and print production by Viscom Design Associates
10 Devonshire Road
Singapore 239846

Art direction by Sylvia SH Tan

Printed on Karma(R) 148gsm matte art paper from Potlatch
Printed and bound in Singapore

Library of Congress Catalog Card Number: 96-93027
ISBN 0-9655807-0-9

The Watercolor World of Cheng-Khee Chee

徐請沂水彩畫輯

陸儼少題

Introduction by Lok Tok

Singapore Art Museum
Chee Studio, Duluth, Minnesota

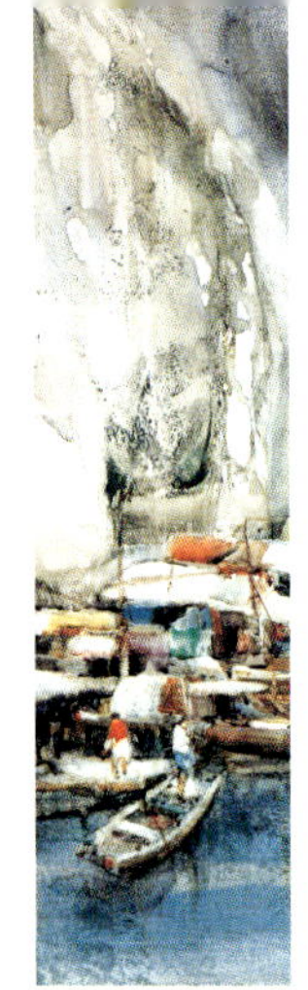

C o n t e n t s

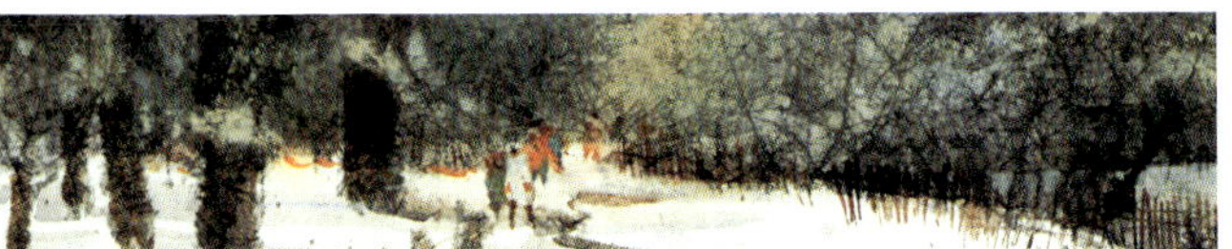

目 录

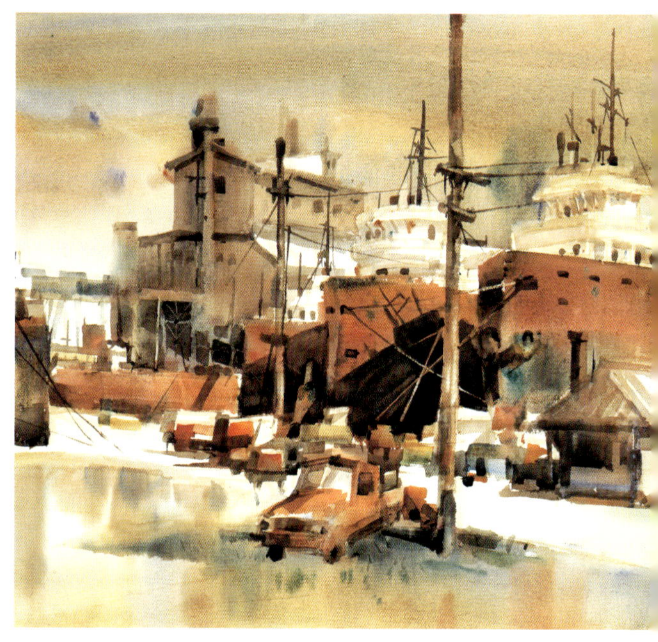

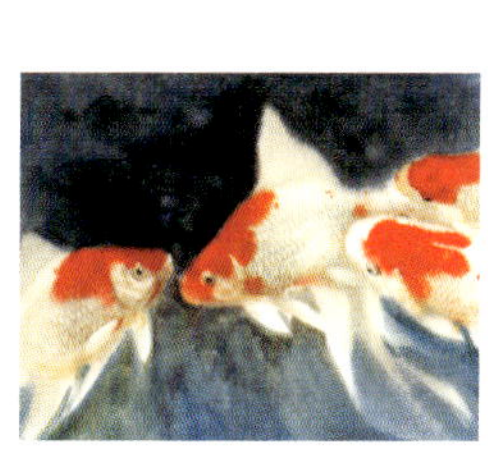

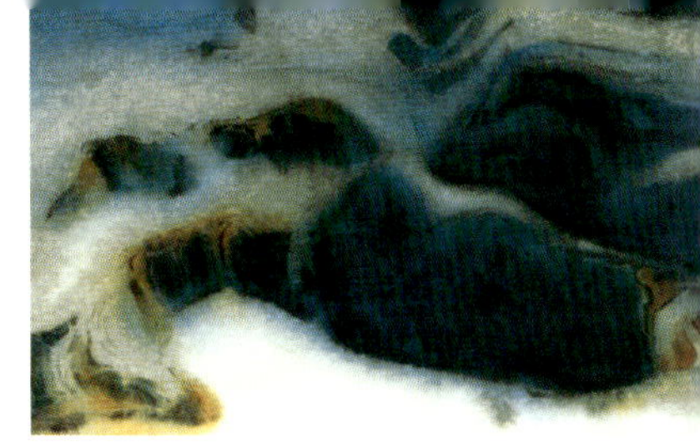

Foreword

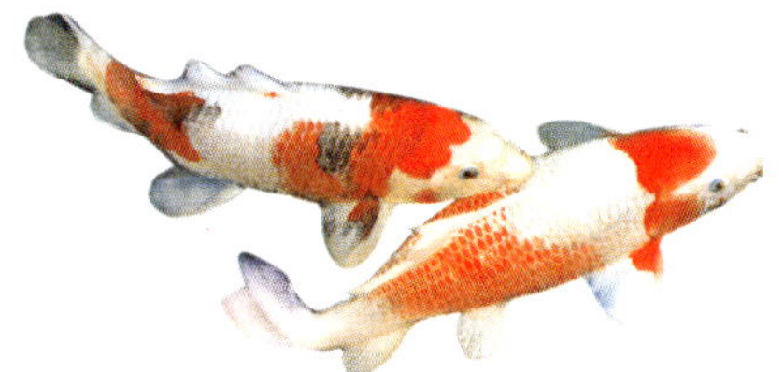

Cheng-Khee has won so many prestigious awards as a watercolorist that it seems superfluous to sing his praises, yet being Chinese, I enjoy adding flowers to embroidery.

Cheng-Khee was one of those artists favored by gods. Not only does he have the artistic talent, he was blessed with a favorable environment to nourish and develop his talent. He grew up in Penang, which after World War II became a flourishing centre of art activities. At that time there was a remarkable art patron, Mr Loh Cheng Chuan, whom all visiting artists looked for support. Mr Loh liked Cheng-Khee, and introduced him to many visiting artists. Cheng-Khee was fortunate also to come under the influence of many eminent artists of the region, including Yong Mun Sen, Tan Choon Ghee, Georgette Chen, Chuah Thean Teng, Kuo Ju Ping, Liu Kang, Cheong Soo Pieng and Chen Wen Hsi. However, what fired his imagination to become a watercolorist was a painting demonstration by Chinese-American watercolorist Dong Kingman at Han Chiang High School in Penang in 1953.

Cheng-Khee attended Library School at the University of Minnesota and worked as a librarian for some time after receiving his Master's Degree. In the meantime he continued to pursue watercolor painting. Eventually his talent matured and received broad national acclaim. He finally became a professor of art teaching watercolor painting at the University of Minnesota.

It is impossible for a Chinese painter with a foundation in Chinese education not to be influenced by Chinese thinking and the Chinese artistic tradition, especially in calligraphy and brush painting. However, the trend for Chinese painters in our time is to become international. Cheng-Khee's success is very much due to the fact that he is a very innovative international watercolorist, working mostly in the Western tradition, but enriched by the finer points of the Chinese painting tradition.

Cheng-Khee's work is international in the best sense. His mastery of the watercolor technique is brilliant, and the praise lavished on him is well deserved. It is with pleasure that I welcome his paintings to the Singapore Art Museum.

Dr Earl Lu
Chairman
Singapore Art Museum

前言

徐靖沂是一位获得许多重要奖项的杰出水彩画家，由我来赞美他，几乎是多馀的事，但身为华人，总是乐于锦上添花。

靖沂是一个得天独厚的艺术家。他不但先天赋有艺术才华，后天也得到良好的滋长环境。他十四岁在槟城长大。第二次世界大战后的槟城是一个繁荣的艺术活动中心。骆清泉先生是当时一位非凡的艺术护法和领导人。许多外地来访的画家都受惠于他。他很赏识靖沂，每每介绍他和这些外来的画家认识，使他得益良多。靖沂也很幸运地得到许多星马杰出画家的影响和启发，在槟城的有杨曼生、张荔英、蔡天定、陈存义、郭若萍等；在新加坡的有刘抗、钟泗滨、陈文希等。一九五三年美藉华人水彩画家曾景文先生在槟城的韩江中学作水彩画示范，这燃点起靖沂对水彩画热爱的火花，也启发了他的艺术想象力。

靖沂在美国明尼苏达大学攻读图书馆学硕士学位，毕业后留校任职。他同时在工馀之暇，不断从事水彩的探索和创作，作品渐臻成熟，获得画坛的肯定和赞许，明尼苏达大学也因此聘请他兼任水彩画教授。

一位受华文教育的华人画家，他的作品免不了受中国思想和艺术传统的影响，尤其是中国的书法和绘画。不过，当代华人画家的创作趋向是国际化。靖沂的成功可以说大部份由于他是一位杰出的国际水彩画家。虽然他的作品多数来自西方水彩的传统，但是中国绘画传统的影响使它们更加丰富多彩。

靖沂的作品是真正国际化的，他的水彩技法是高超的，赞美他的成就是他应得的，我热烈欢迎他的作品来新加坡美术馆展出。

卢明德医生

新加坡国家美术馆 主席

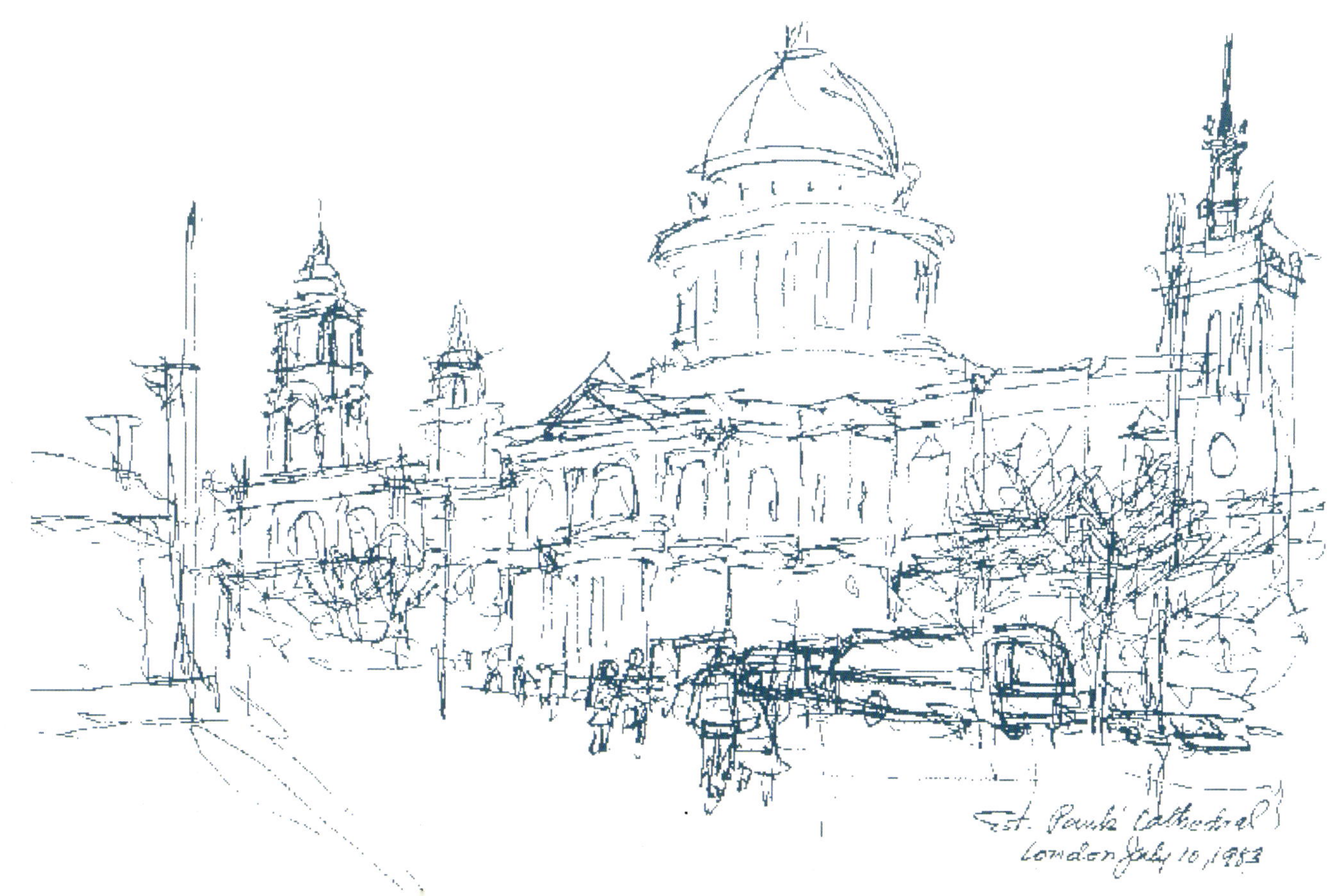

Introduction

Master Watercolorist Cheng-Khee Chee – Artist Who Advances the History of Watermedia by Lok Tok

Betsy Robinson, President of the Sumi-e Society of America, wrote: ' ... (Cheng-Khee Chee's) work embodies just about all the characteristics of spirit, poetry and the essence of truth... He belongs to no particular school or style and most of his work now transcends definition as either "Eastern or Western" ... It is also clear that just to learn brush strokes is not enough. The underlying mentality and philosophy of this art must also be absorbed. Cheng-Khee Chee's own spirit, his creativity and individuality are unique to him but his roots are so clearly in oriental brush painting. I believe that this brush painter's connection to the beauty and power of nature is precisely what makes his paintings so great and truthful.'

Time flies, history marches on, and art advances at a great pace. In 1986 I wrote an article about my friend Cheng-Khee Chee entitled "Professor Cheng-Khee Chee's World of Watercolor." Today, ten years later and in conjunction with his one-man exhibition at the Singapore Art Museum, he retrospectively selected his favorite award-winning paintings together with works of recent experimentation in a hard cover book to be published shortly. This is a great event in the art world, and I am very excited about it! Ten years may not be a long time, but Cheng-Khee's artistic accomplishments are impressive. As I read the published material and record of awards and activities, and view the empathic new work of this ten-year period, I am so overwhelmed by feelings of excitement that I must express them in writing.

The factors in Cheng-Khee's success are many and his artistic accomplishments numerous. He has a unique environment, great talent, broad knowledge, rich virtue, lofty ideals, great passion, unyielding determination, and indomitable spirit. He is farsighted, open-minded, and compassionate. He reveres tradition but is not limited by it. Instead, he synthesizes the ideas and techniques of both Eastern and Western traditions and comes up with his own innovations. His subject matter is varied, his techniques are diversified. Through this article, I would like to share with readers some of my personal observations and feelings.

His Unique Personal Environment

Cheng-Khee was born in 1934 in Fengting, a picturesque town on the southeast coast in Xianyou County of Fujian Province in China. It is surrounded by mountains, rivers, and green fields. His mother, who excelled in embroidery and needlepoint, was perhaps his first influence in art. He attended grade school there. Like all school children in China, he learned calligraphy and gained a firm foundation in Chinese brushwork. He emigrated to Penang, Malaysia in 1948 and was brought up by his uncle Lim Cheng-Leong. Penang is a beautiful island praised as 'The Pearl of the East'. It is populated with people of different races, including Chinese, Malay, Indian, and European.

After World War II, many famous Chinese scholars and artists came to Penang. My father Loh Cheng Chuan organized the Penang Art Society in 1953 and served as its president for many years. The Society held regular annual exhibitions and sponsored many cultural activities. My father also hosted many visiting artists and helped to organize their exhibitions. They all became his friends. The art community started to blossom. Professor Xu Beihong (1895-1953) graced the sign of the Penang Art Society with his calligraphy. My father enthusiastically promoted young talented artists. He encouraged Cheng-Khee to participate in Penang Art Society's annual exhibitions. They became very good friends.

Malaysia was still a British Colony at the time. The English watercolor painting strongly influenced the Penang art community. The self-taught watercolorist Yong Mun Sen (1896-1962), whose work was characterized by boldness and spontaneity, had a profound influence on Cheng-Khee. Tan Choon Ghee (b. 1930), a watercolorist educated in England, was Cheng-Khee's grade school art teacher. Georgette Liying Chen (1907-1992), an oil painter educated in Paris and New York, and Hu Chengxiang, a graduate of the Shanghai Art Academy in traditional Chinese painting, were his high school art teachers. Under these accomplished artists, he received excellent training and established a firm foundation in drawing and painting. He was also inspired and encouraged by many elder artists such as Chuah Thean Teng (b. 1914), Kuo Ju Ping (1908-1966), Lee Cheng Yong (1913-1974) and Khaw Sia (1913-1984) of Penang, and Liu Kang (b. 1911), Cheong Soo Pieng (1917-1983), Cheng Wen Hsi (1906-1992) of Singapore. The natural beauty of Penang and its rich artistic environment nourished his interest and passion for art and inspired him to pursue art with great enthusiasm and determination. Even when he was a student at Han Chiang High School, he organized the Han Chiang Art Club, utilizing all his spare time to paint. Many of its members later became active and accomplished artists. When in high school, he worked with all media. However, it was a painting demonstration by Chinese-American watercolorist Dong Kingman during his US State Department-sponsored goodwill tour in 1953 that set Cheng-Khee on his way to becoming a watercolorist.

Cheng-Khee faced a difficult decision when selecting a college major. In his heart he wanted to be an artist, but in reality it was difficult to make a living as an artist. He finally decided to go to Nanyang University in Singapore to study Chinese language and literature in the hope of becoming a high school teacher. Upon graduation, however, he was hired as a teaching assistant by the University because of his outstanding academic record. He was later transferred to the library to work as assistant librarian in charge of general affairs and preservation. In the meantime, he continued to paint and practice Chinese calligraphy in his spare time. He grew to enjoy his work in the library, and, because of a

水彩巨匠徐靖沂教授

——推动水彩历史向前的画家　　骆拓

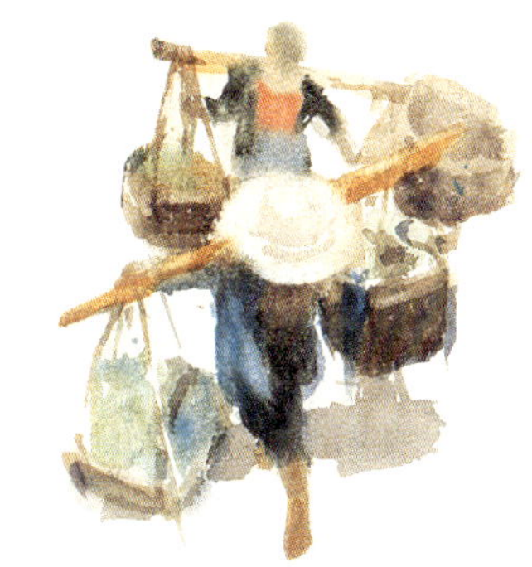

一、引言

美国水墨画会主席蓓诗、罗冰森撰文：「徐靖沂的作品包涵真、善、美的特征，他的画不属於任何派别或风格，多数作品已经超越东方或西方的定义，他开拓了许多新的技法。你可以意识到单凭学习笔划是不够的，还要吸收艺术中潜在的思想和哲理。徐靖沂自身的精神，创造力和个性是他独有的，但是很清楚地，他的根是扎在东方的绘画里。我相信他的画笔和自然的美及力量的结合，正是使他的作品真实和伟大的因素。」

历史在发展，时间在向前，艺术更是日新月异，一九八六我为好友名画家徐靖沂教授撰写「徐靖沂教授的水彩世界」，十年后适逢新加坡国家美术馆为他举办个人展览之际，他精选历年佳作和近期探索的成果，出版精装画集。这是艺坛盛事，激奋友心也！十年不算漫长，但靖沂的艺术成果更臻辉煌，变化巨大，拜读这期间的资料、报刊论文，获奖纪录及动人新作，真是美不胜收，心情澎湃激动，非倾谈不快。

靖沂的成功条件和艺术造诣是多方面的：他有特殊的环境，过人的资秉，深厚的学养，超逸的品德，崇高的理想，澎湃的激情，坚强的意志和无畏的精神。他视界广，见解高，领悟深，不受派别成见的束缚，能够兼容并蓄，融汇贯通，集中西绘画之长而溶於一炉，突破传统，别创新意，题材广泛，技法多变。现藉此文向读者谈谈自已的感受和认识，给大家对靖沂的成就和欣赏增添一些资料。

二、特殊环境

靖沂一九三四年诞生於中国福建仙游枫亭，依山面海，景色绮丽，民风厚重善良。他从小生活在如画的水乡，与水结下不了之缘。六十多年来所寓居的城市皆是水天相连，沐浴着他的学习、生活和事业，这也许是他和水彩结缘的客观原因。他的母亲善於针线，可以说是他爱好美术的最早影响。他在枫亭受小学教育，在书法方面也打下了良好的基础。

一九四八年靖沂定居马来西亚槟城，这是他成长的美丽小岛，素有东方花园，明珠之誉。当年茂密的热带花草树木，青山流泉，小溪幽径布满岛屿，一片明媚宁静，堪称世外桃源。二十多万居民包括华、巫、英、印、以及其他欧亚移民，和睦相处，共同经营这个可爱的乐园。

第二次世界大战后，中国著名的艺人学者，群贤毕至，鼎盛一时。槟城以先翁骆清泉先生经营的南国旅社和家舍为群英汇聚之所。先翁组织槟城艺术协会，举办许多展览和文化活动。徐悲鸿师亲为协会题匾。星马港台大陆艺术名家都与之结下笔墨因缘。由三十年代至五十年代，艺坛一片朝气，靖沂恰逢其盛，是他年青茁壮成长的良好环境。先翁鼓励后进不遗馀力。他赞赏靖沂的才华，极力鼓励他参加槟城各届的展览，与之结下忘年知交。

星马当时还是英国殖民地，英国水彩影响画坛很大，风行一时。槟城自学成功而以大写意水彩见长的杨曼生给靖沂的影响最深刻。留英的水彩画家陈存义是他的小学老师。留法的油画家张荔英和上海美专毕业的国画家胡呈祥是他的中学老师。在这三位良师的教导下，他在素描和绘画方面打下了良好的基础。其他当时画坛上的老前辈如蔡天定、郭若萍、许西亚，以及新加坡的刘抗、陈文希、钟泗滨、陈宗瑞等等也给他很大的启发和鼓励。槟城的环境和他强烈的兴趣及天赋培养他追求艺术的激情和坚毅的性格。他在韩江中学读书的时候，已经组织了韩中美术研究会，课馀时间和同好出外写生，互相观摩。许多会员后来都成为星马活跃的画家。

靖沂在中学时期对水彩、油画、粉画、水墨画各个画种都感兴趣。一九五三年美藉华人水彩画家曾景文先生周游欧亚作友谊访问时来槟城展览，并在韩江中学作水彩画示范。这可能是引导靖沂此后专心从事水彩探索和创作的重要因素之一。

当靖沂要上大学的时候，他面临一个困难的选择。依照他的兴趣，应该攻读艺术，但是当时艺术家的生活非常艰苦，而且攻读大学艺术学位，必须出国留学，经济不允许。经过多方考虑，他终於选择当时初开办的南洋大学，攻读中国语言文学系。在课馀之暇，仍不忘绘事，勤力赞研画理，练习书法和绘画。

大学毕业后，由於他的成绩优异，留校当任助教，后来借调图书馆工作。那时南大缺少图书馆专业管理人员，因为喜欢读书，靖沂对图书馆工作也发生兴趣，於是毅然决定赴美国攻读图书馆学。

一九六二年靖沂远越太平洋去美国的明尼苏达大学攻读图书馆学硕士学位。因为功课繁忙，虽然新的环境激发他绘画的灵感，

shortage in professional librarians, he decided to pursue a master's degree in library science in the US.

In 1962 he went to Minneapolis to attend the Library School at the University of Minnesota. While in graduate school, he had to put his brushes away, despite the fact that he was deeply inspired by the new environment and had a great urge to paint. He started working as a librarian in the University of Minnesota Duluth Campus Library in January 1965. At that time, he picked up his brushes again, and he also got married. He knew that he would be working as a librarian for a long time to support his family, but he never lost his faith and vision of ultimately becoming an artist. Therefore, he set his objective to develop dual careers. During the daytime and weekdays he was a librarian; at night and on weekends he indulged himself in painting.

Minnesota is a beautiful and progressive state. In the north, lies Lake Superior, in the southeast the Mississippi River. Ten thousand lakes are scattered on fertile farm lands. People are warm, honest, and friendly. There is a refreshing and dynamic academic and artistic atmosphere. Again, these qualities are most harmonious with Cheng-Khee's personality. They play an important role in his life and accomplishment as an artist.

In 1979 Cheng-Khee started teaching watercolor painting at the University of Minnesota, Duluth Campus, in addition to his position as Head of Public Services Department in the library. This further encroached on his painting time, but he struggled along to fulfill his responsibilities as librarian, teacher, and artist. He always attributes his success to the understanding, cooperation, and support of his family. As a recipient of the Knickerbocker Artists' 'Grand Prize Gold Medal and Purchase Award,' he was asked to say a few words at the award banquet in Washington, DC. At the end of his remarks, he asked Sing-Bee to join him at the podium and said, 'And if I have any ability at all, I owe that to my wife Sing-Bee. She encourages and makes time for me to paint to develop my ability. Our neighbors felt sorry for her because she was the one who took out the garbage, mowed the lawn, raked the leaves, shovelled the snow, and drove the car, but she performed these chores with joy in her heart, because she wanted me to have more time to

paint. We share our vision, and we chase our dreams together.' He then presented her with the prize. How true it is that 'behind every successful man there is always a woman'.

His Academic and Artistic Development

During Cheng-Khee's high school and college years, academic and artistic activities started to blossom in Malaysia and Singapore. While at Nanyang University, first as a student and later as a librarian, he had the opportunity to study systematically the Chinese classics, pre-Qin philosophers, and representative literary works of the dynasties. He carefully examined the philosophies of Confucianism, Taoism, and Buddhism. This knowledge helped shape his way of thinking, his outlook on life and world, and his artistic concepts. Based upon these, he carefully studied the life and work of great Chinese master painters. He admired Shi Ke (active during Five Dynasties 907-960) for the bold and free spirit emanating from his vigorous temperament. He revered Liang Kai (active during 13th century) for his refreshing, unrestrained splash ink style. Mi Fei (1051-1107) and Mi Youren's (1086-1165) spontaneous expression of their personal observations and ideas inspired his creativity. He respected the Northern Song masters Li Cheng (active 960-990), Fan Kuan (active 990-1030) and Guo Xi (active 1060-1075) for the panoramic and monumental scale of their works that were 'as fine as the creations of nature'. They learned from nature and established their own unique styles. He adored the Southern Song masters, such as Xia Gui (active 1190-1225) and Ma Yuan (active 1190-1264) for their extreme simplicity. Their paintings interweave positive and negative spaces. The untouched paper expresses the most profound feelings. These masters along with many other innovative, expressive, and spontaneous zen and literati painters provided Cheng-Khee with endless creative inspiration.

Cheng-Khee arrived at the United States during the period that was considered the renaissance of American watercolor. Each year the Tweed Museum of Art on the University of Minnesota, Duluth Campus, held the American Watercolor Society traveling exhibition. The 50 paintings in the show were among the best and most representative of contemporary American watercolor. Cheng-Khee spent much time studying these paintings, which greatly expanded his horizon. Also, there were some advantages in being a librarian. First, he was at the source of information; he had access to the rich collections of the University Library. Second, his browsing of images in publications year after year had built up a rich visual data bank in his subconscious mind. Third, the disciplines of librarianship made him more organized, thorough, and analytical in arranging his goals and objectives. Above all, his job as a librarian enabled him to support his family. Whatever time he had left was his 'quality time' to paint. His sole purpose in painting was to express himself and to produce better paintings. To this end, he not only painted but chose every opportunity to enlarge his knowledge of the outstanding watercolorists in the West.

The great American watercolorists Winslow Homer (1836-1925) and John Singer Sargent (1856-1925) established the foundation of American watercolor. They were followed by Thomas Eakins (1844-1916), Maurice Prendergast (1859-1924), John Marin (1870-1953), Edward Hopper (1882-1967), Charles Burchfield (1893-1967) and Andrew Wyeth (b. 1917). Cheng-Khee admired these masters and carefully studied their works.

In 1983, Cheng-Khee led a University of Minnesota class to England to paint and study English watercolor. He was able to see the finest examples of the great masters from J. M. William Turner (1775-1851) and John Sell Cotman (1782-1842) to Sir Russell Flint (1880-1969) and Edward Seago (1867-1956) in major British museums and galleries. When he returned to the United States, he studied all the material about English watercolor he could get hold of in the University libraries. Cheng-Khee also admired the German expressionist Emil Nolde (1867-1956) for his bright, rich and bold colors and Cezanne, (1839-1906), Klee (1879-1940) and Chagall (1887-1985) for their poetic quality.

The American Watercolor Society, founded in 1866, and The National Watercolor Society, established in 1921, have been strong advocates and promoters of the watercolor medium. In the 1970's

觉得非画不可，也只好暂时放下他的画笔。一九六五年一月他开始在明尼苏达大学的都鲁市学城任职。这时候他重新提起画笔，同时他也结了婚。他知道必须在图书馆工作一段相当长的时间去维特他的家庭，但是他始终没有失去成为画家的理想和信心。於是他尽量利用时间，白天和周日勤力工作，晚上和周末醉心专注地作画。明尼苏达在美国中西部，号称万湖之州，是宁静安祥的土地。它北邻加拿大，有浩渺澎湃的苏必烈湖，东南则为举世闻名的密西西比河环抱，一万个湖泊散落在肥沃美丽的农田间。风光旖旎，民俗纯朴，学术气氛浓厚，这与靖沂温厚古朴，脚踏实地，激情於内的性格至为相融。

一九七九年开始，除了担任图书馆的读者服务部主任外，靖沂受聘在大学美术系兼授水彩画课程。这一来更加缩短了他的绘画时间。他只好快马加鞭去完成任务。俗语说：「一个成功男人的背后，一定有一个女人在支持。」靖沂每每庆幸他有一个美满幸福的家庭，能够了解他的苦心孤诣，支持他实现绘画的理想。一九九三年他获得尼葛巴葛美术协会全国年展金牌奖的最高荣誉。在华盛顿的颁奖典礼上，他被会长邀请上台说几句话。他在结语的时候请夫人王声美上台，然后激动地说：「如果有什么绘画才能的话，应该归功於我的妻子声美。她鼓励我，同时尽量争取时间让我去画画，去发展那才能。当我们的邻居看到她倒垃圾，割园地的草，扫秋天的落叶，铲冬天的积雪，天天当车夫接送子女的时候，他们都为她感到可怜。但是她斡这些琐碎的家庭工作时却是满怀喜悦，因为她要让我有更多的时间画画。我们有共同的眼光和理想，我们一起在追寻共同的梦。」说完了话他把奖金交给声美。在他们俩位的熏陶下，子女也都发奋勤学，大有成就，於是靖沂可以以愉快兴奋的心情去追求他的理想。

三、学养基础的建立

南洋大学培植了许多杰出人材，校友遍全球，在政经、文化、艺术各方面都有巨大的贡献。靖沂是当年南大的高材生。他自中学到大学是星马文化艺术兴旺的年代，时代思潮错综复杂，在大环境里始终不渝地修身、养性、沉浸於无涯的学海。在南洋大学期间，他饱读先秦百家、唐宋文学诗词，有系统地探讨儒家、道家、佛家的哲学思想，形成思维深度和与众不同的观念，铸成他的艺术观和人生观。他追求庄子的人性，清静无为的自由心胸和性格的自我解放。在老庄、佛家和儒家精神的熏陶下，他对中国古代大师的成就悉心深入研究。对五代宋初石恪用笔简练，粗旷磅礴，一破前人束缚的作风，至为钦敬。对梁楷继石恪大刀阔斧立意清新，自创减笔疏体，泼墨的洒脱风格，至为佩服。米沛、米友仁父子的湿淋淋米点，充沛淋漓，因蕴化醇，天籁成趣，给他无限的灵感。他崇尚北宋李成，范宽和郭照，喜欢他们作品的气势磅礴，生活气息浓厚。他们师法自然，又能创造异乎常人的独特风格。他仰慕南宋大师马远、夏娃的晶荧洗练，虚实相生，无画处皆成妙境，墨不多而空灵溢於画外的特点。这些大师们给靖沂取之不尽，用之不竭的创作灵感的源泉。

靖沂到美国的时候，正逢水彩画蓬勃发展，复兴鼎盛的时期。他任职的明尼苏达大学都鲁市学城艺术馆一年一度展出美国水彩画会选送全国展览的作品约五十幅。这是美国最有代表性的水彩杰作。每次展出时，他在艺术馆细心研究，留连忘返。多年的观赏，给他大开眼界，因为在图书馆工作，明尼苏达大学典藏超过百万册的图书任由他涉猎。他如饥似渴地阅读有关绘画的图书和杂志。其馀的时间见缝插针，狂热地作画。

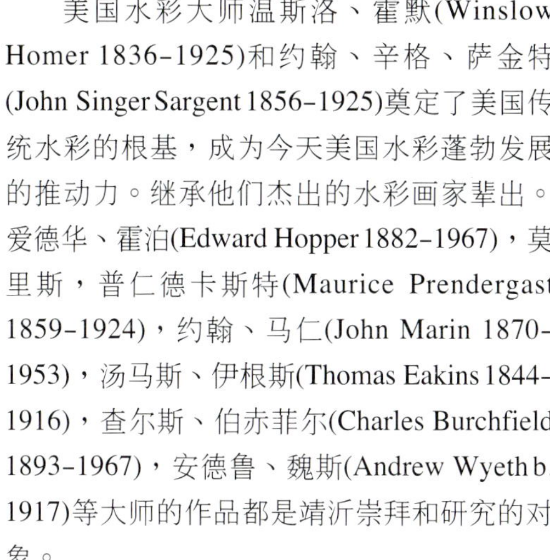

美国水彩大师温斯洛、霍默(Winslow Homer 1836–1925)和约翰、辛格、萨金特(John Singer Sargent 1856–1925)奠定了美国传统水彩的根基，成为今天美国水彩蓬勃发展的推动力。继承他们杰出的水彩画家辈出。爱德华、霍泊(Edward Hopper 1882–1967)，莫里斯，普仁德卡斯特(Maurice Prendergast 1859–1924)，约翰、马仁(John Marin 1870–1953)，汤马斯、伊根斯(Thomas Eakins 1844–1916)，查尔斯、伯赤菲尔(Charles Burchfield 1893–1967)，安德鲁、魏斯(Andrew Wyeth b. 1917)等大师的作品都是靖沂崇拜和研究的对象。

一九八三年靖沂带领明尼苏达大学美术班去英国考察写生。在英国各重要的美术博物馆饱赏英国水彩大师的作品。从威廉、特纳(J.M. William Turner 1775–1851)，约翰、郭特门(John Sell Cotman 1782–1842)，到威廉、罗素，弗林特(Sir William Rusell Flint 1880–1969)和爱华，西果(Edward Seago 1910–74)，美不胜收。回美之后，搜集图书馆所藏有关英国水彩的资料，悉心研读。他对德国表现主义画家埃米尔，挪迪(Emil Nolde 1867–1956)华丽的色彩和大胆的作风有浓厚的兴趣。对塞尚(Cezanne 1839–1906)，克莱(Klee 1879–1940)和雪加尔(Chagall 1887–1985)等富有诗意的作品也非常欣赏。

美国水彩画会(American Watercolor Society)成立於一八六六年，百馀年来推动发扬水彩媒介，不遗馀力。后起之秀的全国水彩画会(National Watercolor Society)，对提倡水彩艺术也做出很大的贡献。一九七〇年代以后，美国各地新的画会应运而生，如雨后春荀，生机勃发。一九九六年美国美术家杂志列出全国性，区域性，和地方性的水彩画会共一百三十多个。这些画会每年举行展览，开办短训班，蔚为风气。这些活动也很受社会和美术爱好者的热烈支持。过去二十多年水彩图书杂志的出版事业欣欣向荣。水彩颜料、纸张、工具的改良和新产品的涌现，供应服务的普及，这一切都为画家具备优良的创作条件及推动的力量。目前美国水彩画种的兴盛势力，有如千军万马，不克阻挡。画坛也达到了百花齐放，百家争鸣的自由局面。

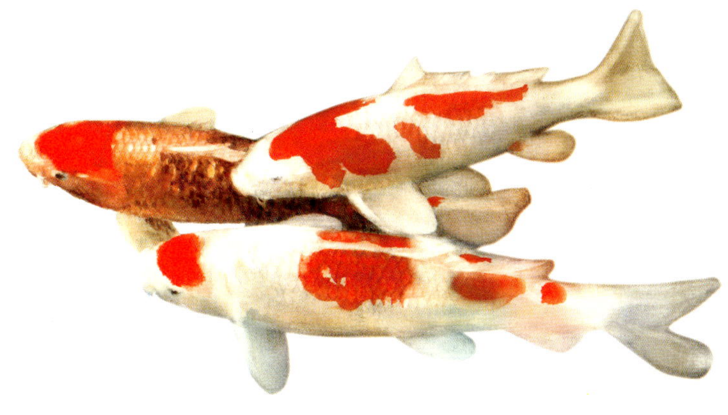

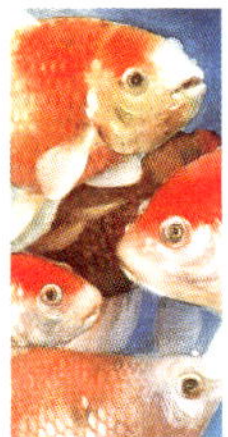

new watercolor societies sprang up like mushrooms. The *American Artist* listed over 130 national, regional, state, and local organizations in 1996. It has become a phenomenon that these organizations hold regular annual exhibitions and sponsor workshops. These activities are usually well attended and supported by communities and art lovers. During the past 20 years, the publishing of books, magazines, and instructional video on watercolor painting has also prospered. New and improved products, together with excellent supplier services, also contributed to the popularity and momentum of the watercolor medium. It has been declared that watercolor has come of age. Today watercolorists are enjoying the freedom of creativity and 'one hundred flowers are blooming and one hundred thoughts prevailing.'

Under the tremendous momentum of watercolor movement, Cheng-Khee actively participated in all kinds of activities. At first he took painting workshops to enrich his knowledge in color and design and sharpen his skills in handling the medium. These workshops also fired up the flame of his passion for painting. In the meantime, he actively participated in national juried exhibitions. After working very hard for ten years, his paintings started to receive national recognition. In 1975 his paintings were accepted by the American Watercolor Society's Annual National Exhibition, Watercolor USA, and others. By the early 1980's he was elected to signature membership in most of the important national watercolor organizations, such as the American Watercolor Society and the National Watercolor Society. In 1979 he started teaching watercolor painting at the University of Minnesota. In 1981 he was promoted to Assistant Professor of Art to teach regular watercolor courses in the Art Department. In 1988 he was promoted to Associate Professor. It is not very common in the United States that a self-taught artist becomes a professor of art. It is obvious that his accomplishments in art are outstanding.

The Formulation of His Painting Concepts

Among the many teachers and friends of Cheng-Khee, Edgar Whitney perhaps had the most direct and profound influence upon him. In the summer of 1978, 'Ed' went to Duluth, Minnesota to serve as Juror of Awards for the Midwest Watercolor Society's Second Annual National Exhibition and to conduct a one-week painting workshop. The exhibition was held at Tweed Museum of Art of the University of Minnesota, Duluth. In the process of jurying the awards, Ed asked Cheng-Khee to accompany him at the museum. They looked at each of the one hundred pieces in the show. Ed painstakingly and patiently analyzed the merits and weaknesses of each work. Cheng-Khee felt he had learned more about design and art appreciation on that day than in the previous ten years. Afterwards Cheng-Khee attended Ed's workshop to put the design theories into practice.

Cheng-Khee was also deeply indebted to Ed's profound statements: '... substances obeying their own laws do beautiful things,' and 'Wet method is the most forthright subscription to the nature of watercolor. It gives the medium a greater chance to obey its own laws, achieving lovelier effects than you can paint'. These statements helped him connect the creative process to the Taoist philosophy and to the innovative painting methods practiced by the early Chinese masters mentioned previously. He was inspired to formulate his own goal in painting: 'to pursue the essence of Tao, the state of effortless creation beyond craftsmanship and artistry.'

For the past twenty years, Cheng-Khee has been experimenting, exploring, and searching for the most natural way to express his specific subjects and inner feelings, to synthesize the concepts and techniques of both East and West traditions, and to combine realism and abstraction to push the watercolor medium to its limits. He hopes that ultimately his paintings will be neither of the East nor the West, neither realism nor abstraction, but the presence of all elements that communicate on a universal level. After many years of practice, Cheng-Khee concluded that the watercolor medium is closer to Tao than any other medium. The very flowing movement of washes has a strong evocative power. The interpenetration of colors creates mysterious precipitations and nuances. In watercolor the artist can let the medium obey its own laws and create wonders in the same way that nature creates her own works. He therefore formulated the principle of 'Beginning with abstraction and ending with realism.' He considers the act of watercolor painting a dynamic process of interaction, interchange, interbreeding, interconnection, and integration of abstraction and realism, emotion and reasoning, accident and intention, subjectivity and objectivity, imagination and reality. This gives the artist utmost freedom and flexibility in the process of painting. An artist begins a painting improvisationally and in the very act of painting brings it to the finished state.

In order to work in this process effectively, he insists that an artist should possess the following four prerequisites:

1. Thorough knowledge of the subject matter (the outer world)
2. Strong feelings toward the subject matter (the inner world)
3. Thorough understanding of design (elements and principles)
4. The skills for expressing the subject matter in the most natural way

The synthesis of the outer world and the inner world forms the inspirational basis for painting. This inspirational basis combines with knowledge, experience, and personal cultivation to become the source for the contents of paintings. The design principles guide the artist in making better pictures. The skills include the ability to draw and the ability to handle a specific medium. The natural way is the essence of his process in handling the watercolor medium. In watercolor painting oftentimes the process directly influences the content or sometimes determines the content.

Cheng-Khee's roots are deep in the Chinese tradition, yet he was nourished by nutrients from all over the world. He brilliantly synthesizes the concepts and techniques of both eastern and western traditions to come up with his own innovations.

Varied Subject Matter and Diverse Techniques

Cheng-Khee strongly believes artists should not be content with the specific subject matter in which they excel, or with the specific techniques they have mastered, merely to repeat themselves within an established style. He feels artists should be sensitive

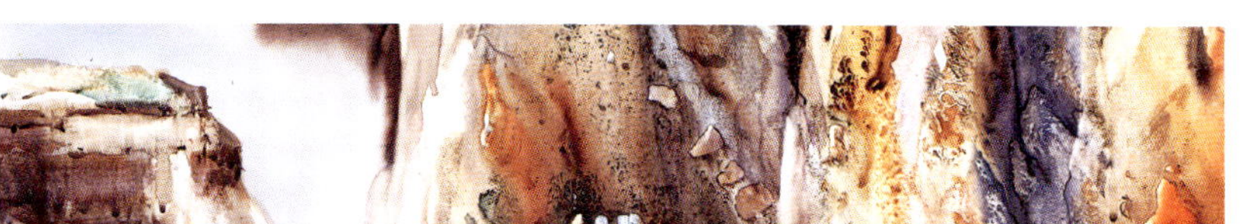

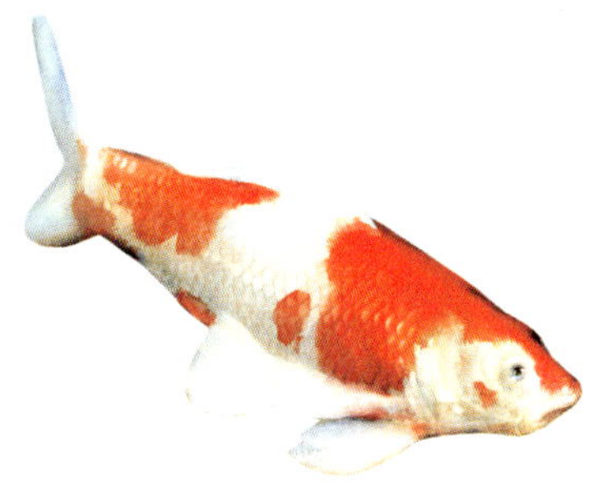

在席卷美国的水彩热潮带动下，靖沂决心投入历史巨浪里，积极参加许多活动，最初参加了水彩训练班，开拓眼界，建立信心，寻找自已的艺术发展途径。一九七三年他参加林基教授(Gaell Lindstrom b.1919)在明尼苏达大学主持的夏季水彩训练班，整整一个月。一九七七年他参加艾格、威尼先生(Edgar Whitney 1891-1987)的短训班，一九七九年他参加曾景文先生的短训班。虽然他没有直接受教於程及先生，但是程老的理念和风格，也是靖沂所钦佩的。这些水彩训练班加强了靖沂对水彩技法、色彩、构图设计的认识，燃点了他创作激情的火花，从此埋头作画，并积极参加全国性的展览。八十年代开始他已被选美国水彩画会，全国水彩画会以及其他重要画会的署名会员。一九七九年开始在明尼苏达大学教授水彩。一九八一年升任助理教授。一九八八年升任副教授。以一个自学成功的画家受聘为大学美术教授，在美国还是罕见，可见他在艺术上有超人的成就。

四、绘画理念的形成

在靖沂的许多师友中，给他最大影响的可算艾格、威尼先生。一九七七年美国中西部水彩画会第二届全国展览在明尼苏达大学都鲁市学城艺术馆举行。艾格、威尼专程由纽约来主持评选工作，在整个评奖过程中他特意邀请靖沂一起工作，共同认真地研究分析每幅入选的作品，不厌其烦，详尽地指出每张画的优点和存在的问题。参与这复杂细致的工作，使靖沂受益不浅，他说：「这一天里我对构图设计和美学原理的认识，胜似十年的探索」。接着他又参加艾格、威尼的水彩训练班。艾师的画多数用湿画法，直接影响靖沂对湿画法产生了浓烈的兴趣。艾师认为：「物质顺从自身的规律而产生美的东西」，「湿画法最符合水彩的本质，因为它让媒介有较大的机会去顺从自身的规律而产生了比你所画的还更可贵的效果。」这个本来简单的道理，却给靖沂绘画的理念起了很大的启发作用。它点破了道家哲理和绘画创作的重要关系。正如中国哲理「天籁」、「极致」、「笔笔诱法」，随笔墨颜色应运而生的「天趣自然成」。靖沂对水色自身的分合游动，凝聚汇彩，堆积沉淀，展现预计不到的效果感到无限兴奋。他认为比「胸有成竹」，计划在先更出奇迹和可贵。当物质顺从自然发生和发展时，立即采取高度灵活手法，因势利导，取舍胸中丘壑，塑造成高於预计在先的美妙画面，能运用此中奥妙，必然会画出富有生命力的作品。这给他指出了创新的途径，攀登艺术的高峰。

经过多年的实践，靖沂认为水彩是最接近道家哲理的媒介。只要给它制造适当的条件，任何艺术效果都可以顺理成章，无为而获。基於水彩创作过程的特性，他提出了「抽象的开始，具象的结束」的原则。他认为物象从抽象到具象是一个无序与有序相统一的生发过程。他把水彩创作的过程看成是有象与无象，抽象与具象，偶然与必然，主观与客观，激情与理性，互相生发，富有生机的过程，这给绘画赋予最大的灵活性。画家从充分发挥想象到即势成形之间，让自己的感情韵律通过笔触和水色运作，结合成一个充满生气的过程。把这个过程，包括偶然的效果，在画面上保存下来，而达到气韵生动的境界。

靖沂认为这个「抽象的开始，具象的结束」的原则也应该应用在传统的水彩画法上。这就是说要画一幅好的具象的写实作品，也必须先有一个好的抽象的构图设计。画家要分析画面物象的设计要素如点、线、面、色彩、肌理、形状、明暗关系等等，然后根据设计原理、组织画面，而达到一幅杰出的，具象的写实作品。

一个画家要实践「抽象的开始，具象的结束」的原则，而达到运用自如，炉火纯青的地步，靖沂认为应该具备以下四个条件：

1. 对题材、物象要有充分的了解和知识。
2. 对题材、物象要有强烈的情感。这情感包括喜、怒、哀、乐、爱、憎等等。

以上两个条件：前者代表外在世界，后者代表内心世界。两者的结合，建立起创作的灵感。这和一切生活经验，学识修养汇流成为创作的源泉。这源泉给画家供应取之不竭的创作内容。

3. 充分了解美学上构图设计的原理。怎样把设计要素，根据设计原理，谱写成一幅抽象的，有机组织的图画。
4. 掌握熟练的表现技法。这里包括素描锻练和处理媒介特性的能力，充分地表现作品的内容。

以上两个条件是表现内容的手段，也就是创作的过程，也就是属於形式。在水彩画的创作上，表现方法往往直接影响内容，甚至於形式决定了内容。

靖沂几十年扎根在东方的绘画里，研究中国古代的书法和绘画，这是西方画家做不到的事，东方画家又没有适合的环境长期生活在西方的文化里，他是在绘画的理念上和技法方面揉和二者於一炉的出色画家。

五、题材丰富，技法多变

靖沂认为画家应该通过绘画，反映时代，表现生活和个人对事物的感受和愿望。画家不但在观察事物上要有敏锐的眼光和伟大的胸怀；在创作技法上也要有勇於探讨，大胆尝试的精神。不断探索寻求新的表现方法，灵活地发挥灵感，创作出多变而富有时代气息的作品。靖沂取材广泛，表现技法也因画而异。从金鱼、锦鲤、蝴蝶花、玫瑰、向日葵、荷花、睡莲到福建故乡、长江、漓江、水乡、游艇、星马旅游、美国著名的世

to changes around them and, like scientists, be constantly exploring, experimenting, discovering, and developing new concepts, ideas, and ways of expression. Cheng-Khee's subject matter – from goldfish, koi, irises, roses, sunflowers, lotuses, to his hometown, watertown, Li River, Yangzi River, Southeast Asian scenes, canyons of the Southwest, boats, harbors, beaches, streets, alleys - is greatly diversified, and his techniques are also varied. The various concepts and techniques he has developed over the years can be described as follows:

1. Traditional/Academic Watercolors

Although Cheng-Khee stresses innovation, he never overlooks the importance of the traditional/academic approach to watercolor painting. The excellent design, the paint quality, the control of washes, the choice of subject matter, all reflect his solid foundation and craftsmanship. 'The Ore Carriers' is such an example from his earlier work. He applied warm dominant strong color to the big shapes of the imposing ore carriers. The subtle variation of red, sienna, umber, tonal values, and shadow patterns separate shapes and express spatial relationships. He uses strong calligraphic lines to tie everything together to achieve unity and harmony. This is a very strong painting. It was awarded his first Gold Medal in the Allied Artists of America's 1980 Annual National Exhibition in New York City.

There are many other fine academic watercolors such as the 'Watertown Series,' the 'Hangzhou Alley Series,' the 'Rainy Day Series,' and 'Fenting - My Hometown'. They are all award-winning paintings. They show Cheng-Khee's great facility in the drawing and handling of the medium.

2. The Crinkling Technique

Cheng-Khee combines his dexterity in Chinese calligraphy, sensitivity with the watercolor medium, and subtlety of the texture achieved by crinkling the sized Masa paper to come up with a sophisticated visual language. He uses this unique language to express views of the four seasons and other highly textured subject matter. The results were often described as 'divine', 'remarkable', 'wonderful', and 'dreamlike'.

'Winter Pleasure' received First Prize in the New Orleans Art Association's 1986 Annual National Art Exhibition. The painting vividly captures the spirit of winter activities in the snow-covered woods. It makes viewers feel they are there. They can hear people humming, talking, and bursting into laughter. They can also hear the sound of ski rubbing against the snow. Three-fourths of the page is devoted to the highly textured, white-blanketed woods and only one-fourth to the snow-covered ground where he strategically places the skiers in a semicircle. This is a bold and refreshing design concept. The grouping and interaction of the skiers successfully brings out the dramatic quality of human activities. This element, in turn, brings the entire picture to life and adds the warmth of humanity to the cold winter.

'Autumn 1983' is another masterpiece. It received First Prize in the Sumi-e Society of America's 1984 Annual National Exhibition and Gold Award in the Georgia Watercolor Society's 1985 Annual National Exhibition. This is a scene of golden autumn. Trees with red leaves, yellow leaves, and green leaves bask in the bright sun. Cheerful people are enjoying their walk through the woods. The crinkled texture that forms the foliage of trees is so exquisite and natural, a perfect collaboration between the artist and the medium itself. The white shape of the path dotted with colorfully dressed people forms the center of interest. Although four-fifths of the painting is devoted to trees and shrubbery, it still conveys a feeling of spaciousness. Tender feelings and beautiful design make this an inspiring painting. There are many other excellent paintings done in crinkling technique. Cheng-Khee has perfected the method to a high level of sophistication.

3. Marbling and Monoprinting Technique

Cheng-Khee is very observing and perceptive. He is sensitive to and often inspired by very common things around him such as the water stain on walls caused by a leaky roof, the texture of a peeling surface, the beautiful colors of gem stones, the ripples in water, the moss on pebbles, the violent spray of the ocean, the dramatic storm, the turbulent blizzard. Cheng-Khee is also a very thoughtful person. He has dreams, fantasies, imagination, and vision. He contemplates the infinity of time and space; he ponders spiritual, supernatural, and mystical experiences. All of these often defy description or expression in realistic images. Instead, he searches for feelings or concepts in the abstract images evolving from the process of marbling or monoprinting. 'The Lost Horizon' series of 1983 and the 'Rhythm of the Shore' series of 1996 are fine examples of his use of these processes. Sometimes he imposes realistic subject matter upon the abstract images to combine dreams with reality, to arrive at realism from abstraction, as in 'The Koi Pond' and 'The Canyon with Juniper'.

4. Saturated Wet Technique

The saturated wet technique is Cheng-Khee's important contribution to the watercolor medium. Cheng-Khee started painting wet-in-wet in 1977 after attending Edgar Whitney's workshop. After working a few years with this technique, he discovered that if you keep the paper wet in the entire process of painting, you can wipe out color at will and repaint if necessary. This quality gives artists utmost freedom and flexibility when comes to painting complex light-value positive shapes surrounded by dark-value negative space. The process can be reversed by painting the background first and then wiping out positive shapes. It also allows the artist to make numerous corrections without muddying the painting. He did many paintings of koi, goldfish, and flowers with this method. He divides the painting process into two stages. In the first stage he aims at creating an abstract under-painting. He starts with emotion and energy, encourages accidental effects, watches the abstract relationship of color, texture, shapes, and tonal value. In the second stage he makes a quick

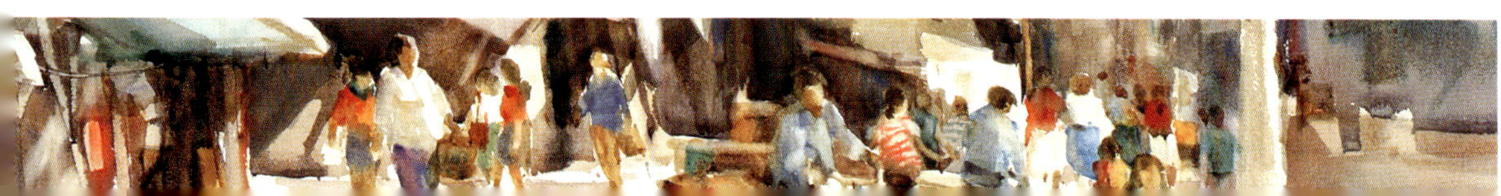

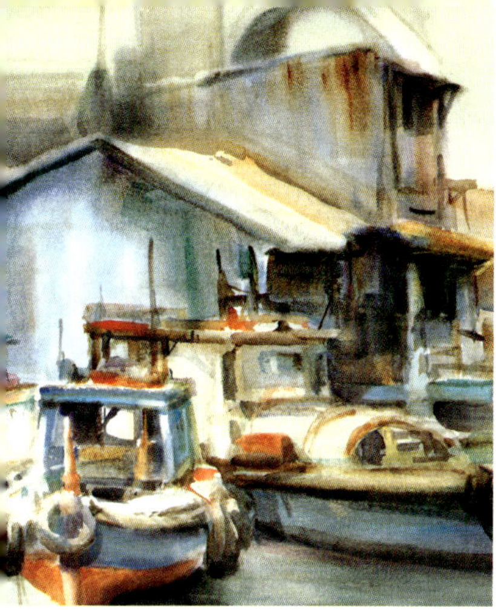

界奇景大峡谷，无不入画。现就各种不同技法及题材分析阐述如下。

1　传统水彩

靖沂立意创新，但不忽略传统。他在传统水彩方面也下了刻苦的功夫。他所画的许多传统水彩，层次安排，颜色和水份控制，造型严紧，构图取舍均按规范进行，这是他功夫扎实，根基深厚的原因。继而是干湿相间画法，在水和颜色的处理运用有重大的进展，打开了走进纯湿画法的大门。

「铁矿船」是靖沂比较早期的作品，层次分明，大胆采用大块浓烈色彩，以暖调子为主表现都鲁铁矿的雄伟船队。他在很接近的红赭色调里去区分层次的变化，辅以粗线条和强烈的对比，使画面协调统一，至为动人。此画一九八O年在纽约美国美术家联盟(Allied Artists of America)全国联展获水彩组金牌奖。

传统水彩还有许多佳作：「水乡组画」，「杭州后巷组画」，「雨天组画」等等都是全国得奖的精湛之作。这充分表现他素描功力的深厚和技法运作的熟练和扎实。

2　揉纸法

「揉纸法」也是他的出色贡献。虽然许多画家都在运用，但目标不同，效果各异。靖沂的中国书法素养使之能够娴熟控制飞白破笔，融和於水彩的技法色彩，用得非常灵活。他表现树林和四季景物最为特色。颜色层次有条不紊，以揉出的纹理，揉挤敷彩，轻者如纱，重者如层岩重叠，冷暖相间，粗笔细笔交织，在碎乱如麻中去求宏大统一。美国艺术界誉之为「神奇作品」，「梦境式的大自然」，「超乎常规的奇迹，妙极了！」。

「冬天乐」获得新奥良美术协会(New Orleans Art Association)一九八六年全国综合画种展览全展第一奖。画面把渡假欢乐的人群和大雪弥漫的银装树林表现如置身其境。你仿佛可以听到喧哗的歌声，欢悦的谈笑和雪筏的喳喳声。使严冬的寂静充满了热烈温暖的节奏。茂密的森林占去画面四分之三的位置，这是画家有胆略的安排。他成功地运用「反虚为实」，「知黑守白」的哲理。在仅留的四 分之一空白处，他点上了滑雪的人群，并美妙地刻划了生活的细节和感受。在最前面的二位主人翁赋予故事性，穿红衣的是正在学滑雪，似乎是滑倒了无数次，所以分外小心。这戏剧性的刻划，点活了整个画面。色调的安排也妙不可言，他大胆地以暖色为主调，表现冬雪的寒冷，极难也！一九八三年的作品「秋」连续得了美国墨画会全国联展第一奖和乔治亚州水彩画会全国联展金奖。金色的秋天，盖满红叶、黄叶、绿叶的树丛被阳光烘托得暖洋洋。轻松愉快的人们载欣载奔，其乐无穷。揉出的纹理很自然，不雕不琢，顺理成章，与大地、林木神遇而并化，参造化而与天地精神相通。环抱空白处的人行道感觉宽敞舒畅。五分之四的茂密树林并不减弱它的空旷通爽。完美的构思，出色的经营是使画面动人的原因。

3　拓印法

靖沂善於抓住生活的细节加以发挥，夸张，升华，将屋中漏痕，瘢剥之形，水的涟漪，青苔的滴翠，海边激浪，都成画家童话梦境，玄虚幻象；寿山石不同色泽，斑块，纹理，自然天成的一切，无不是他遐想，幻觉，演化的对象。以宏大的宇宙，神奇的时空，创出不可思议的图象。以赞叹生命和自然的奥密，泼出，染出，诱发，皴扫出奇幻的画面。「缥缈」，「岸边旋律」，「古柏幽谷」，「锦鲤荷塘」等作品均出自偶然天成的「幻象」，以颜色的浮动，水波的荡漾，整理成胸中乾坤，抽象的开始，经画家的匠心经营而达到具象的结束，这是「拓印法」。他以「自适其适」「纯素之道，唯神是守」，「机心存於胸」的哲理去谱成幻象，狂想的梦幻曲子。

4　纯湿画法

靖沂的极端湿画法，也叫纯湿画法是他对水彩画的重大贡献，是揉低法，拓印法深入发展的必然收获，是抽象到具象，偶然与必然，主观与客观，激情与理性的互相发生，富有生机的遇程，充满了灵活性和戏剧性。他一九七七年开始运用湿画法，经过多年的实践，发现只要浸湿重磅画纸，在整个绘画的过程中保持它的湿度，便可以任意擦掉纸上的颜色，重新画过。这个性能对处理画面有深色背景空间环绕着淡色物象的情形，便可以自由放胆，先画出整个背景，然后根据构图形势，洗出物象的形体，再加工完成。他用纯湿画法创作了许多金鱼、锦鲤和花卉的作品。在创作的过程中往往是形式去影响内容的发展，甚至决定和改变构思立意的初衷。当你把水和色泼到画纸上，片刻便出现非人工所为的偶然效果。许多幻形出现，浓彩丰盈氤氲，淡彩晶明透彻，水色重叠聚散，占片混合渗透，飘游莫测。画家激情焕发，迅速以主观意念去疏导，辅之以笔，海绵等工具，把偶然性化成必然性，把瞬息抓住的意念推进，改变成客观的现实画面。抽象开始达到了具象的结束，表现出理想的画幅。

靖沂这种大胆尝试，即刻有了突破，画出意想不到的「金鱼组画八五年一号」的巨幅作品，精彩动人，获得一九八五年美国中西部水彩画会(Midwest Watercolor Society)全国联展第一奖。他以粗大笔触大刀阔斧和细致入微相配合，画得非常协调，完美而自然，仿佛可以听到鱼群在水中拍动的节奏声

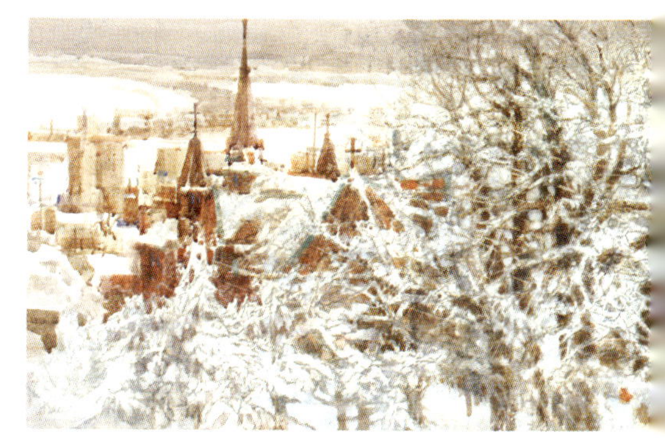

design decision to impose subject matter on the existing under-painting before the paper dries up. This time he works with reasoning, intention, realism, and objectivity. This is a big breakthrough for him, and so far this way of working is uniquely his.

'Goldfish 85 No. 1' received the top honor in the Midwest Watercolor Society's 1985 Annual National Exhibition. He combined dynamic big brush strokes for the big fish shapes with a minutely detailed rendering of their eyes and scales. One almost can hear the sound that comes from the fish movement. The fish scales are as shiny as silver, the red markings on the head and body are bright and translucent, the fins look like a silken blouse, the tails are long gauze skirts. They look as if they were cheerfully engaged in a waltz. The design, the paint quality, the feeling of fish and water make the painting a masterpiece which has surpassed the quality of other fish paintings in watercolor.

After the 1985 goldfish series, Cheng-Khee devoted much of his time studying goldfish and koi as subject matter, and further perfected the saturated wet technique. His paintings have become progressively complex and sophisticated. 'Koi 90 No. 9' received the Silver Medal in the American Watercolor Society's 1991 Annual International Exhibition, and 'Koi 92 No. 1' the Grand Prize Gold Medal in the Knickerbocker Artists' 1993 Annual International Exhibition. This is a multimedia exhibition. A watercolor painting's surpassing oil, sculpture, and other media to be awarded the Grand Prize is an undeniable indication of a major artistic achievement. The painting also received the $10,000 Purchase Prize for Excellence, the highest price ever given to a purchase award in watercolor. The painting became the first work in the Knickerbocker Artists' Collection.

5. Improvisational Splash Color Technique

Throughout his life, Cheng-Khee has related to mountains, water, shores, rocks, waves, surfs, spray and gulls. These have become an important part of his experience and are reflected in many of his paintings. Initially he painted the rock texture in the traditional 'built-up' method. But with the versatility of watermedia, he was convinced that with proper material and technique he could create the rocky shores and mountainscapes in the more 'natural way'. This moment came when he acquired a John Pike palette in 1980. After using the palette for a few painting sessions, he discovered exciting 'paintings' of rocky shores and mountainscapes on the mixing surface of the palette, just as he had envisioned. So he started searching for a painting surface as smooth as plastic, yet able to retain paint so it will not be washed off. He finally found the Strathmore 500 series high-surfaced illustration board most satisfactory. He also discovered that applying a diluted acrylic gel medium to the paper enhanced results. When sweeping a broad brush charged with color over the gel-medium-coated surface, the paint is immediately repelled, which creates tensions and other unexpected and exciting textural effects resembling rocks and mountains.

After many paintings, he feels that the best approach to this method is to work improvisationally. He starts the painting with strong emotion and energy, and with great speed. He works at white heat for about twenty minutes, trying to cover the entire sheet of paper. This encourages his subconscious mind to work. He uses no preliminary sketches, nor does he have any preconceived plan of composition. He is concerned only with achieving accidental relationships of warm and cool colors, variety of shapes, light and dark value patterns, and texture. Gradually, through the very act of painting, he discovers the subject matter, which combines dream with reality, emotion with reason, abstraction with realism. At this point he exerts more conscious control and guides the painting to its finishing stage. It is a process of searching for the unknown. The painting develops in the very process of painting.

This is a risky painting method, but the unexpected results are very gratifying. This is the ultimate collaboration between the artist and the medium. This is perhaps Cheng-Khee's greatest contribution to the watermedia. The 'Li River' series, the 'Yangzi River' series, the 'Lake Shore' series, and the 'Along the Colorado River' series are all outstanding paintings. They were inspired by nature, but they are more beautiful than nature. Contemplating these series of paintings makes viewers feel they are in a fairyland.

At the invitation of the Western Colorado Watercolor Society, Cheng-Khee served as Juror of Selection and Awards for the 1994 Annual National Exhibition, and directed a one-week painting workshop in Grand Junction. After completing his assignment, he explored the Southwest Region along the Colorado River down to southern Utah and Arizona. The spectacular, magnificent, and wondrous view of the canyons and the ever-changing mood of nature strongly inspired his creative passion. His 'Southwest Series', and 'The Spirit of Southwest Series' have entered a deeper level in the realization of his creative concepts. This development reveals plans for even more ambitious artistic adventures.

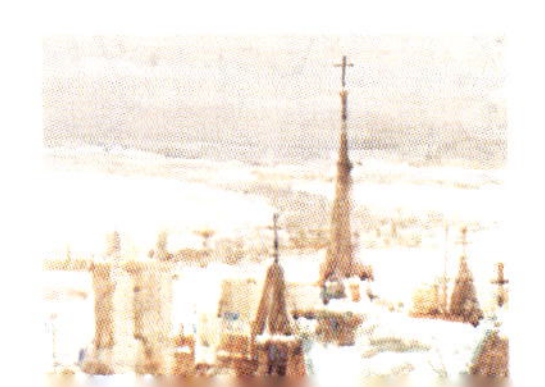

Concluding Remarks

The rapid advancement of transportation and communication technologies has shortened both time and space. Science and technology have never had national boundaries, and the national uniqueness in art and literature will also fade in light of the shrunken time and space. The interpenetration, interbreeding, and integration of the concepts and processes of different art forms resulting in mixed media works have been apparent for many decades. In the watercolor world, the term 'watercolor' has been gradually replaced by 'watermedia'. The definition has been expanded from the narrower meaning of transparent watercolor to any painting done in water-soluble pigments on paper. This includes not only such media as gouache, tempera, and acrylic, but also the entire field of East Asian ink and brush painting.

Cheng Khee inherited the glorious traditions of Chinese, European, and American master watercolorists. In turn, step by step, he has broken new grounds for the watercolor medium through his talents, vision, imagination, ambition, and determination. The record of his artistic research and exploration is invaluable, and his accomplishments have been highly regarded and recognized nationally and internationally.

The introduction of plurality in creative concepts and processes has liberated artists and opened up a whole new frontier for inquisitive minds to probe and explore. Cheng-Khee is a serious explorer. His rich experience in painting has built a solid bridge for him to cross to future endeavors. His achievement of yesterday has established a firm foundation upon which to build new monuments. He is certain to climb new peaks and help advance watermedia to new heights, and be highly esteemed in the history of art.

音。构图的安排，颜色和水份的控制，层次浓淡深浅的推移，虚实的处理都恰到好处。背景点、染、扫、擦技法清新纯熟。大胆之处气势如脱缰之马，空虚之处如蝉衣之通透，鱼尾与水融和无隙。鱼的头部和鳞片刻划入微。美妙之至！那银光闪烁的光泽，鲜红欲滴的头顶红帽子和身上透明呈水晶体的红斑，质感的表现强极了！那透明如纱的长鳍似舞衣的阿袅，那拂水的长尾若华尔兹舞姿之翩跹。这杰作在水彩领域的成就已超越前人，而树立了自己的强烈风格，已远非人们理解的传统技法规范。

这之后靖沂用大部份时间深入研究湿画法的变化和技巧互相制约的发挥，作品越来越臻精湛。他的「锦鲤组画九O年九号」获美国水彩画会一九九一年国际年展银牌奖。「锦鲤组画九二年一号」获一九九三年美国尼葛巴葛美术家协会(Knickerbocker Artists U.S.A.)国际综合媒介作品展览全场冠军金牌奖和购藏奖。水彩画能够超越油画、雕塑和其他画种而获得全场冠军，是难能可贵的事。可见他的湿画法已经达到生烟御风，凌云如龙，出神入化的境界。

5 即兴泼彩法

靖沂一生与山、水、岸、石、浪、涛、海鸥结了缘。这些題材是他生活经验中重要的一部分，反映在他的许多作品中。开始画这些题材时，他用传统的积色法；但是知道水彩的多方面性能，他坚信只要找到适当的材料和技法，那丰富的山石肌理便可以应运而生，不劳而获。

一九八O年初靖沂采用美国水彩画家约翰・派克(John Pike 1911-1979)的塑料调色盘。画了几幅画后，他发现调色盘有自然凝聚成山石、流水、高山幽谷、烟云出没的图象，这正是他预想的效果。他仔细推敲产生这效果的原因。由於光滑塑料调色盘有抗衡阻止颜色迅速粘附的力量，加以引导，便出现意想不到的纹理图象。经过多次的试验，他发现光滑的广告画卡纸，刷上一层冲淡的丙烯调色剂((Acrylic Gel Medium)，待干后用大扁笔大胆刷上颜色，可以得到最好的肌理效果。经过无数次的实践，他觉得用泼彩法时最好是胸无成竹，无題而为，乘兴而就。让激情焕发，急速泼彩，谱出偶然的感怀。凭着画面抽象幻象的形成，注意冷暖、干湿、涩滞、浓淡、厚薄、虚实的对比关系，或粗旷细腻，或宁静激荡，当机立断，在杂乱中理出章法，去芜存精，促它变化凝形。这种画法难度高，冒险性也大；但意想不到的画面带来无限的快慰。这是人性与物性的巧妙结合，巧夺天工，而达到气韵生动的境界。

「漓江组画」、「杨子江组画」、「湖岸组画」、「西北组画」等大量作品，都是瞬息万变，游动凝形，咫尺天涯的神化之作。他表现的比现实更完美，更引人入胜。这是画家把对现实的感受，概括升华而表现出高於现实的艺术真实。以上一系列的作品令观众身历仙境，宛如童话世界。虽然各自的题材、构图极不相同，但每张作品都是精湛无比。

靖沂善於将颜色在游离的充沛水份中控制得粗细自如。粗大的如巨石下坠，瀑布式地飞泻滚翻。细腻的如屋中漏痕，或幼细如游丝。色彩的凝聚与细小色粒的沉淀，画出了紫、晴紫、蓝、纯蓝、翠蓝、绿、褚石、朱红、暗红及土黄等互相衬托对比的丰富色谱。更大胆巧妙的是以大量浓烈原色的交替使用，和单独突出纯原色的存在，互相辉映，溶之於「脏」颜色的汪洋大海中，达到鲜者更鲜，柔者益柔，深沉之处更凝聚厚重的感染力。

一九九四年靖沂应科罗拉多西部水彩画会(Western Colorado Watercolor Society)之邀，担任该会主办全国水彩展览的评审并主持一星期的水彩训练班。任务完成后，他畅游科罗拉多、尤塔和阿里桑那的峡谷。那峥嵘险峻，奇形怪状的景色，那朝霞暮霭，风雨雷电，瞬息万变的气象，给他无限的创作激情。他的新作如罗汉林列，万佛降临。形态栩栩如生，迫真巧妙，鬼斧神功。「西北组画」、「西北精神组画」是他理念的深入表现，展现了更宏伟的创新前景：

六、结语

由於交通和讯息科技的高速发展，将时间和空间的距离都大大地缩小了。科学和技术从来没有国界之分，文学和艺术的民族色彩也将会随时空的缩短而冲淡。现在各种美术形式在创作的理念和技法的运作上早已开始互相渗透而产生了混合媒介的作品。在水彩画的领域里，「水彩Watercolor」一词也已渐渐被「水的媒介Watermedia」一词取代。在定义上由狭义的透明水彩而扩大到广义的，凡是用水和彩色（包括墨色）画在纸张上的作品。这一新的定义，不但包含了粉画、蛋彩、丙烯等等，也包括了整个东方的绘画。「水的媒介」一词拓宽了艺术追求的范畴，打破了画种的单元性而包溶了艺术处理的多元性。为此带给艺术家无限宽广的前程和多元的研究课题。期待着脚踏实地的，一步一个脚印的勇敢探索者，在无限的境界中去竖立一个个的丰碑。

靖沂继承中国、欧洲和美国先贤光辉的传统，凭他的才华、眼光、理想和努力，数十年如一日，一步一个脚印地追求实践，给我们留下了丰富的、宝贵的艺术纪录和成果。他的贡献得到美国画坛的充分肯定和推崇，也得到国际画家的推荐和尊敬。他的这些艺术的纪录和成果将是他明天去追求探索新的艺术领域的桥梁和竖立新丰碑的基础。明天，我们期待着他的艺术探索的新课题，带给我们更丰硕的成果。在艺术的百花园中，开出一朵朵更美丽的鲜花。把水的媒介带上新的高峰，在美术史上留下光辉的一页。

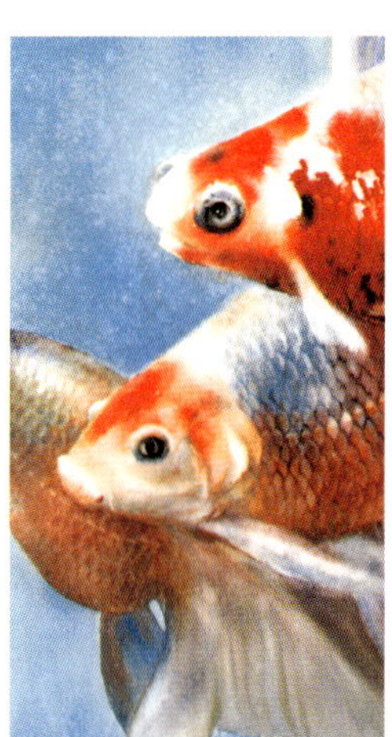

The Watercolor World of Cheng-Khee Chee

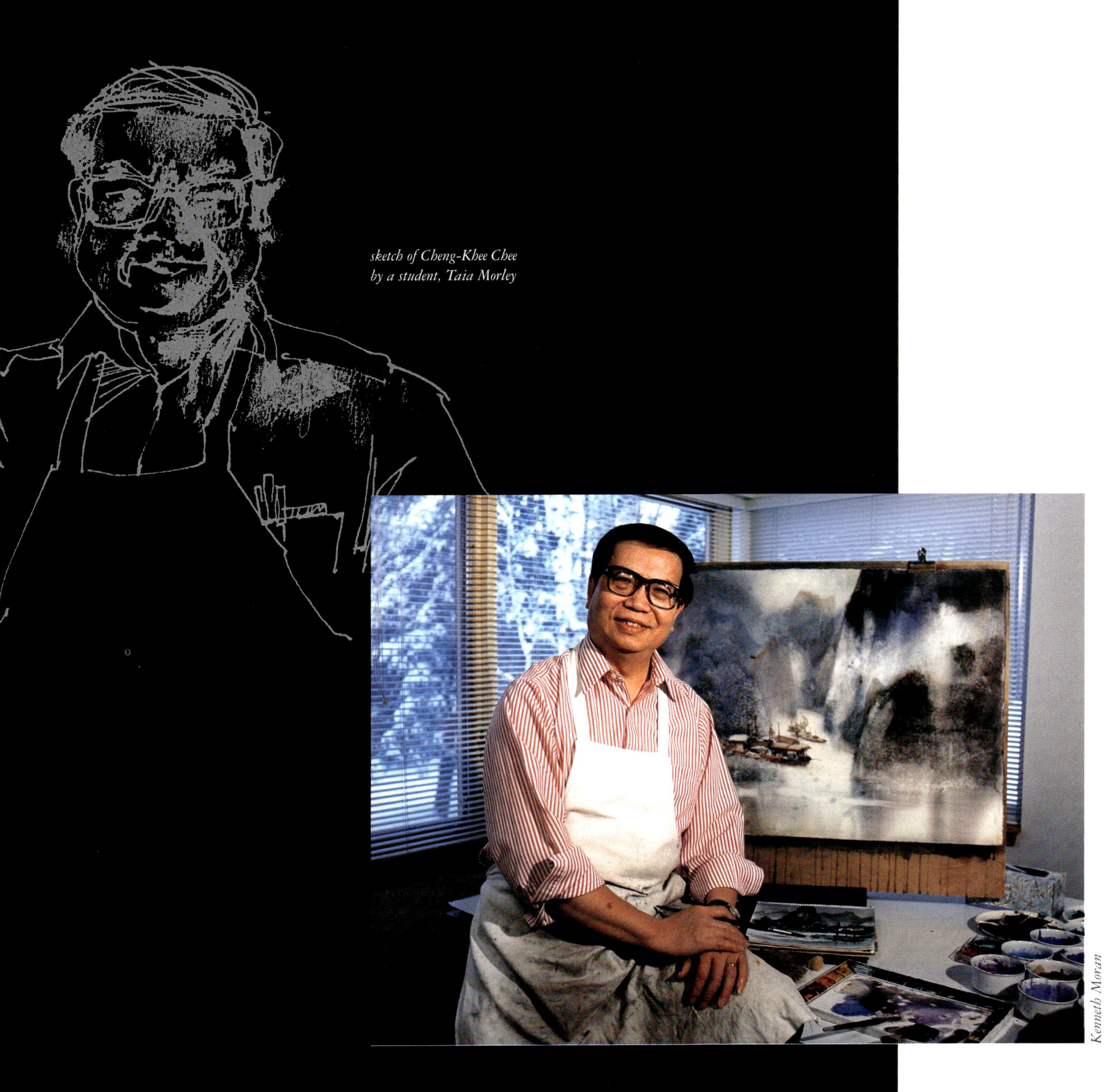

sketch of Cheng-Khee Chee by a student, Taia Morley

Kenneth Moran

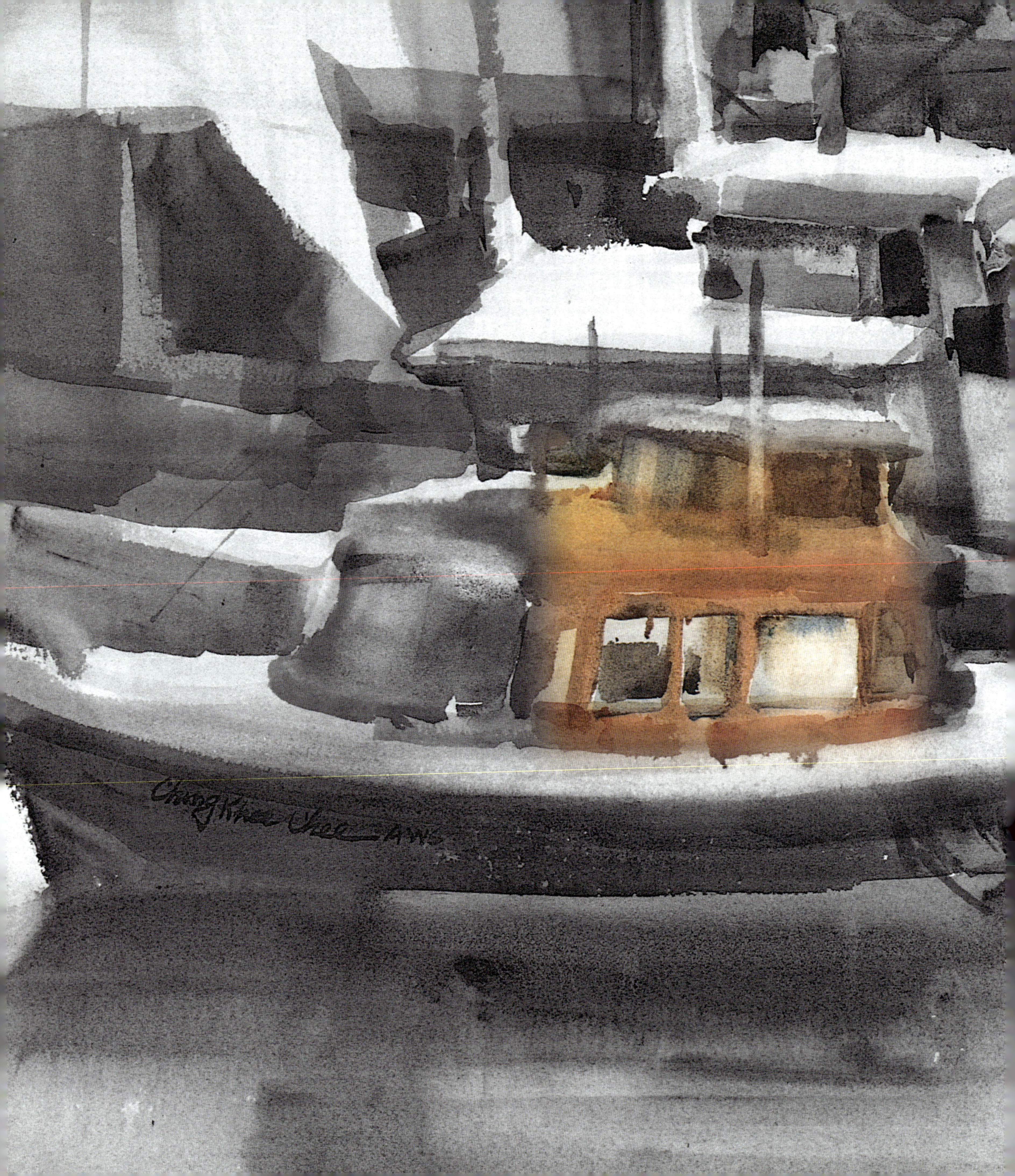

Traditional Watercolor

Traditional Watercolor Technique

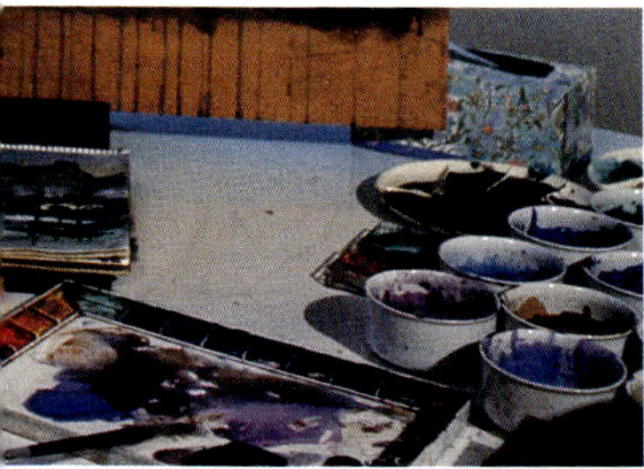

Although striving for innovation, I have never overlooked the importance of traditional/academic approaches to watercolor painting. It is imperative to master drawing skills and techniques of handling the inherent qualities of watermedia such as controlling paint and washes. It is also crucial to have a thorough understanding of design. Before starting a painting, I would analyze its design elements such as line, color, texture, value, shape and then orchestrate these elements into a cohesive painting by applying design principles.

For each traditional watercolor, I generally select a sketch I did on location together with a few photo references as bases. From here I evaluate the design elements, determine the focus point, plan the space division, select a color scheme, and work out a value pattern. I do a half sheet color study first, then progressively work up to a full sheet, and finally a double elephant, the preferred size of my final version of a painting. Often times I have wasted many sheets of paper before arriving at a painting that I feel is my best effort at the time. Although the planning is careful and calculating, I strive for a painting with freshness, spontaneity and vitality.

The end results of my paintings are mostly representational, but I start each painting with an abstract design pattern. I practice art in non-objective, abstract and realistic persuasions. I do not believe in the superficial division of these viewpoints. I paint what I most deeply feel at heart, and what is most true and natural to me. It is my desire to synthesize all three viewpoints in my paintings.

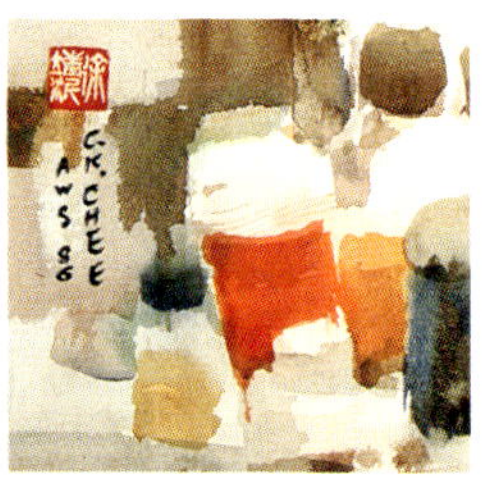

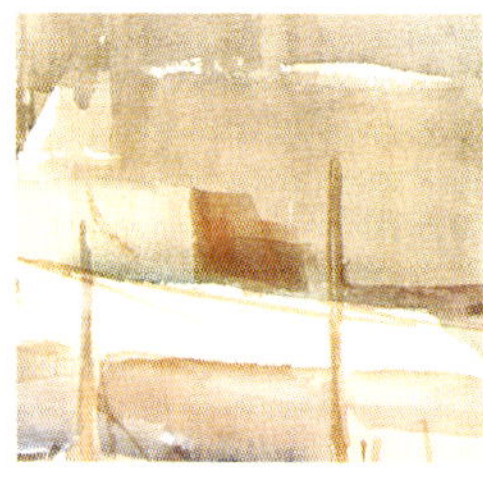

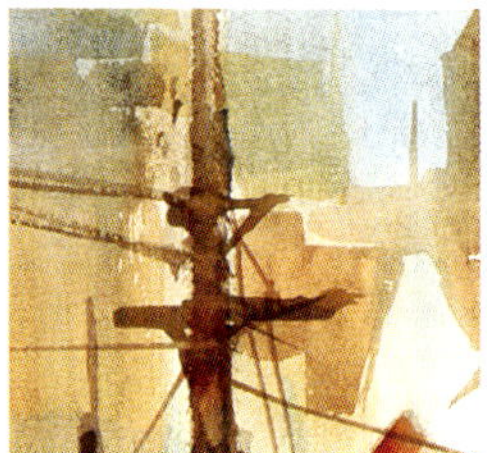

传统水彩

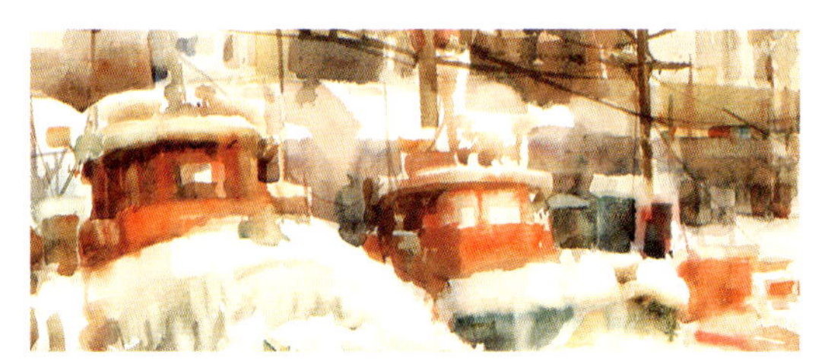

虽然我不断在探索新的题材和表现技法，但是从来不忽视传统水彩的重要性。素描的功夫和处理水彩特性的技能都是非常重要的。造型的准确，颜色的应用，水份的控制，都要达到运用自如，得心应手的境界。再进一步，对构图设计的要素和原理，要有充分的了解。在没有动笔之前，一定要先分析物象的设计要素如点、线、面、色彩、肌理、形状、明暗关系等等，然后根据设计原理、组织画面，使它成为一幅有机结合的理想作品。

我画每一幅传统水彩的时候，都要经过严谨细密的计划。通常我在一幅水彩速写的基础上结合一些参考照片，仔细分析设计要素，决定中心，选择颜色，分割画面空间，拟定明暗关系，先画一个稿本，然后正式创作。经常要画几次，达到满意时为止。虽然准备工作细心策划，但到了画的时候，必须大胆落笔，尽量求明快新鲜，给看画的人有充满活力，一气呵成的感觉。

我的作品大部分是写实的，但也有抽象和半抽象的。我认为一个画家应该画他内心感受最深的题材，应用地认为最自然，最真实的表现技法和形式去发挥，而不应该肤浅地分别他的作品属於抽象或具象。

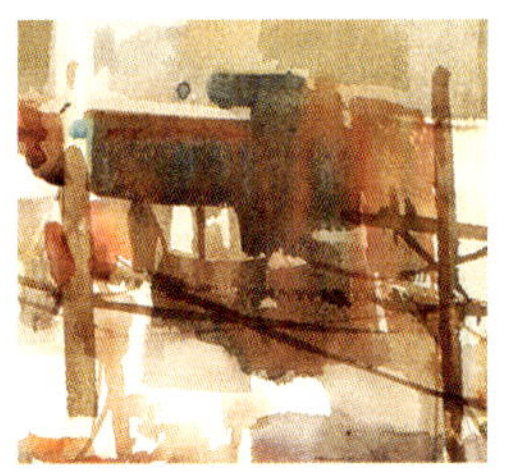
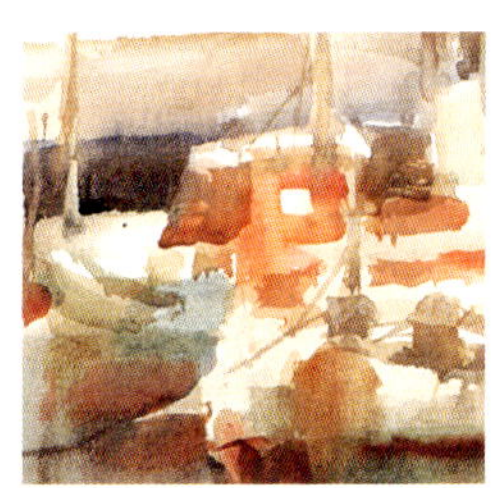
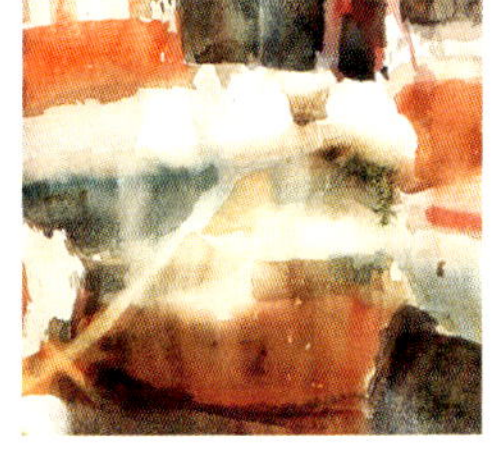

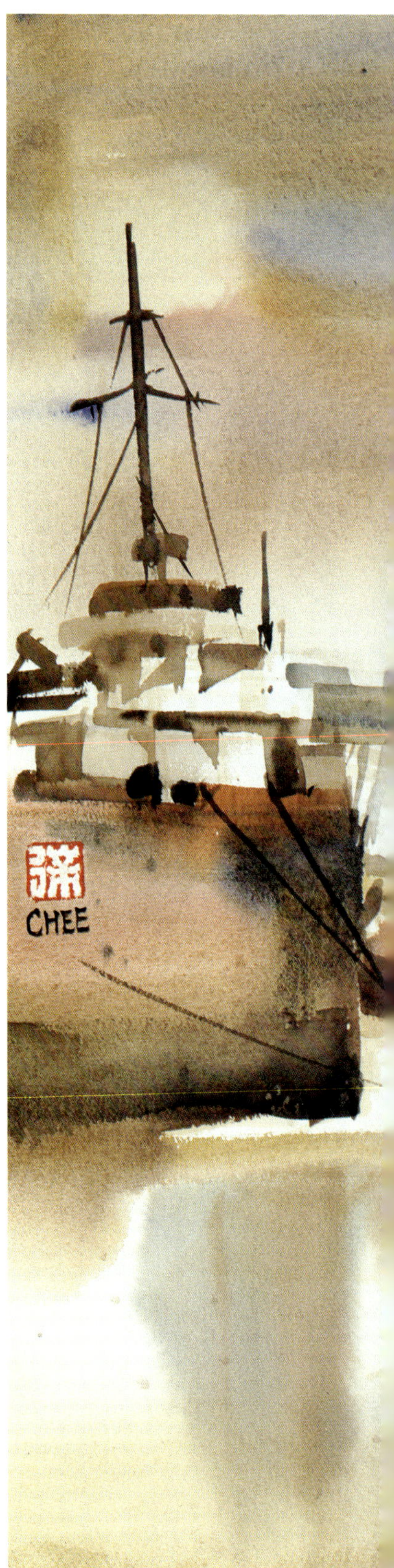

1

Ore Carriers

铁矿船

25" x 40" 63cm x 102cm

1980

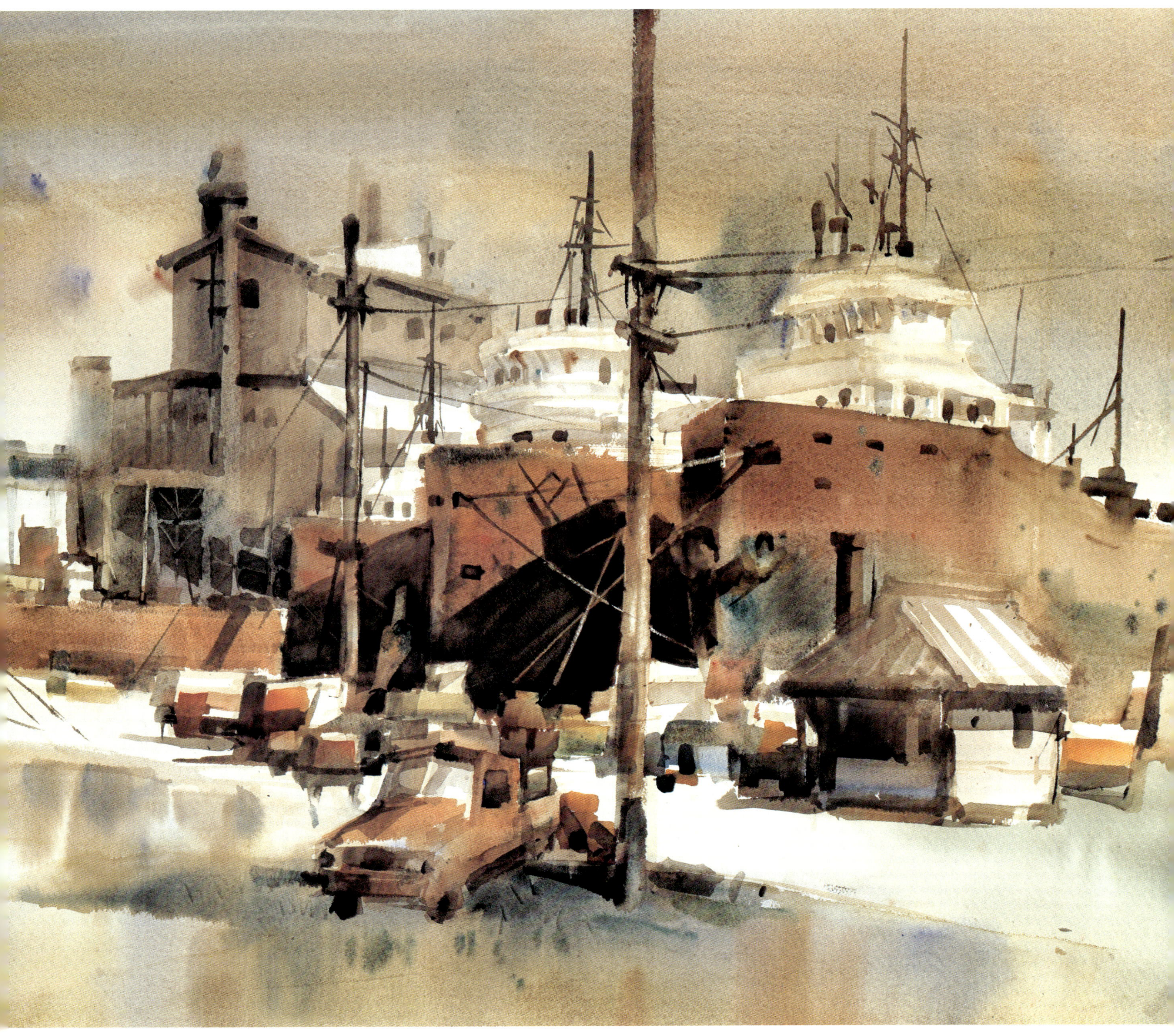

2

The Blizzard

暴风雪

25" x 40" 63cm x 102cm

1980

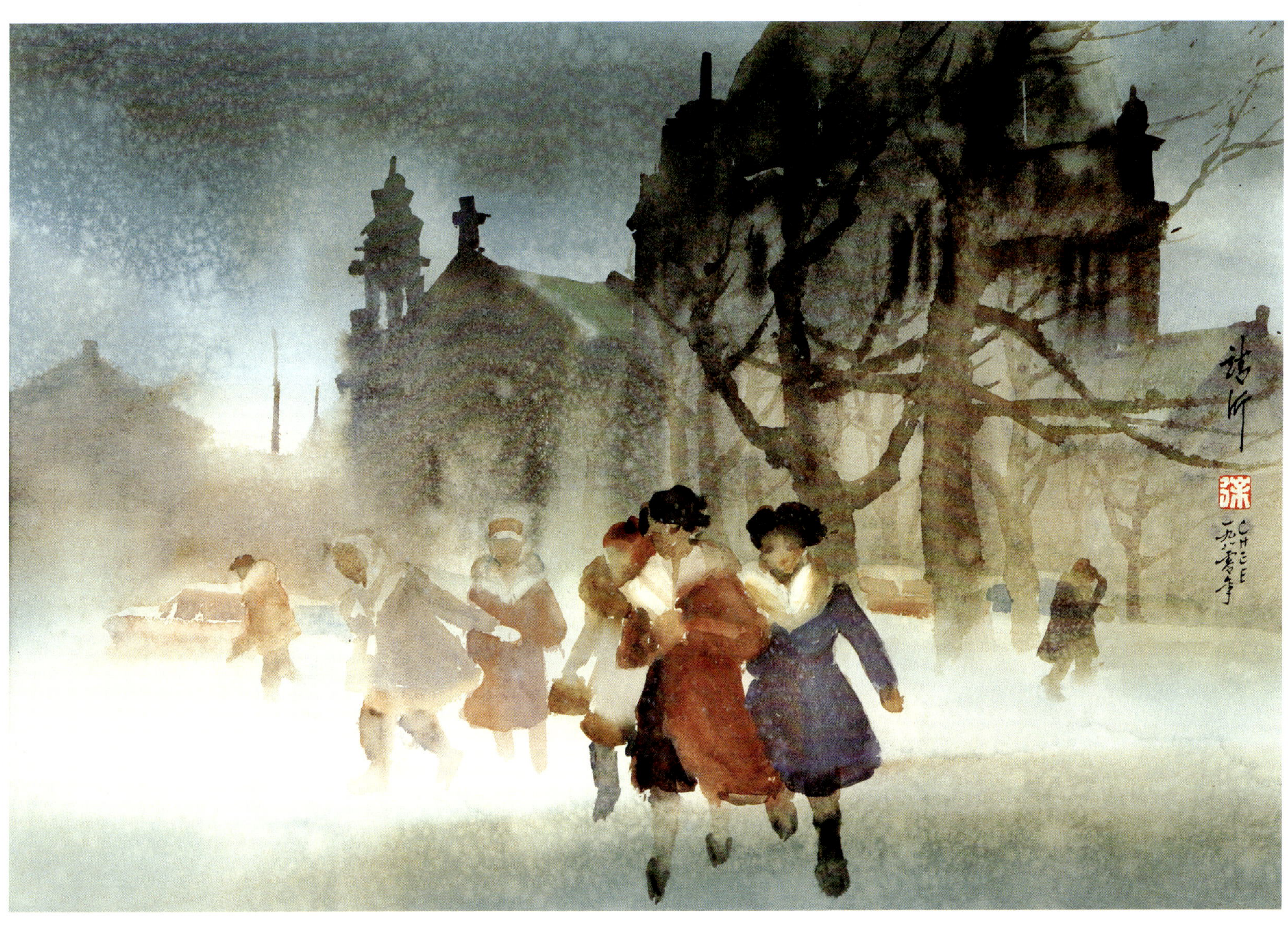

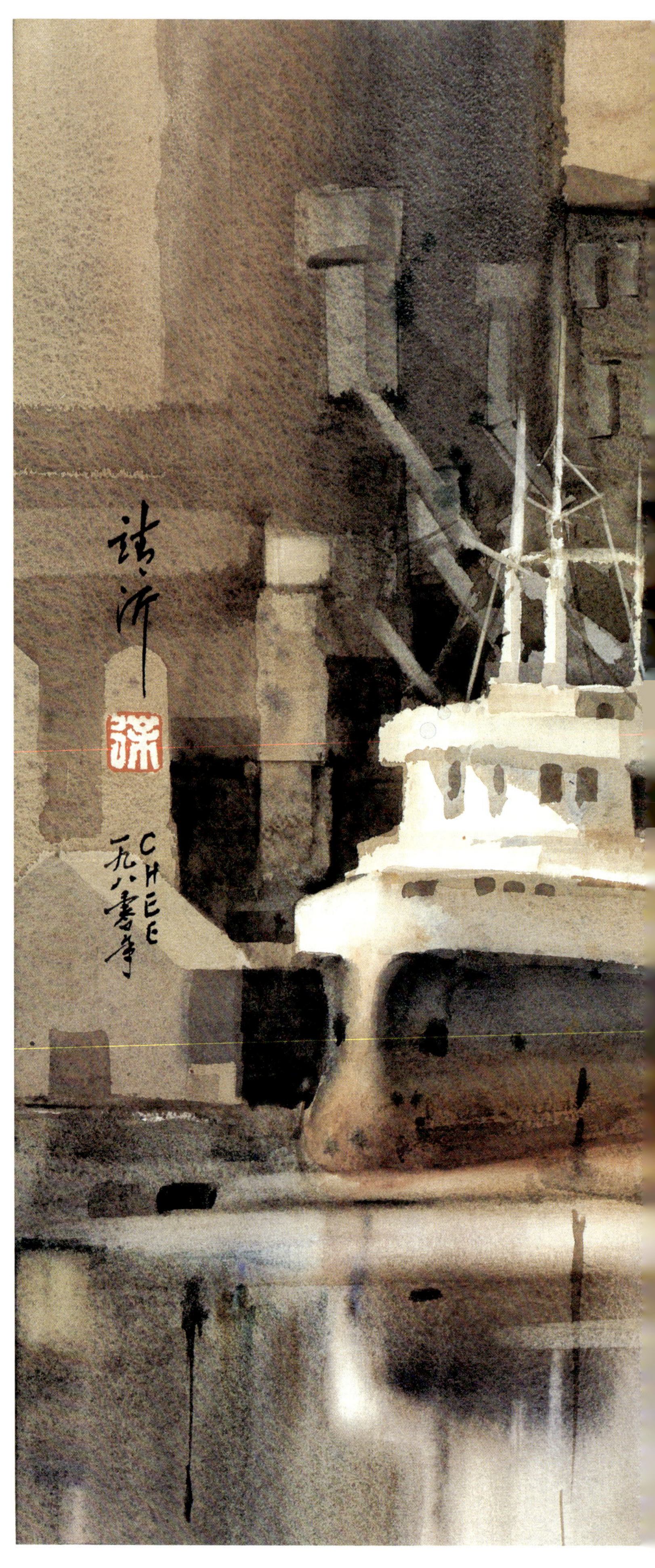

3

GRAIN TERMINALS

谷仓码头

30" x 40"   76cm x 102cm

1980

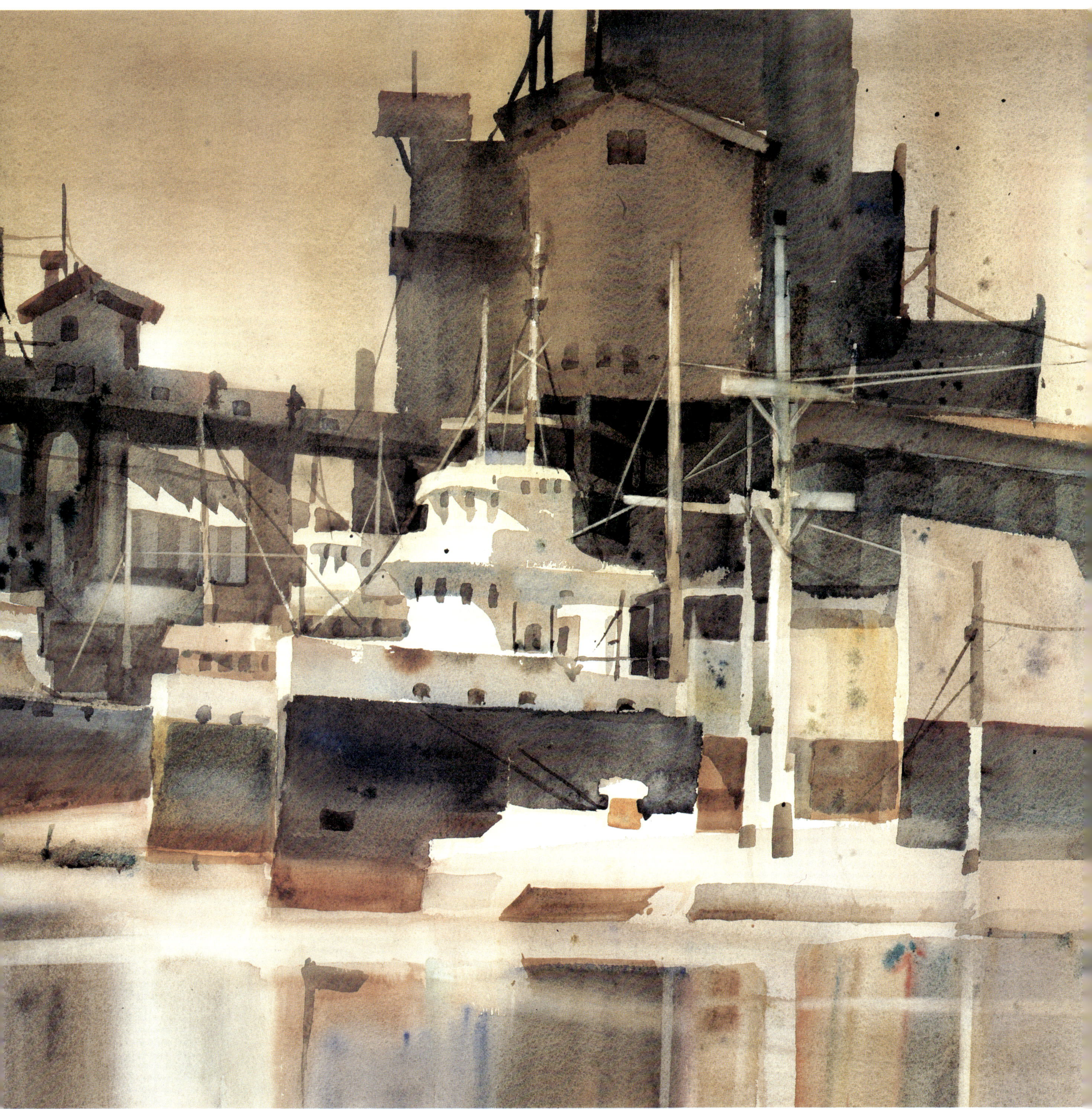

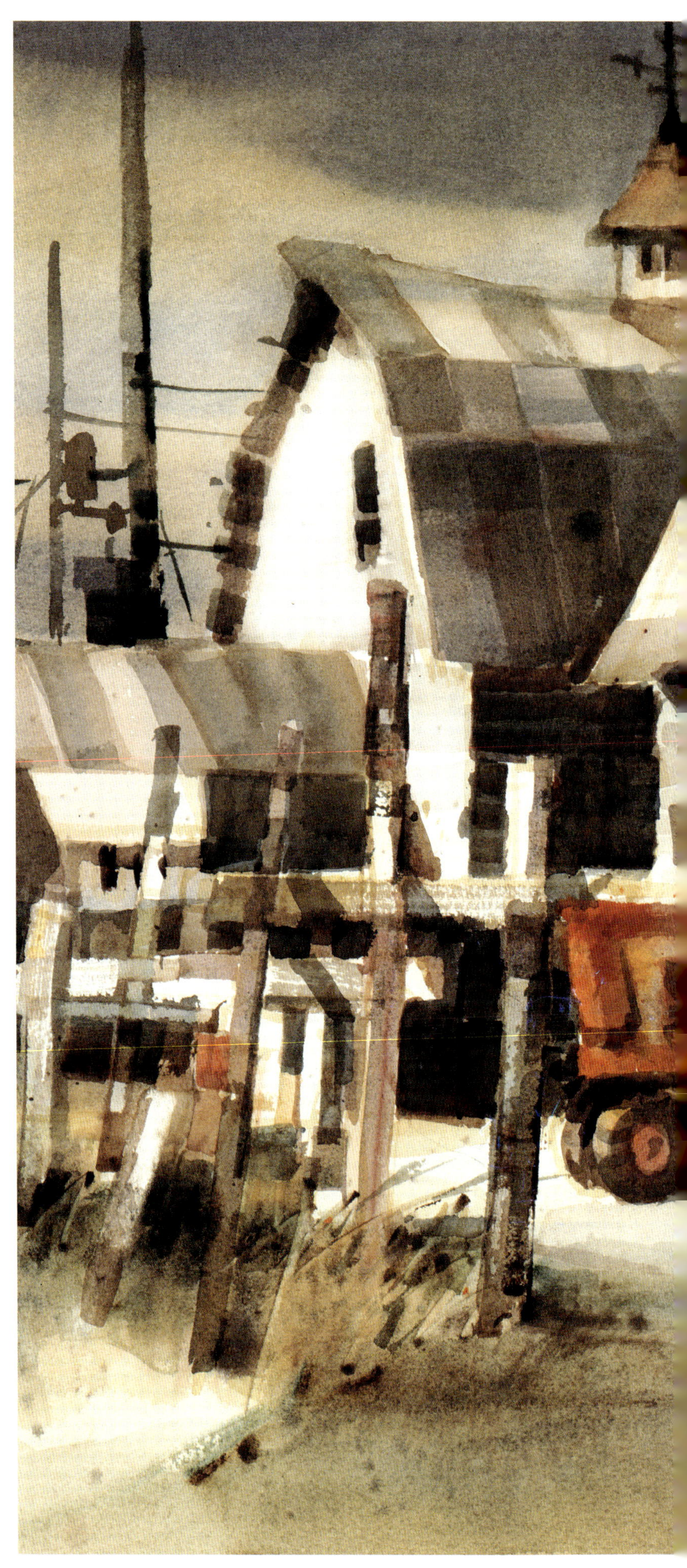

4

FARM AT TWIG

农场

25" x 40"   63cm x 102cm

1980

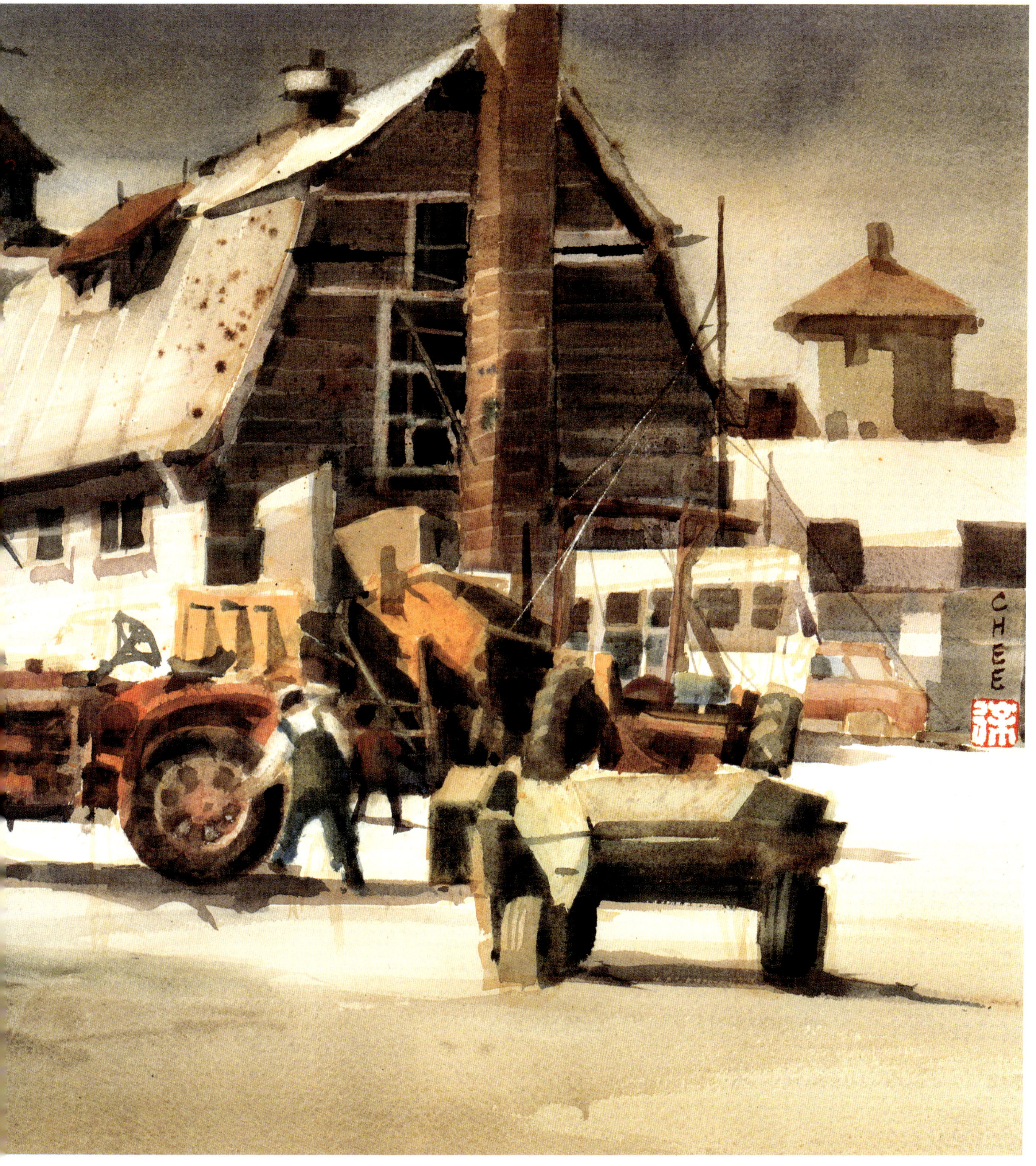
CHEE

5

Rainy Day – New York

纽约雨天

25" x 40" 63cm x 102cm

1981

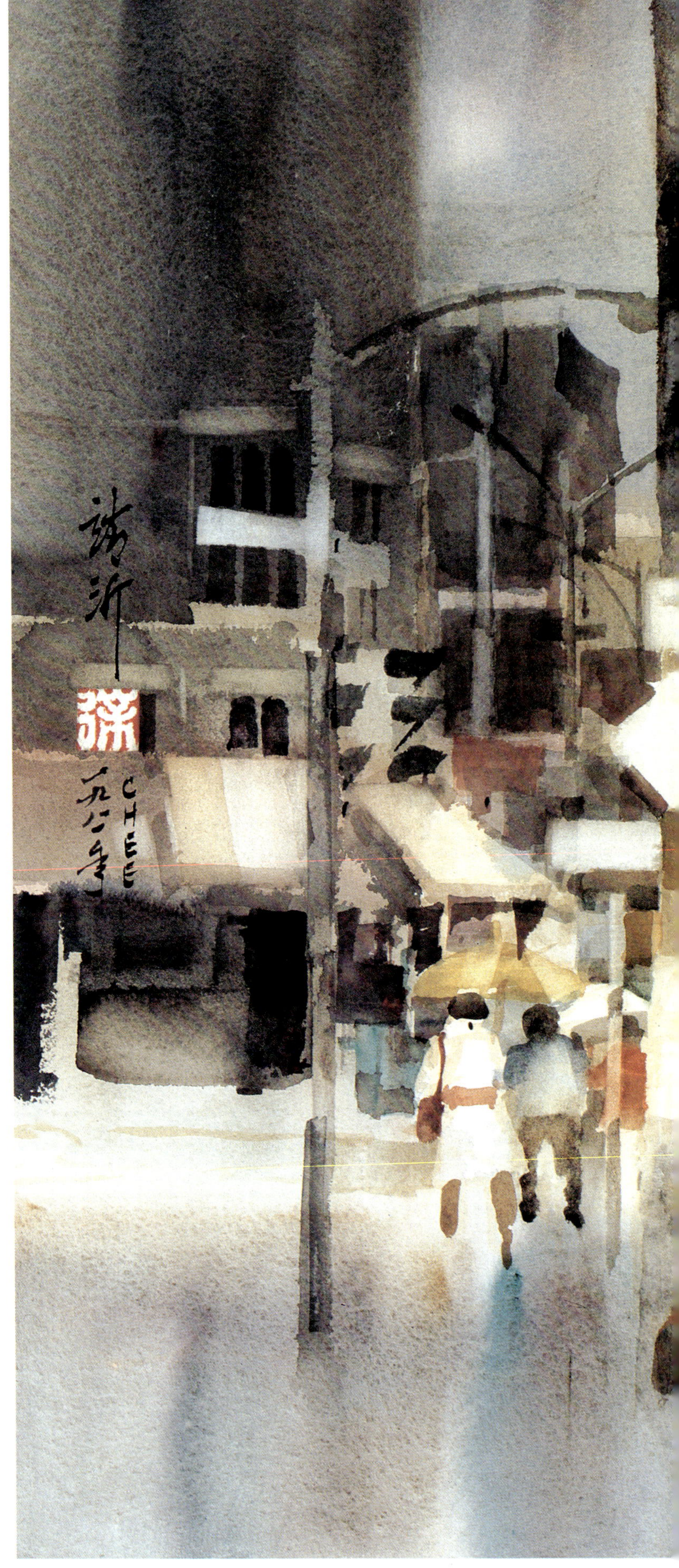

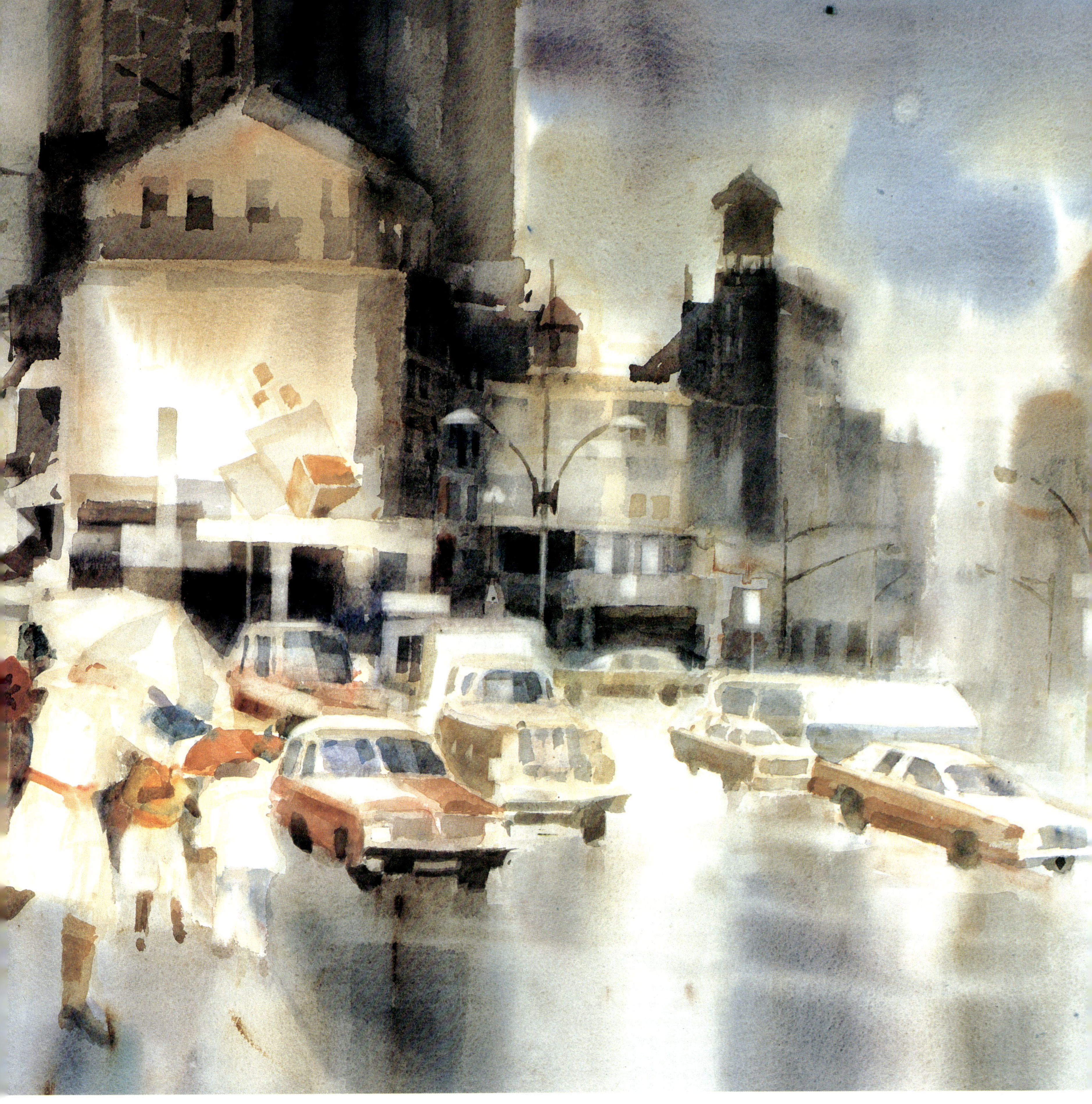

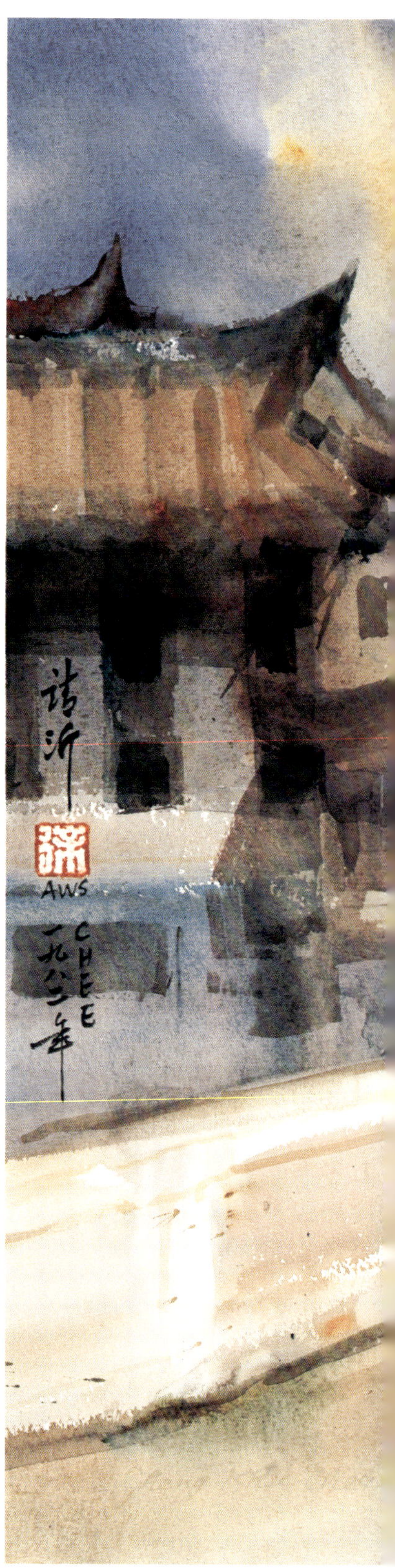

6

Fenting – My Hometown

枫亭一我的家乡

25" x 40"   63cm x 102cm

1982

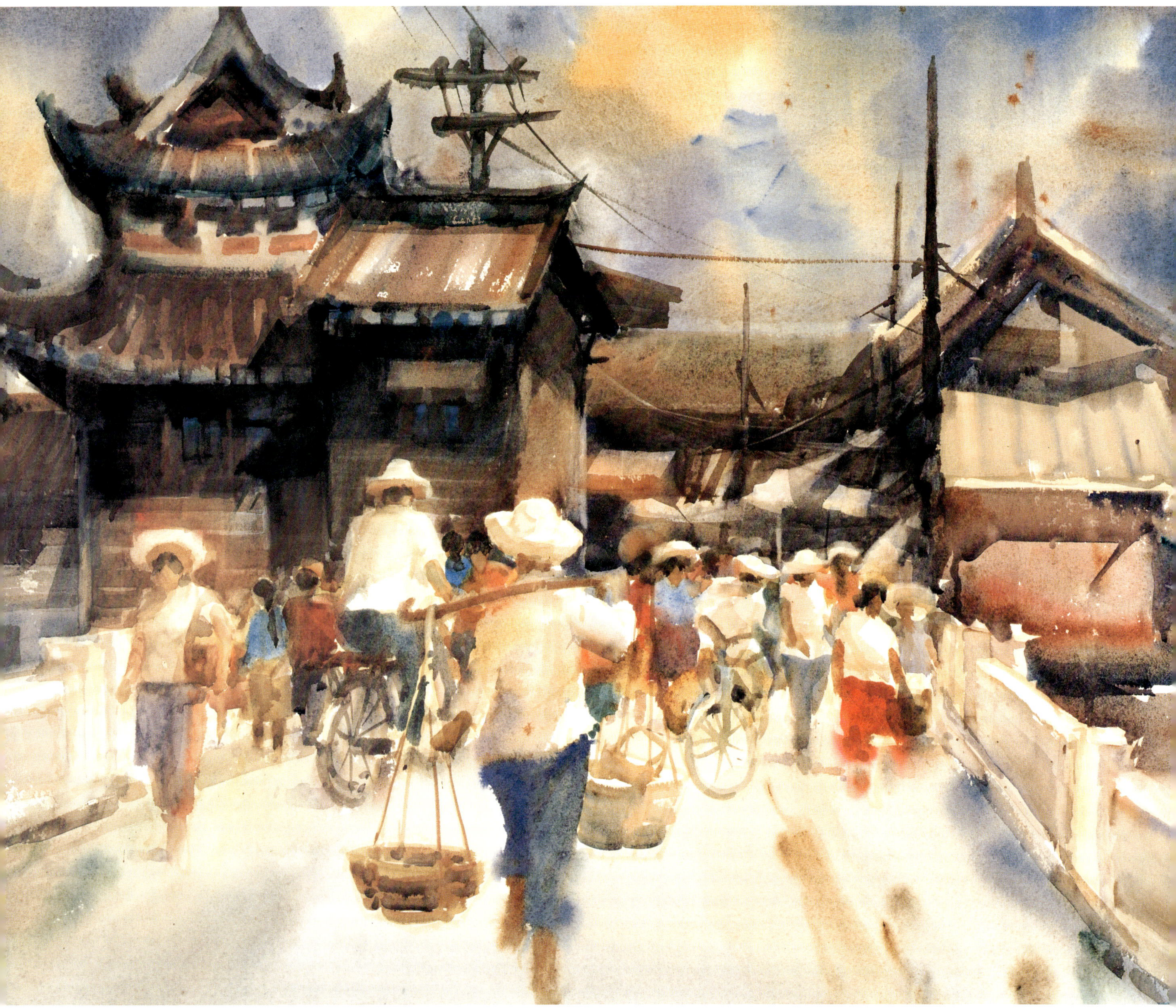

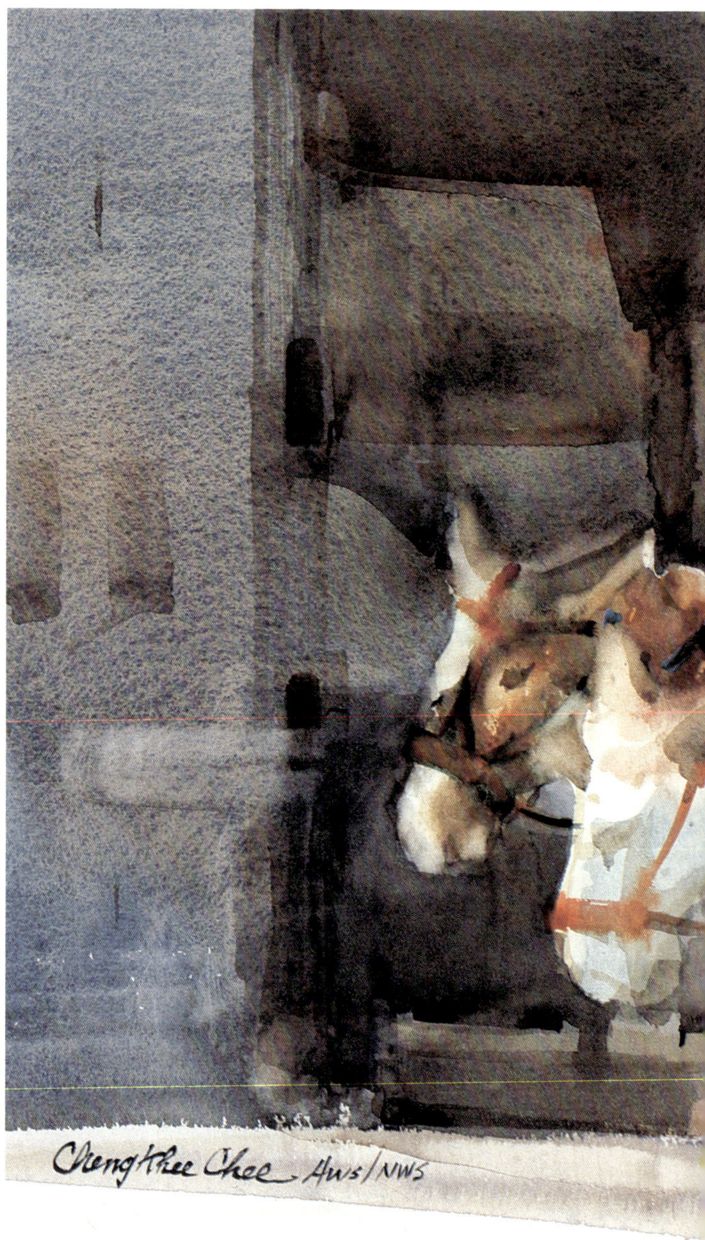

7

Beast of Burden, Xian

西安骡车

25" x 40"   63cm x 102cm

1983

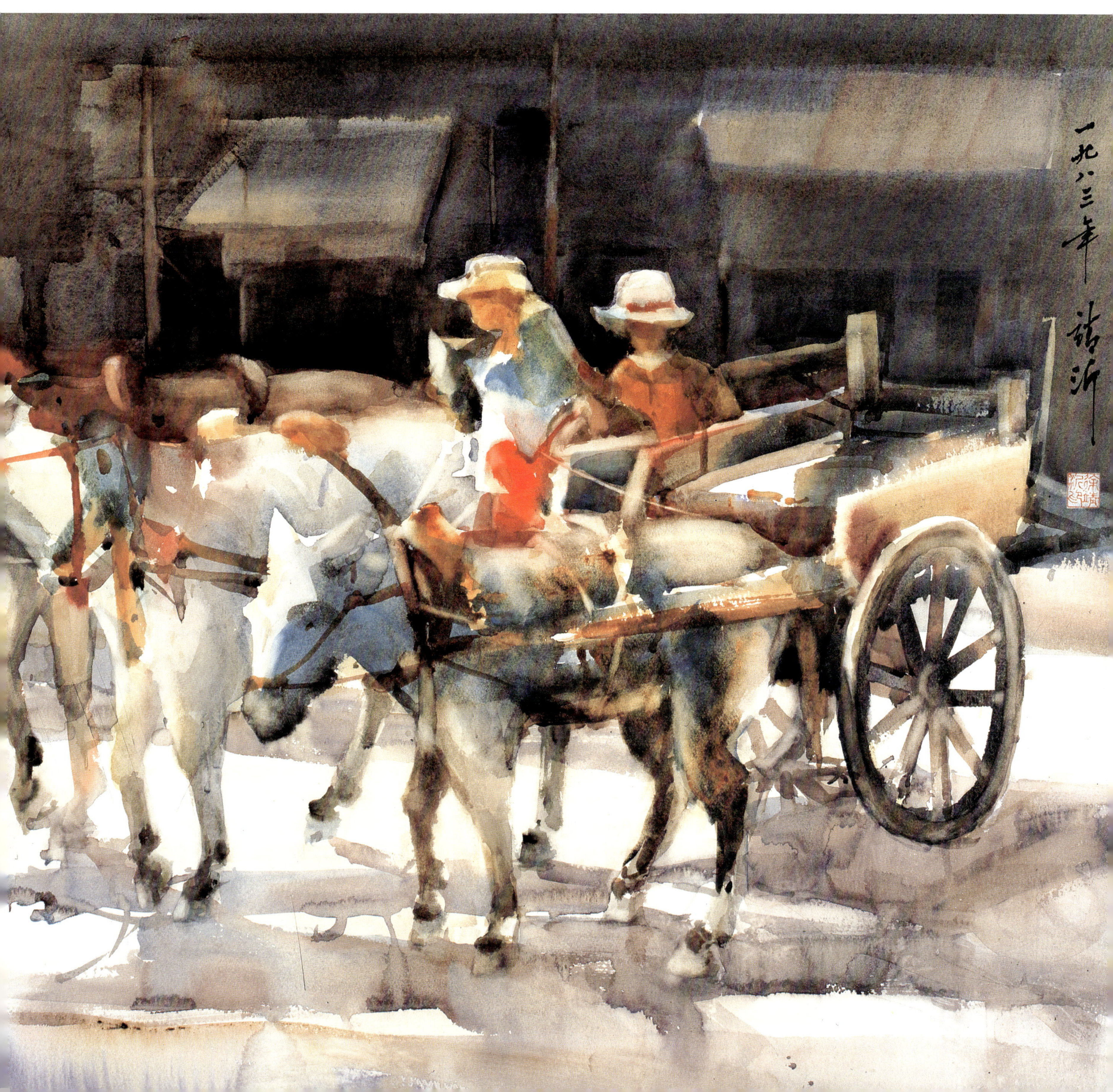
一九八三年

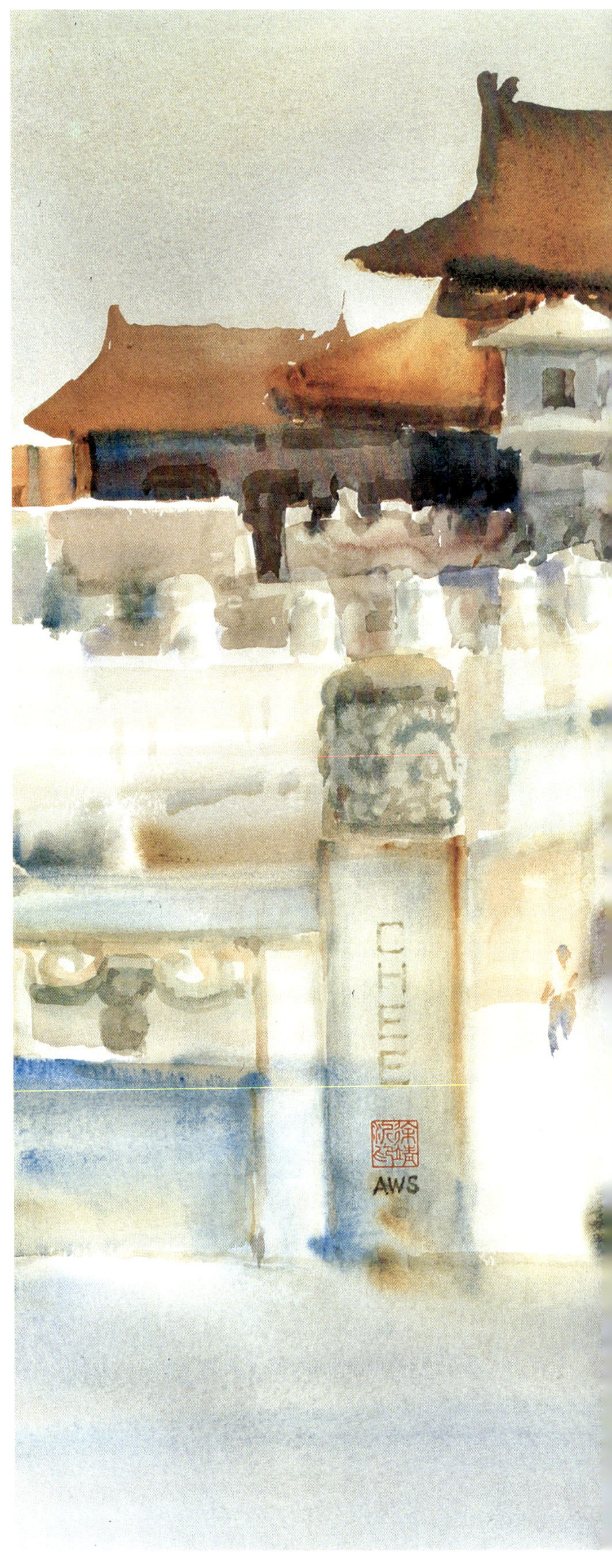

8

Forbidden City

紫禁城

25" x 40"   63cm x 102cm

1983

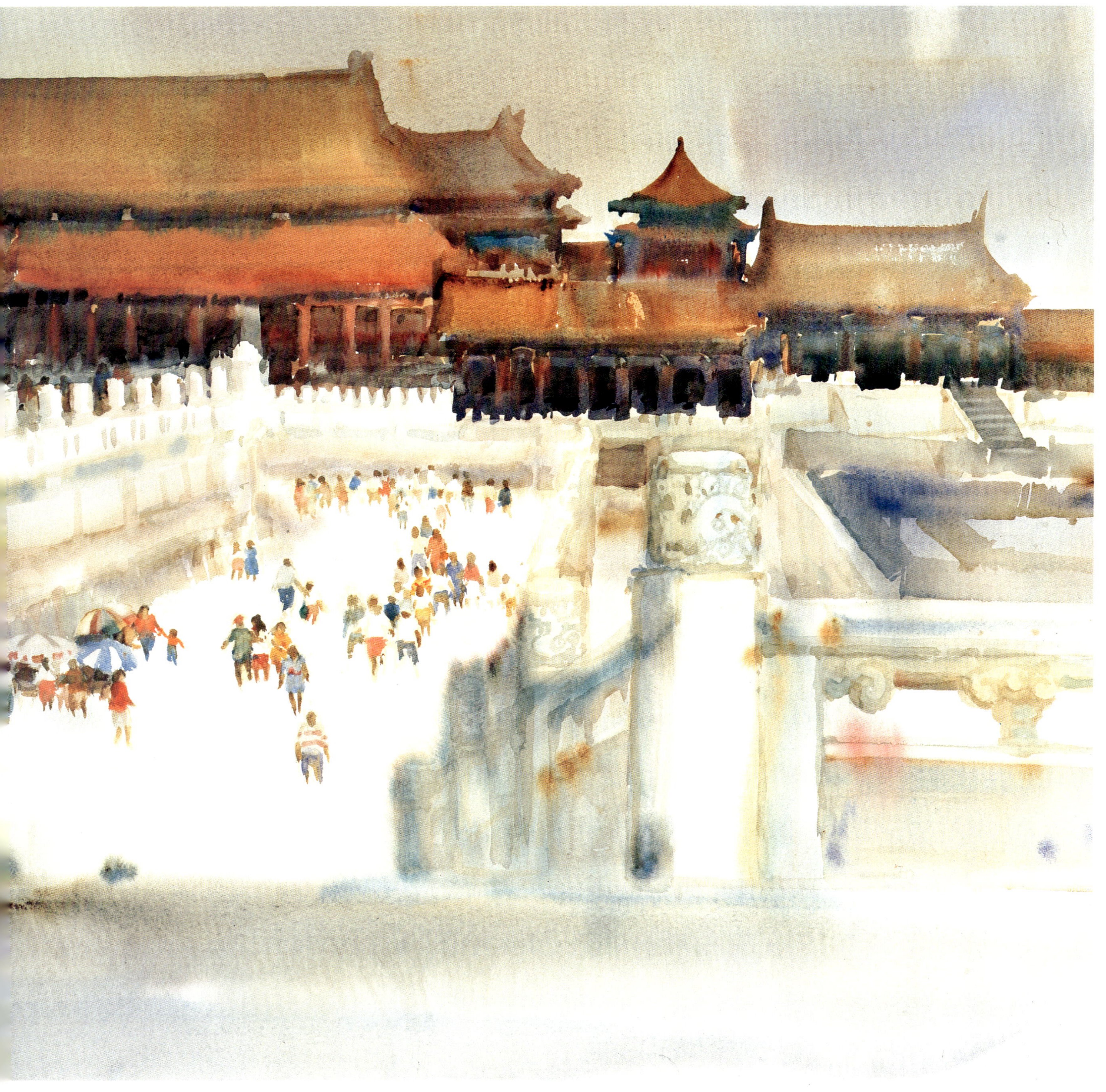

9

ENGLISH FISHING TOWN

英国渔镇

25" x 40"   63cm x 102cm

1984

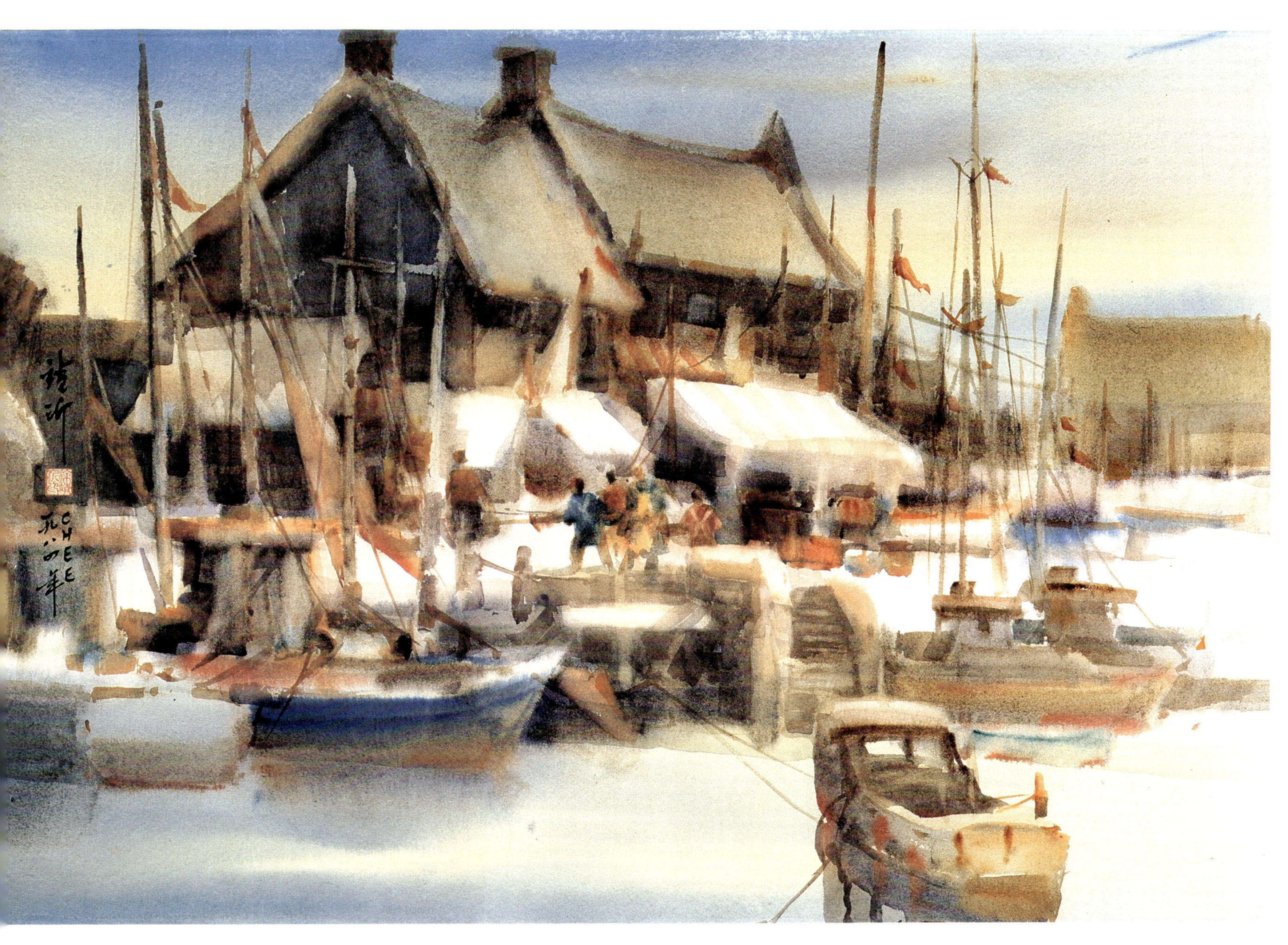
CHEE

10

Duluth Harbor

都鲁码头

25" x 40" 63cm x 102cm

1984

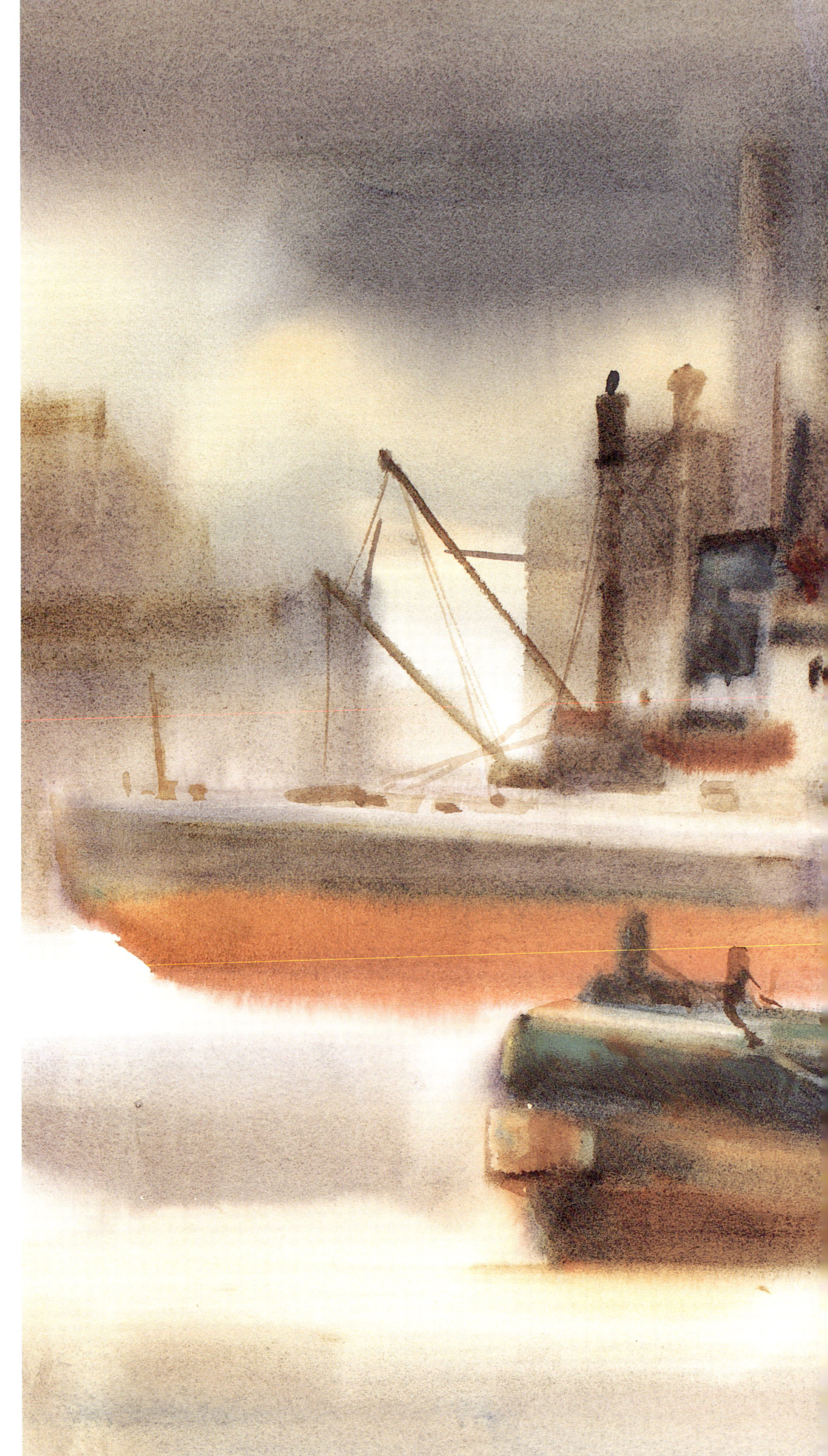

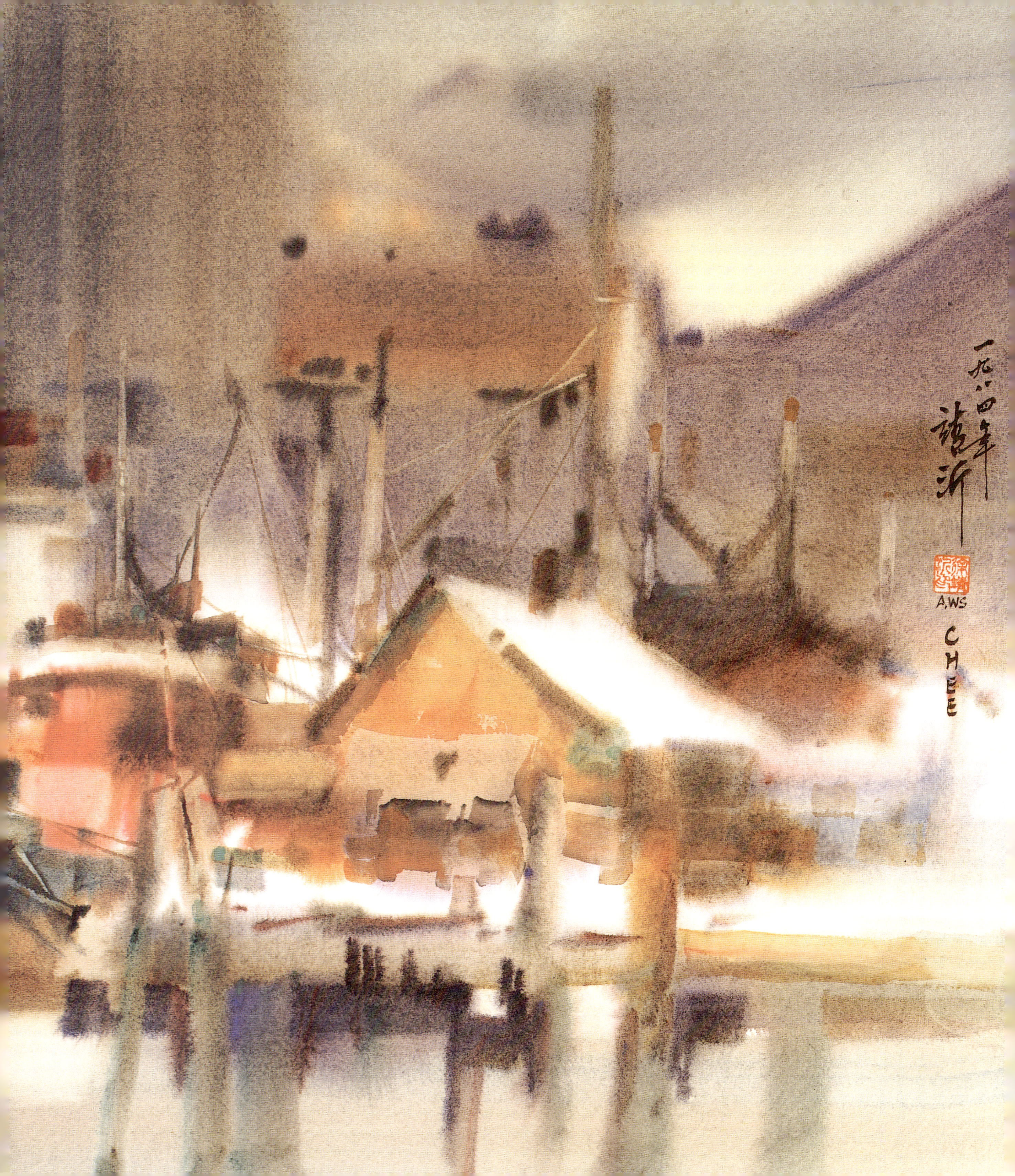
一九八四年
諸沂
A.WS
CHEE

11

WATERTOWN 85 NO.1

水乡85年1号

25" x 40" 63cm x 102cm

1985

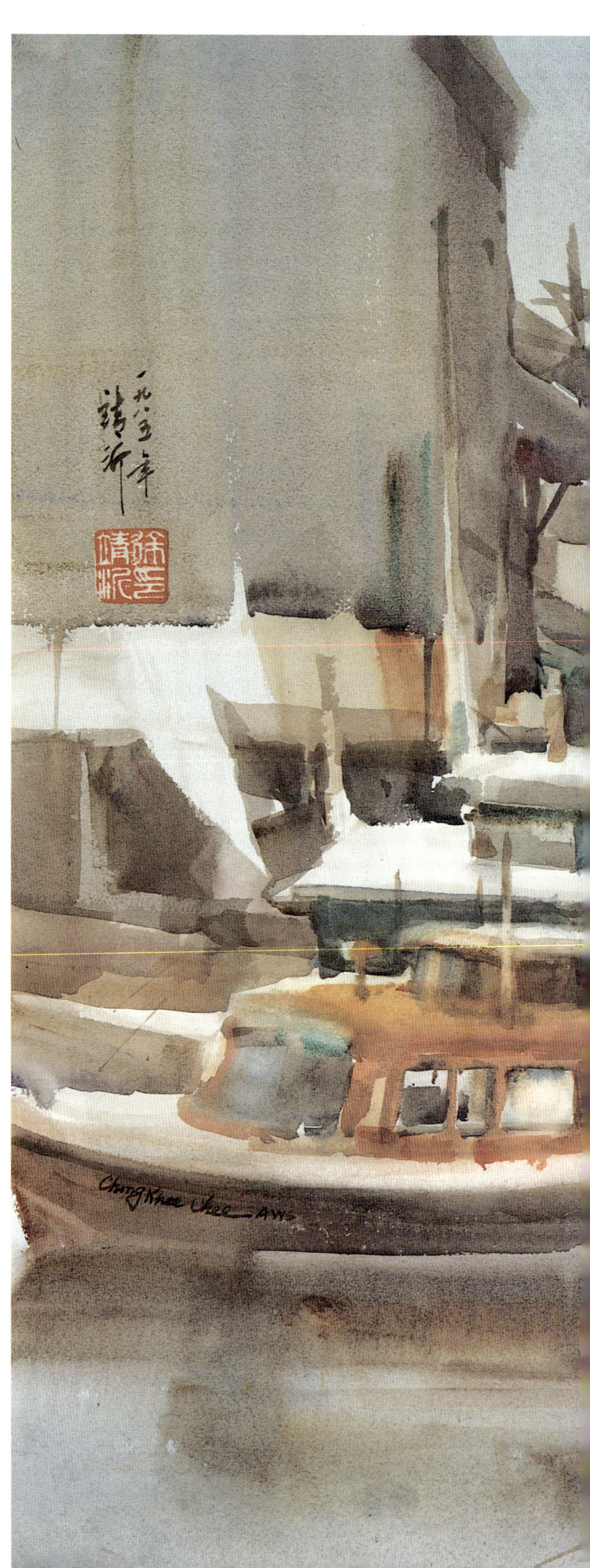

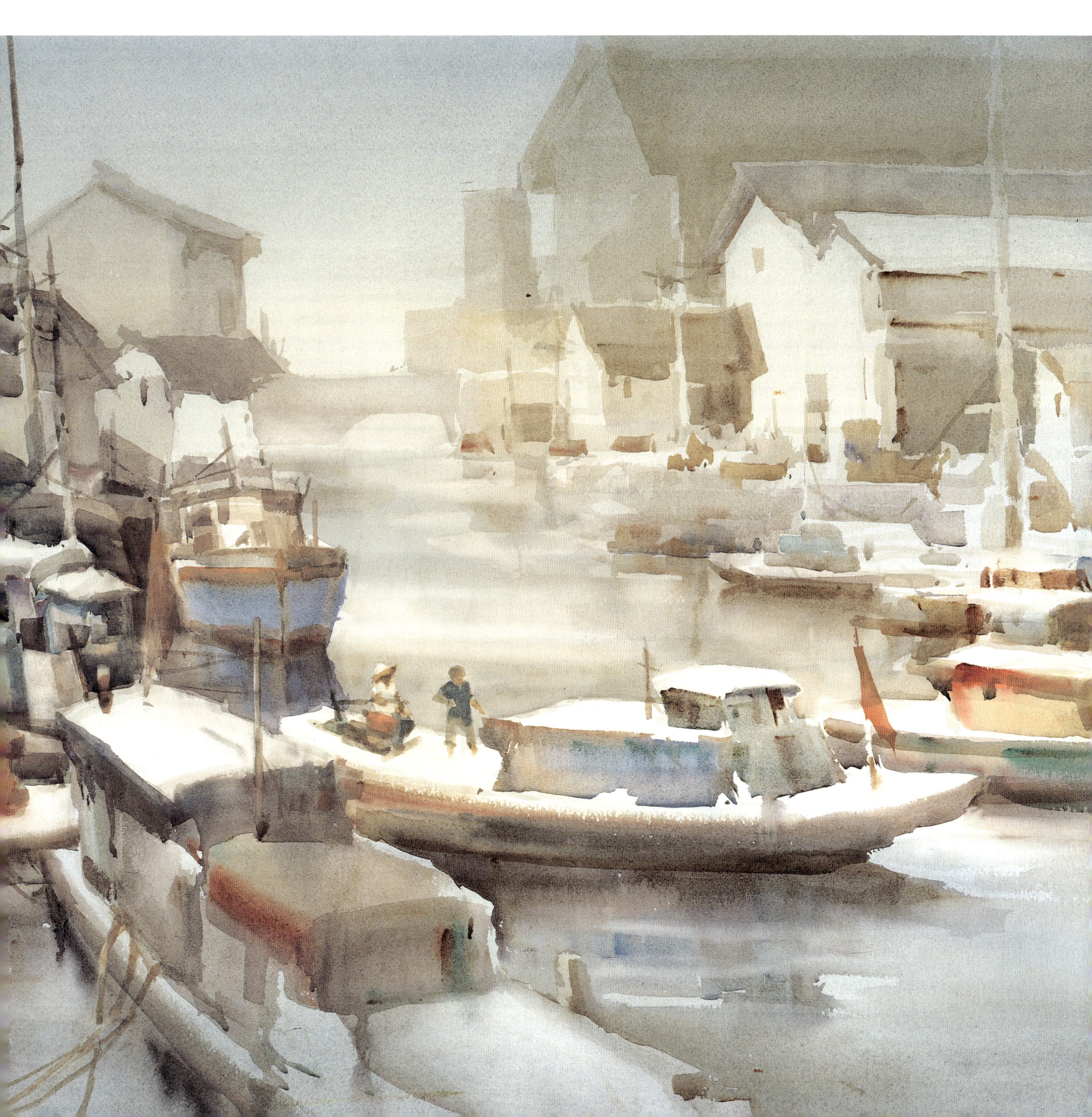

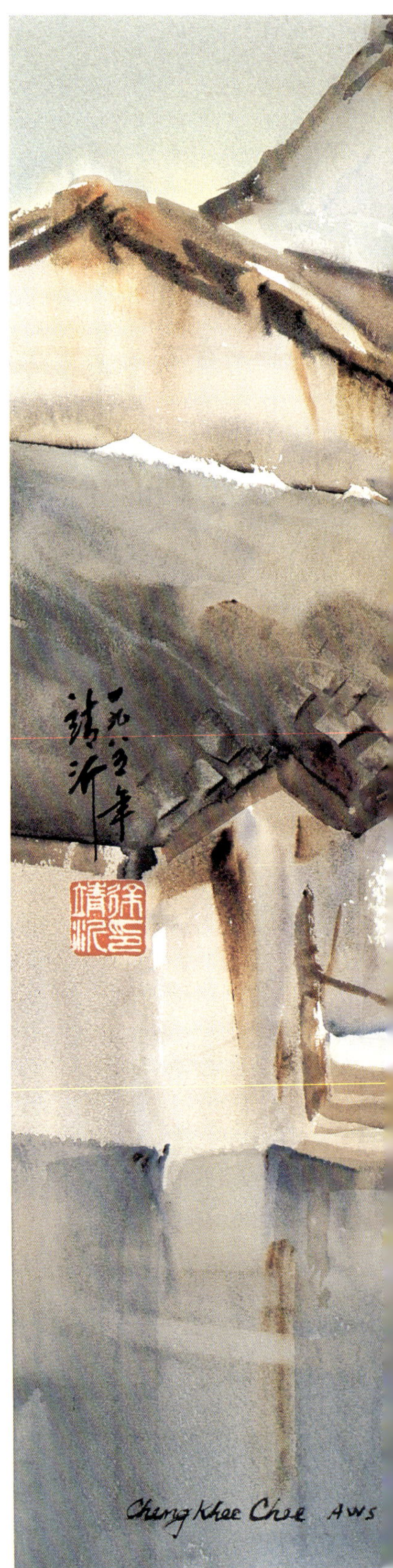

12

Watertown 85 No.2

水乡85年2号

25" x 40"   63cm x 102cm

1985

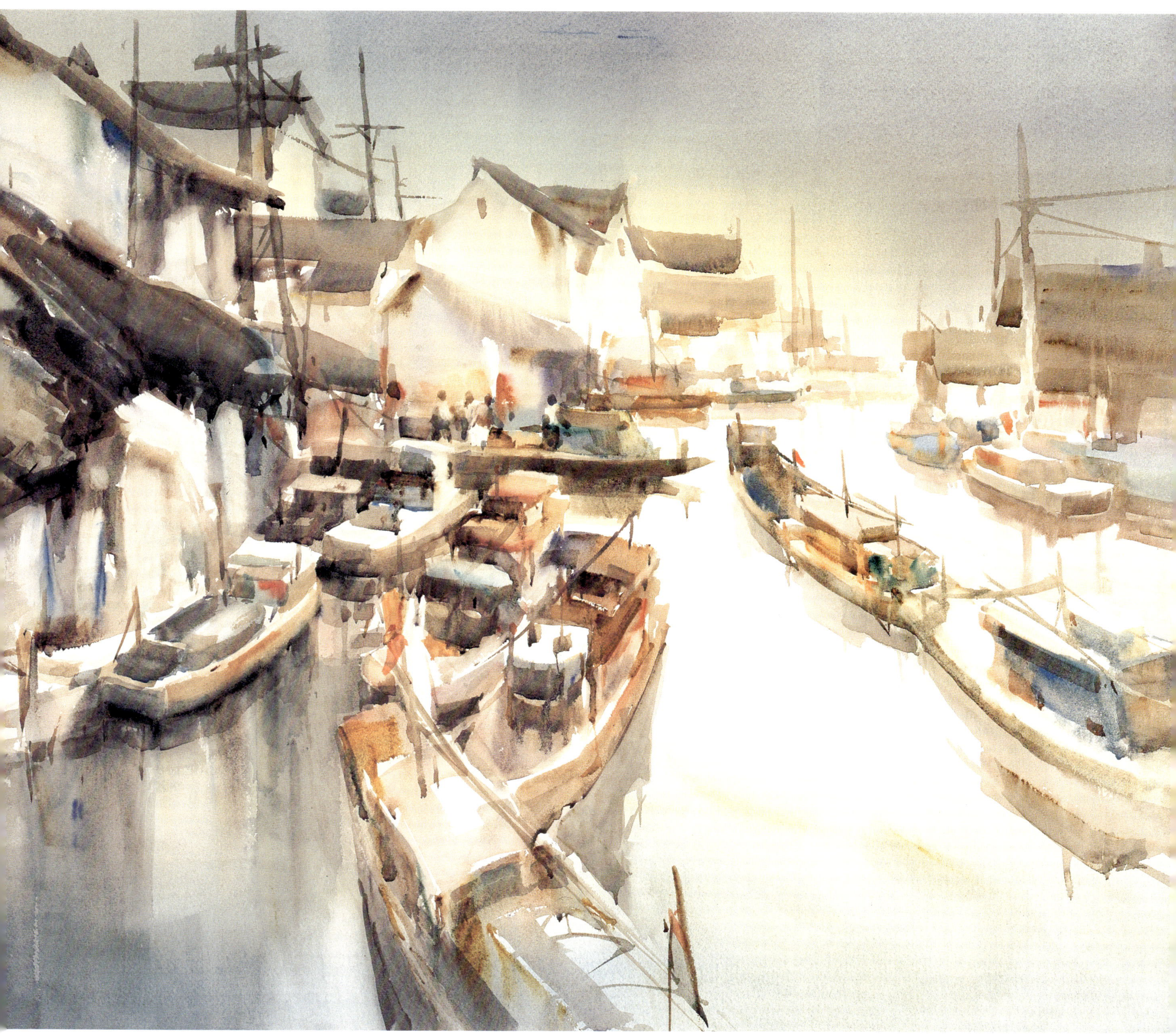

13

HANGZHOU ALLEY 85 NO.1

杭州后巷85年1号

25" x 40"   63cm x 102cm

1985

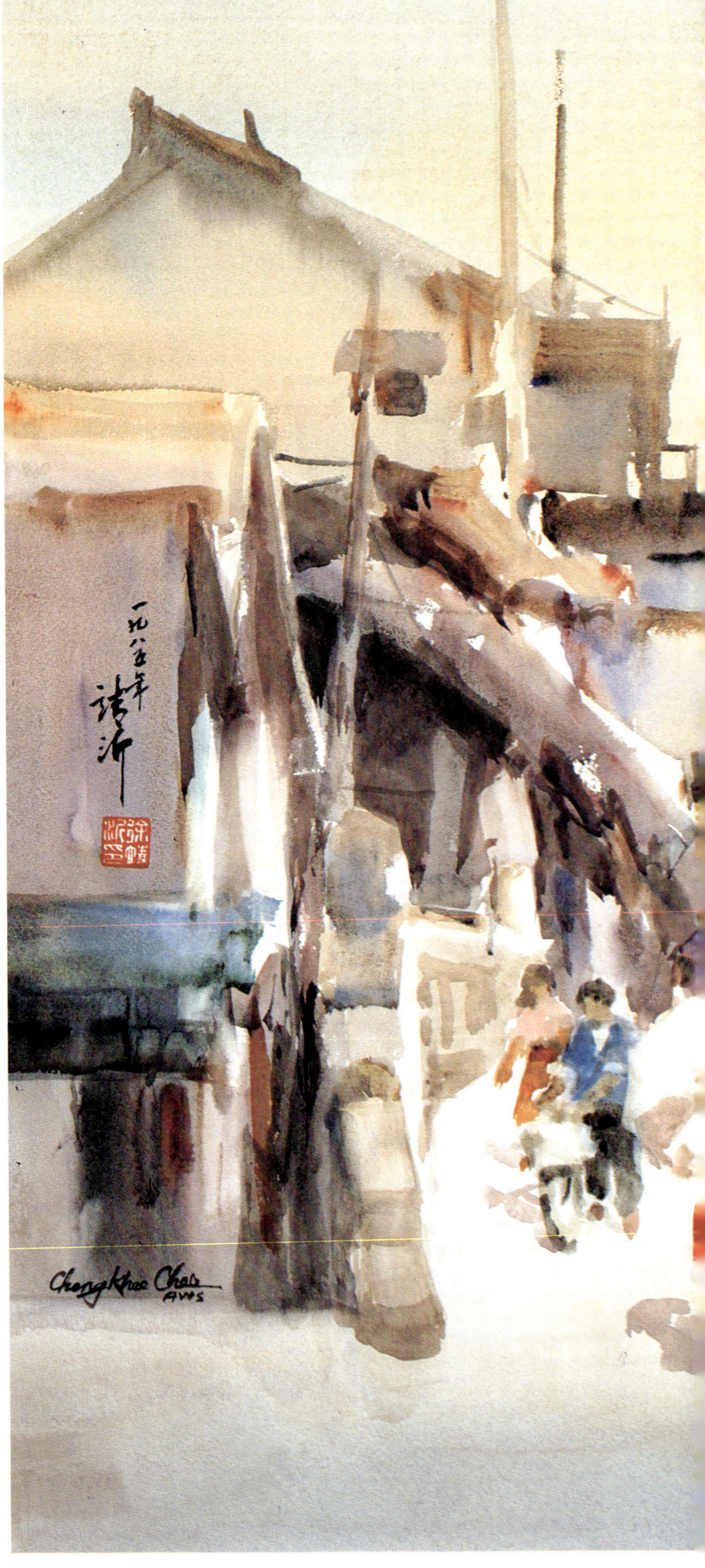

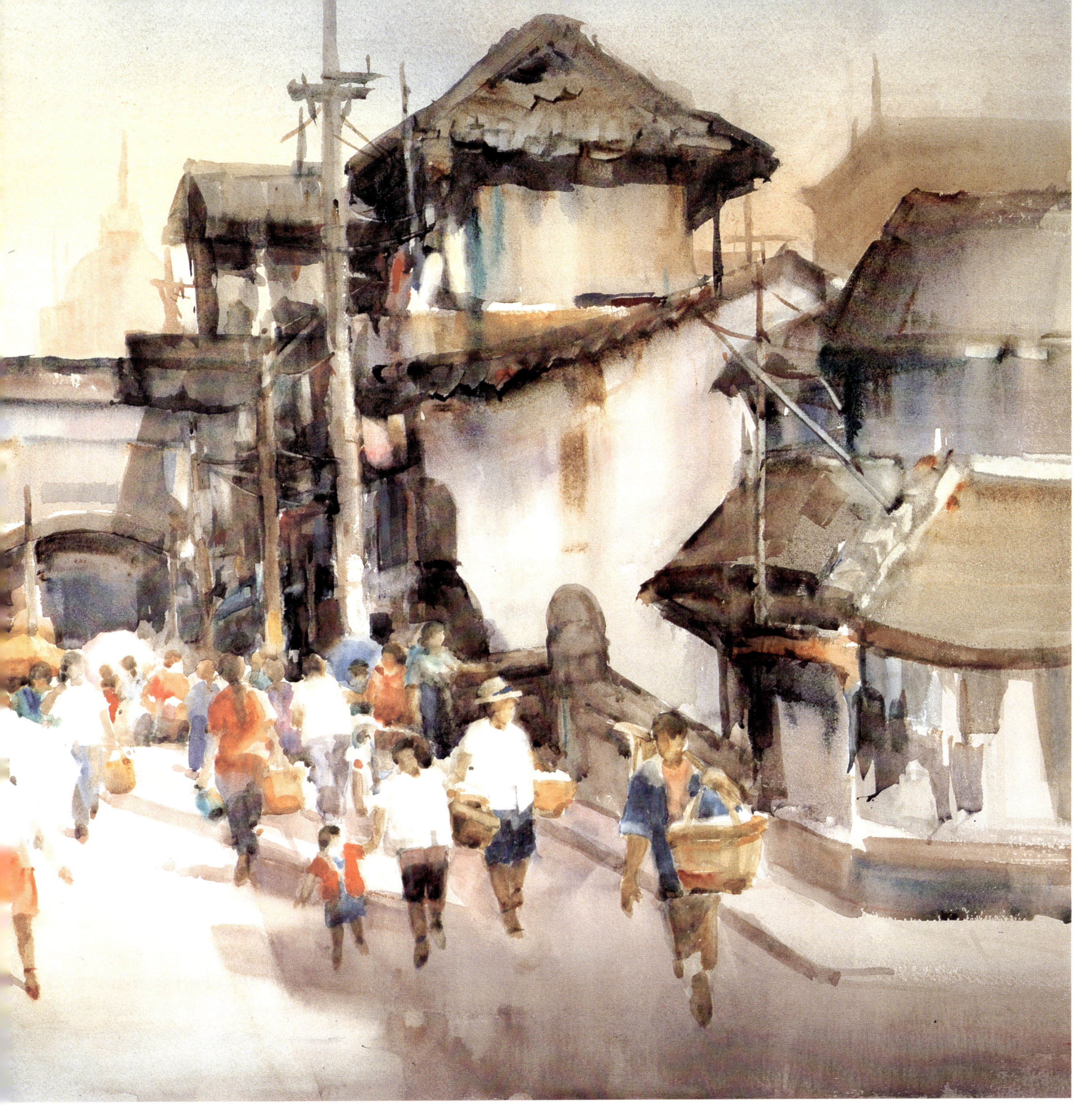

14

HANGZHOU ALLEY 85 NO.2

杭州后巷85年2号

25" x 40"   63cm x 102cm

1985

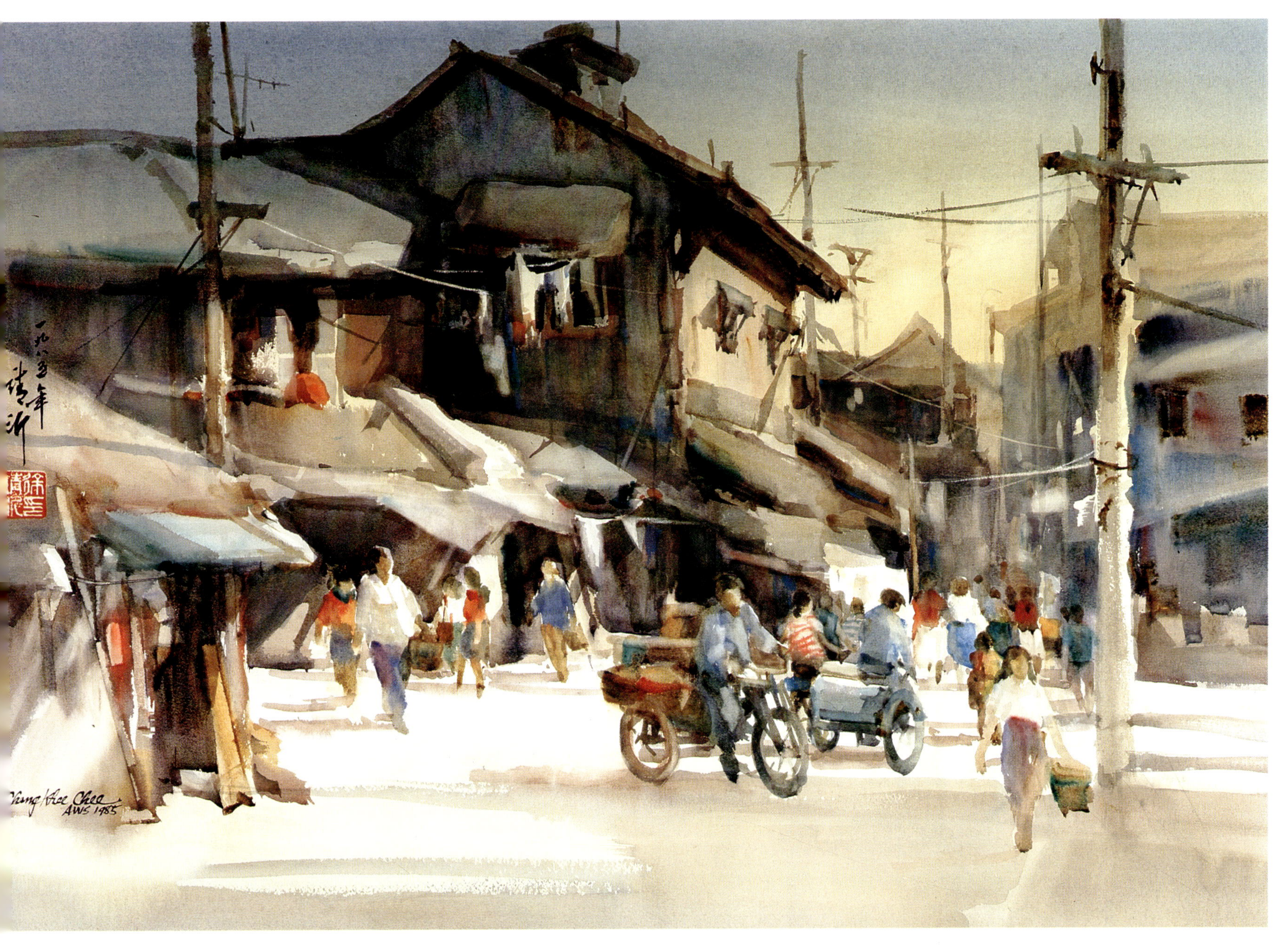
一九八五年
Khee Chee
AWS 1985

15

WINTER HARBOR

码头之冬

25" x 40"   63cm x 102cm

1986

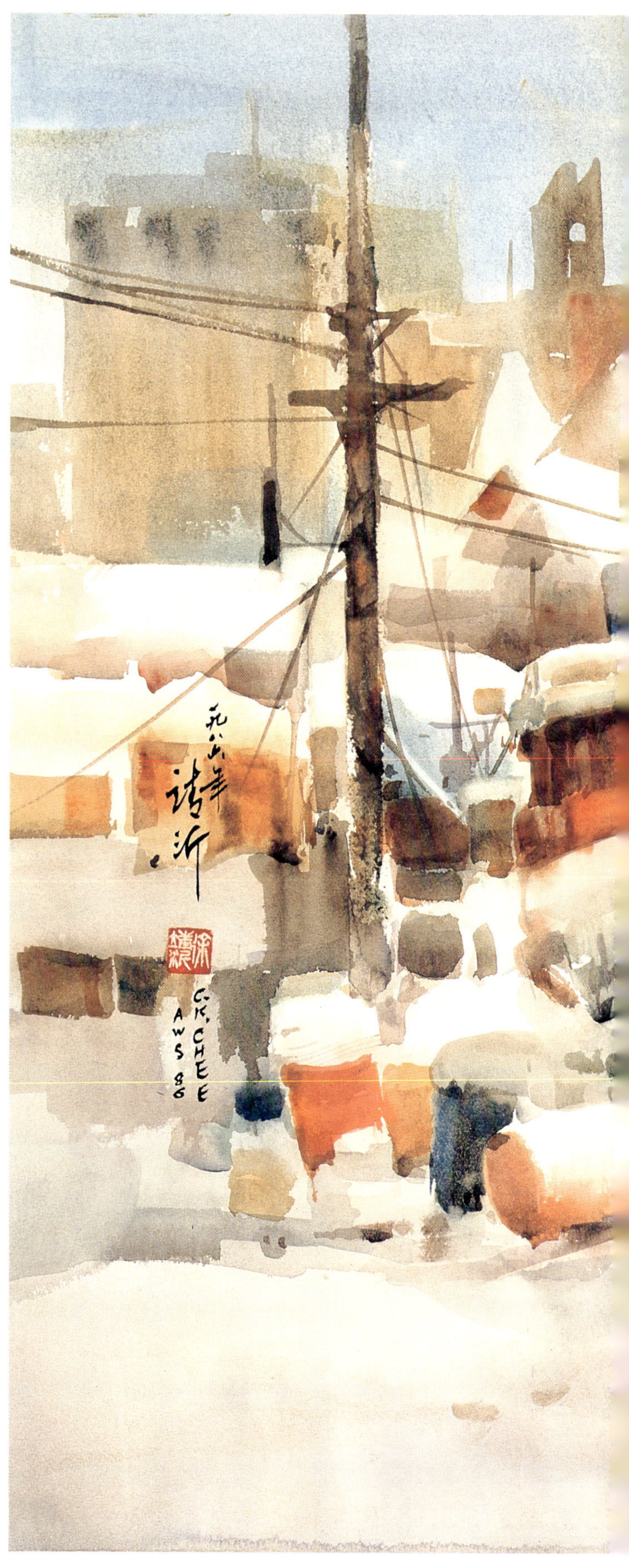

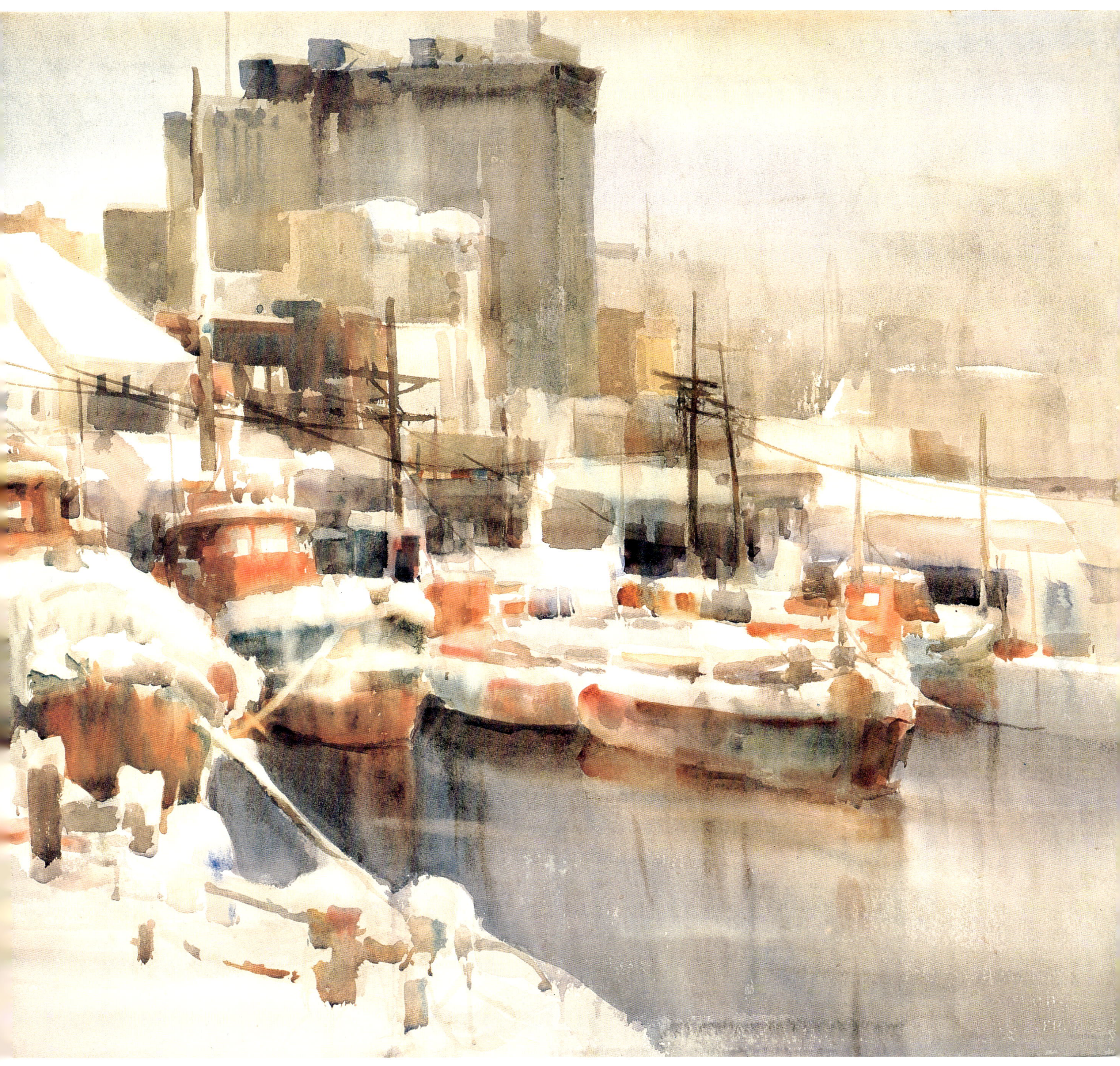

16

HANGZHOU ALLEY 89 NO.1

杭州后巷89年1号

30" x 40"   76cm x 102cm

1989

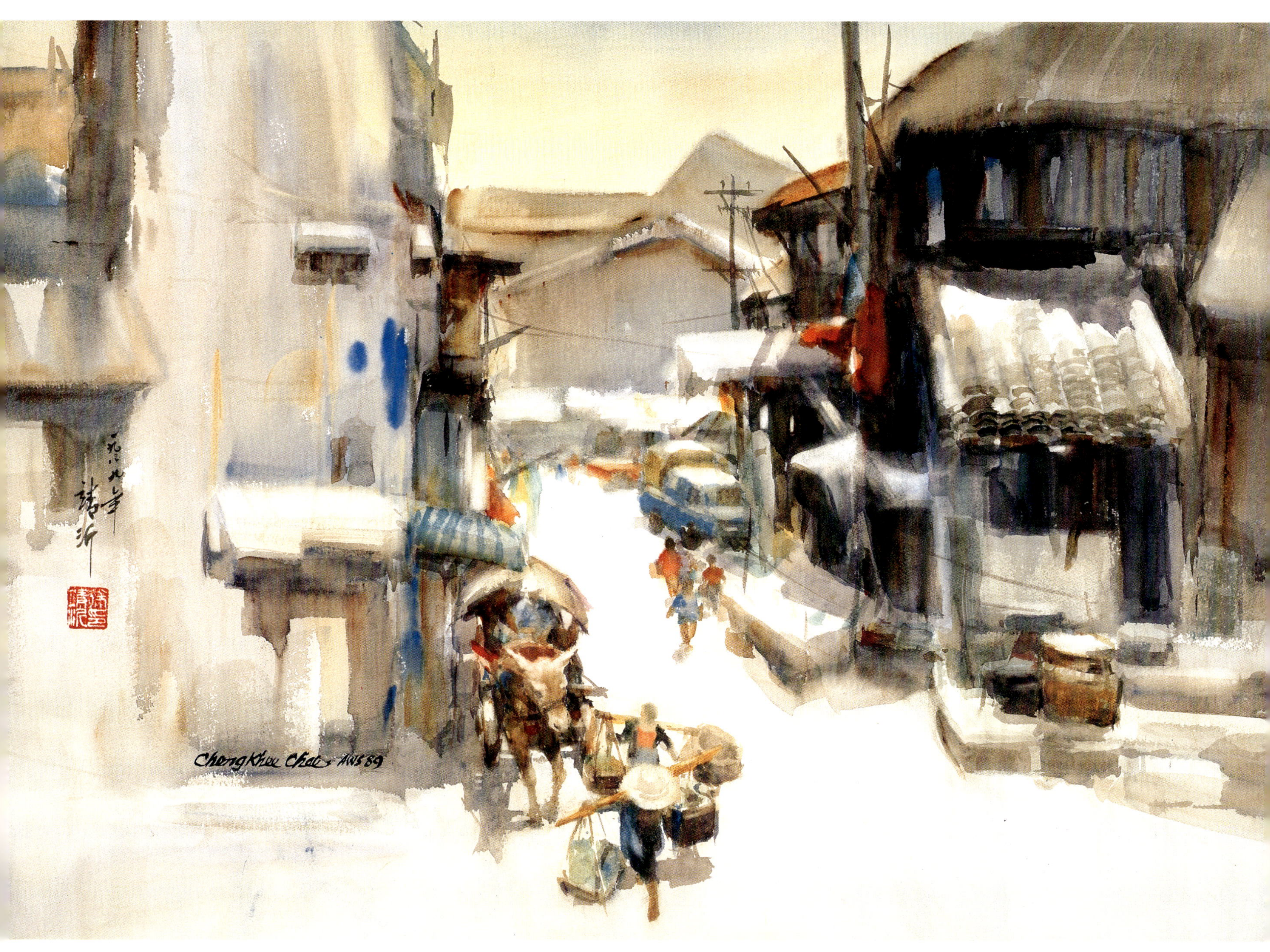
ChengKhee Chee · AWS 89

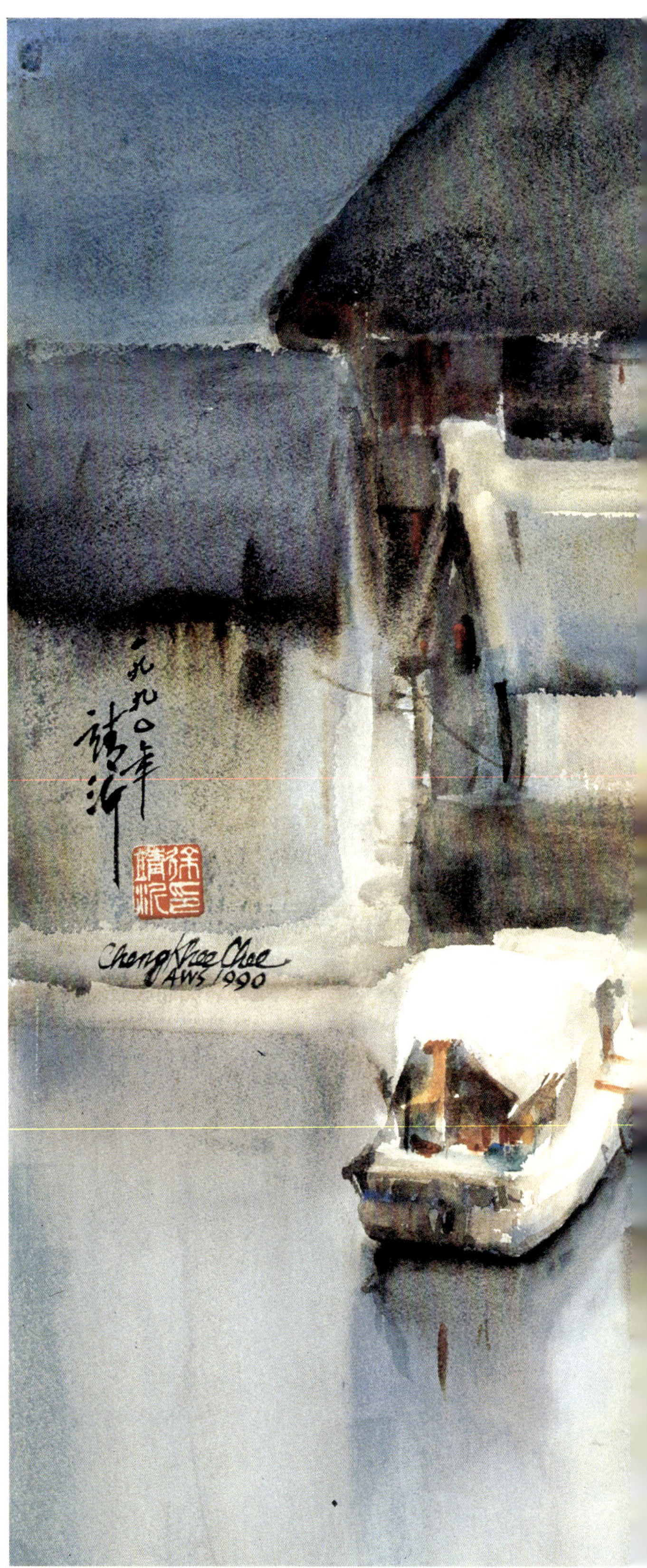

17

Watertown 90 No.1

水乡90年1号

30" x 40" 76cm x 102cm

1985

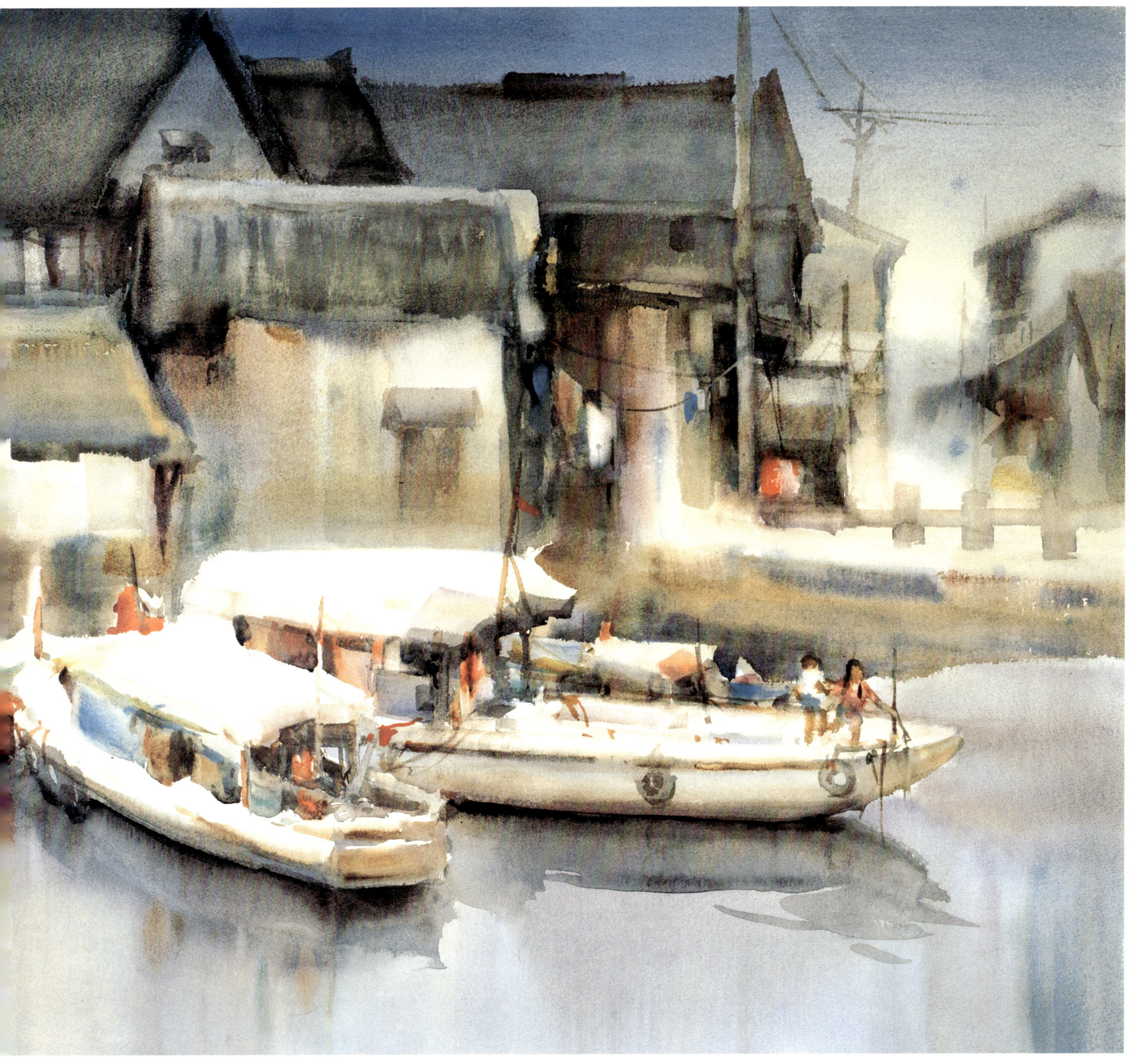

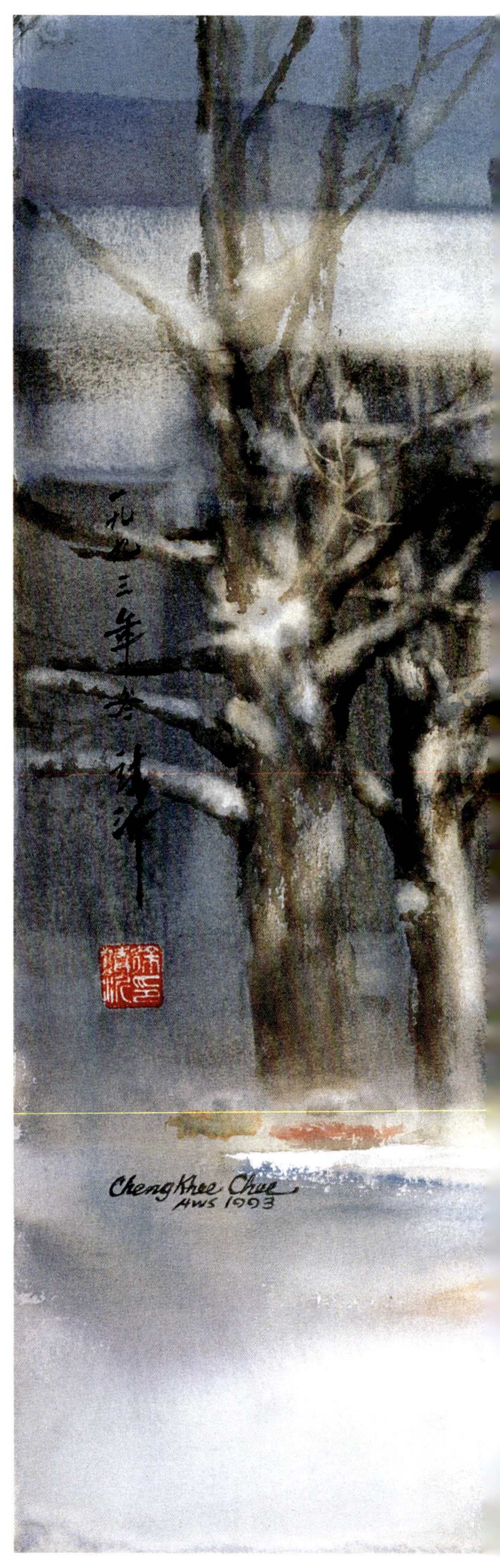

18

DULUTH WINTER 92 NO.1

都鲁之冬92年1号

30" x 40"   76cm x 102cm

1992

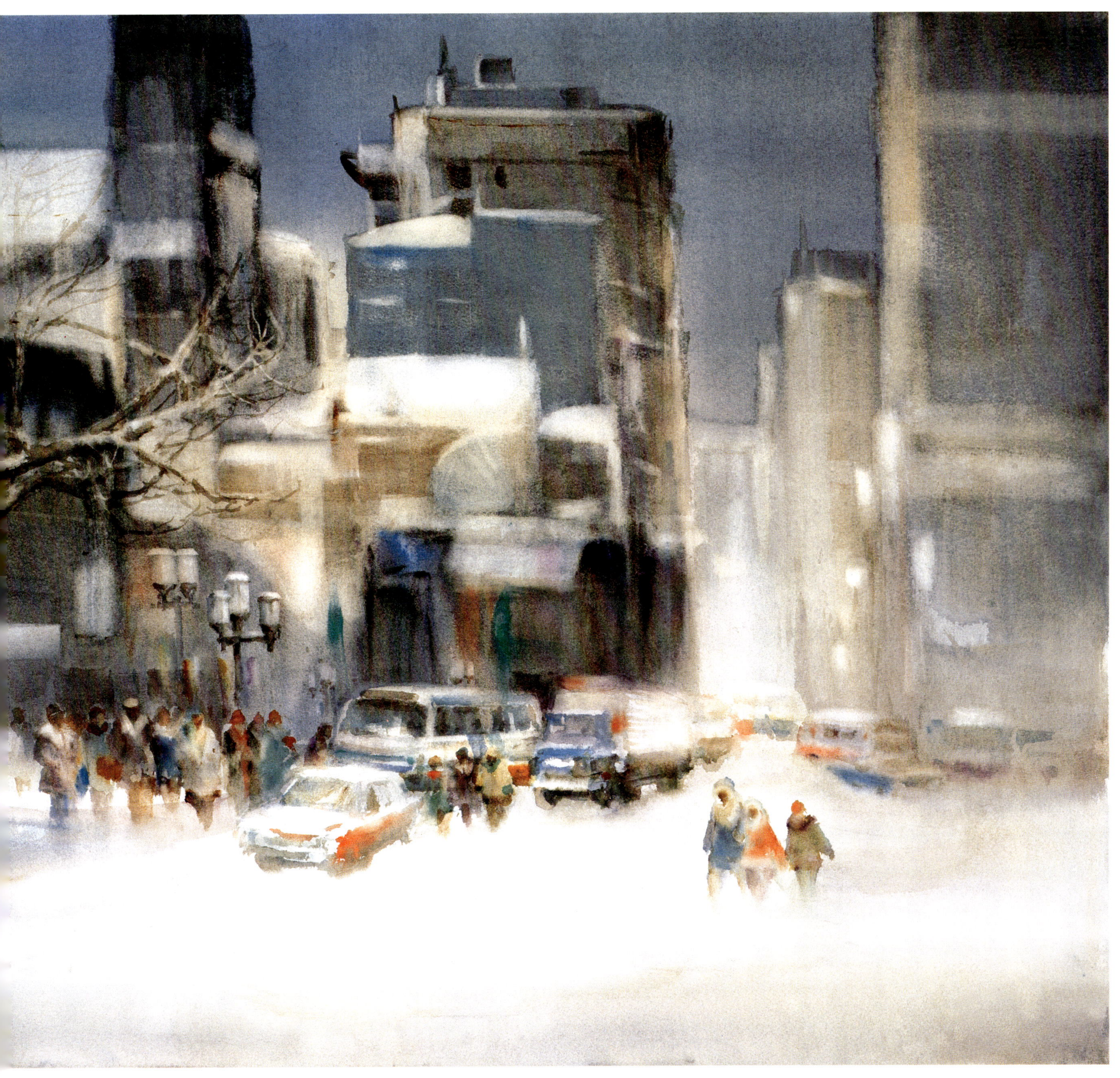

19

Penang Fishing Boats

槟城渔舟

22" x 30" 56cm x 76cm

1993

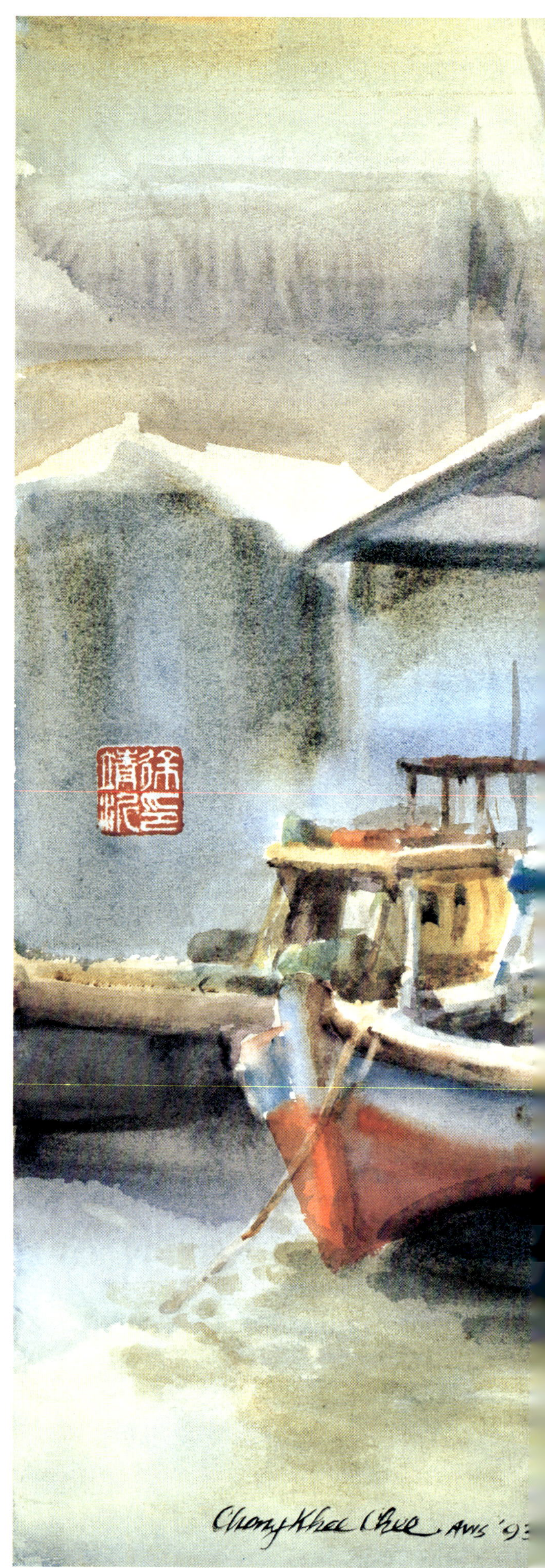

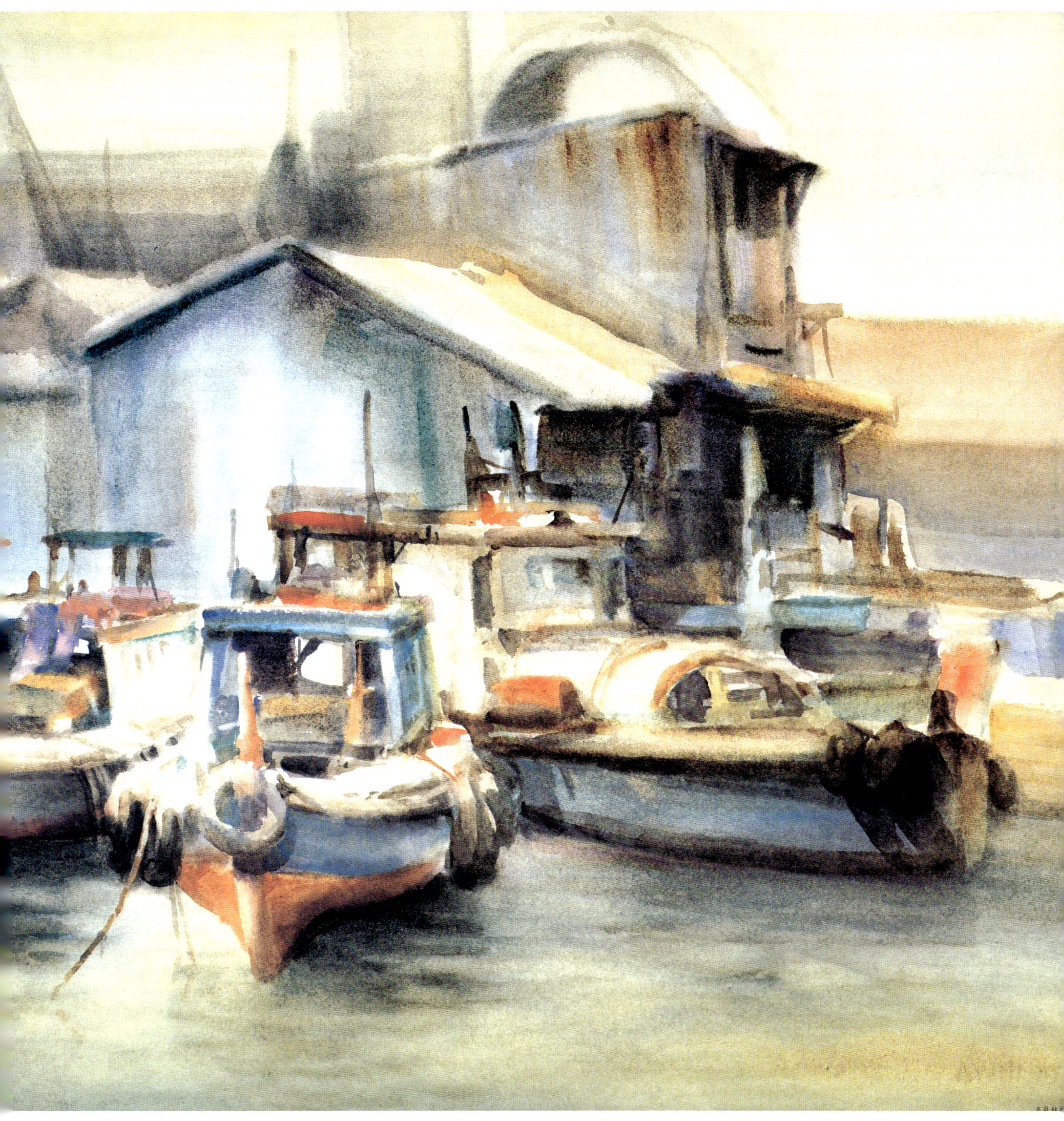

20

Fenting Morning

枫亭之晨

22" x 30"   56cm x 76cm

1993

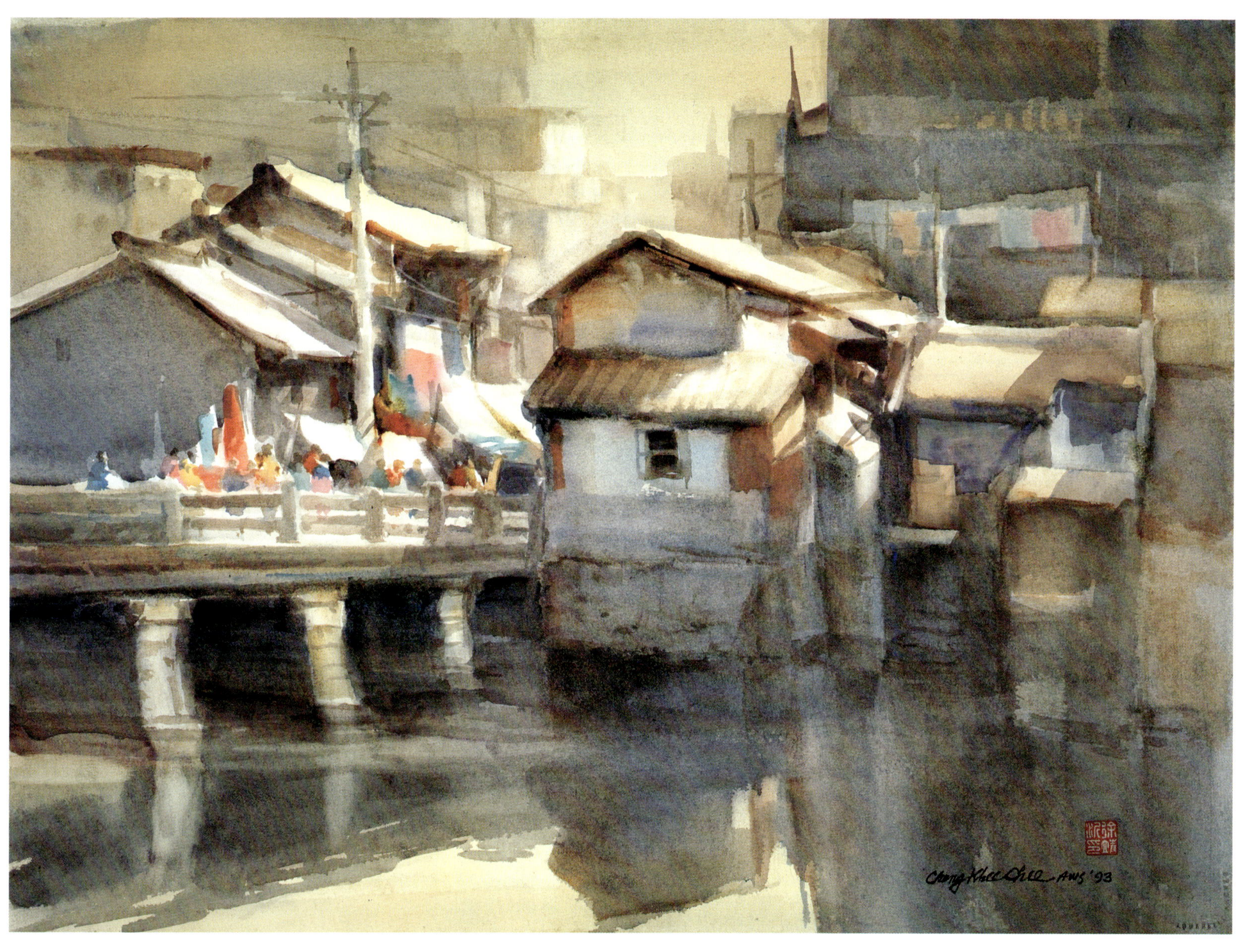

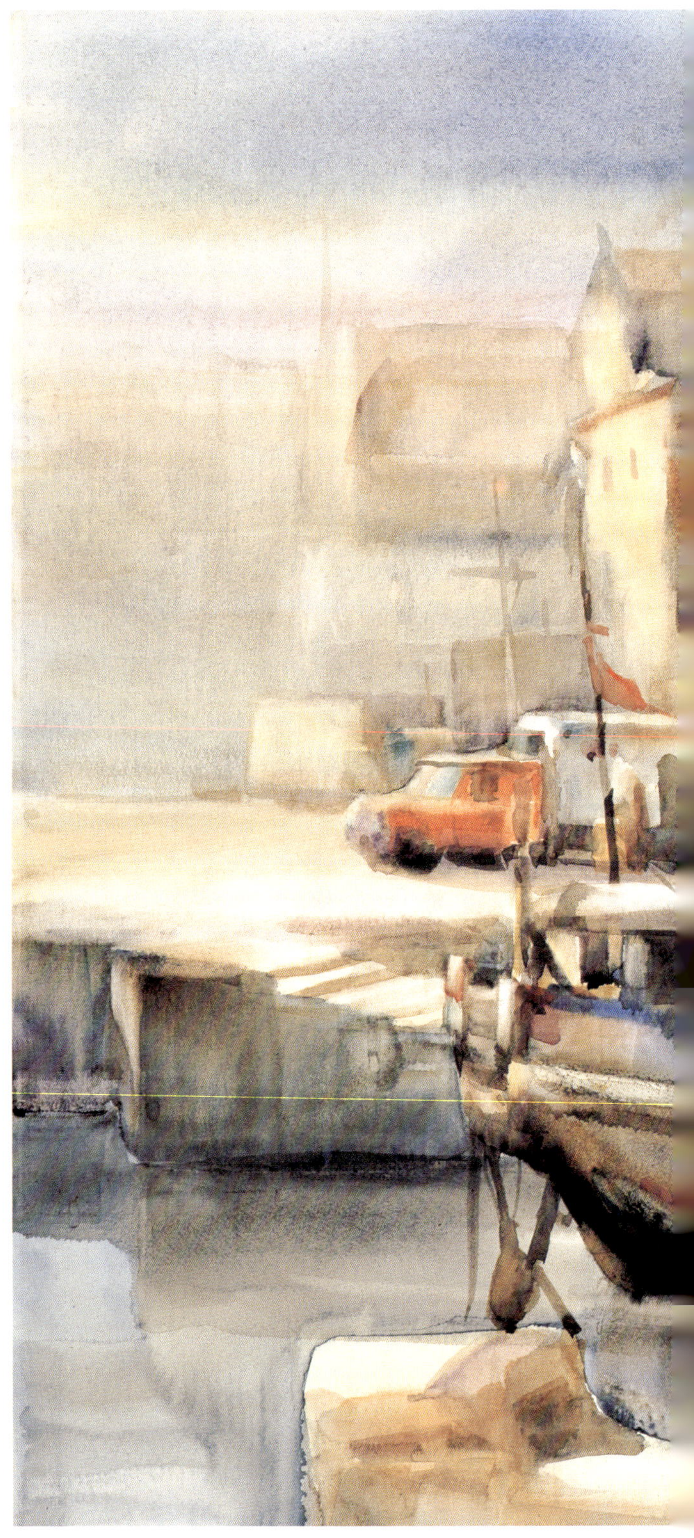

21

MORNING HARBOR

湄洲之晨

30" x 40" 76cm x 102cm

1995

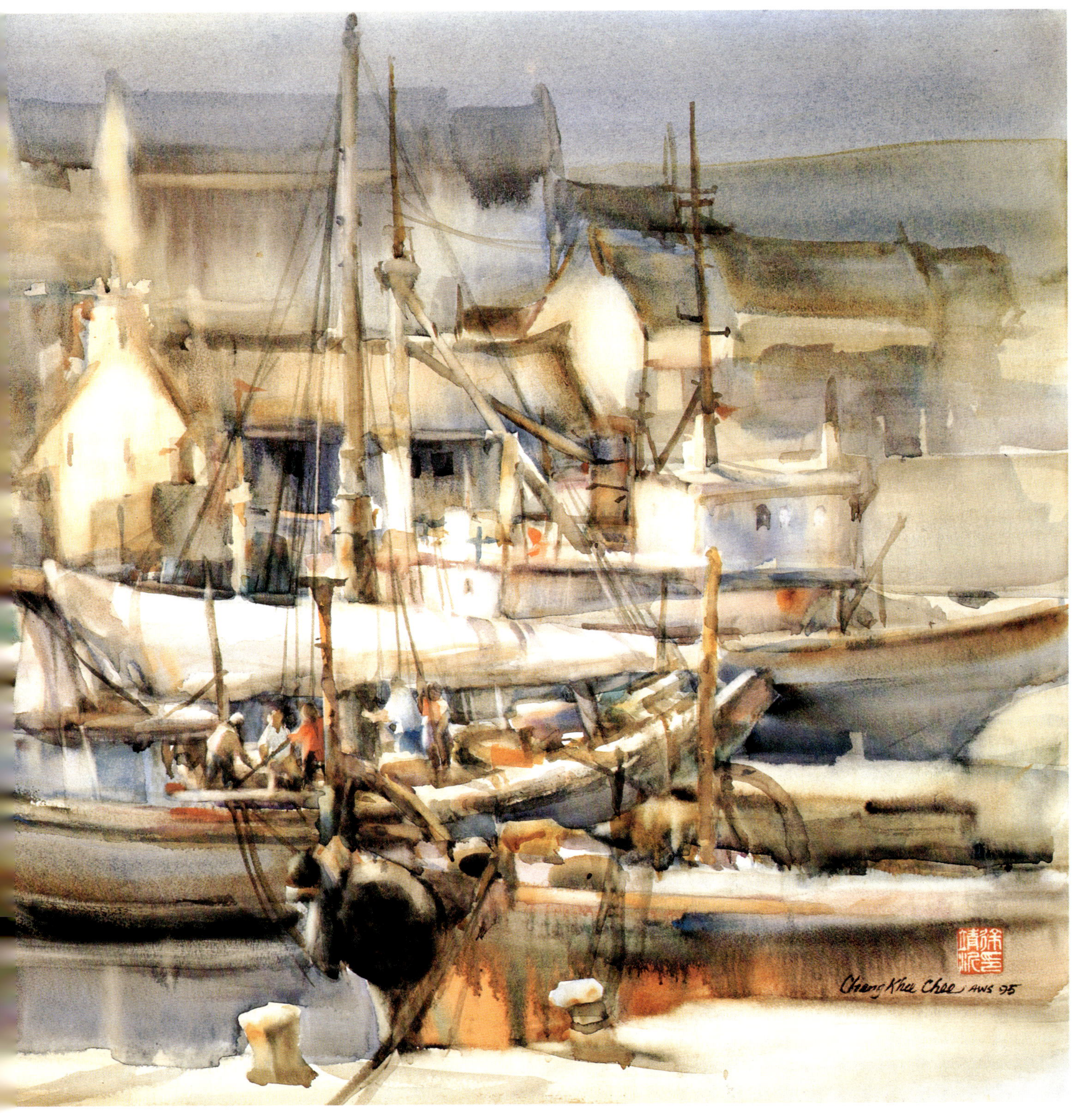
Cheng Khee Chee AWS 95

22

XIAMEN HARBOR 95 NO.1

厦门渡头95年1号

30" x 40" 76cm x 102cm

1995

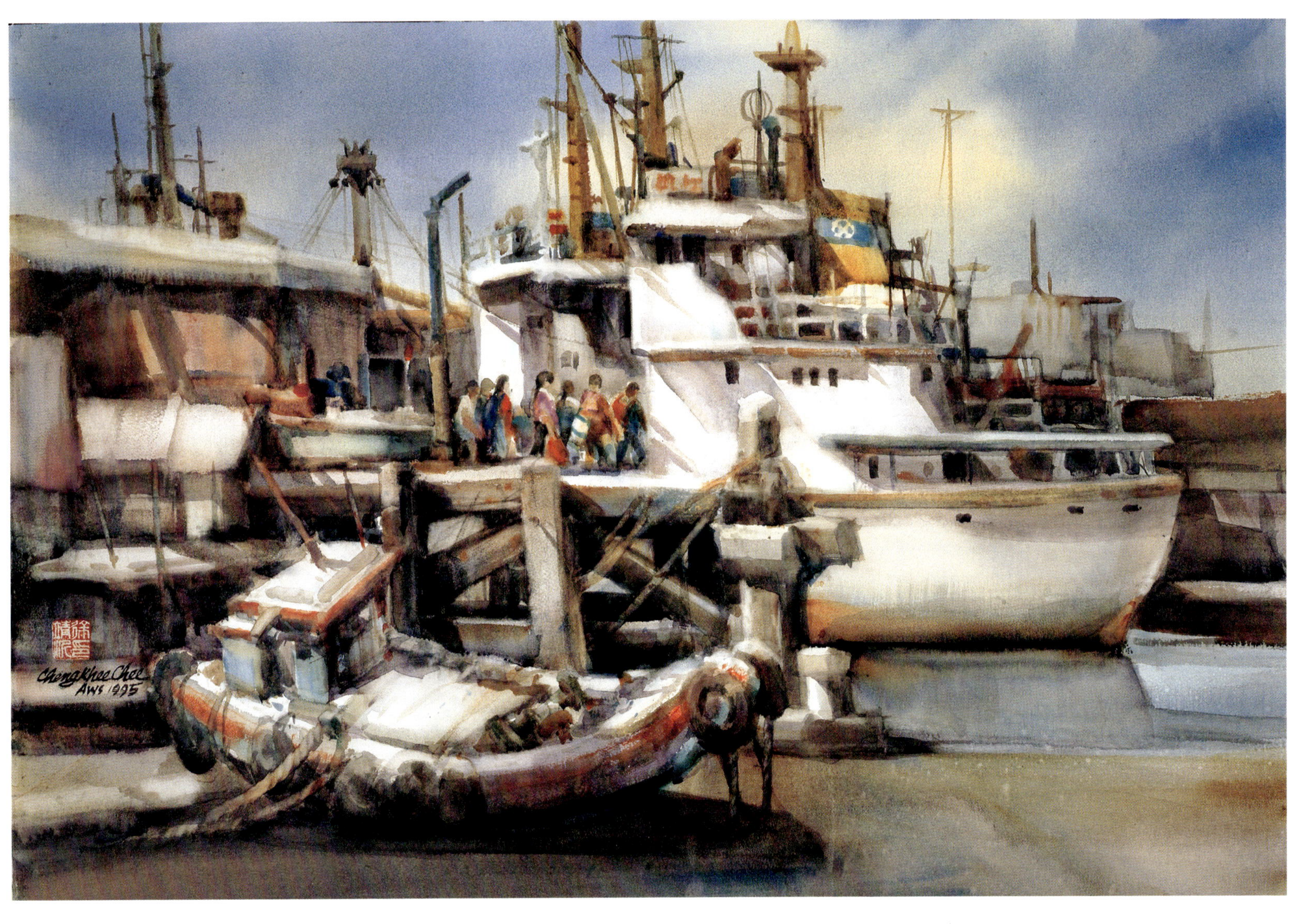
ChengKhee Chee
AWS 1995

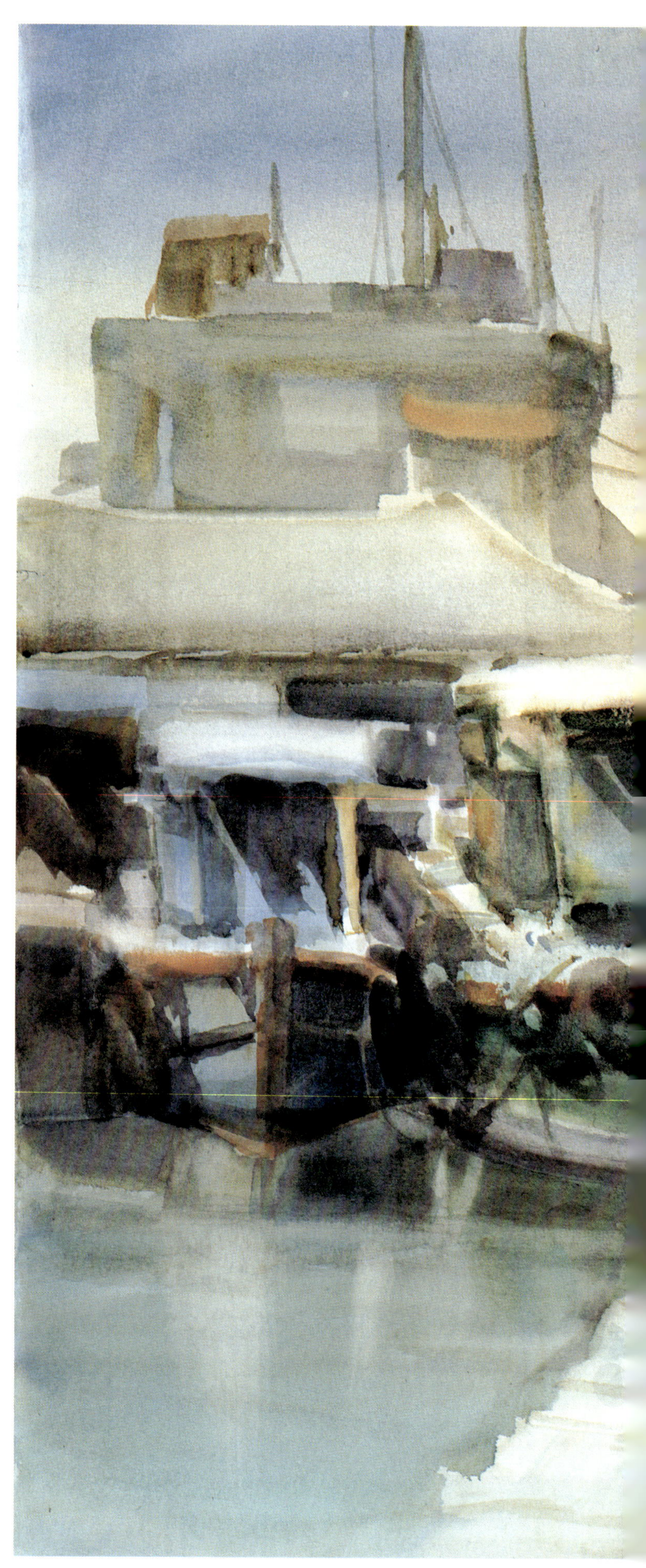

23

XIAMEN HARBOR 95 NO.2

厦门渡头95年2号

30" x 40" 76cm x 102cm

1995

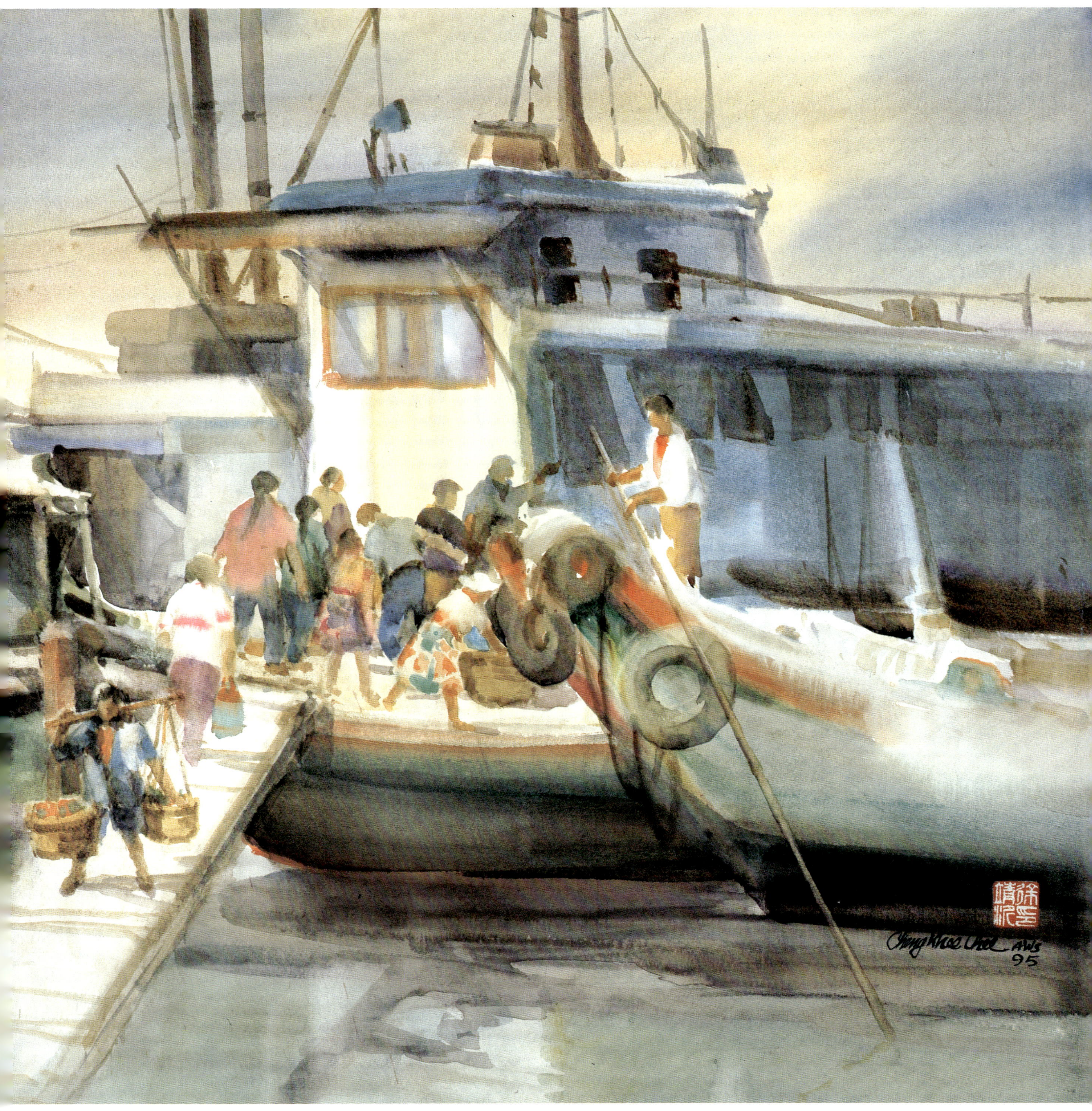
AWS
95

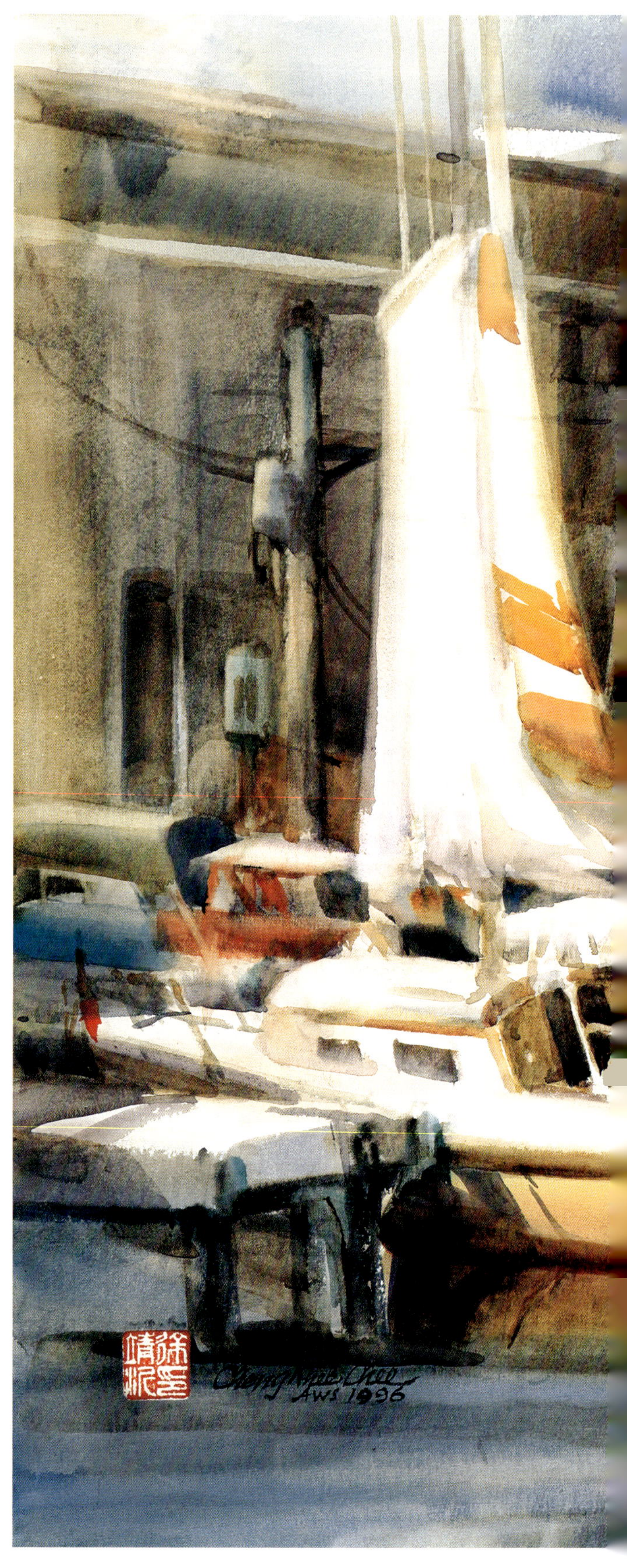

24

Yacht Club

游艇俱乐部

30" x 40"   76cm x 102cm

1996

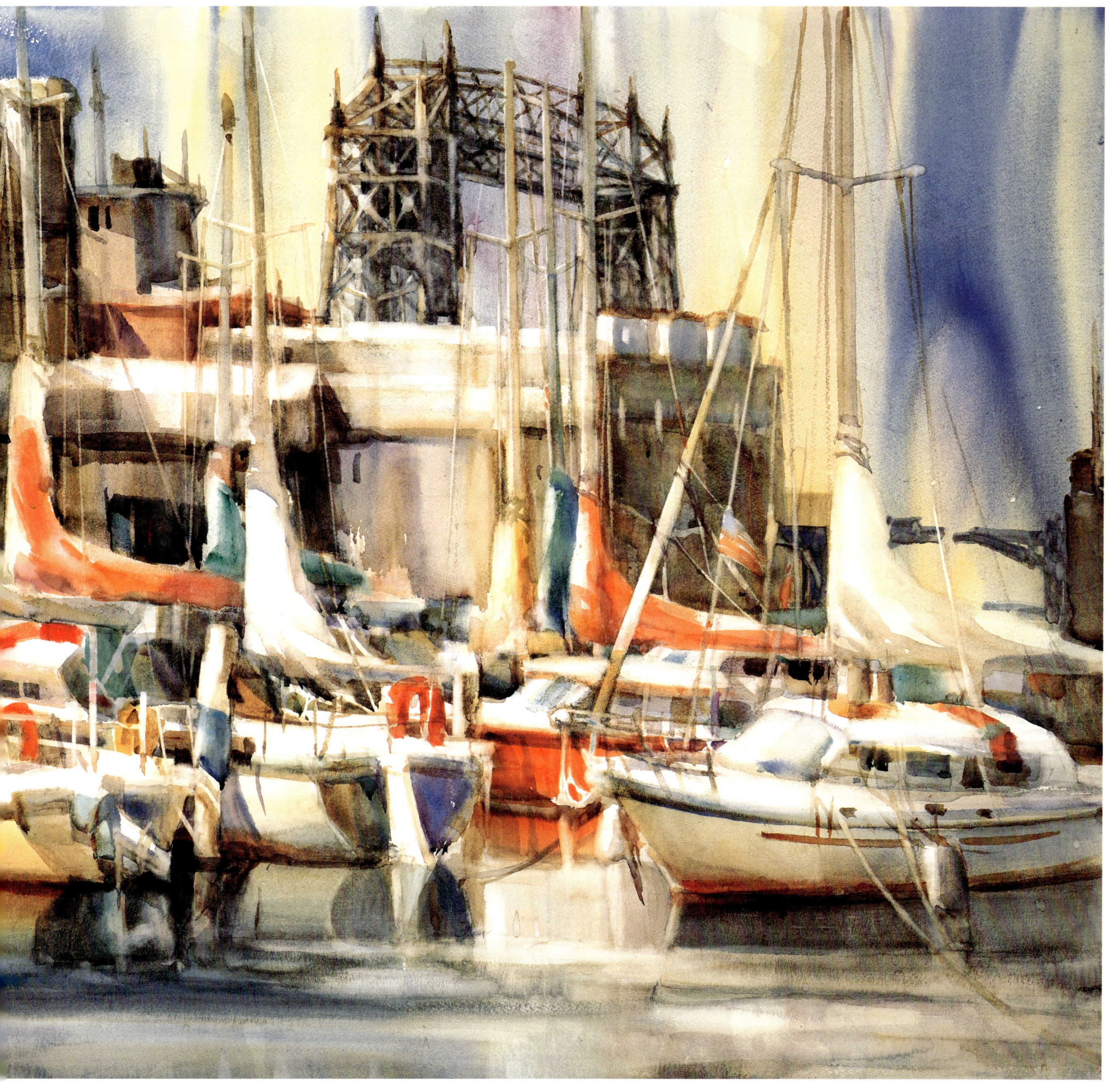

25

Penang Fishing Village 96 No.1

槟城渔村 96 年 1 号

30" x 40"   76cm x 102cm

1996

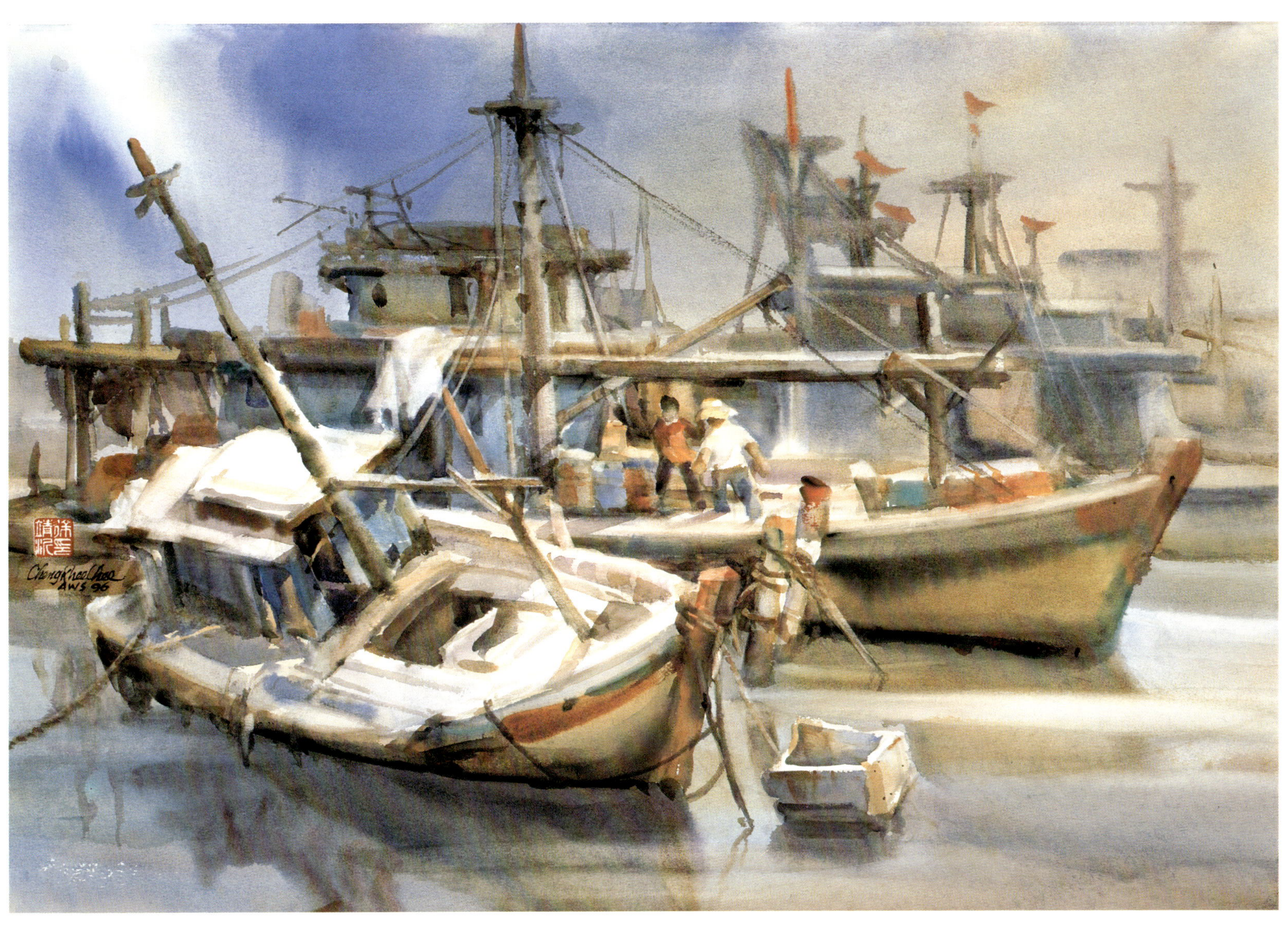
ChengKheeChee
AWS 96

26

Malacca Impression

马六甲印象

30" x 40"   76cm x 102cm

1996

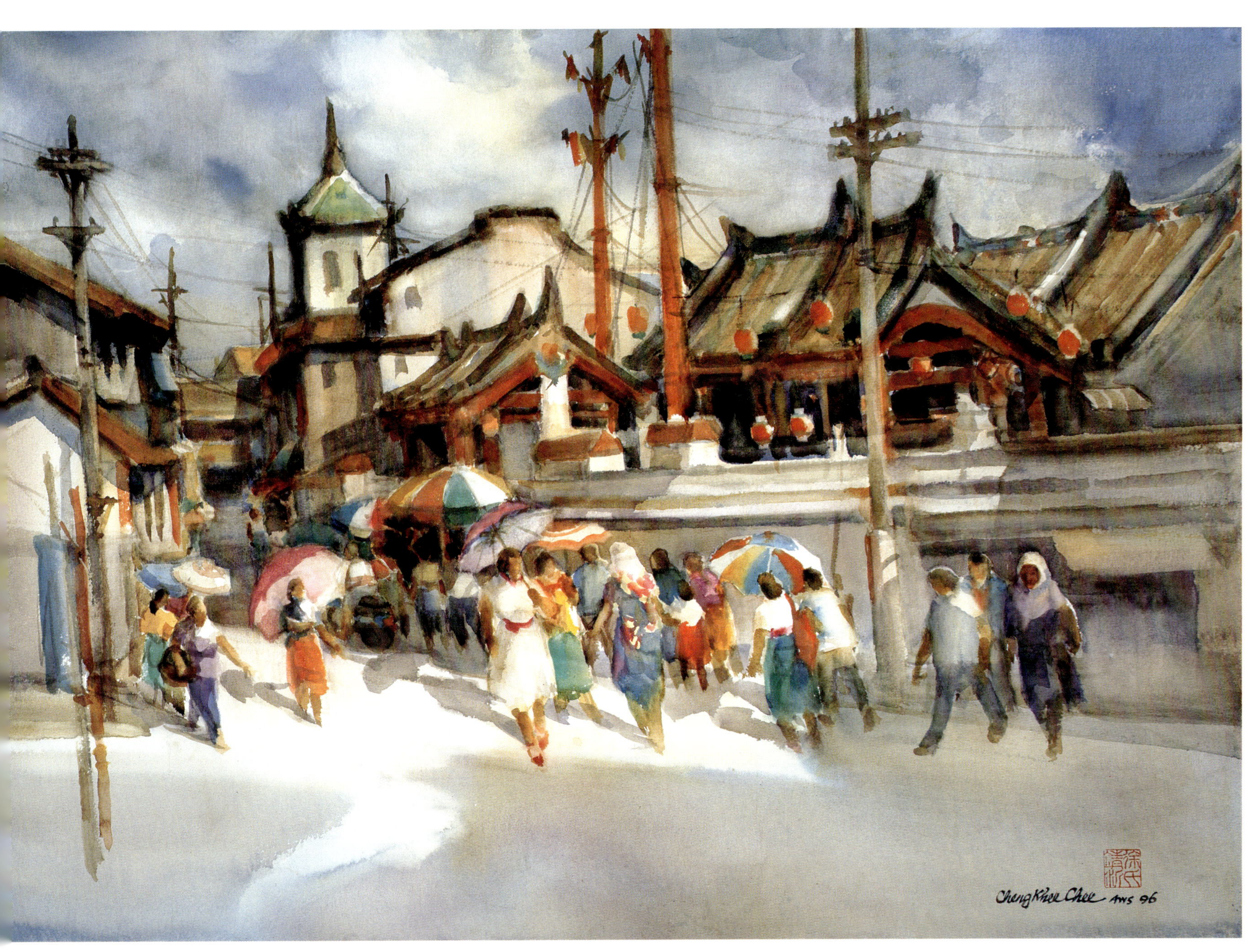
Cheng Khee Chee AWS 96

27

Singapore Impression

新加坡印象

30" x 40" 76cm x 102cm

1996

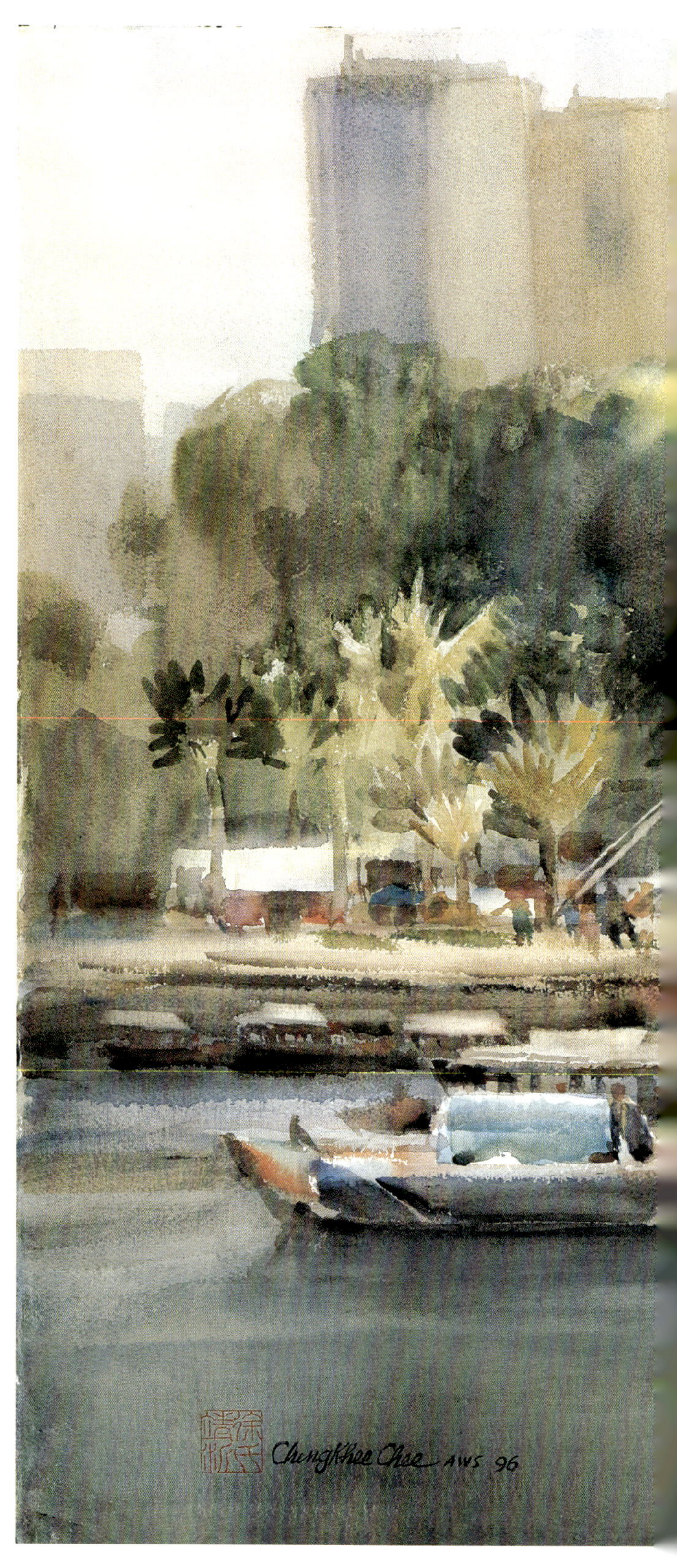

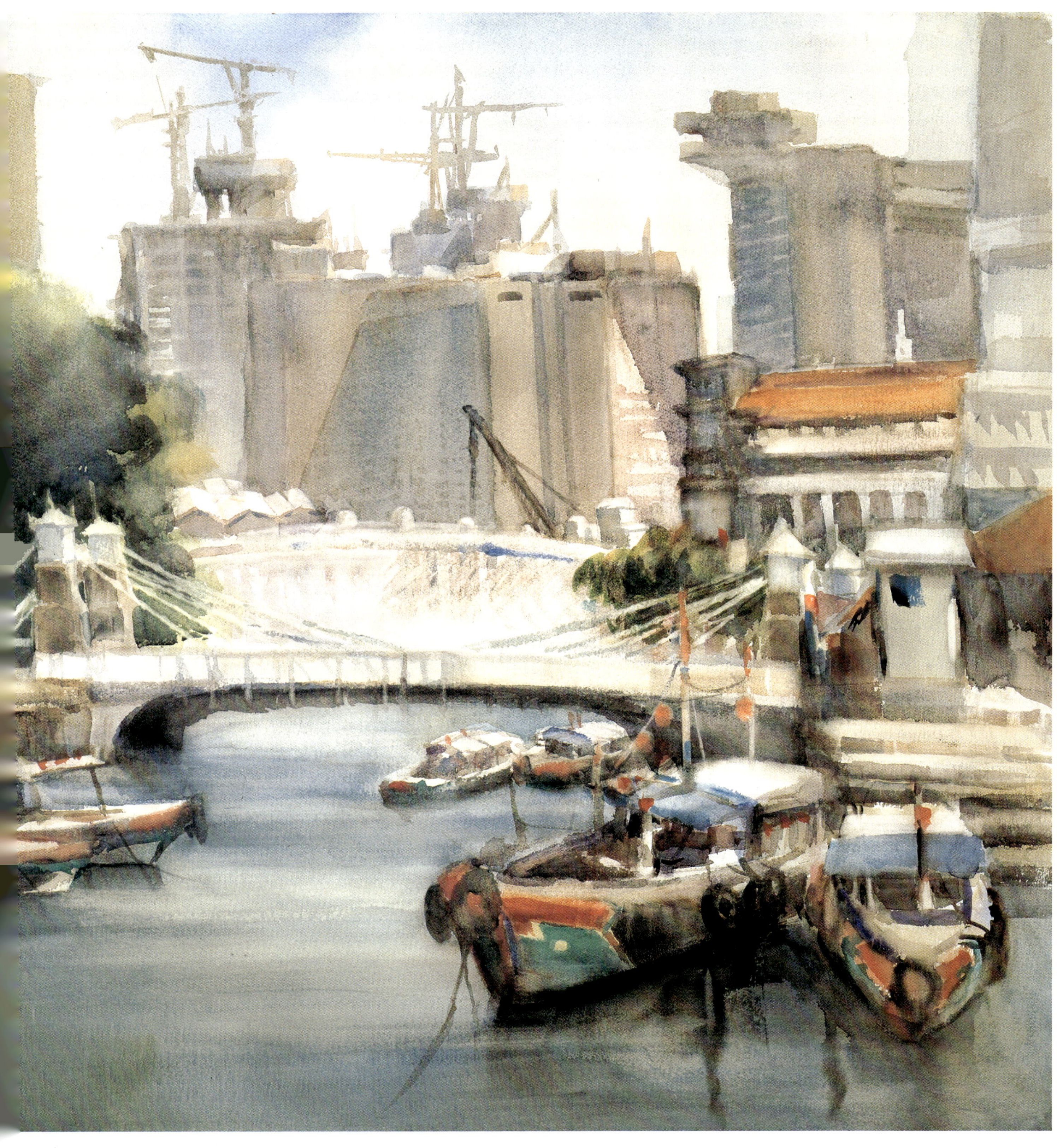

28

KUALA LUMPUR IMPRESSION

吉隆坡印象

30" x 40" 76cm x 102cm

1996

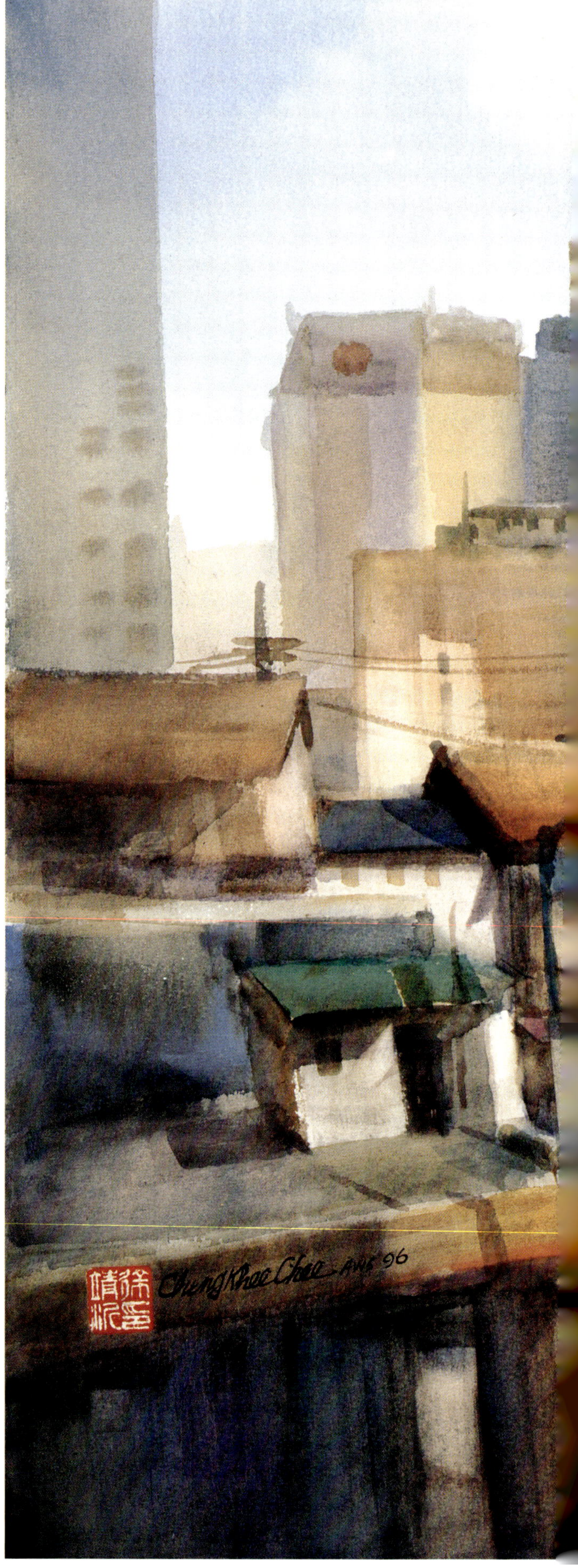

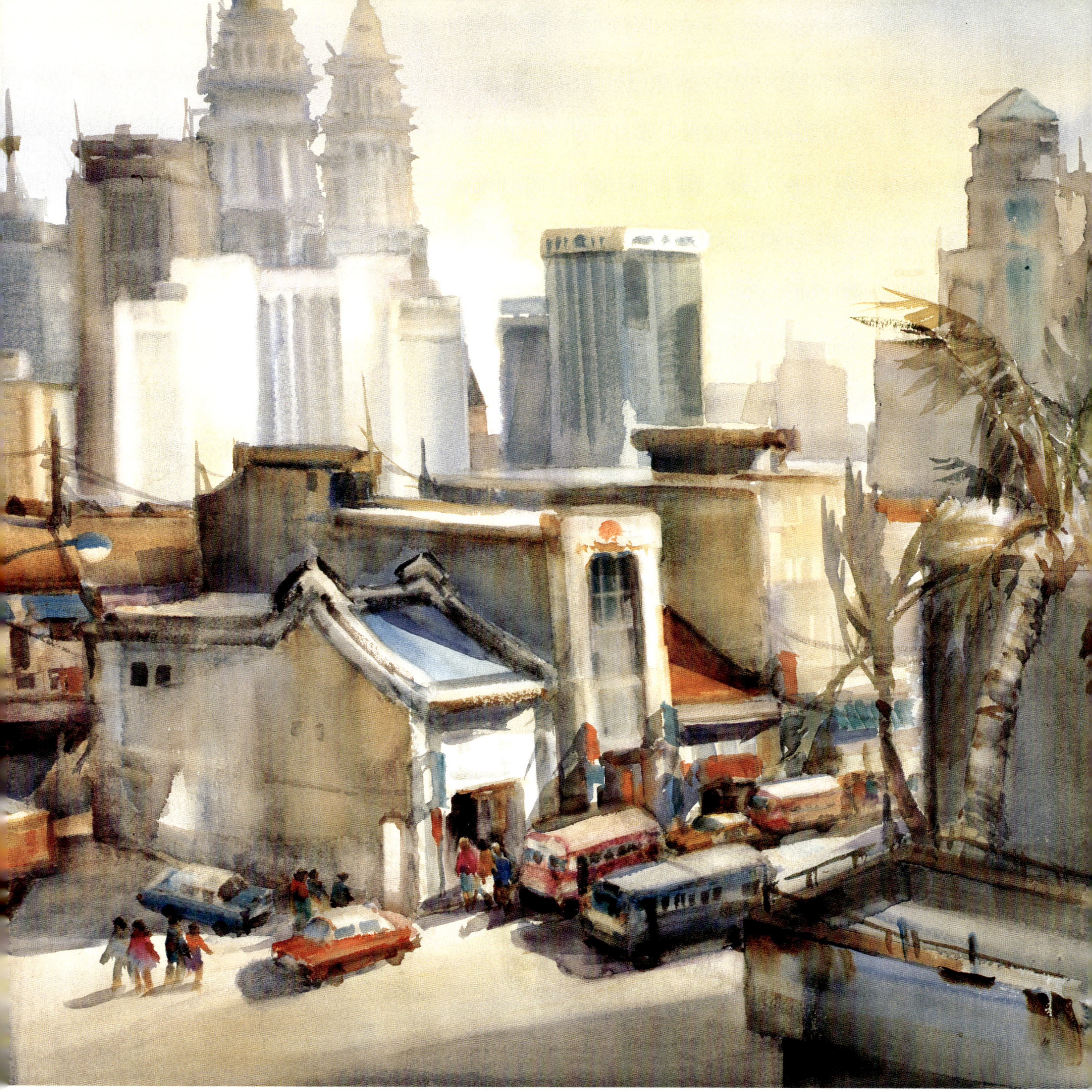

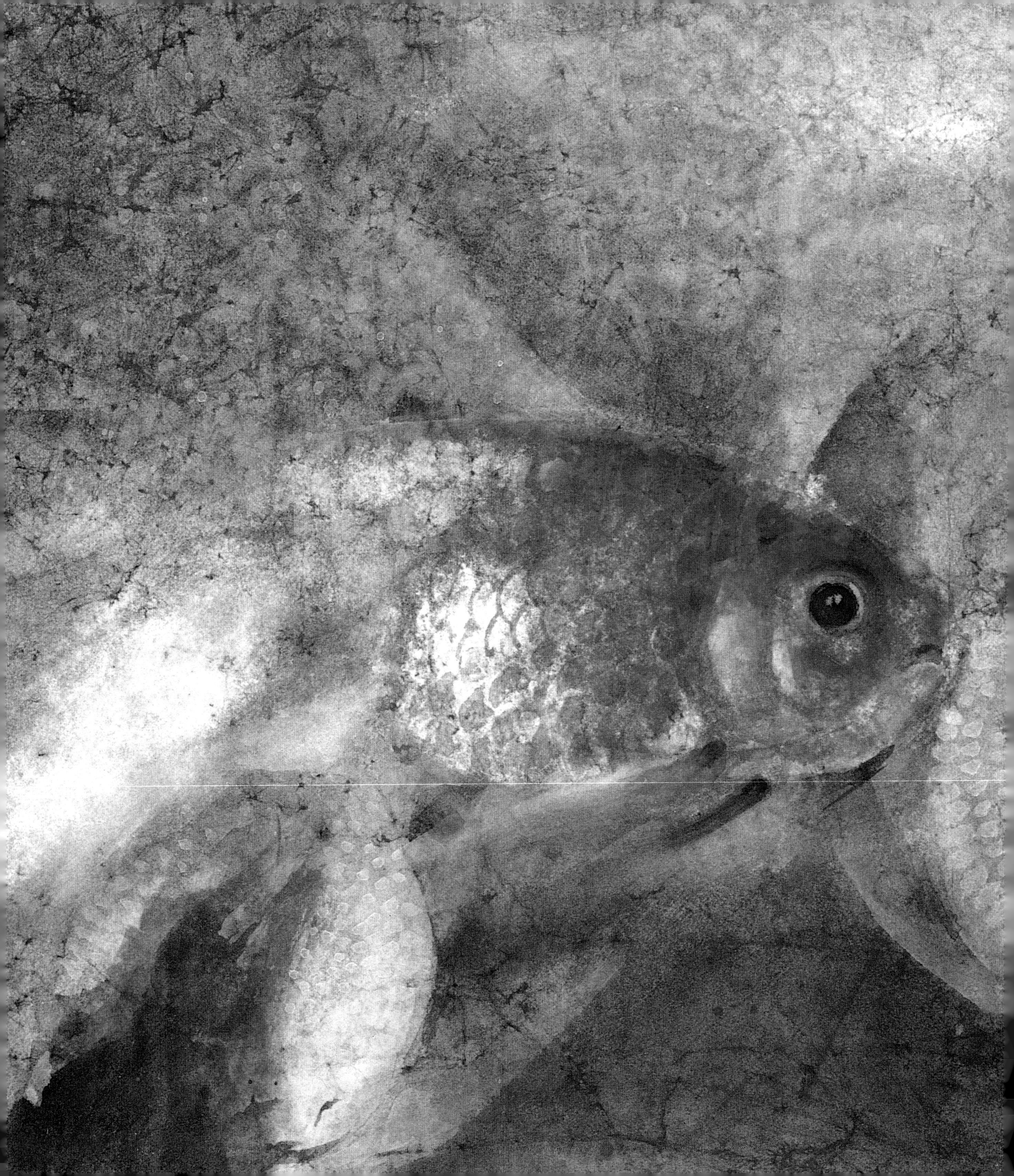

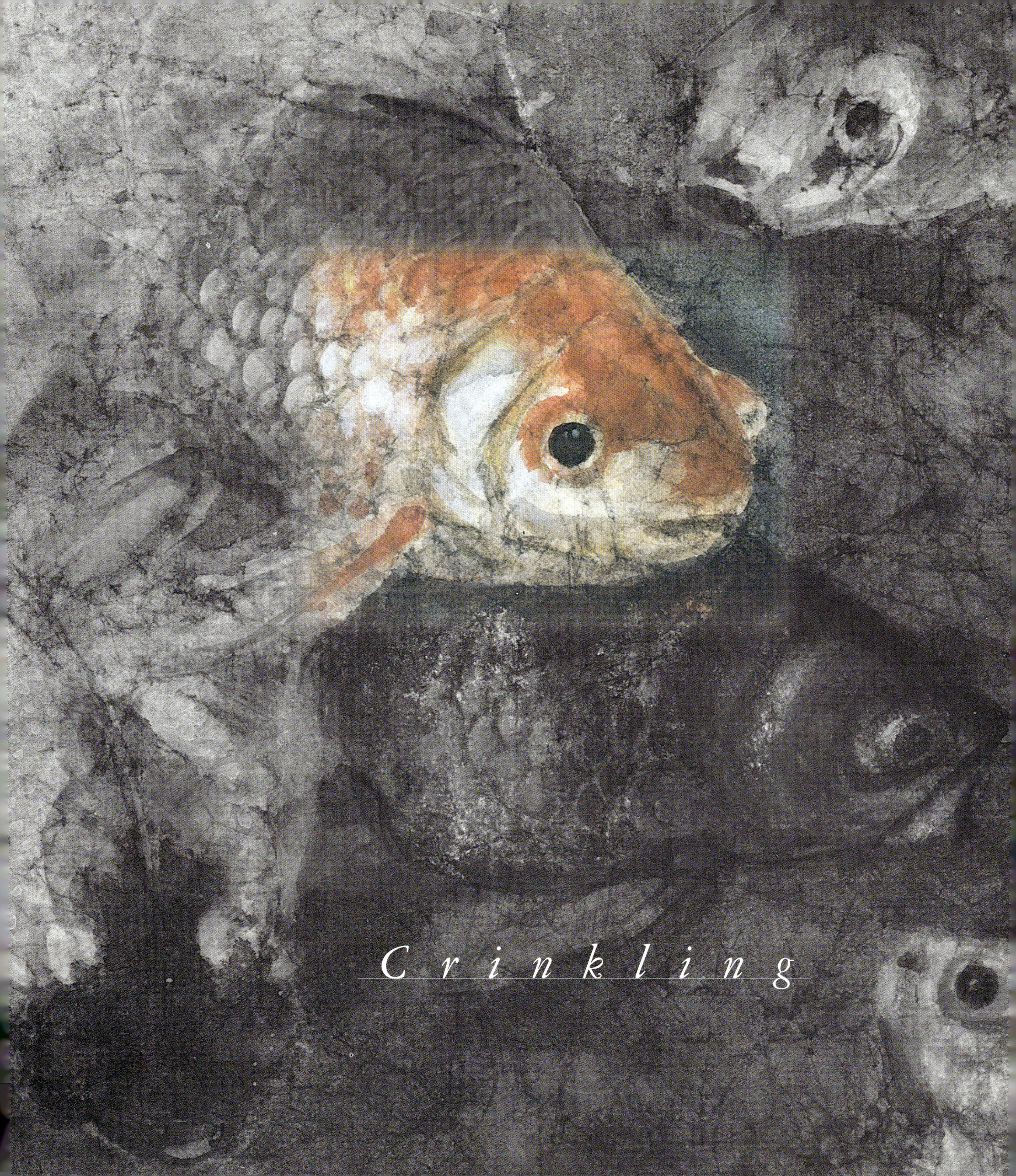

Crinkling

Crinkling Technique with Oriental Paper

Subject Matter and Esthetic Concept

I use this method for painting tree forms and other highly textured subjects. One of the most exciting aspects of Minnesota life is the experience of changing seasons. Colorful thickets of autumn leaves, exciting snow-covered winter trees, exuberant spring blossoms, and luxuriant summer foliage have all stirred my feelings and inspired me to paint. Inspired by Frederick Wong and Tseng-Ying Pang, I have found that crinkling oriental paper, manipulating it to the desired texture, and painting on the wrinkled surface is the most natural way to capture the tree forms. The end result is a combination of East and West, and abstraction and realism. Realistic images are actually built up from an accretion of small abstract fragments.

Tools and Supplies

2" squirrel hair, hake, or other soft-hair brushes
Round Oriental brushes
Masa or sized Xuan paper
Oriental liquid ink (Sumi ink)
Tube watercolors
Mounting board (rag board or watercolor paper)
Mounting paste (Metylan cellulose wall paper paste)

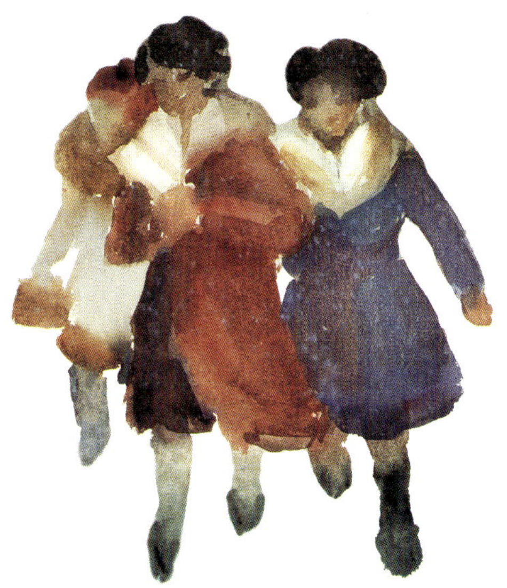

Painting Procedure

1. I soak Masa paper or apply water to both sides of it until it becomes limp and soft
2. I crinkle the paper to form the desired wrinkles, and paint on the wrinkled surface to achieve intriguing textural effects
3. When the painting is finished, mount it to smooth it out. If necessary, I continue to refine the painting after it has been mounted

I use two approaches in this technique. The first one is to do the entire painting in monochrome with Chinese ink, as in the traditional Chinese approach. When the painting is done, I mount it and add colors to enhance. I have found this approach most satisfactory in depicting winter scenes. The second approach is to use colors right from the beginning, painting from light to dark. I have found this approach most suitable for capturing the bright and fresh colors of spring and autumn.

I also use two different ways to mount my paintings. For smaller paintings (say, up to 22" x 30") I mount them on rag cardboards or regular watercolor paper. For larger paintings (say, 22" x 30" and up) and paintings done on fragile Xuan paper, I place the painting face down on a table top, apply paste to the back of the painting, and then place a backing sheet (Masa or similar paper) which is about one inch wider on all four sides. I smooth it down on the back of the painting. I flip the painting over, apply paste along the edges of the backing sheet, and paste the painting on the table top or a heavy board (such as plywood) to dry. When the painting is bone dry, I cut along the edges to free it from the board, and trim the edges of the painting. The painting is then ready for framing.

揉纸法

1. 材料：日本熟纸Masa
墨、水彩或国画颜料
2. 特点：将纸浸湿，揉绉，压平，用扁笔平刷墨或颜色，那绉痕部份分吸收性较强，於是色彩或墨较浓，呈现网络或树的细枝状。
如果纸揉绉后不压平，用扁笔轻轻在纸面上刷过墨或颜色，然后把纸压平，纸面便呈现飞白或浮雕状的纹理。
用这两种笔法效果结合一般用笔方法，交替运用，便能产生各种丰富趣味的肌理纹络。这种画法的目的在求偶然的肌理效果。
3. 画法：根据上述，先画出偶然肌理，然后顺理成章，完成部分画面。如果对肌理效果感到满意，便可以把纸拓平，然后加工完成整个画。据我本人的经验，揉纸法最适宜画四季景色。画冬景时可以先用墨画，然后把画拓平，再上色加工而完成画面。画春秋季节，一般色彩鲜明，我直接用彩色画肌理，然后拓平加工，完成画面。如果画面要以树木配合建筑物，则在揉纸时酌量避免建筑物部分的纸面。
因为这种画法的目的是利用偶然性的效果，开始作画时不太拘泥定稿，应该要随机应变，灵活处理。
4. 画例：冬天乐、圣堡罗教堂、秋

29

St Paul Cathedral

圣保罗教堂

21" x 31" 54cm x 79cm

1978

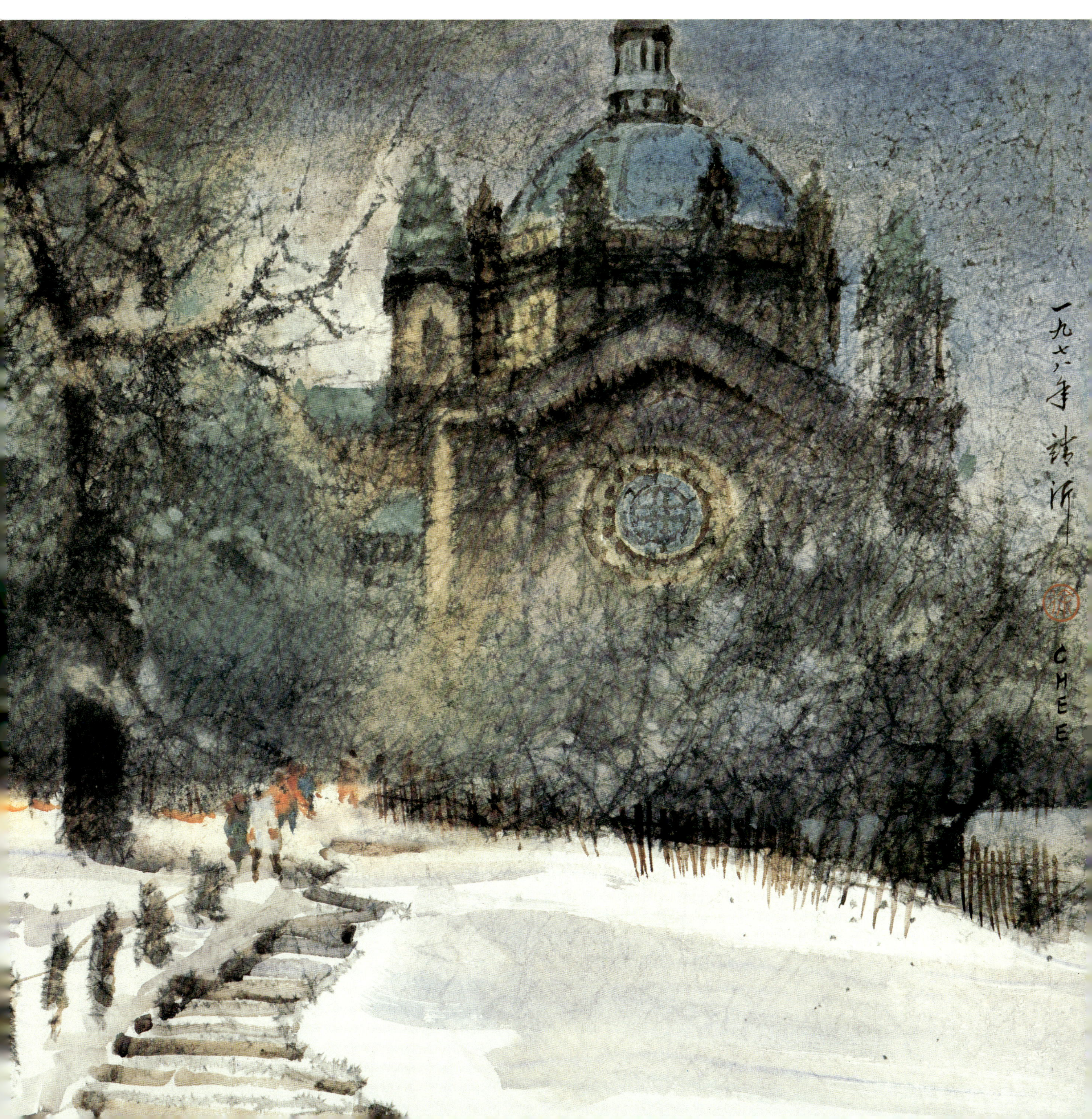
CHEE

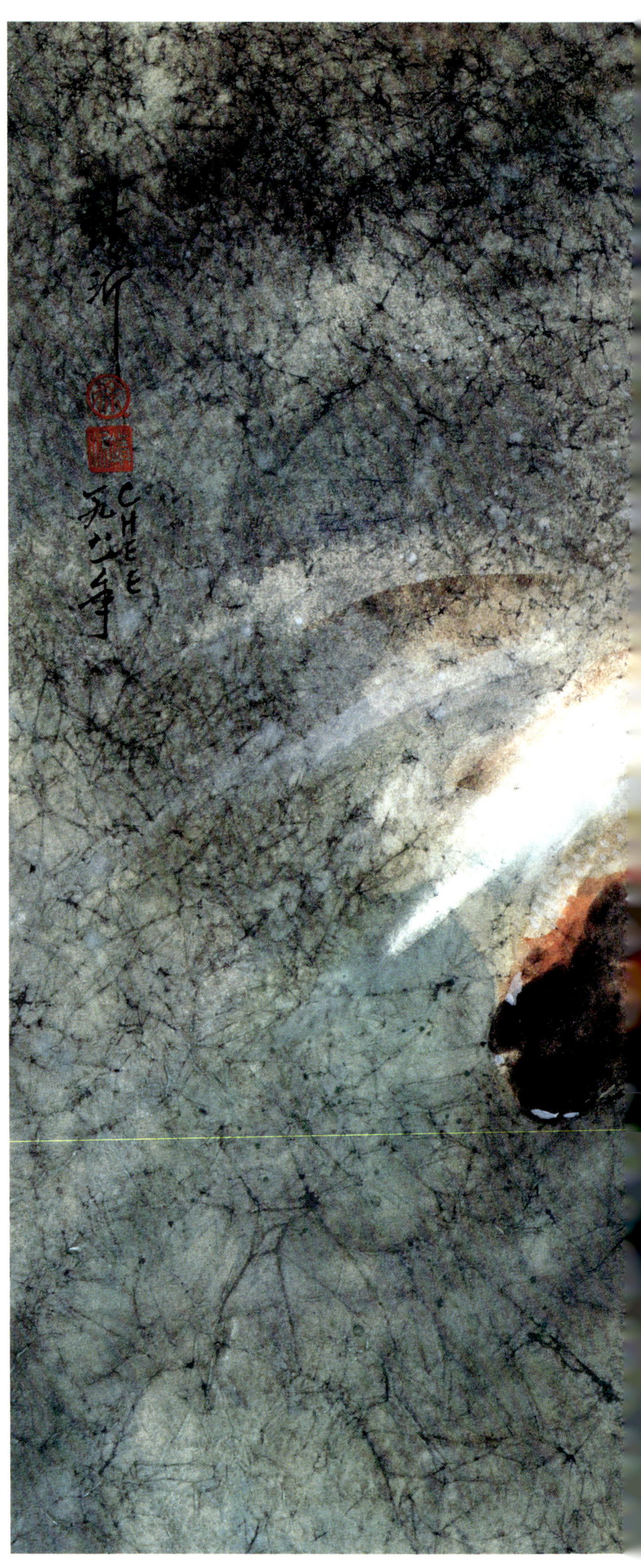

30

Goldfish 81 No.1

金鱼81年1号

25" x 40"   63cm x 102cm

1981

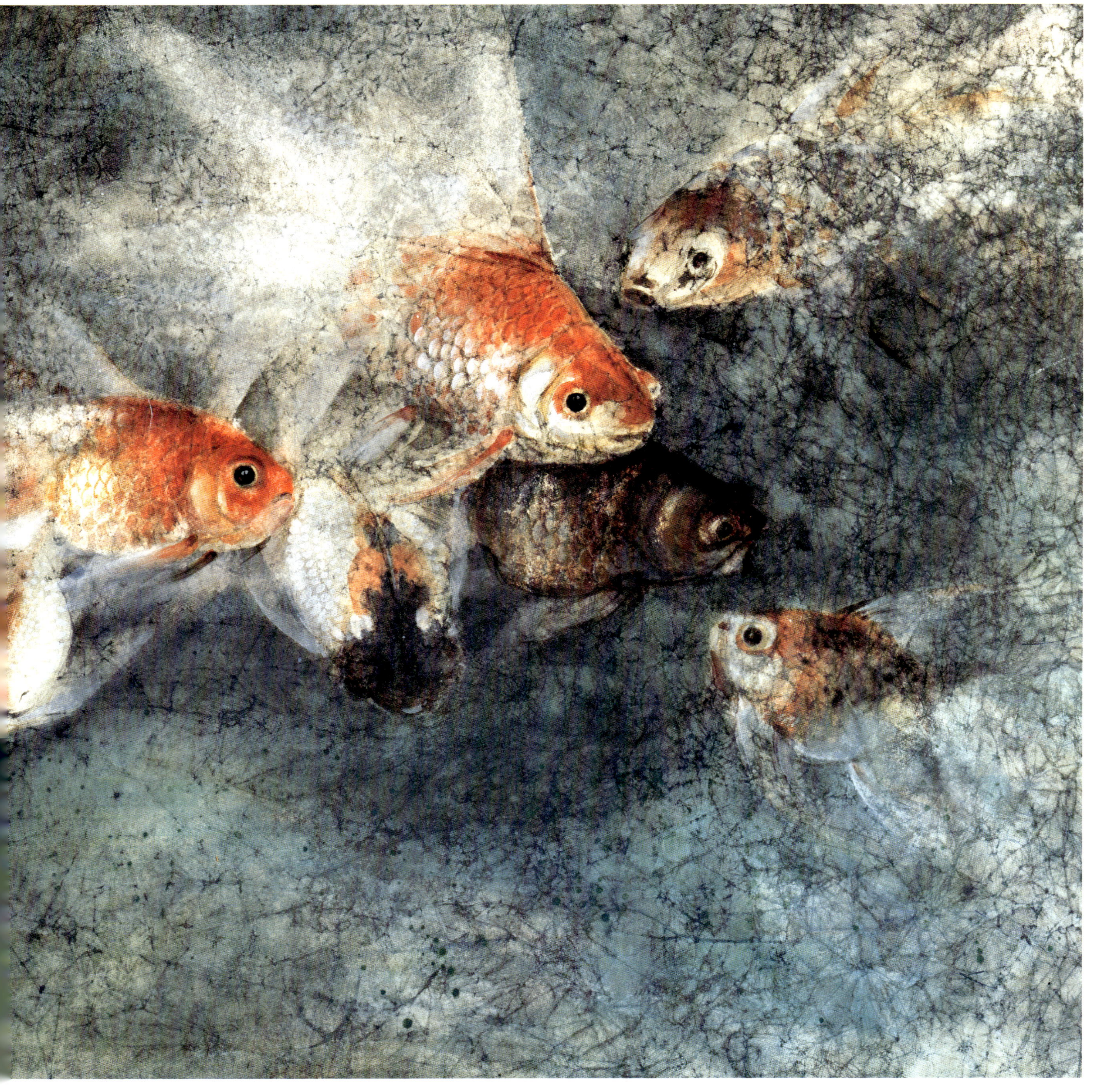

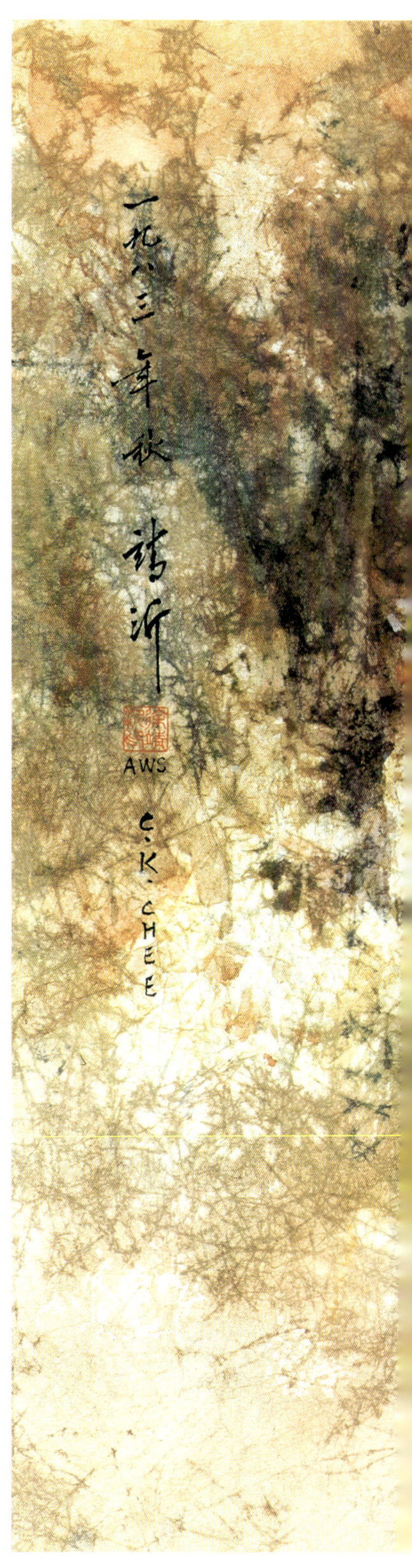

31

Autumn 83 No.1

秋83年1号

25" x 40" 63cm x 102cm

1983

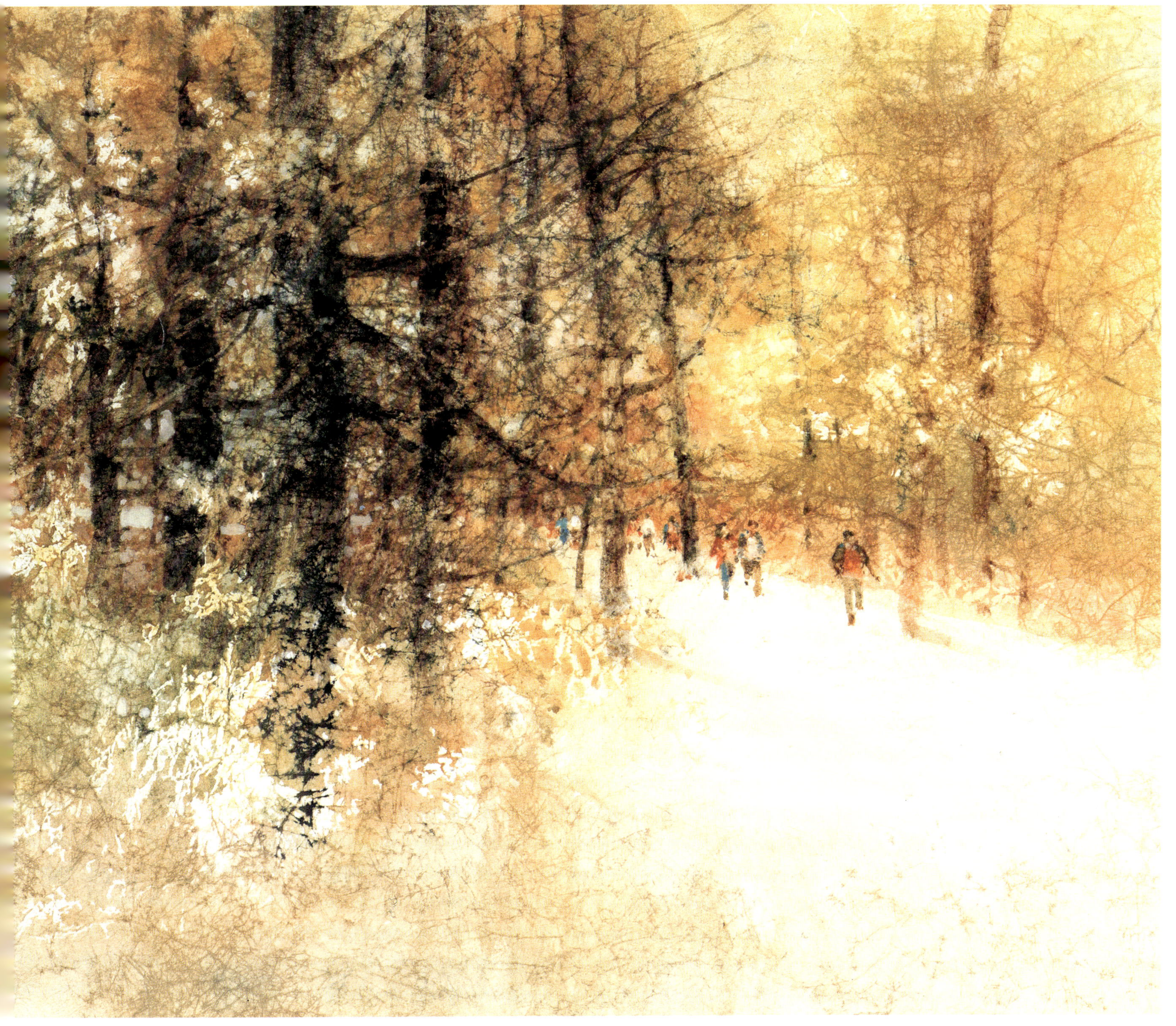

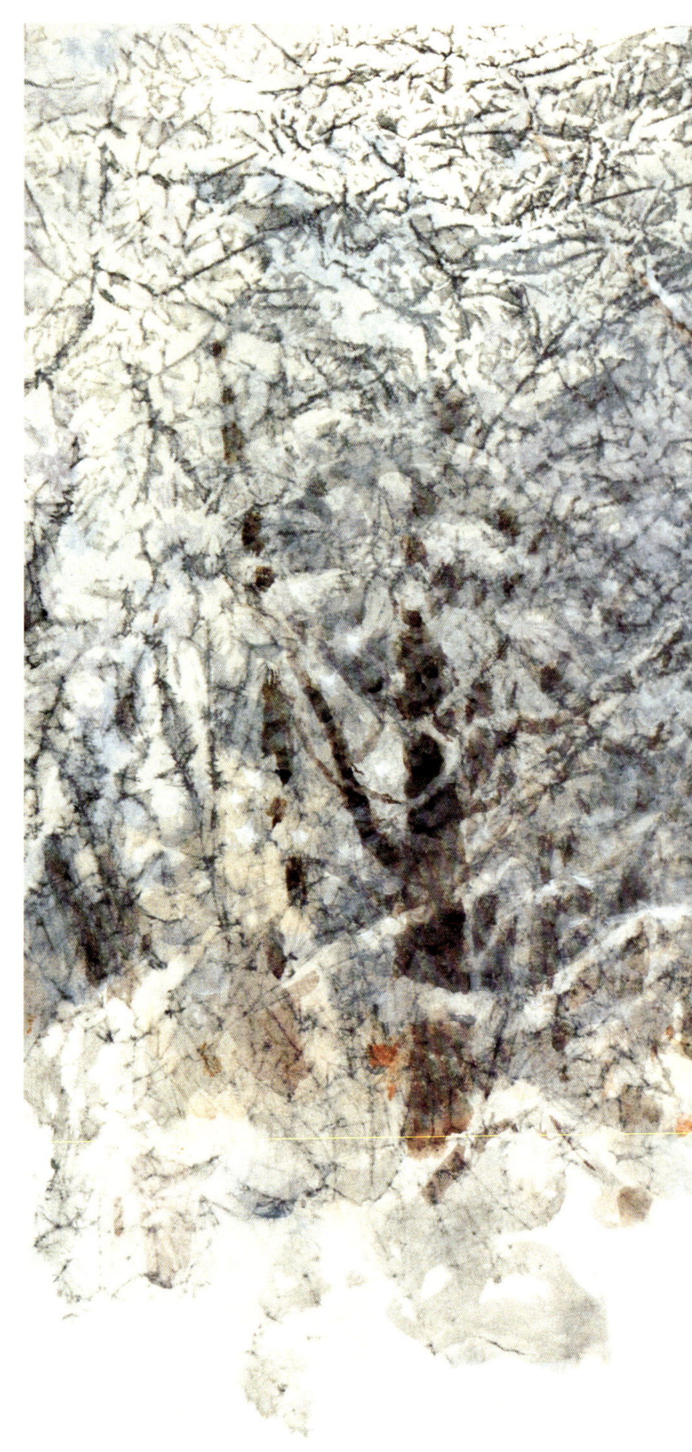

32

WINTER PLEASURE

冬天乐

25" x 40"   63cm x 102cm

1984

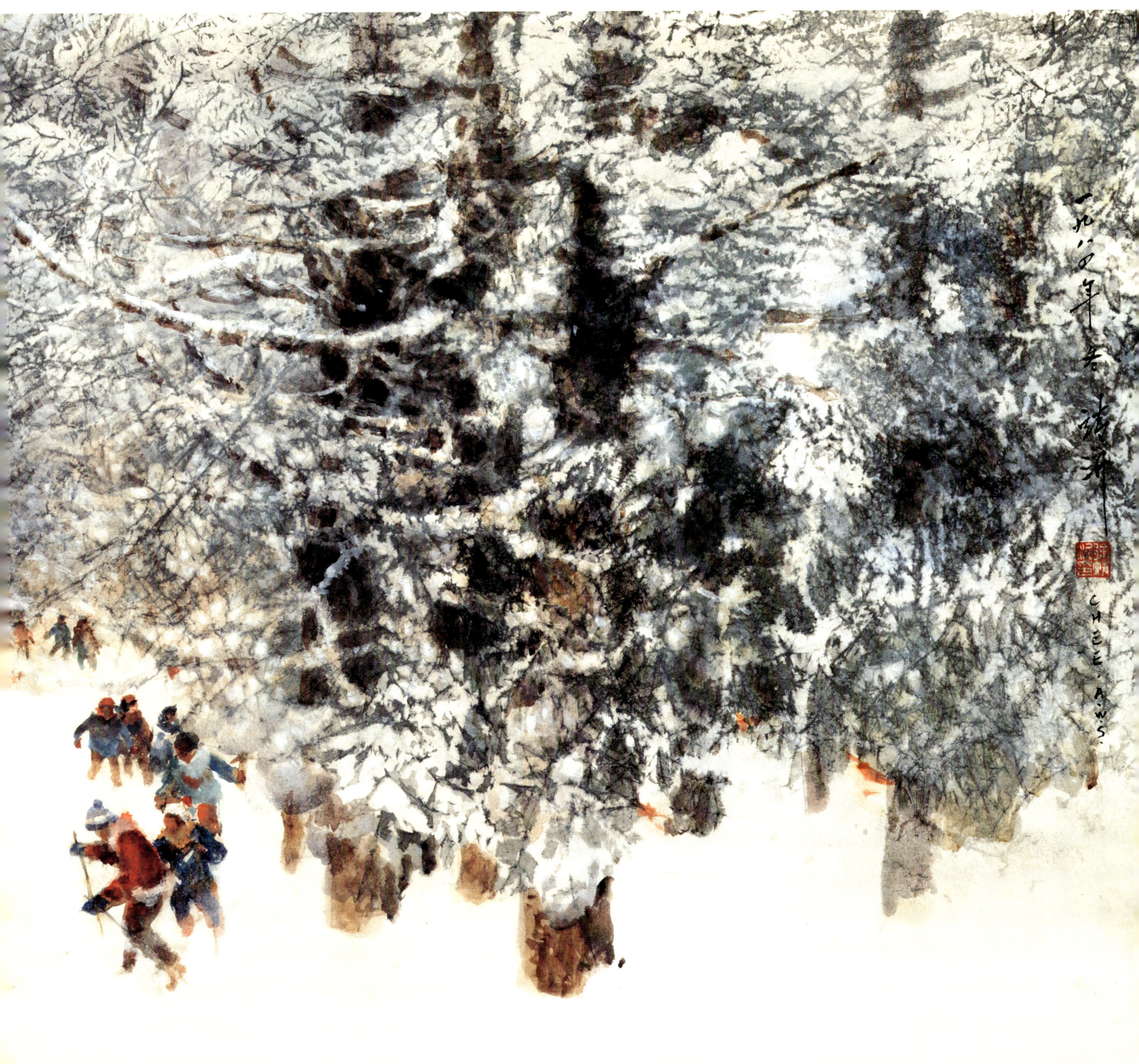
一九八四年春
CHEE, A.W.S.

33

DULUTH WINTER 86 NO. 1

都鲁之冬86年1号

25" x 40" 63cm x 102cm

1986

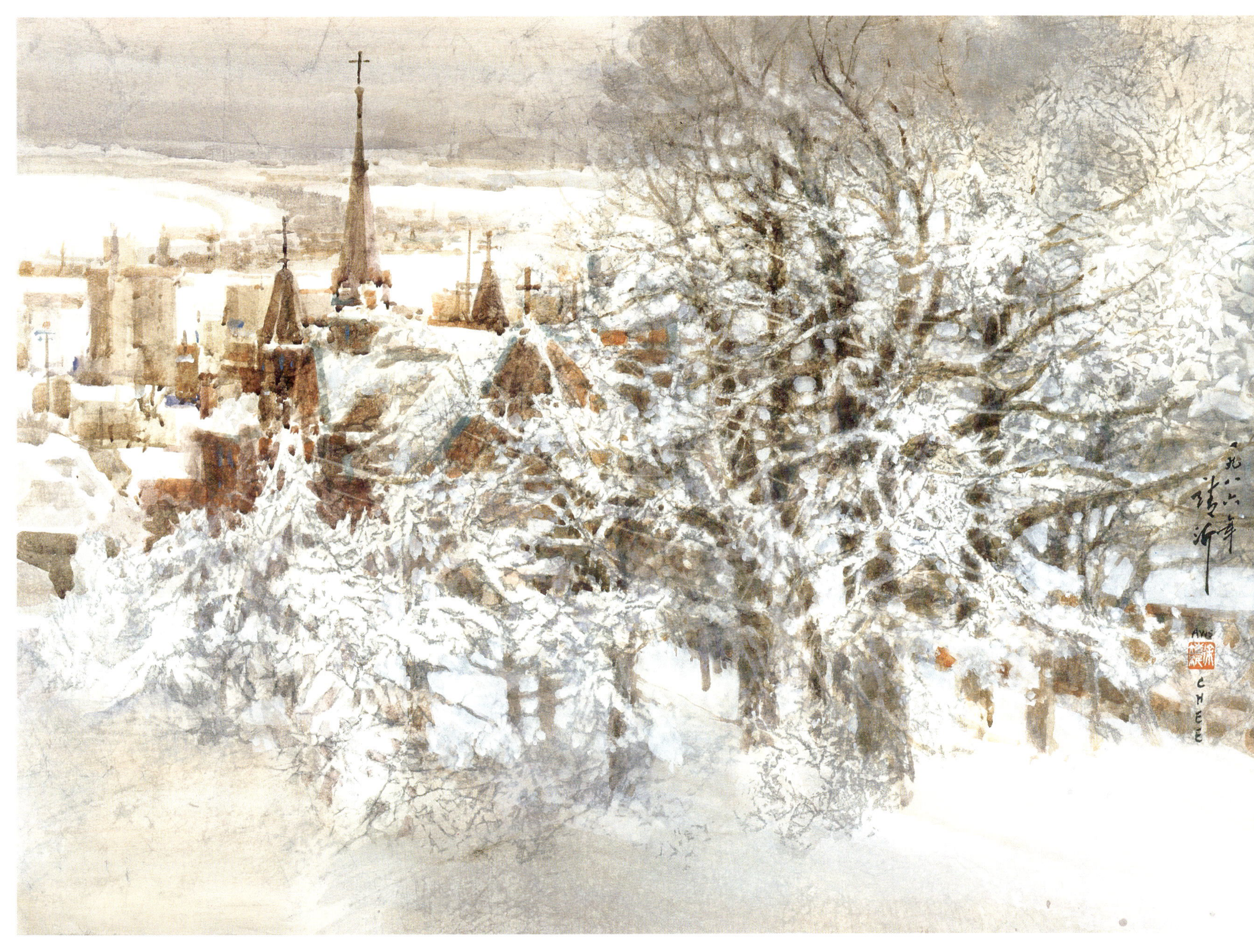

34

Springtime Lake View

湖岸春光

25" x 40"　63cm x 102cm

1987

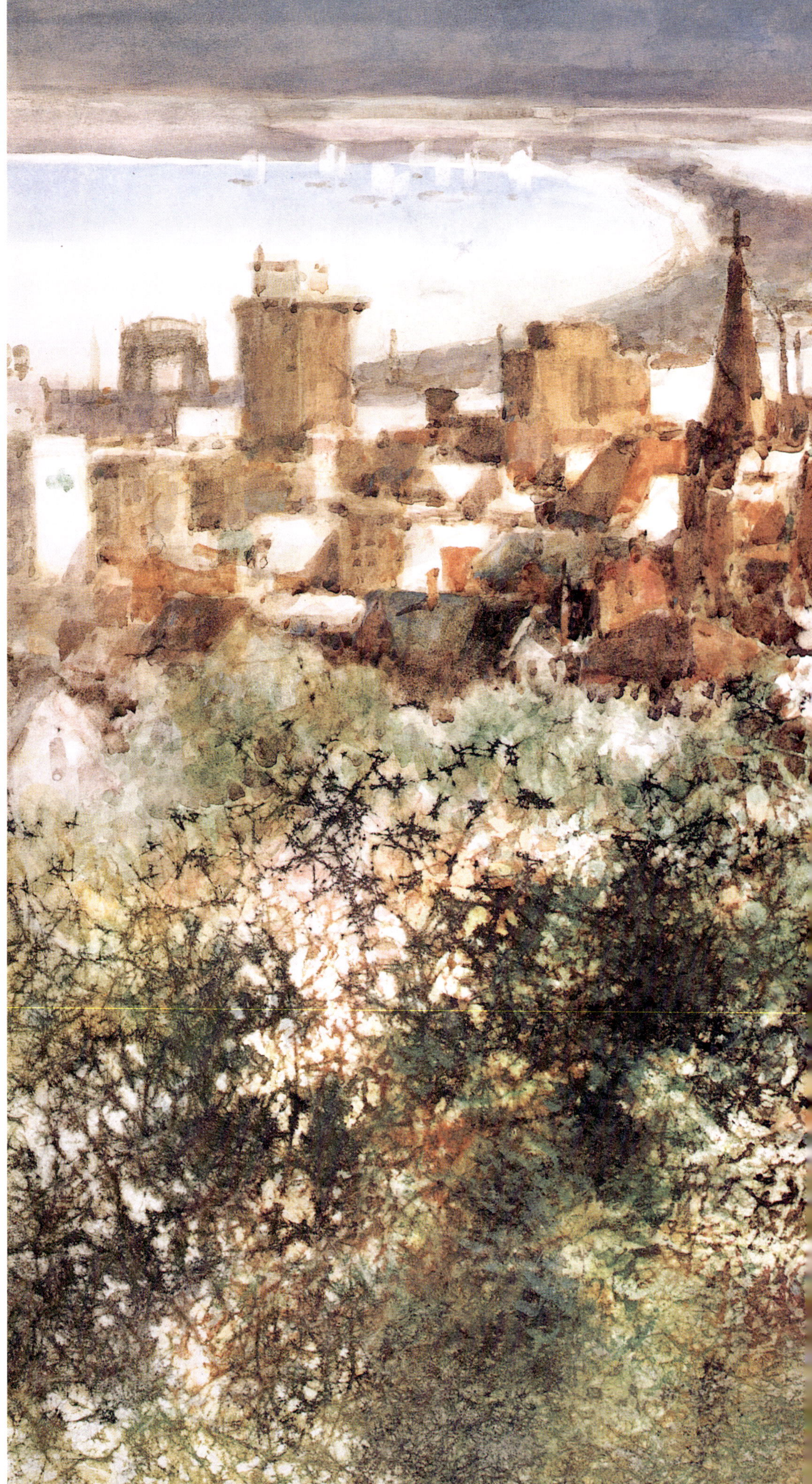

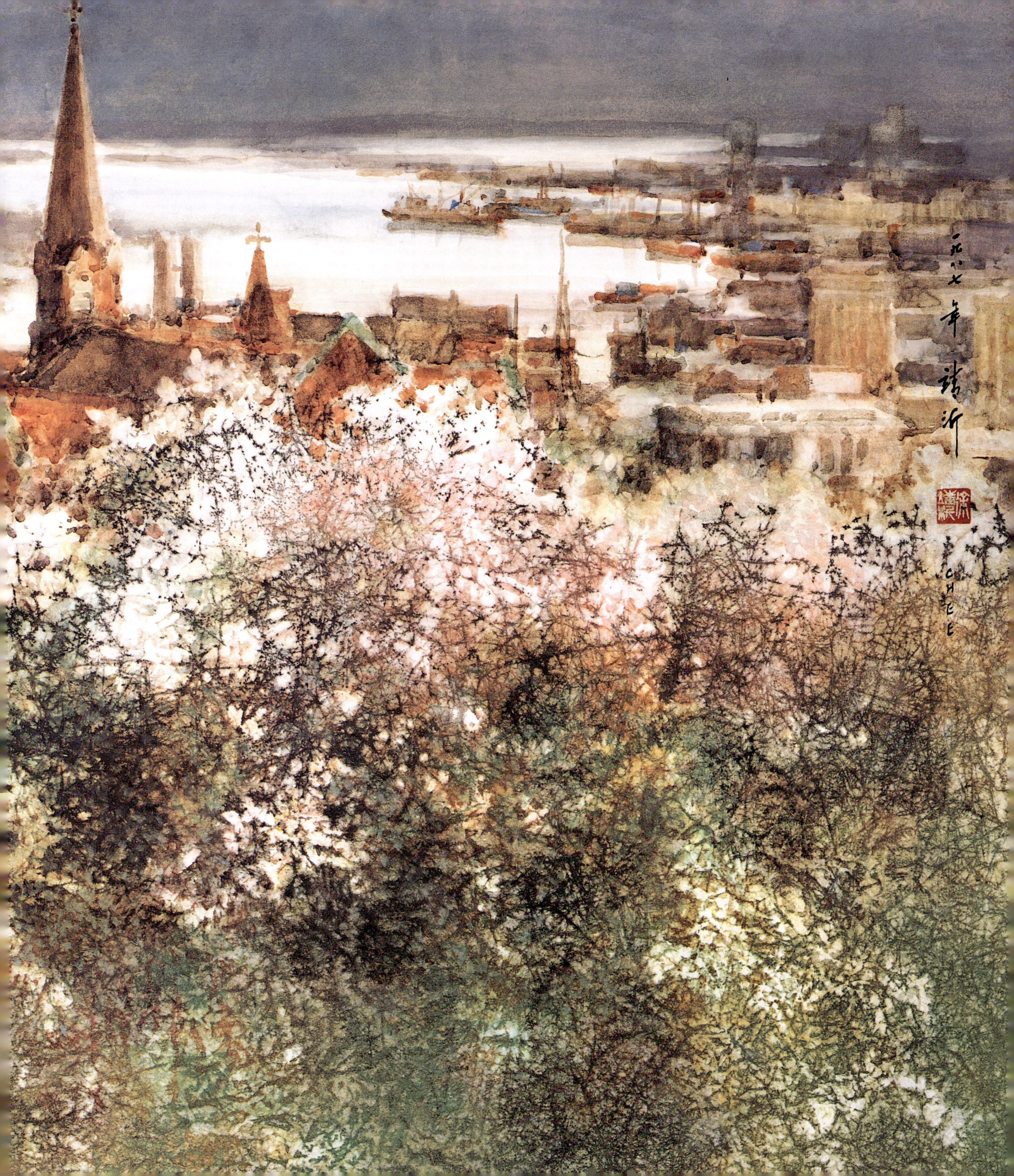
一九八七年
CHEE

35

Spring 96 No. 1

春96年1号

30" x 40"   76cm x 102cm

1996

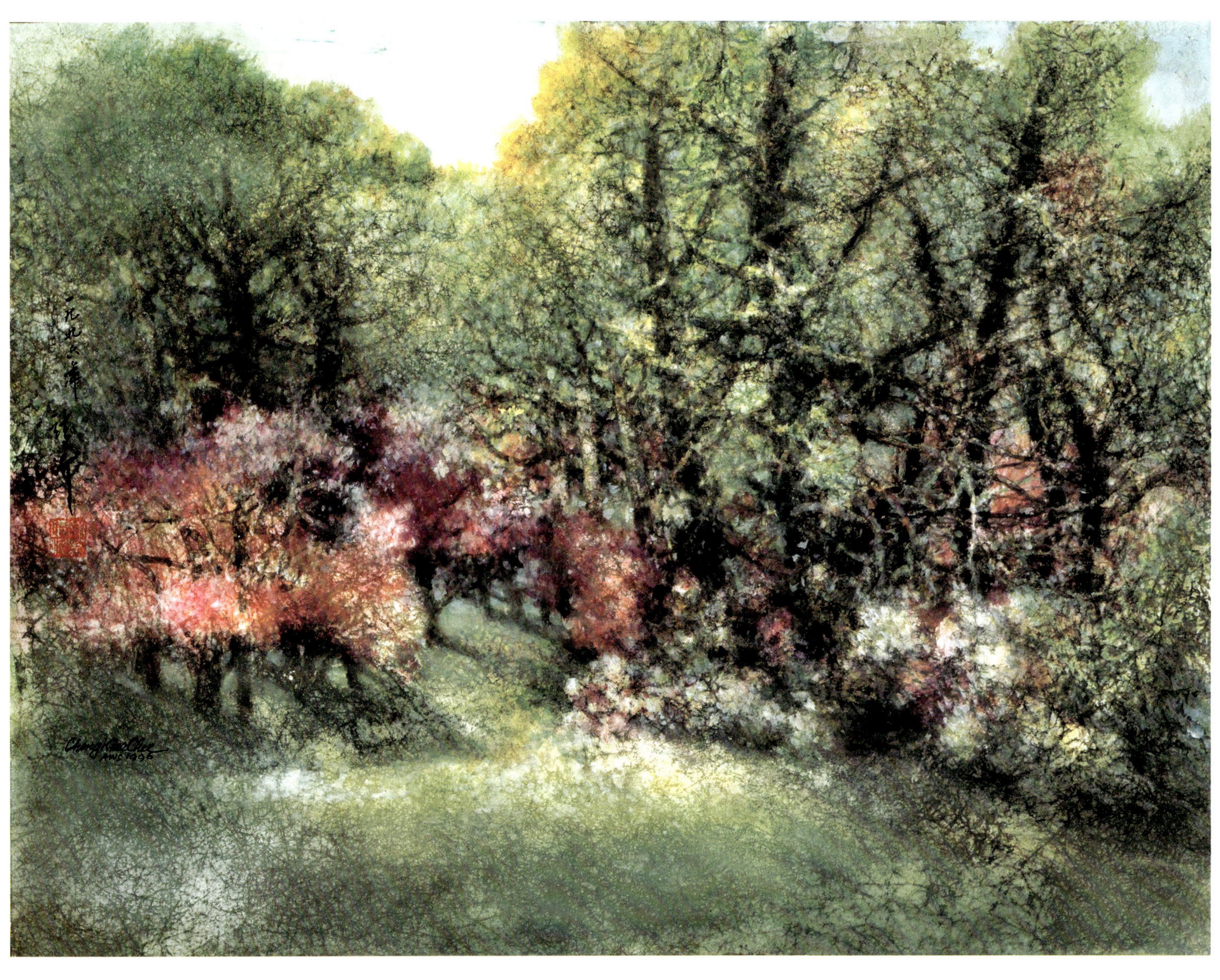

36

Autumn 89 No. 1

秋89年1号

24" x 36"   61cm x 91cm

1989

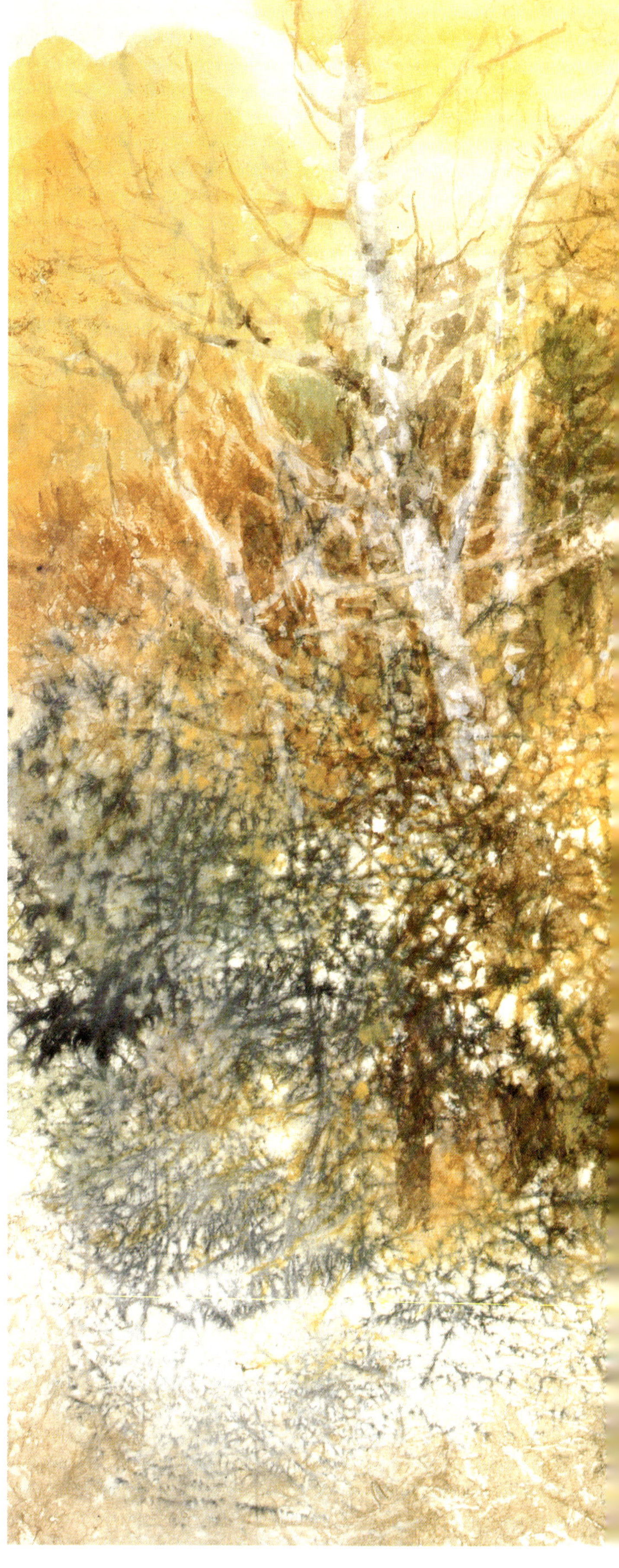

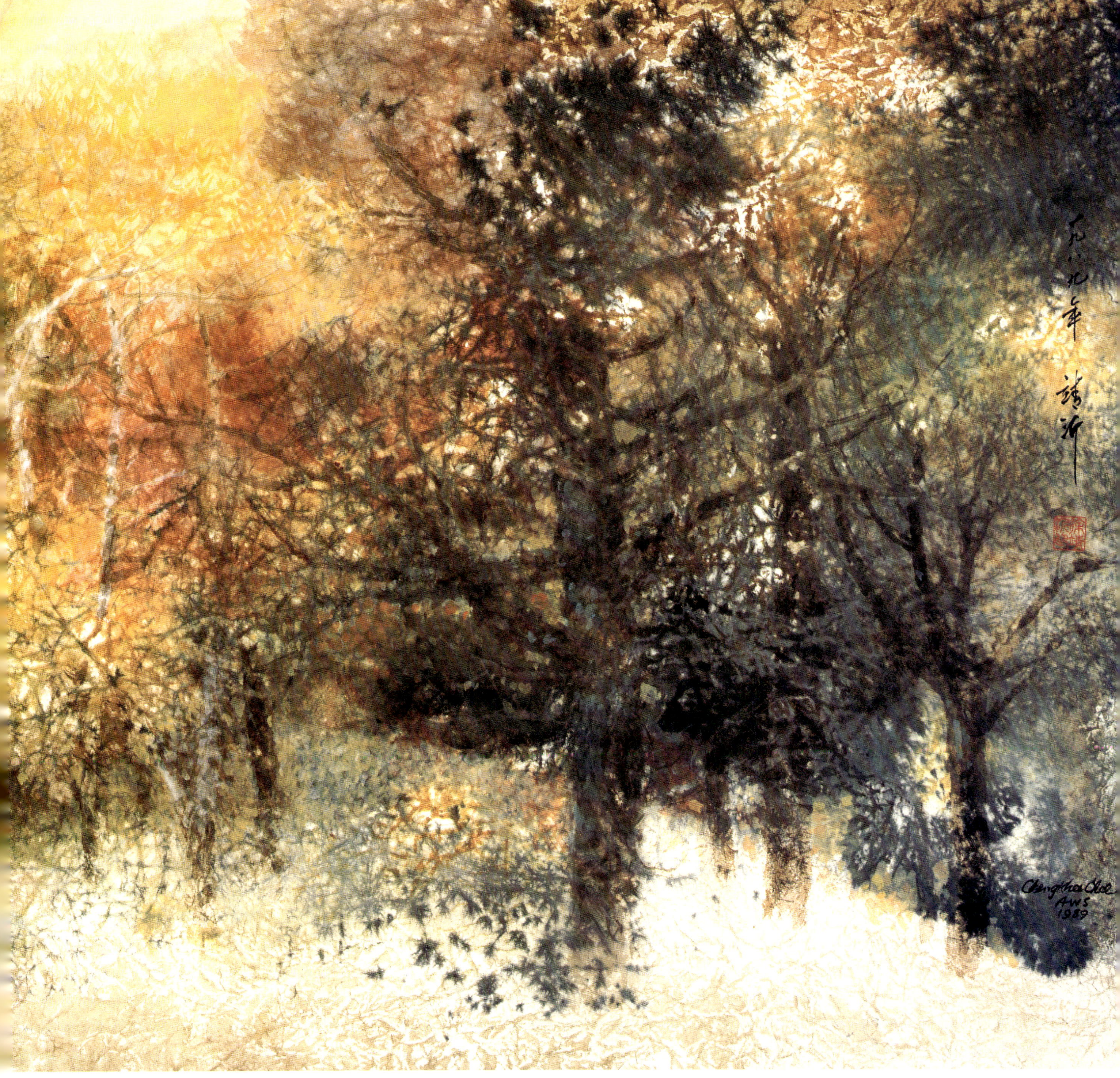
一九八九年
Cheng-Khee Chee
AWS
1989

37

Winter 96 No. 1

冬96年1号

30" x 40" 76cm x 102cm

1996

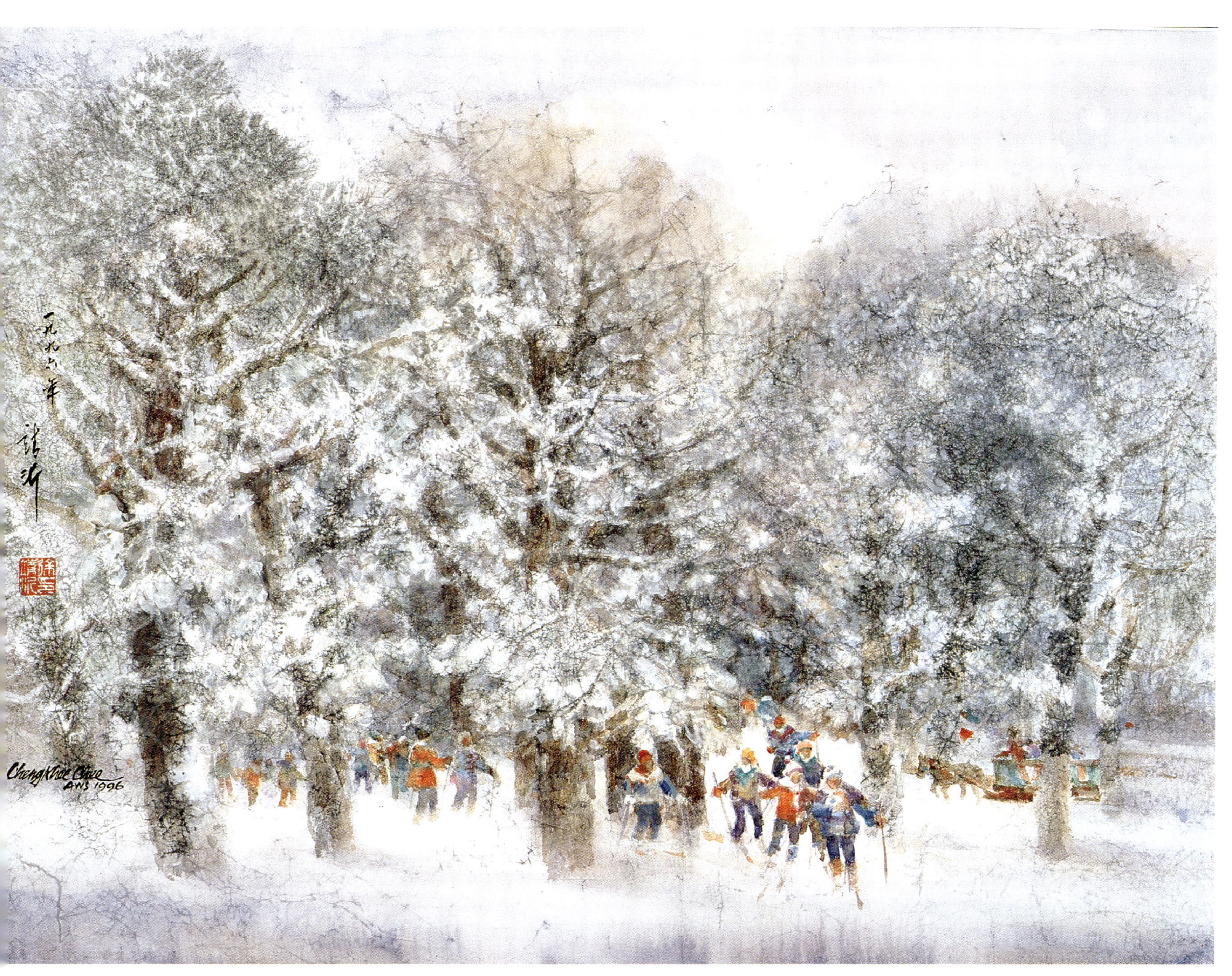
一九九六年
ChengKhee Chee
AWS 1996

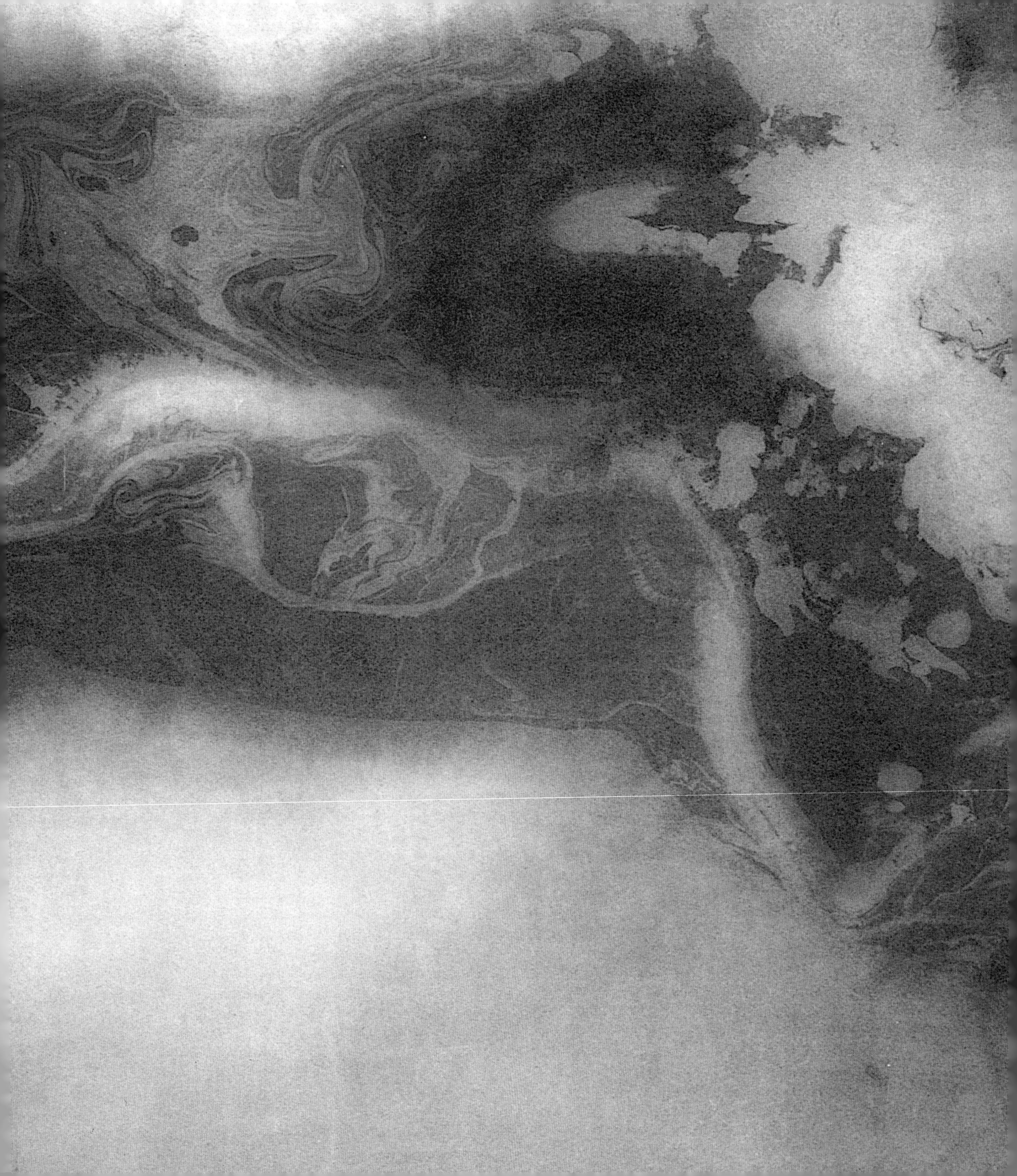

Marbling

Marbling and Monoprinting Technique

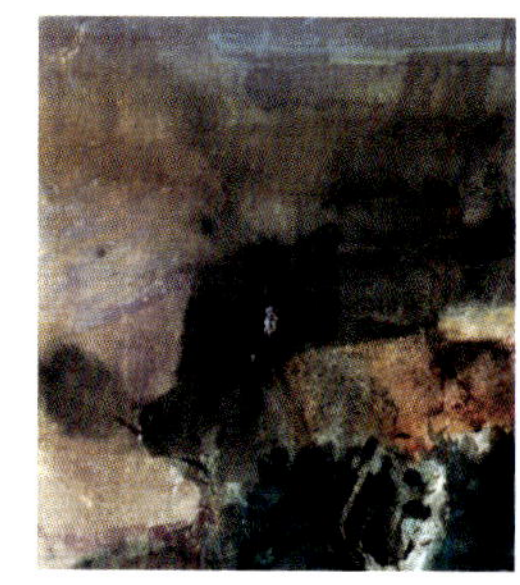

Subject Matter and Esthetic Concept

Like any one else, I have dreams, fantasies, imagination, and vision. I often contemplate the infinity of time and space. I also ponder spiritual, supernatural, and mystical experiences. All of these defy description or expression in realistic images.

The ink marbling technique originated in China over two thousand years ago. It became a sacred art of painting on water practiced by Shinto priests in Japan from the 12th century on. The Japanese term for the process is 'suminagashi', meaning flowing ink. The rhythmic and swirling lines and shapes created by this process invariably suggest the images of moving clouds and water interlocking with mountains and rocks. Inspired by Liu Guo Sung's work, I started to explore this technique and concept in 1982 to express my spiritual, visionary, and dream world (The Lost Horizon Series).

Later on I modify this technique by splashing ink and watercolor on a piece of white enameled masonite, guide the colors and ink to run and mix in the desired way, and transfer the image to a sheet of absorbent rice paper. After the paper is dried, I develop it into a painting. The painting could be abstract, such as 'Rhythm of the Shore', or realistic, such as 'Canyon with Junipers', or a combination of realism and abstraction, such as 'The Koi Pond'.

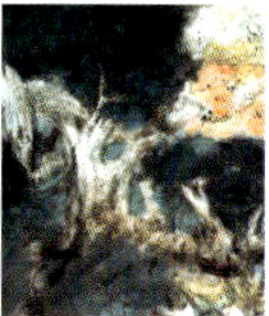

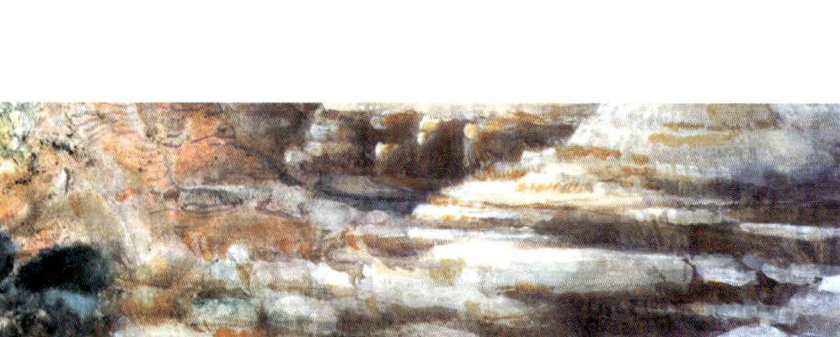

Tools and Supplies

A pan or tub wider than the size of paper
Liquid Oriental ink (sumi ink)
Tube watercolors
Absorbent rice paper such as Xuan, Kozo...
Oriental brushes
Mounting board or masa as backing sheet
Mounting paste (Metylan cellulose wall paper paste)

Painting Procedure

1. I fill a tub with three inches of water at room temperature
2. I drip liquid sumi ink gently onto the surface of water with a brush
3. I manipulate the floating ink gently with a stick to form desired patterns
4. Place a sheet of dry absorbent rice paper over it to pick up the ink patterns. Further manipulation of design patterns can be done by folding the paper to divide it into different planes, and picking up the ink pattern at different time intervals
5. I pick out the most successful piece, adjust the value relationship, and add colors to finish it
6. See A for the alternative method
7. I mount the painting to smooth out and strengthen it

水拓法

1. 材料：宣纸、皮纸、或其他吸水生纸、墨汁、水彩或中国画颜料。
2. 特点：将墨汁滴在清水上面，使它自由浮泛游动；往往出现行云流水，高山幽谷的虚幻图象。将一张生纸盖上去，这图象马上拓印到纸上。
   这种画法的目的是在寻求偶然的效果和动荡飘逸的韵味。
3. 画法：按照上述的方法印制许多图象，选出最满意的拓在画版上加工上色而完成画面。
   用笔或用色加工时要注意细心保留偶然效果的韵味。做到人牲物性自然合作而臻於天衣无缝的境界。上色时尽量选用透明度高的颜色，层层加上，使有厚重感而不损害原来的墨痕。
   另一种画法是将墨和色彩同时泼在塑料版上，使水、墨、色交融。满意之后，将生纸盖上，把图象拓印到纸上，然后冷静思量，细心加工而就。
4. 画例：缥缈组画（抽象）、荷塘锦鲤（抽象和具象结合）、古柏幽谷（抽象到具象）

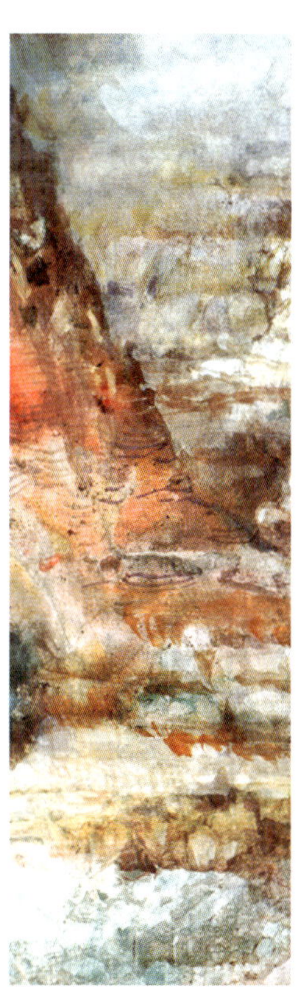

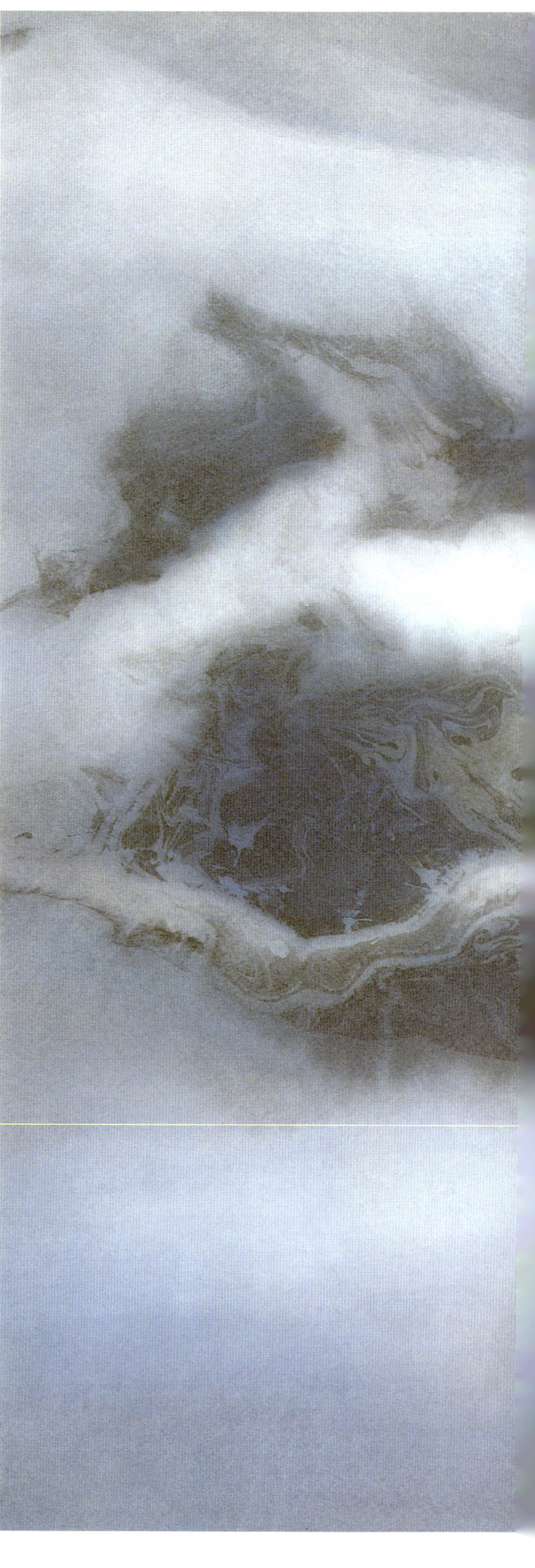

38

Lost Horizon 83 No. 1

缥缈83年1号

24" x 36" 61cm x 91cm

1983

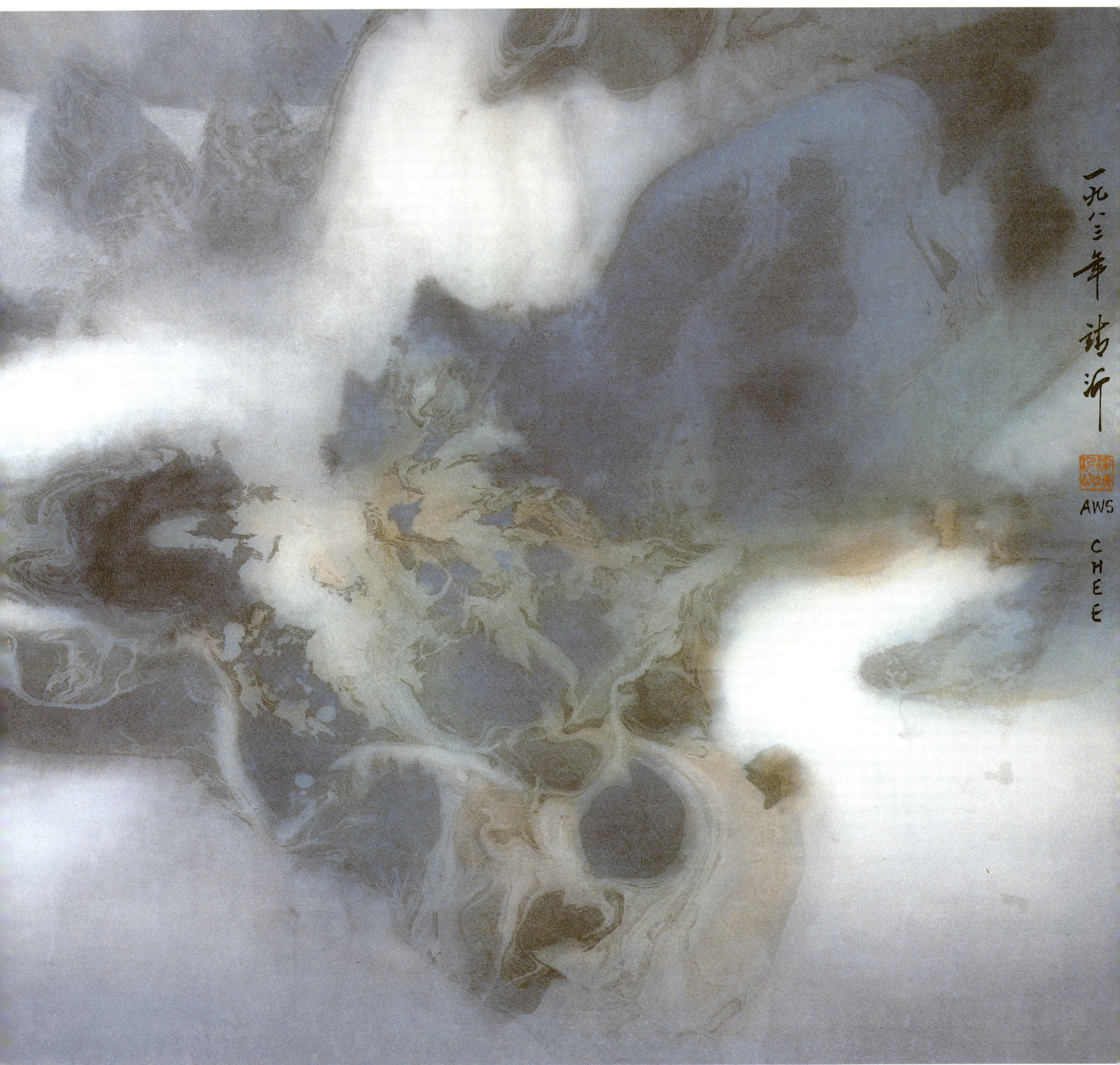
一九八三年
AWS
CHEE

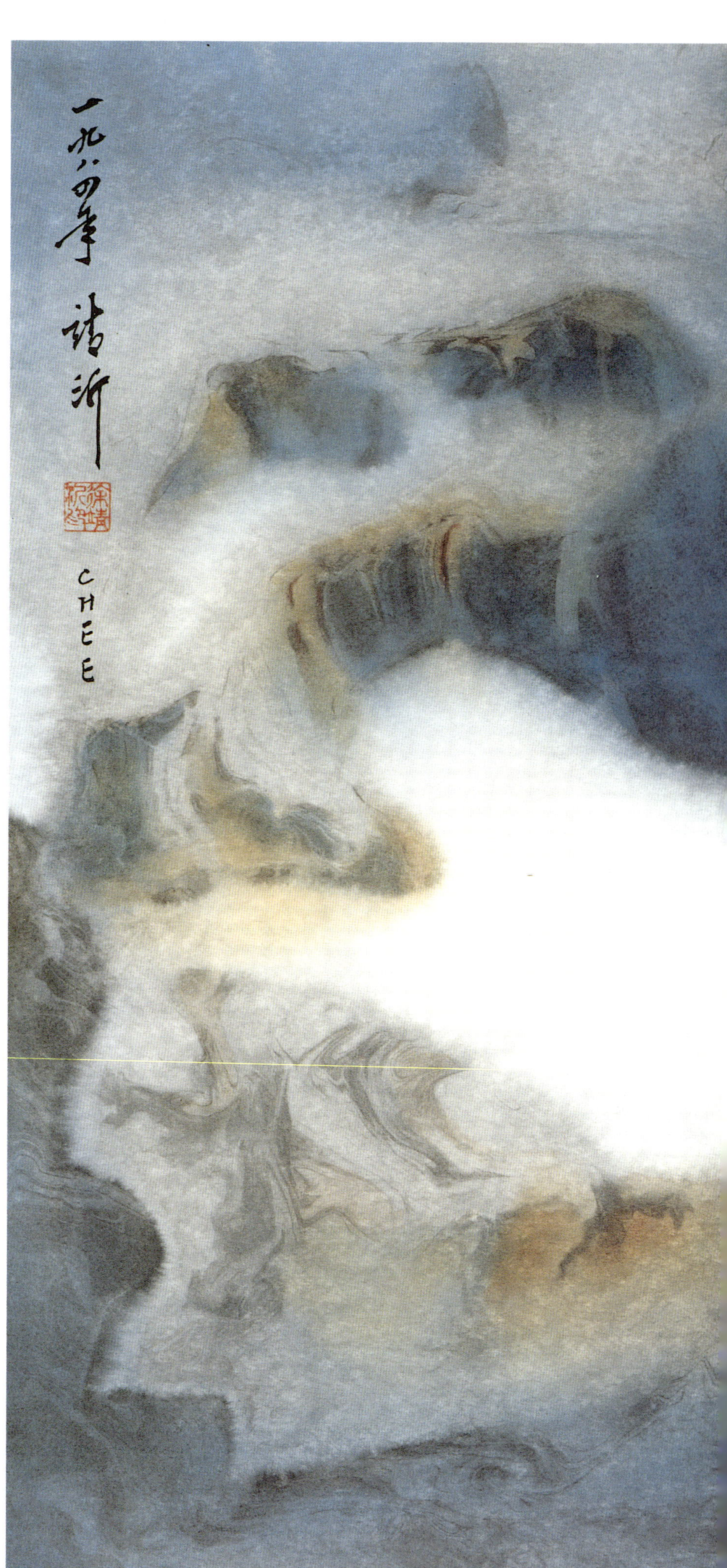

39

Lost Horizon 83 No. 2

缥缈83年2号

24" x 36" 61cm x 91cm

1983

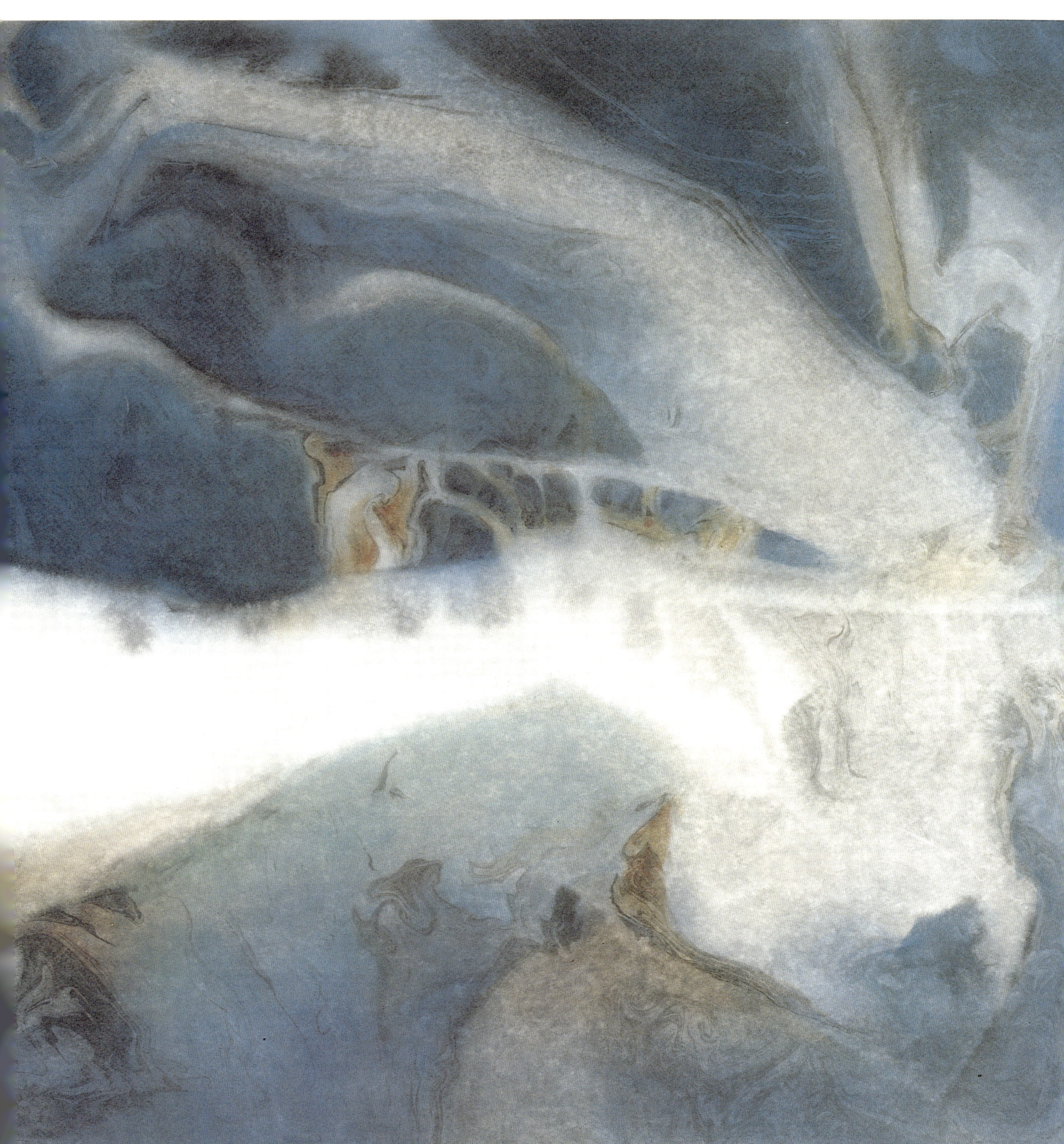

40

Clouds, Earth, Water

云、地、水

24" x 36" 61cm x 91cm

1983

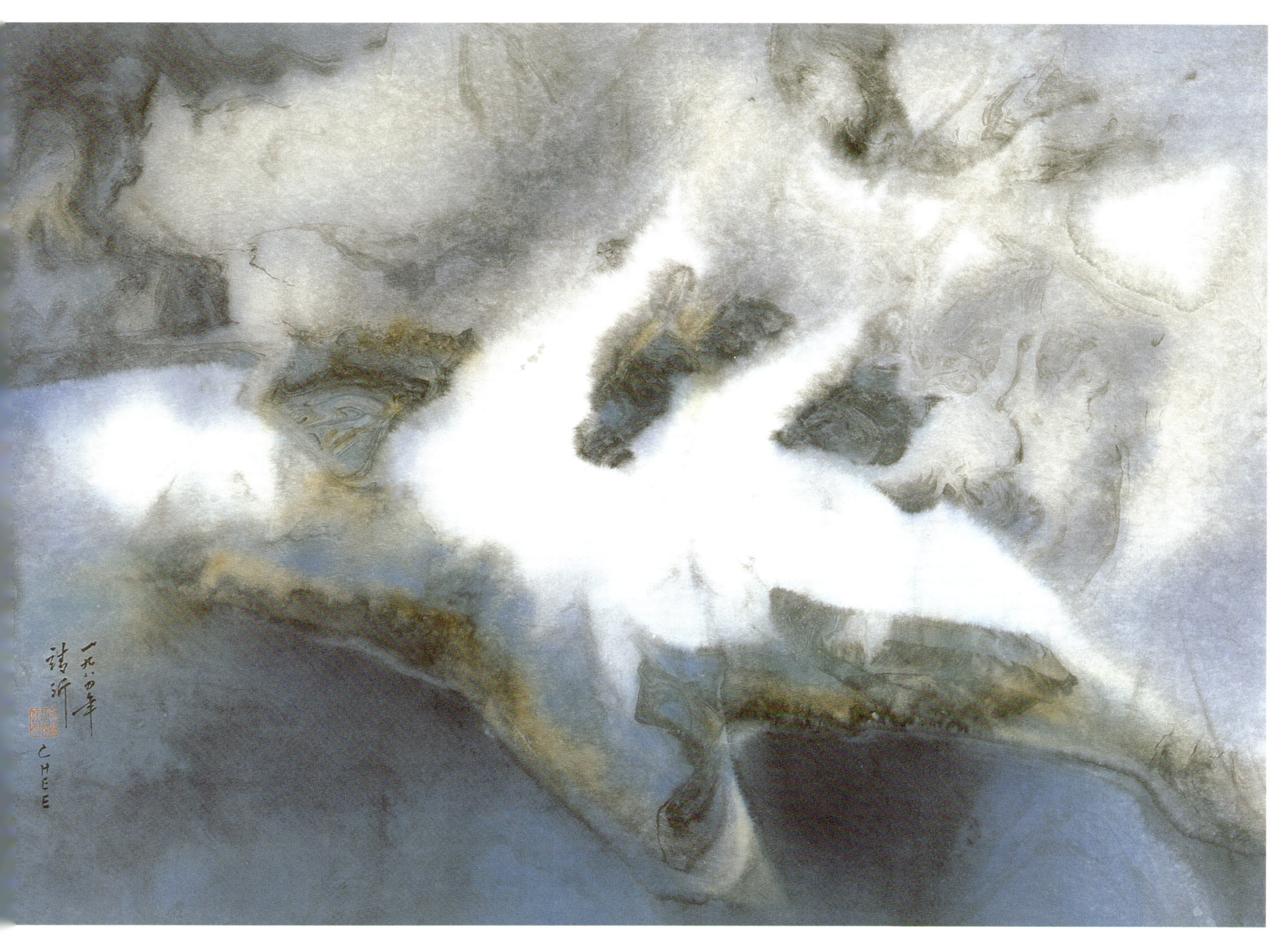
一九八四年
靖沂
CHEE

41

RHYTHM OF THE SHORE

岸边旋律

30" x 40" 76cm x 102cm

1996

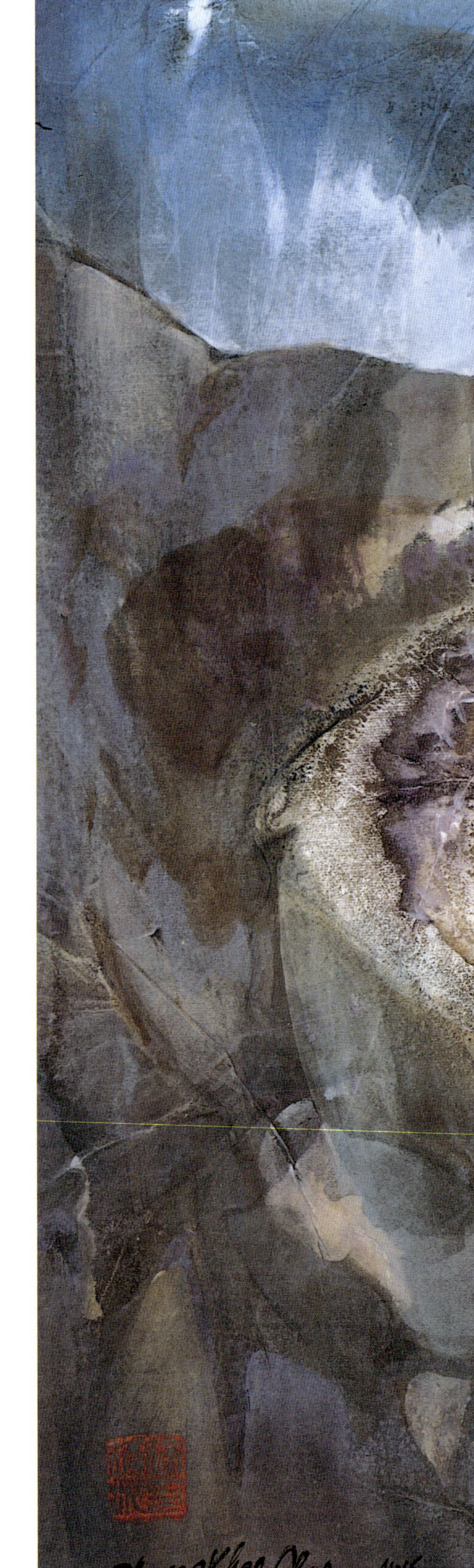

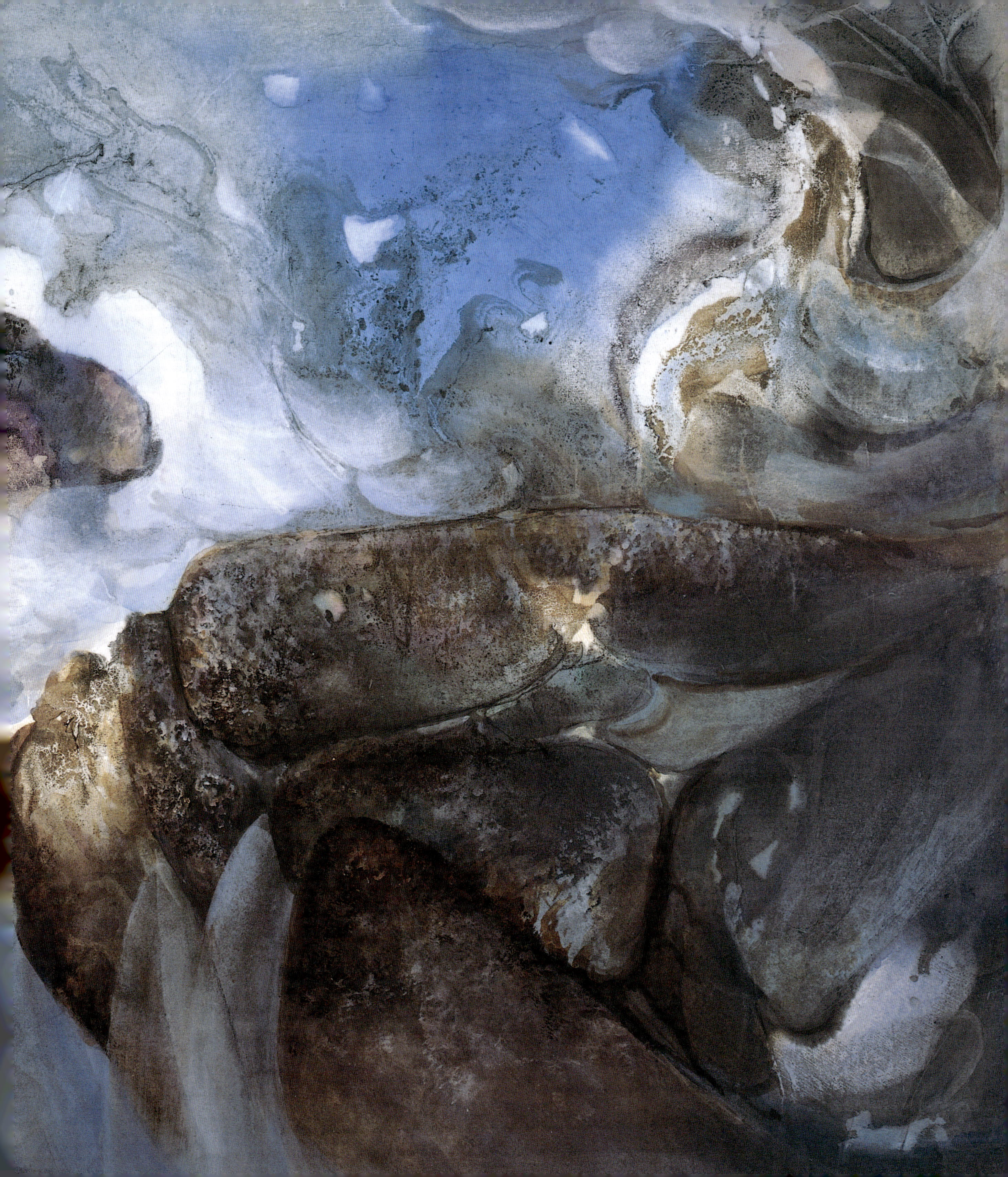

42

Koi Pond

锦鲤荷塘

30" x 40"   76cm x 102cm

1996

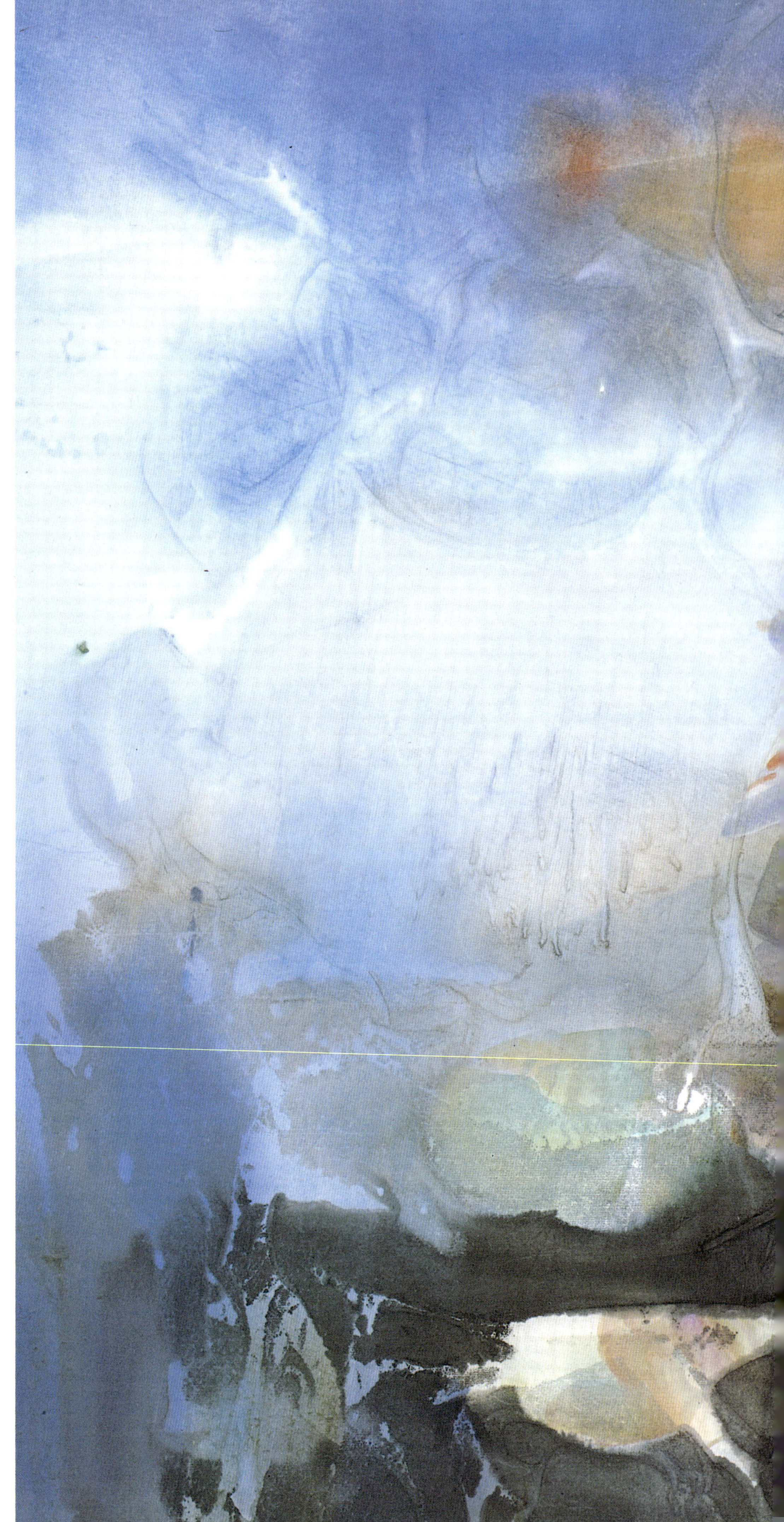

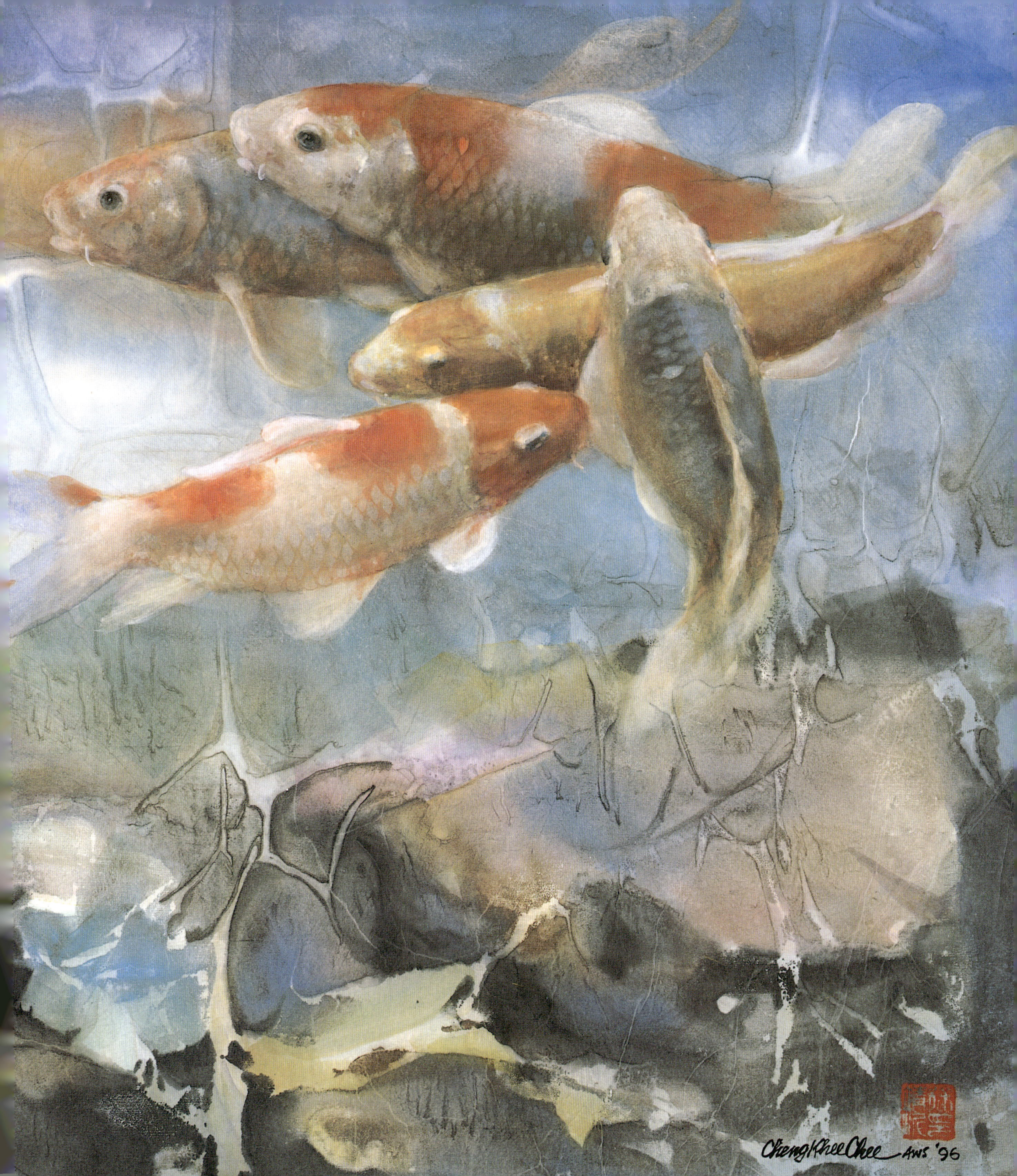
ChengKheeChee
AWS '96

43

Canyon with Junipers

古柏幽谷

30" x 40"   76cm x 102cm

1996

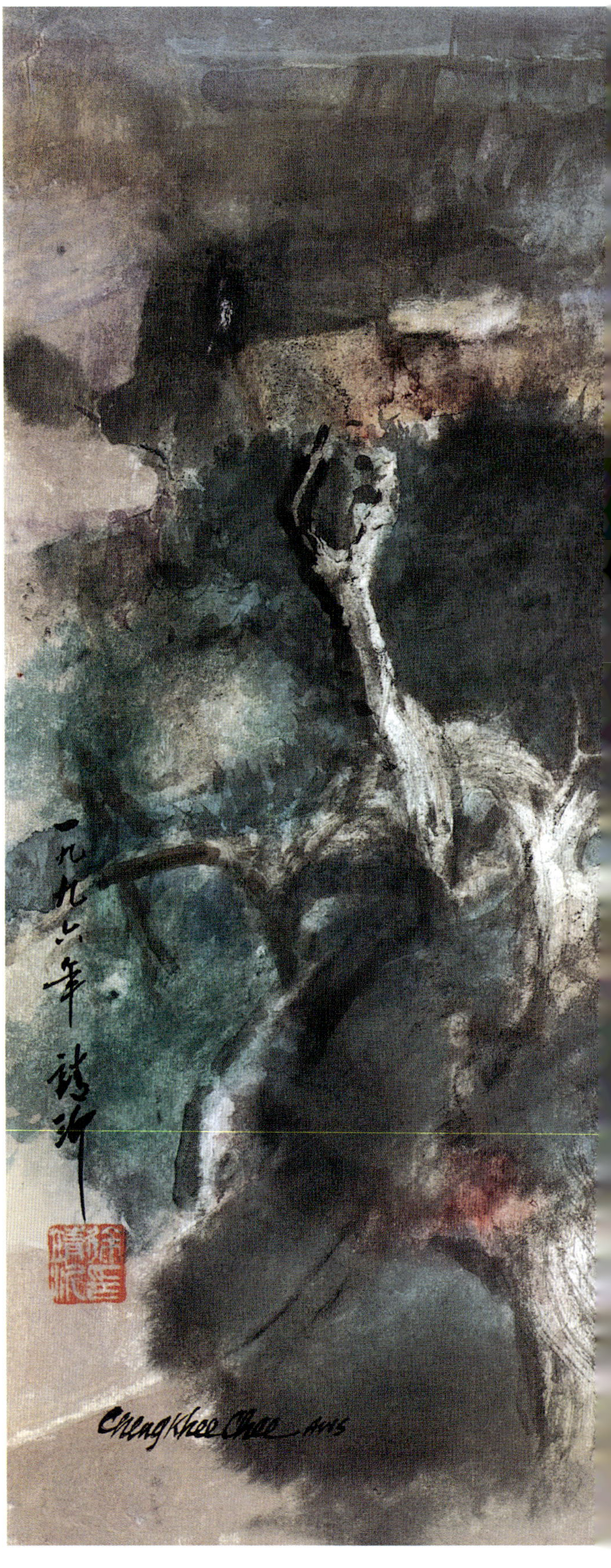

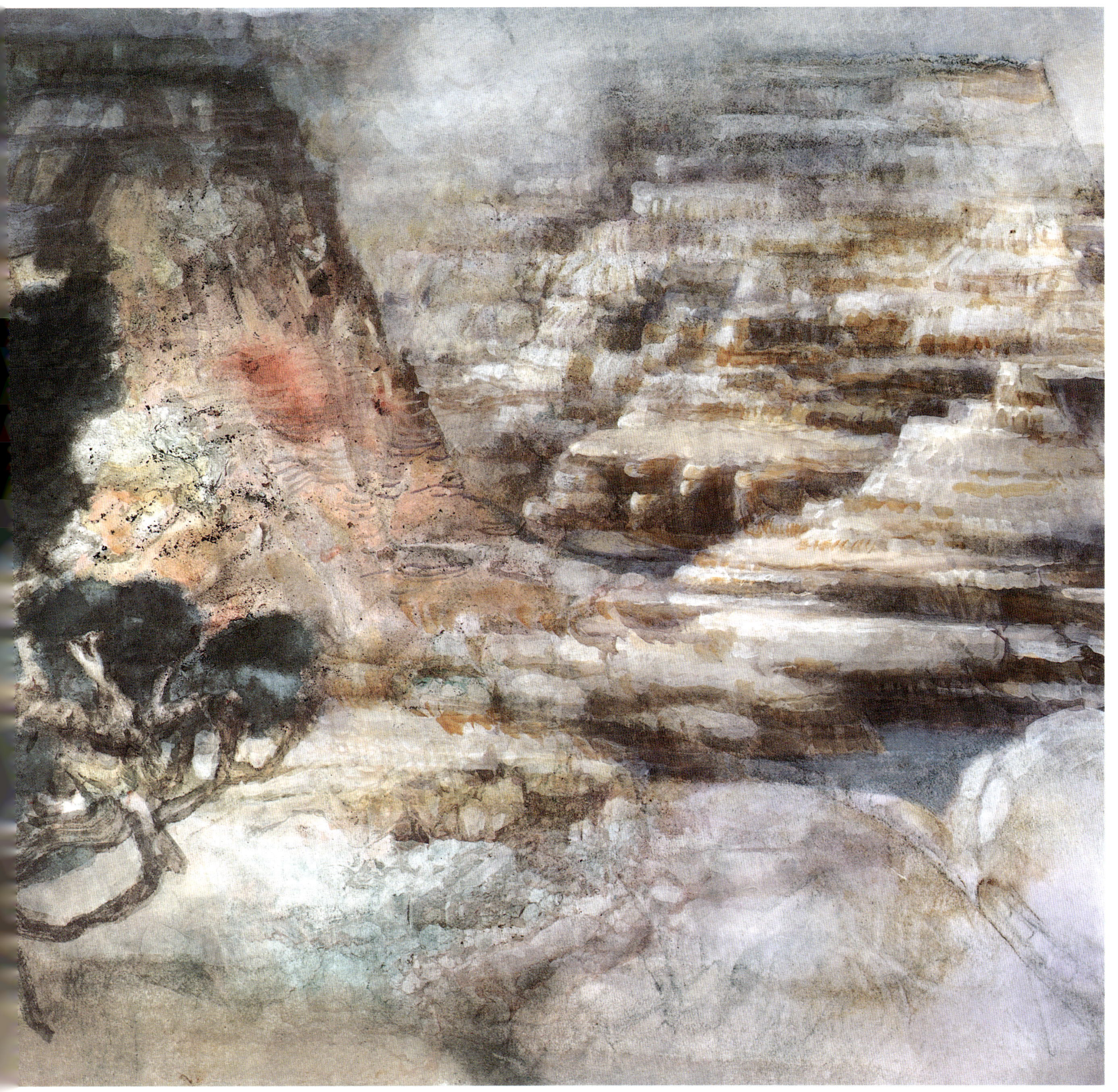

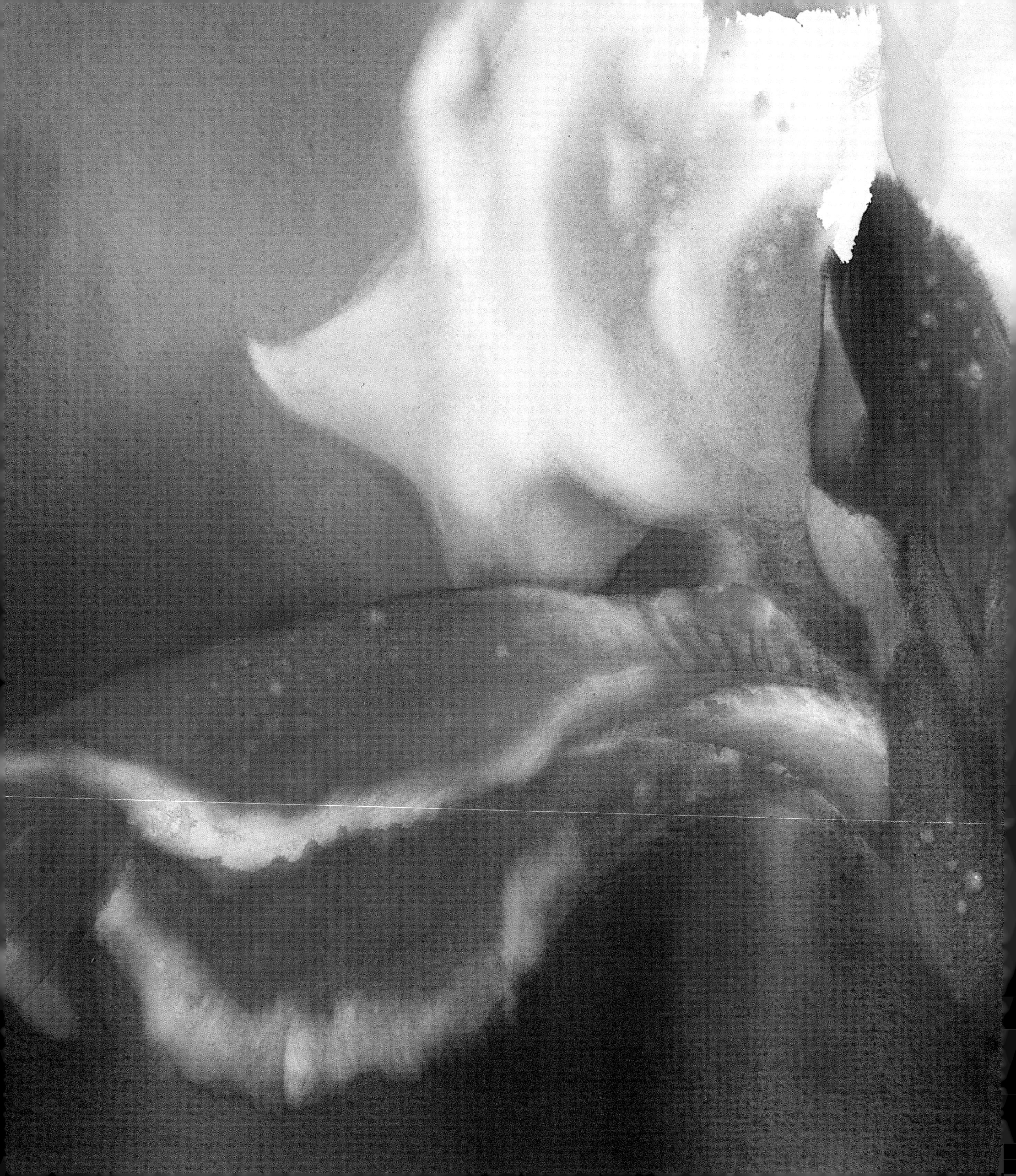

Saturated Wet

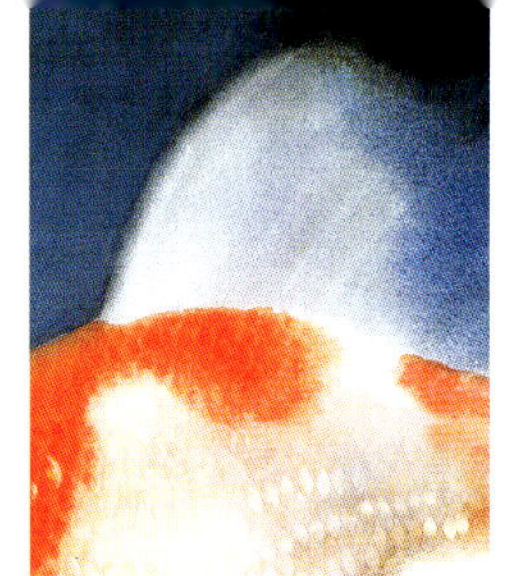

Saturated Wet Technique

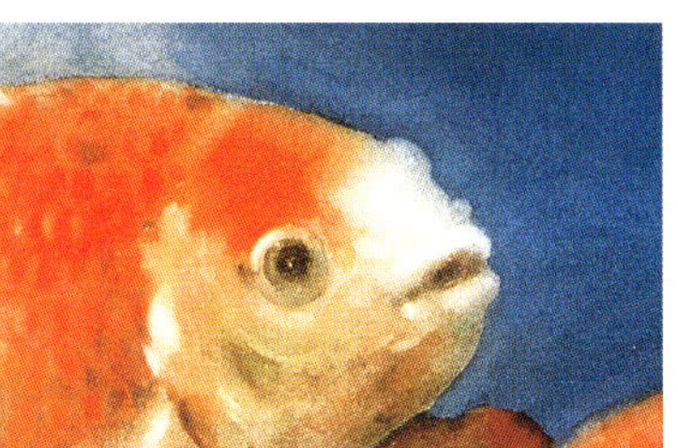

Subject Matter and Esthetic Concept

I use this method for painting subjects such as goldfish, koi and flowers. Their shapes are generally lighter than the negative background, and they have soft edges. The saturated wet paper allows easy lifting, gives soft edges, and maintains a unified background.

Goldfish and koi are an important part of Asian people's lives because they give them pleasure and relaxation. I am very fond of both of them. They are irresistible to paint. I have observed and studied both species for many years in aquariums, ponds, and books and magazines. I have a good grasp of their physiology and habits. This knowledge enables me to take an almost improvisational approach in the process of painting.

When painting fish I try to get the feeling that fish are *in* the water, and the two are inseparable. When painting flowers I try to bring out their soft and gentle characteristics. This can best be achieved in the saturated wet technique.

Tools and Supplies

2" or 3" squirrel, camel or other soft-hair brushes
1" and ½" squirrel, camel or other soft-hair oval
D'Arches, Lana or other cold-pressed paper, 140lb or 300lb
Tube watercolors premixed in dishes

Painting Procedure

1. I soak the paper until it is thoroughly saturated
2. I place the paper on a painting board (Masonite or other) to let it settle until the shine disappears. Excess surface water can be removed by rolling a roll of paper towel over it
3. I premix a large quantity of tube watercolors in dishes
4. I paint the negative background first trying to think only in abstract terms: warm and cool colors, light and dark values, smooth and rough textures. I daringly splash colors on the paper, tilt the board to let them run and mix, and guide them in the direction I want them to flow
5. When I am satisfied with the background painting, I let it settle until the glistening wetness of the surface disappears. I then evaluate its composition, and start lifting shapes off the moist surface
6. Next, I build the forms, and further develop the painting
7. In the final stage I refine the details. For fish scales, I use the stencilling method. I cut scale shapes of various sizes on a sheet of plastic, lift out individual scales with a moist sponge, and touch up with a brush

Timing is extremely important in these steps. If the surface is too dry, colors cannot be lifted; if it is too wet, the colors will run. Under proper conditions, I can lift out shapes to the paper white. If I use sustaining colors such as Winsor blue, the hint of these colors will enrich or add interest to the painting.

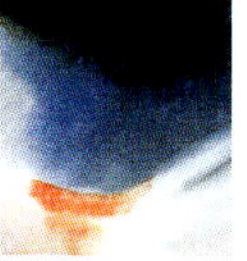

纯湿画法

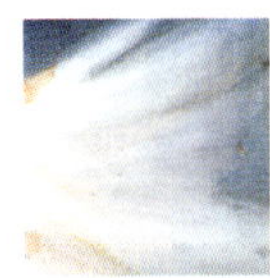

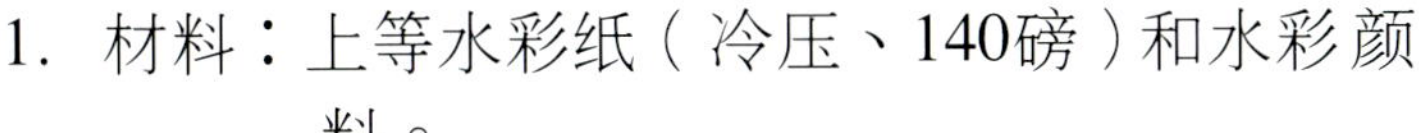

1. 材料：上等水彩纸（冷压、140磅）和水彩颜料。
2. 特点：在湿透了的上等水彩纸上作画，可以任意擦 掉纸上的颜色，增减修改，一直到满意为止。完成的作品色彩柔和饱满，即使经过多次往返修改，画面颜色不会有灰暗污浊的现象。
3. 画法：这种画法的关键在掌握画纸的湿度。未画前先把纸两面都刷上水，让它湿透后才开始作画。在画的过程中根据需要，在纸背和画版之间再加水，保持纸的湿度到完工为止。

   因为这种画法可以任意增减修改，开始的时候不必照顾细节，尽量鼓起激情，大刀阔斧地将不同的颜色布满画面，几乎相等於画一幅抽象表现主义的画。背景画得满意以后，马上衡量构图布局，用海绵或洗乾净的画笔在湿的画面上塑造形象。先是平面洗掉颜色，继而加工加色塑成立体感。细节部分则等待画纸乾了以后加工。
4. 画例：锦鲤组画，蝴蝶兰，玫瑰。

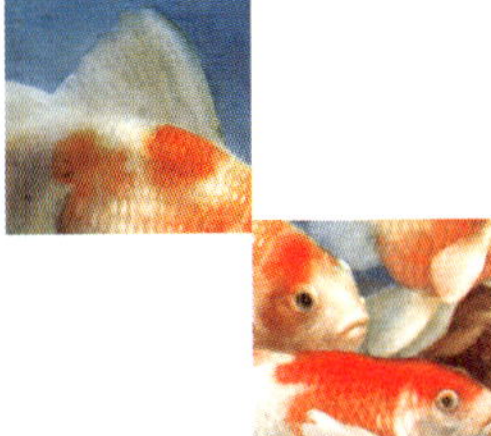

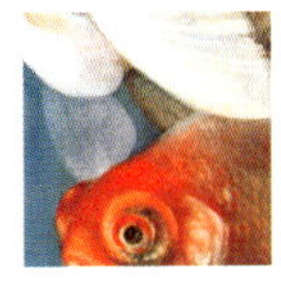

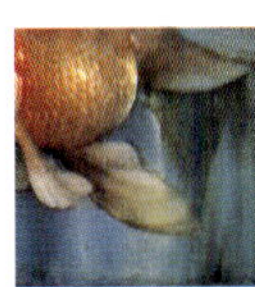

44

Goldfish 85 No.1

金鱼85年1号

25" x 40" 63cm x 102cm

1985

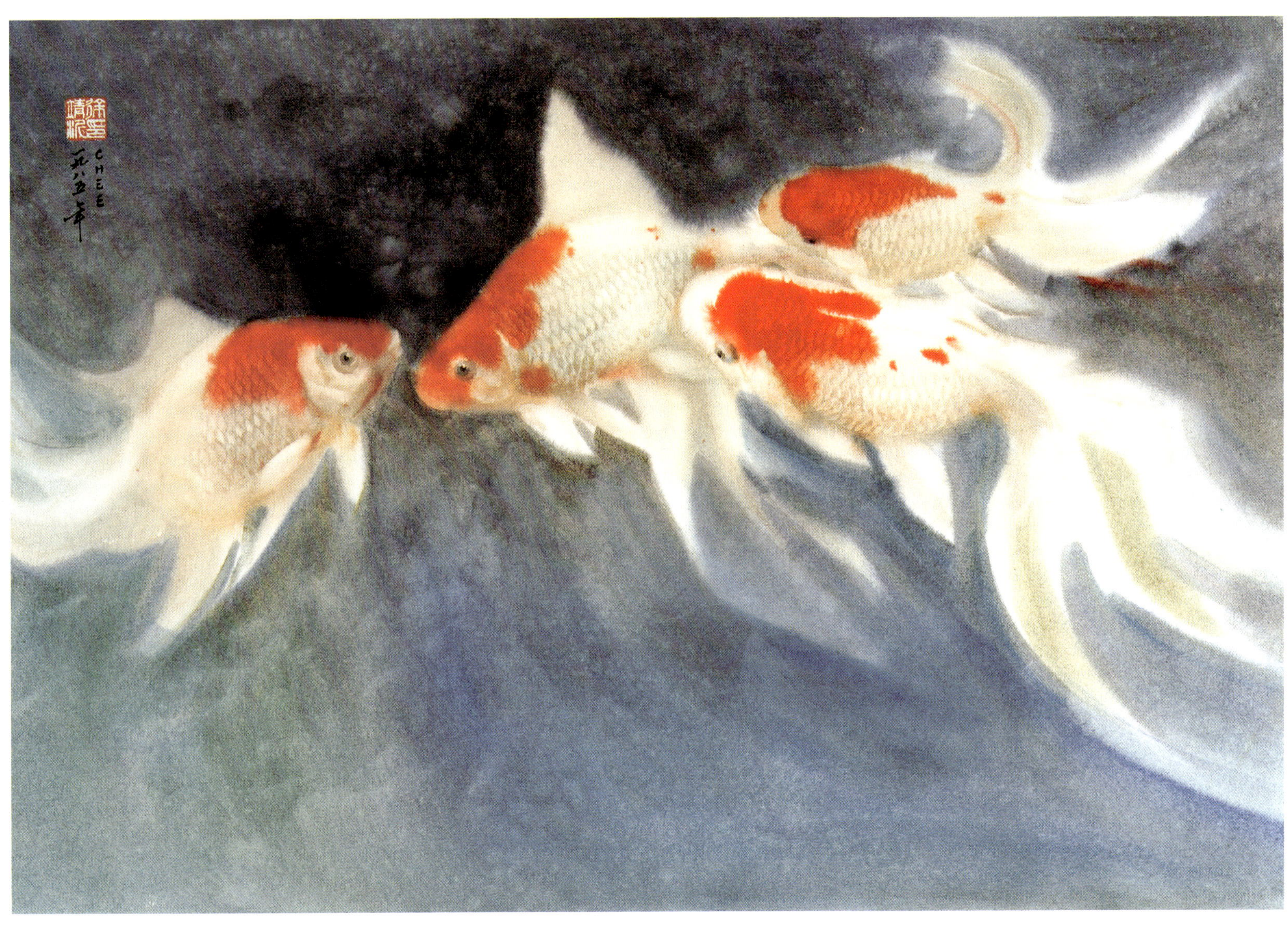
CHEE

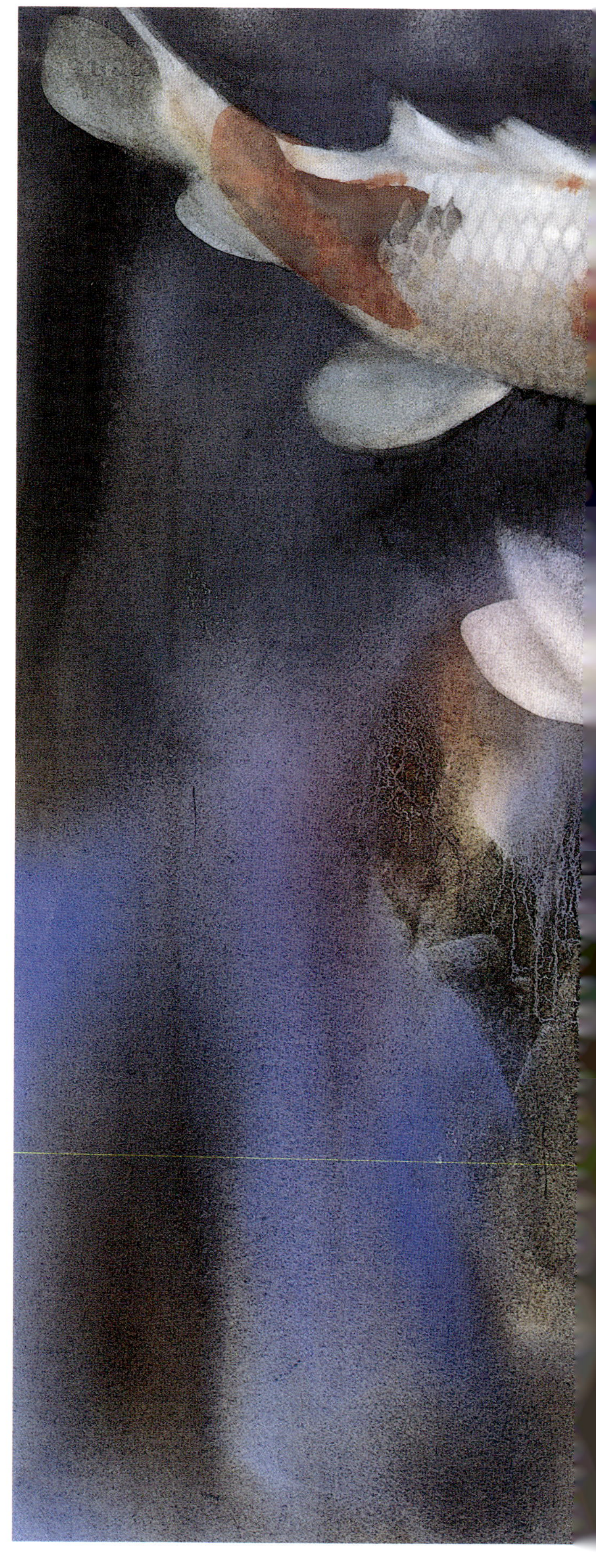

45

KOI 90 NO.4

锦鲤90年4号

25" x 40" 63cm x 102cm

1990

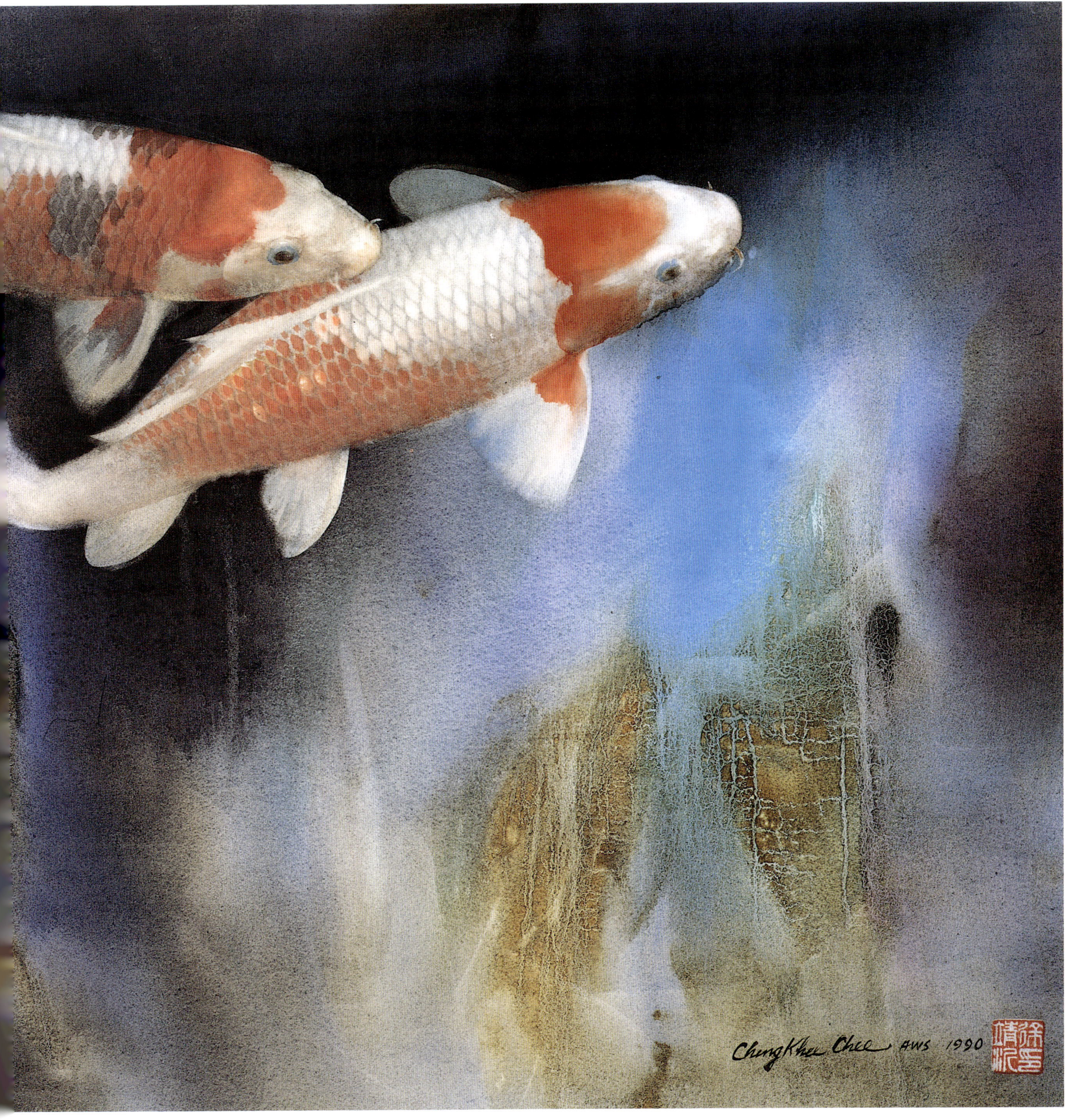
ChengKhee Chee AWS 1990

46

IRIS 90 NO.1

蝴蝶兰90年1号

25" x 40"   63cm x 102cm

1990

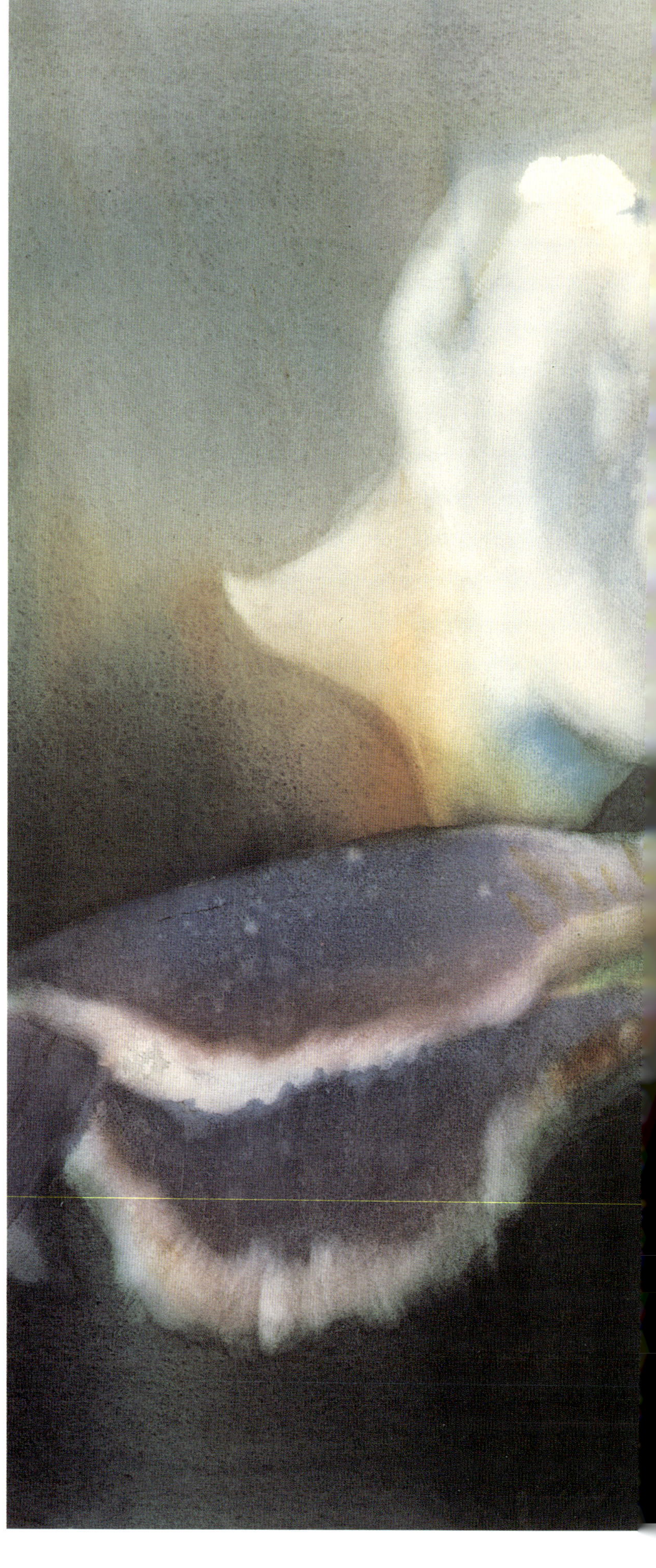

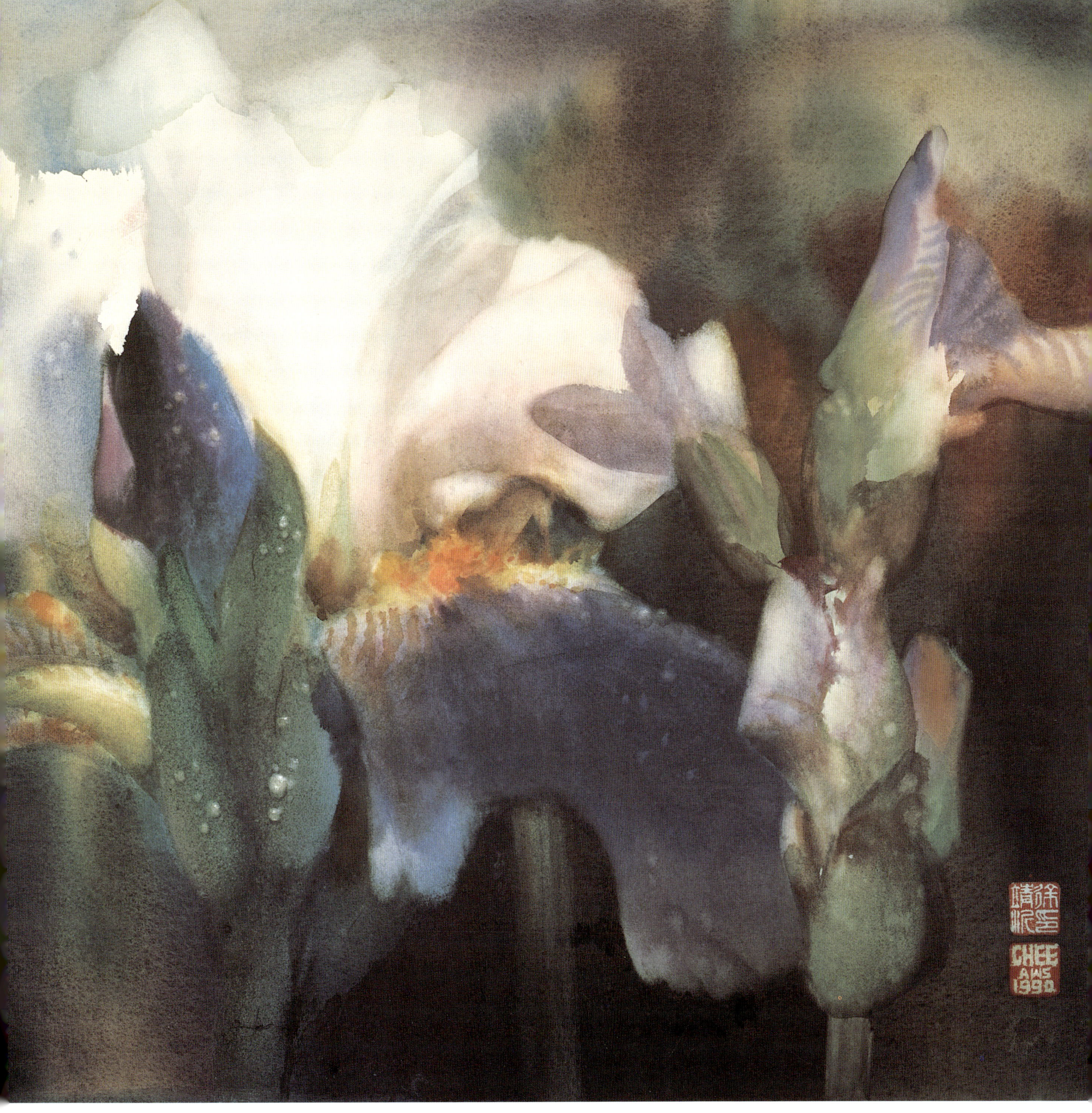
CHEE
AWS
1990

47

GOLDFISH 90 NO.1

金鱼90年1号

25" x 40"   63cm x 102cm

1990

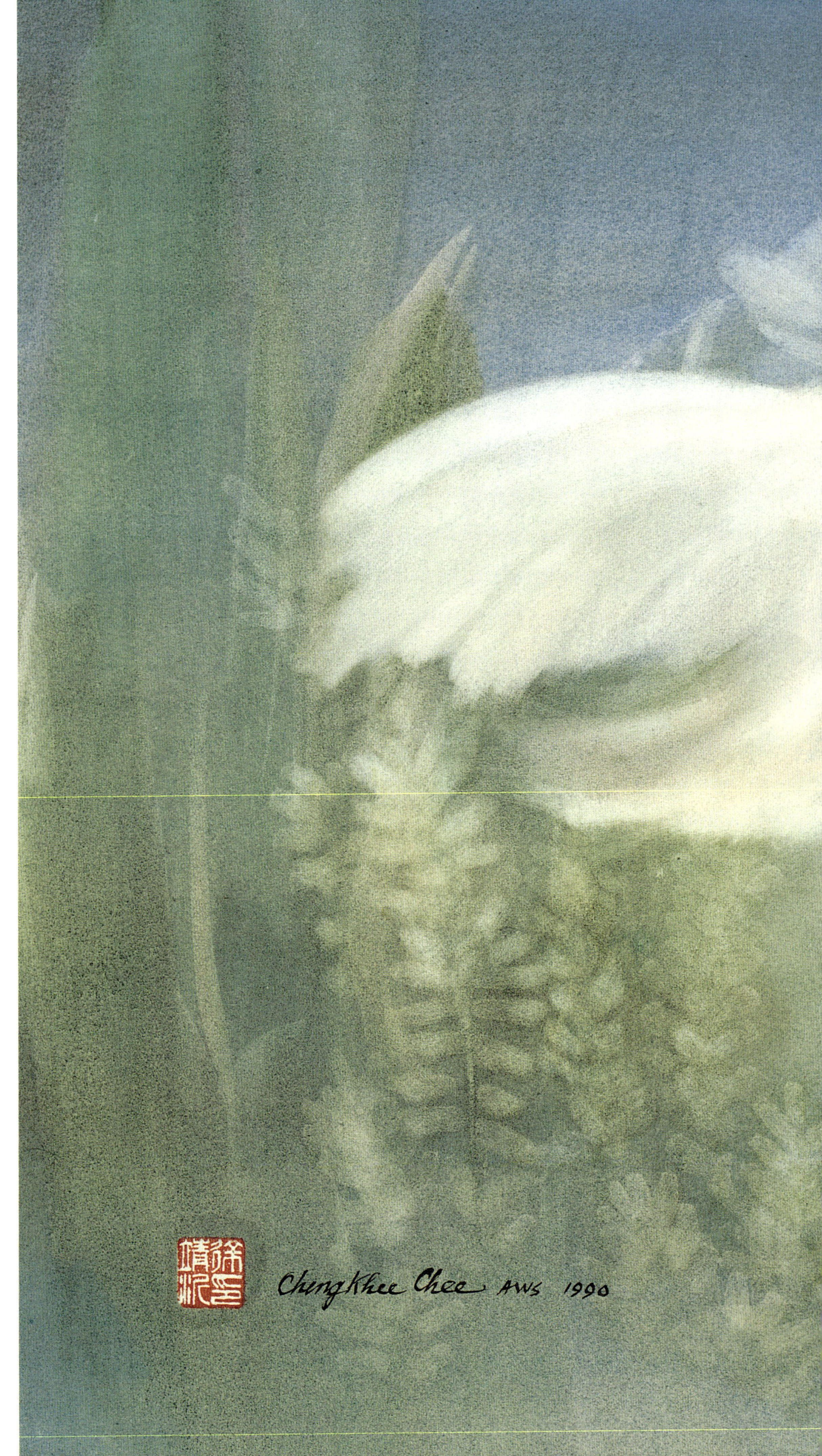

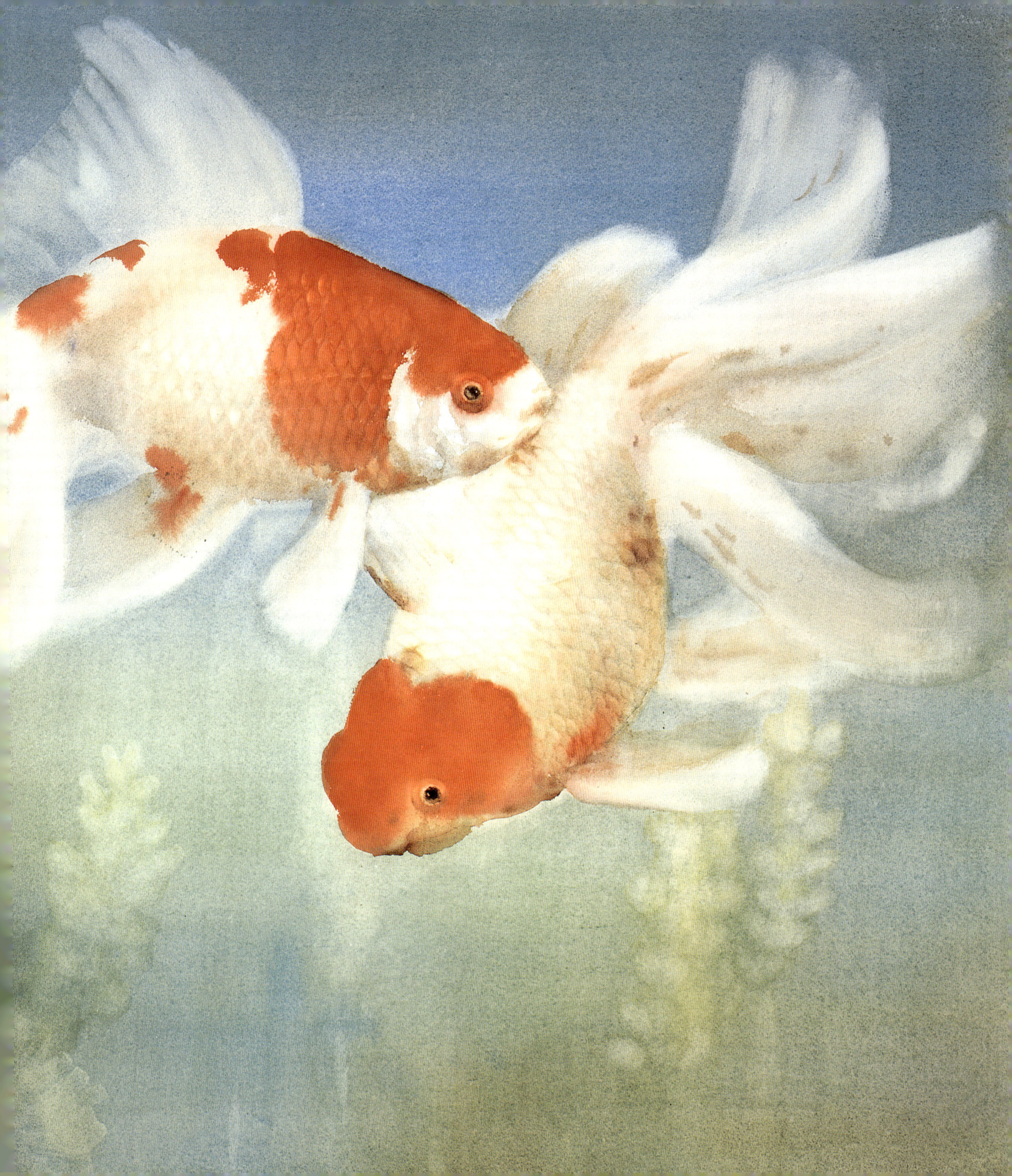

48

KOI 90 NO.2

锦鲤90年2号

25" x 40"   63cm x 102cm

1990

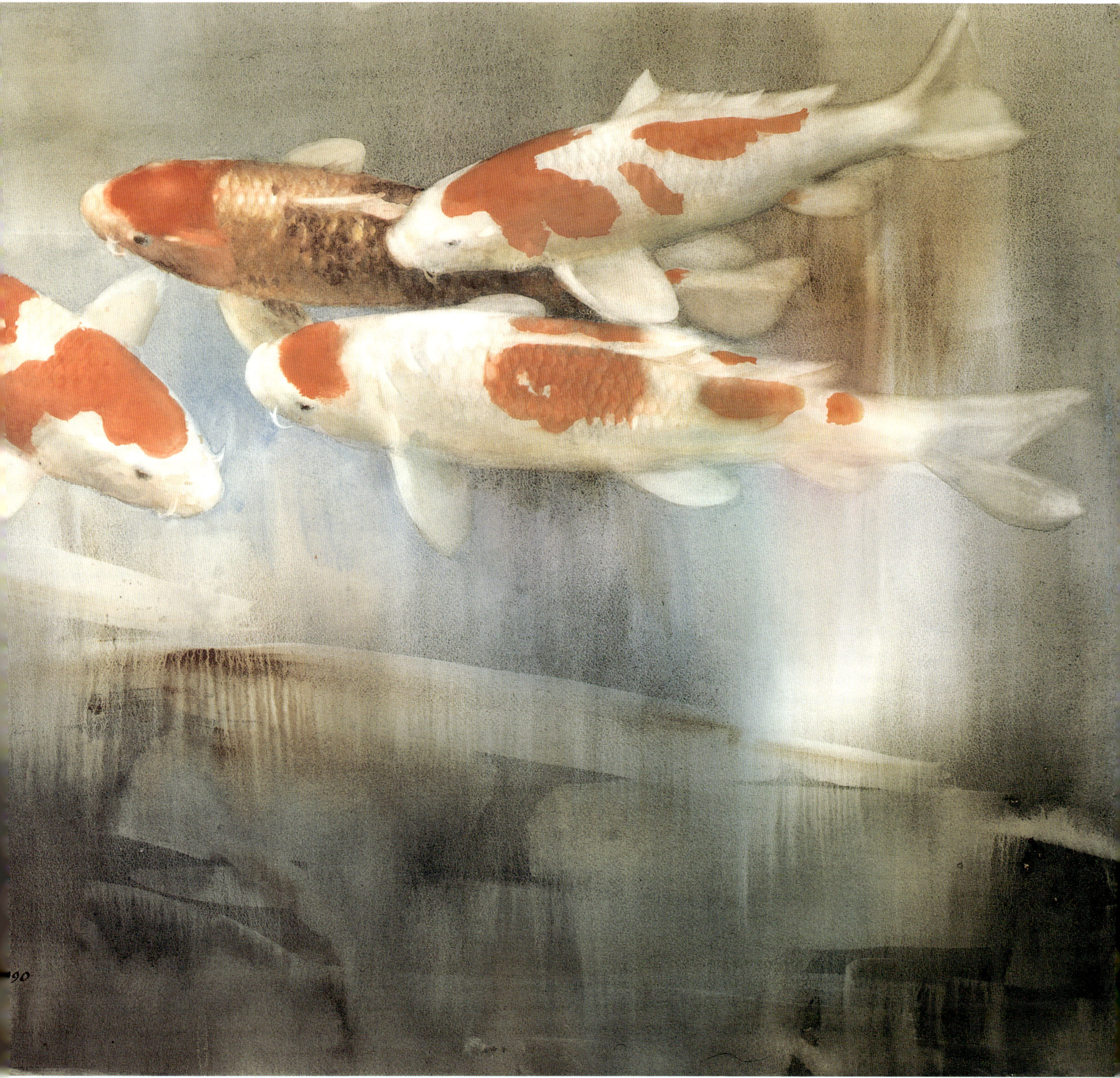

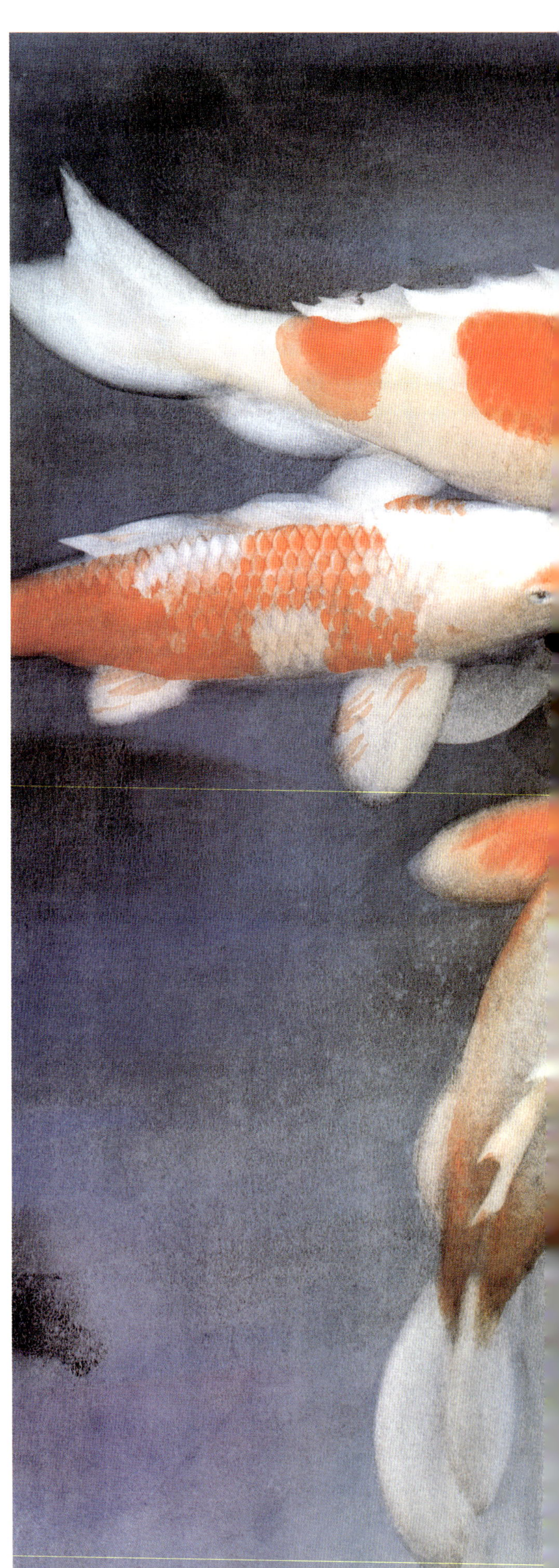

49

KOI 90 NO.9

锦鲤90年9号

35" x 43" 89cm x 110cm

1990

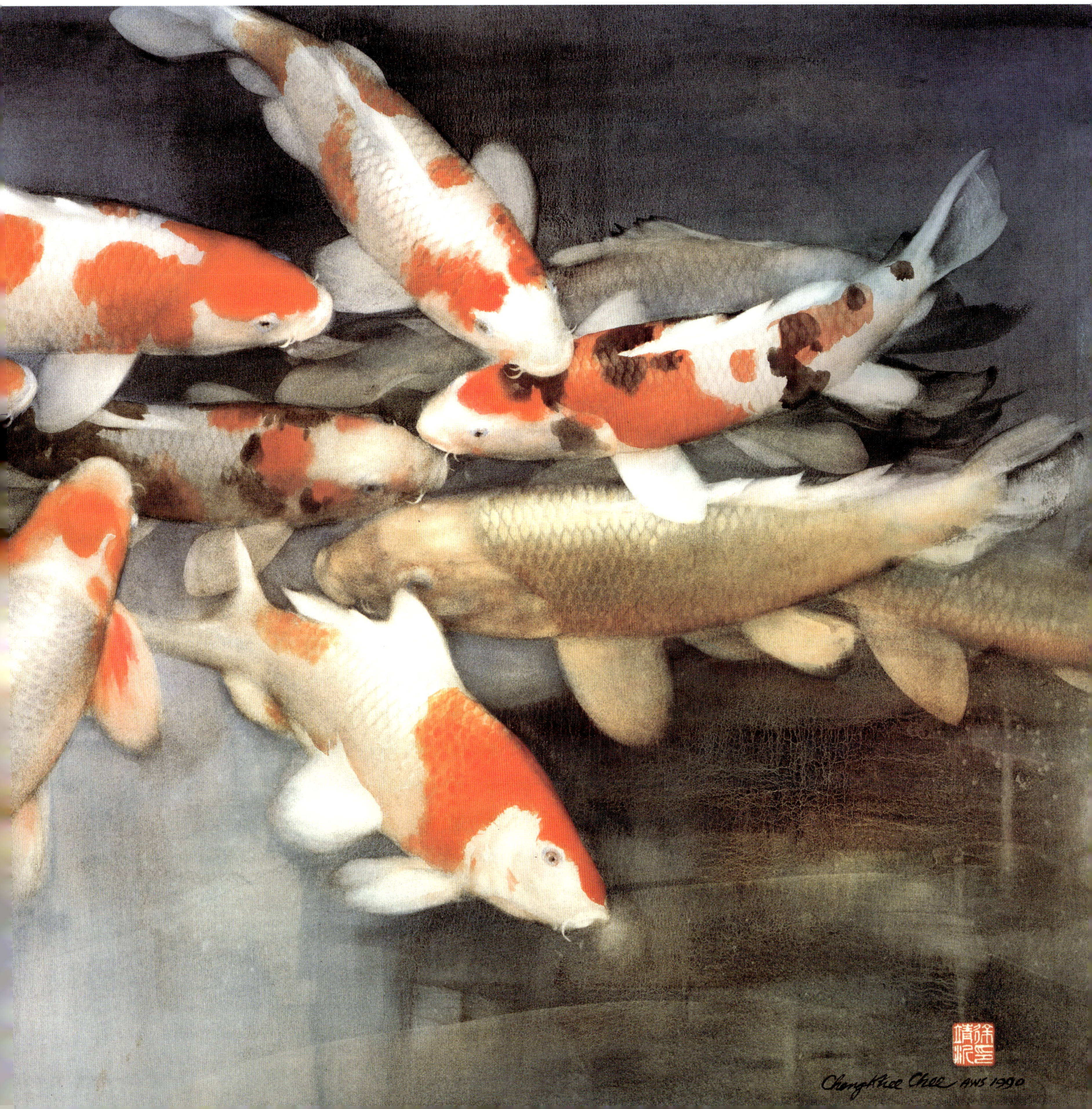
ChengKhee Chee AWS 1990

50

KOI 92 NO. 1

锦鲤92年1号

30" x 40" 76cm x 102cm

1992

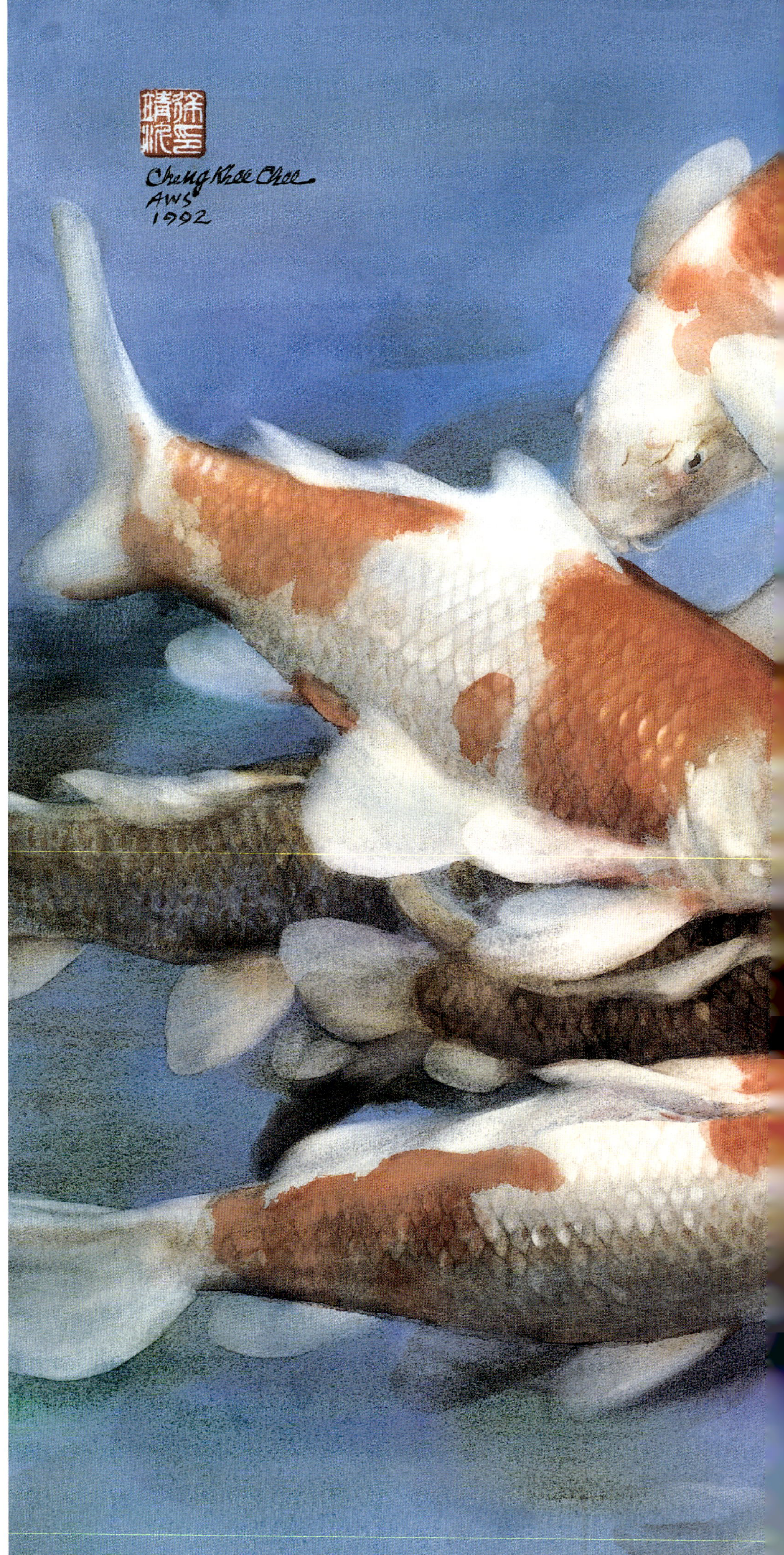

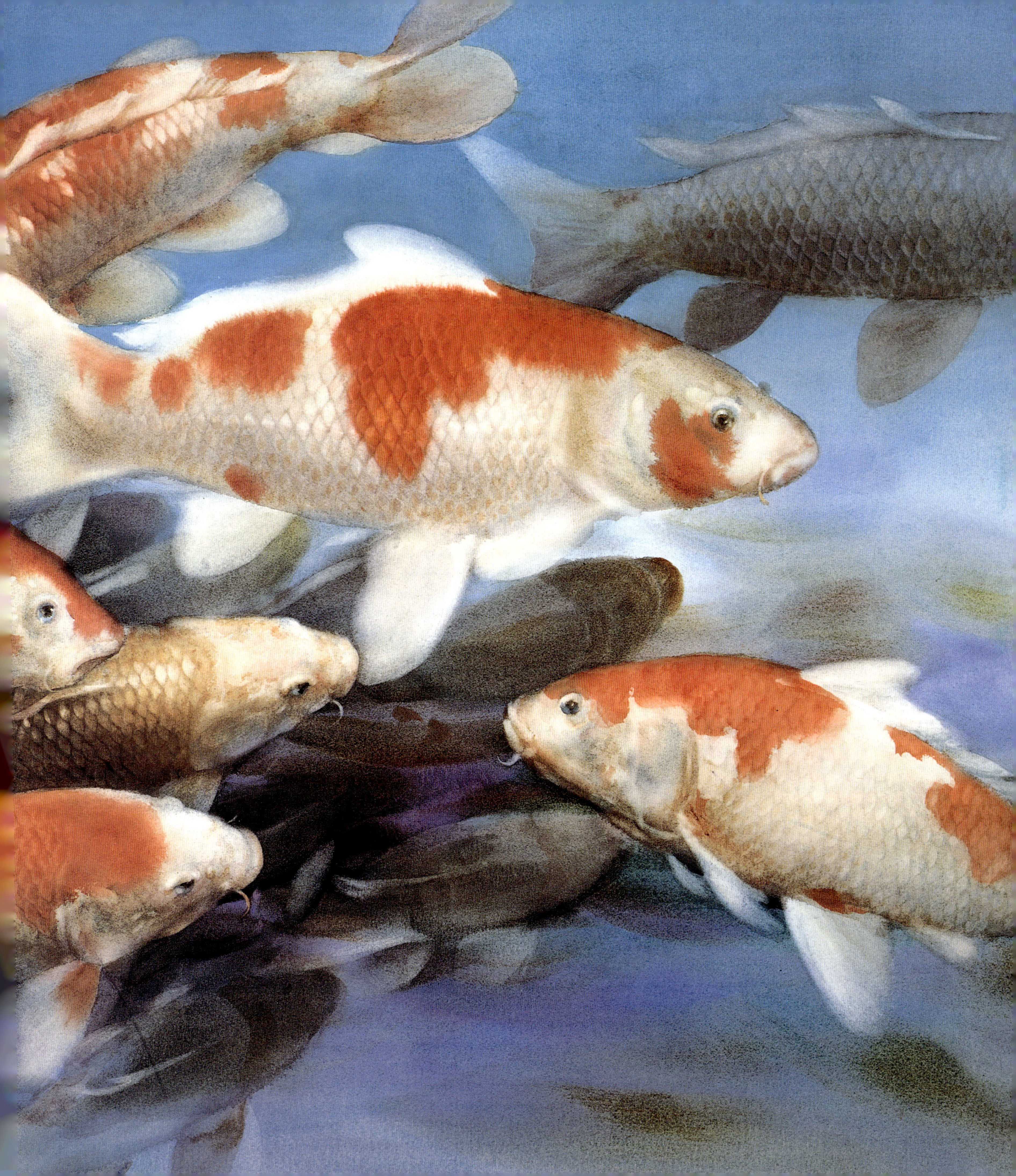

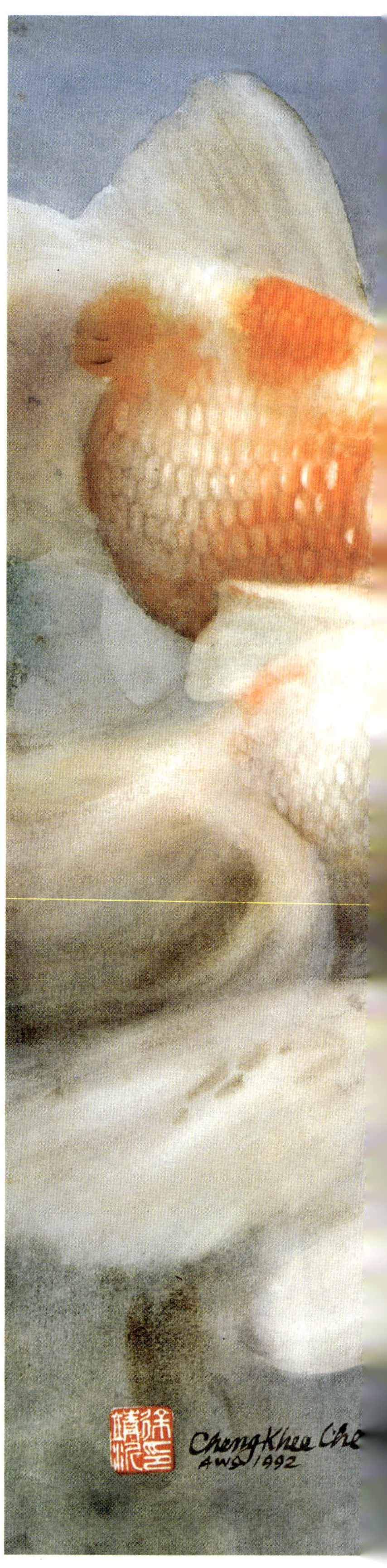

51

GOLDFISH 92 NO. 1

金鱼92年1号

30" x 40" 76cm x 102cm

1992

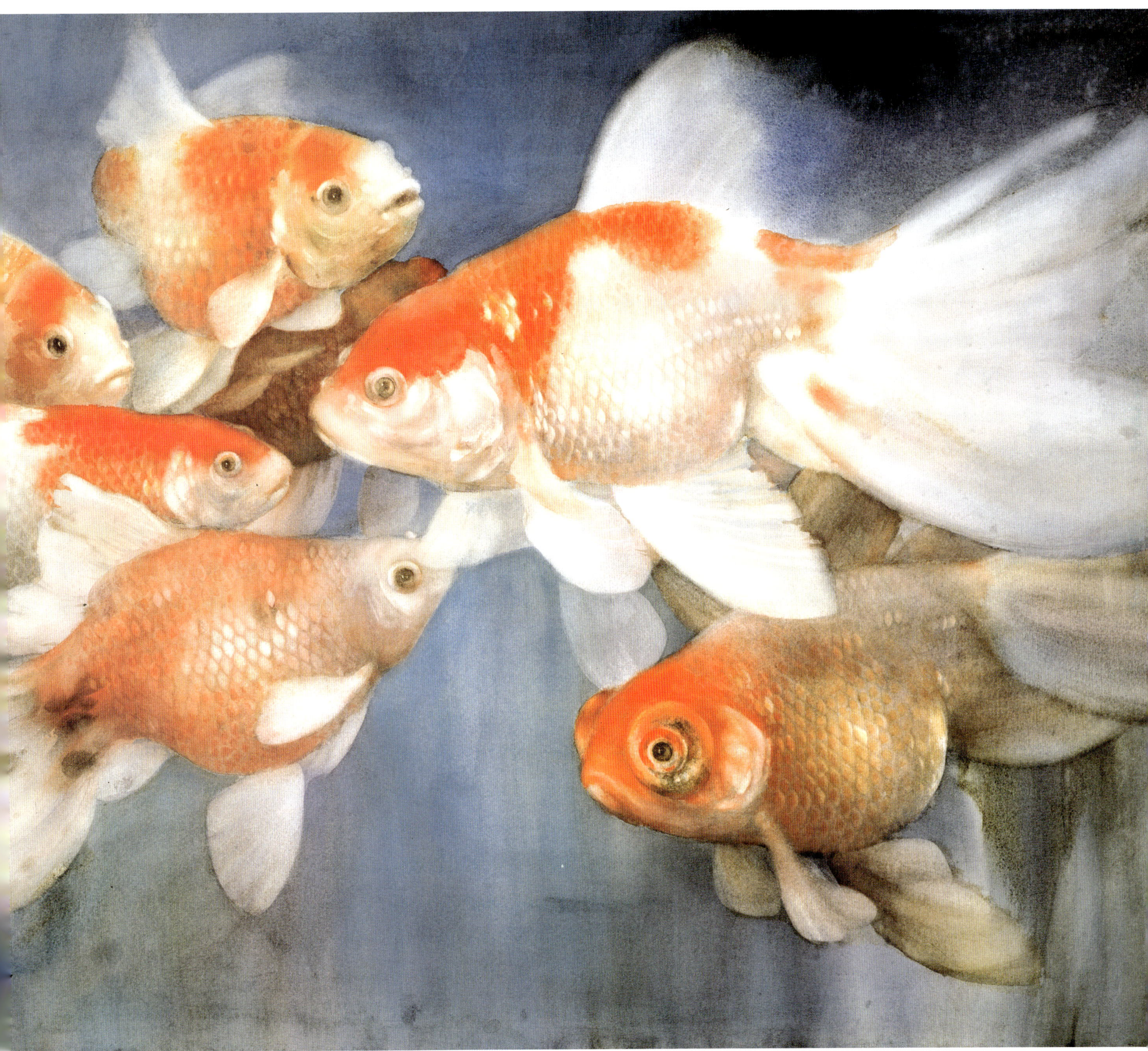

52

Lily Pond with Koi

荷塘锦鲤

25" x 40" 63cm x 102cm

1992

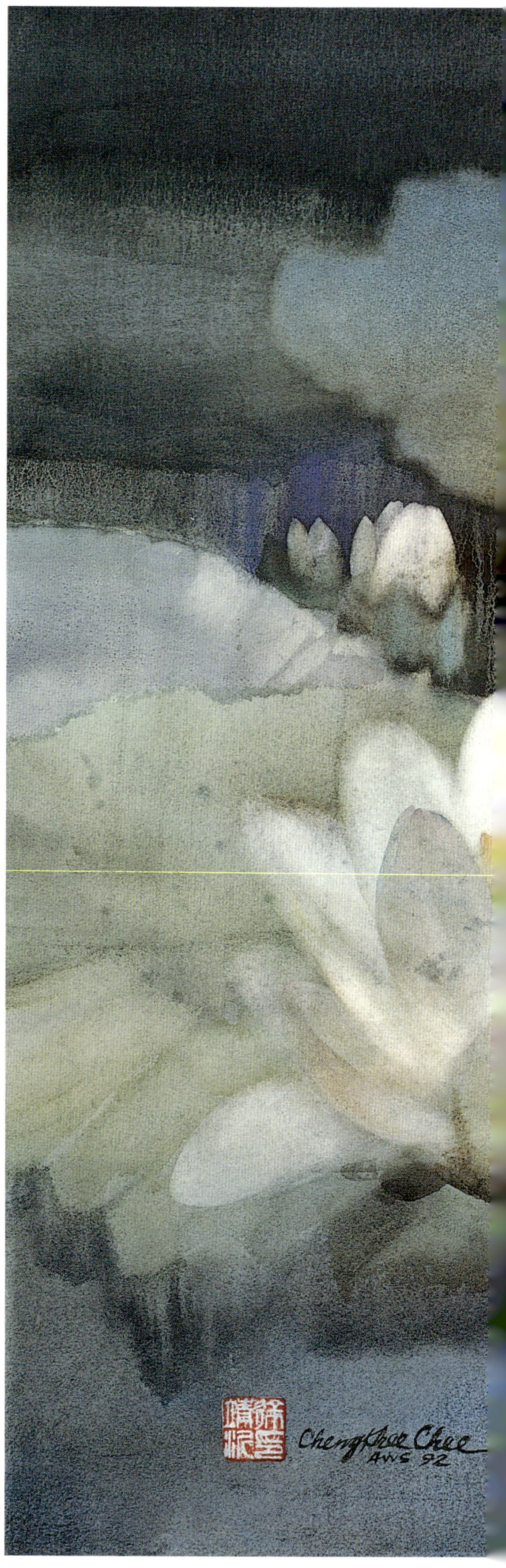

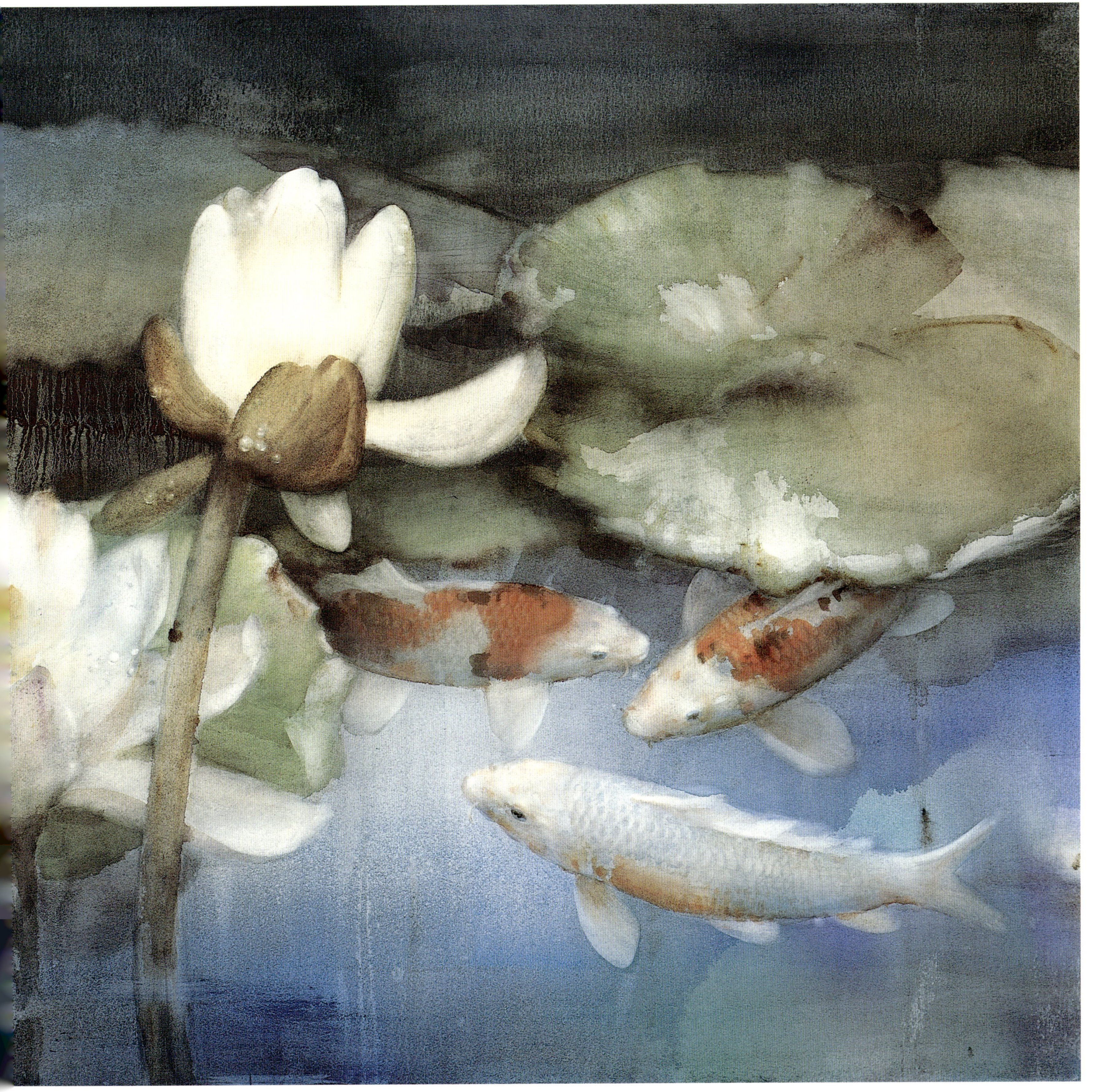

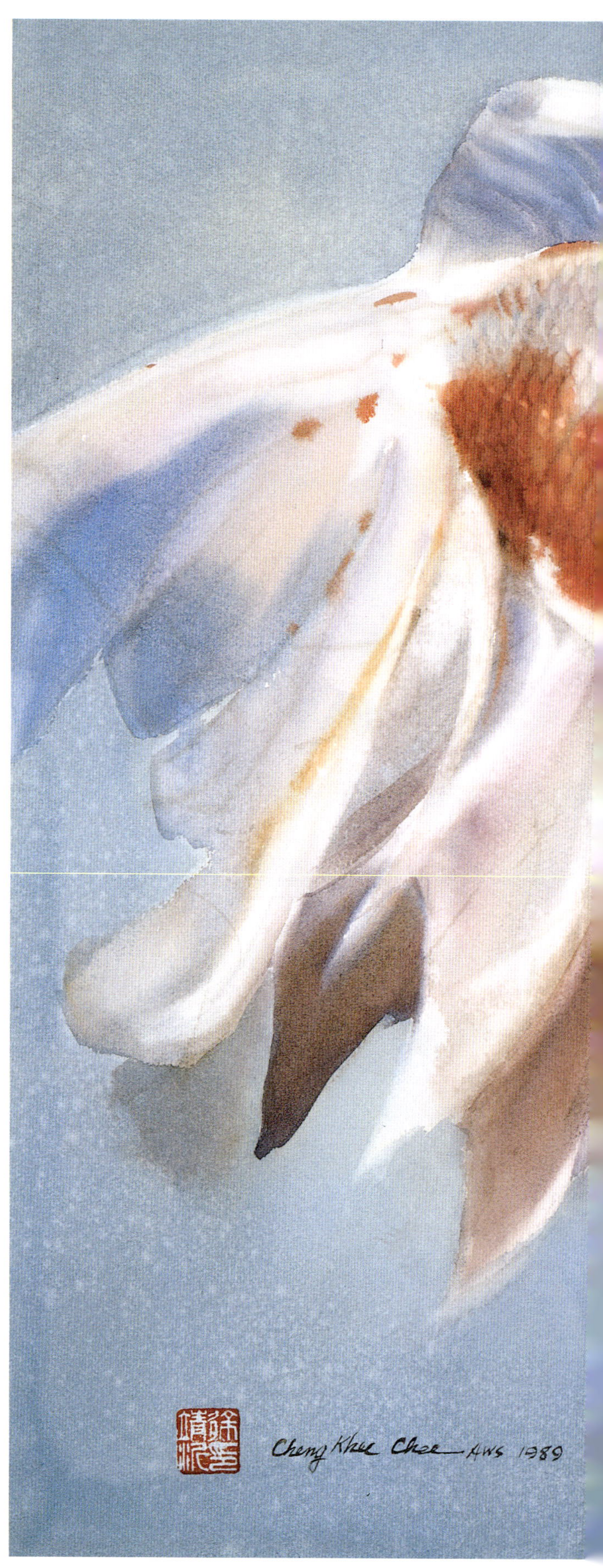

53

GOLDFISH 89 NO. 1

金鱼89年1号

30" x 40"　76cm x 102cm

1989

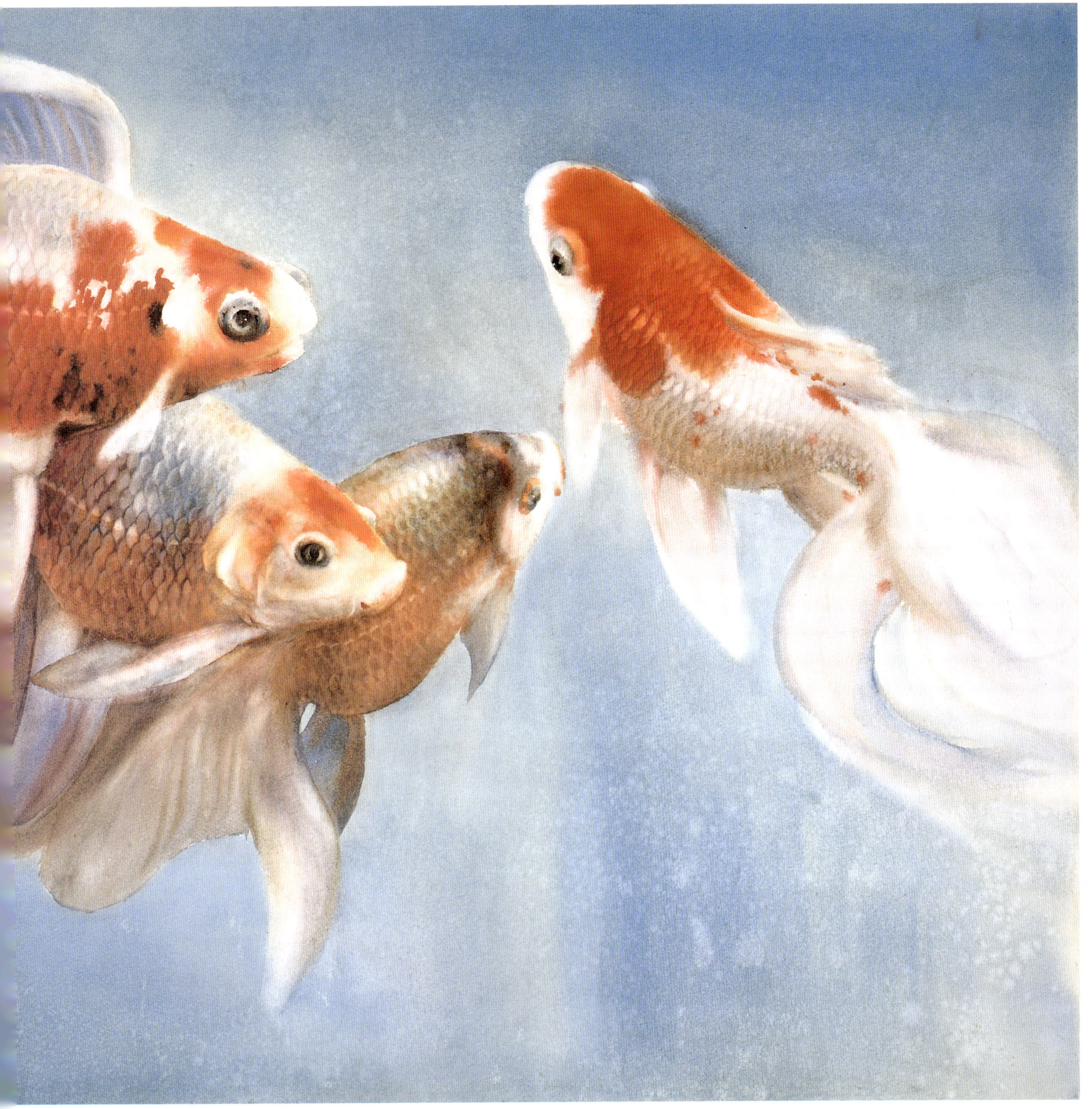

54

Koi 95 No. 1

锦鲤95年1号

30" x 40"   76cm x 102cm

1995

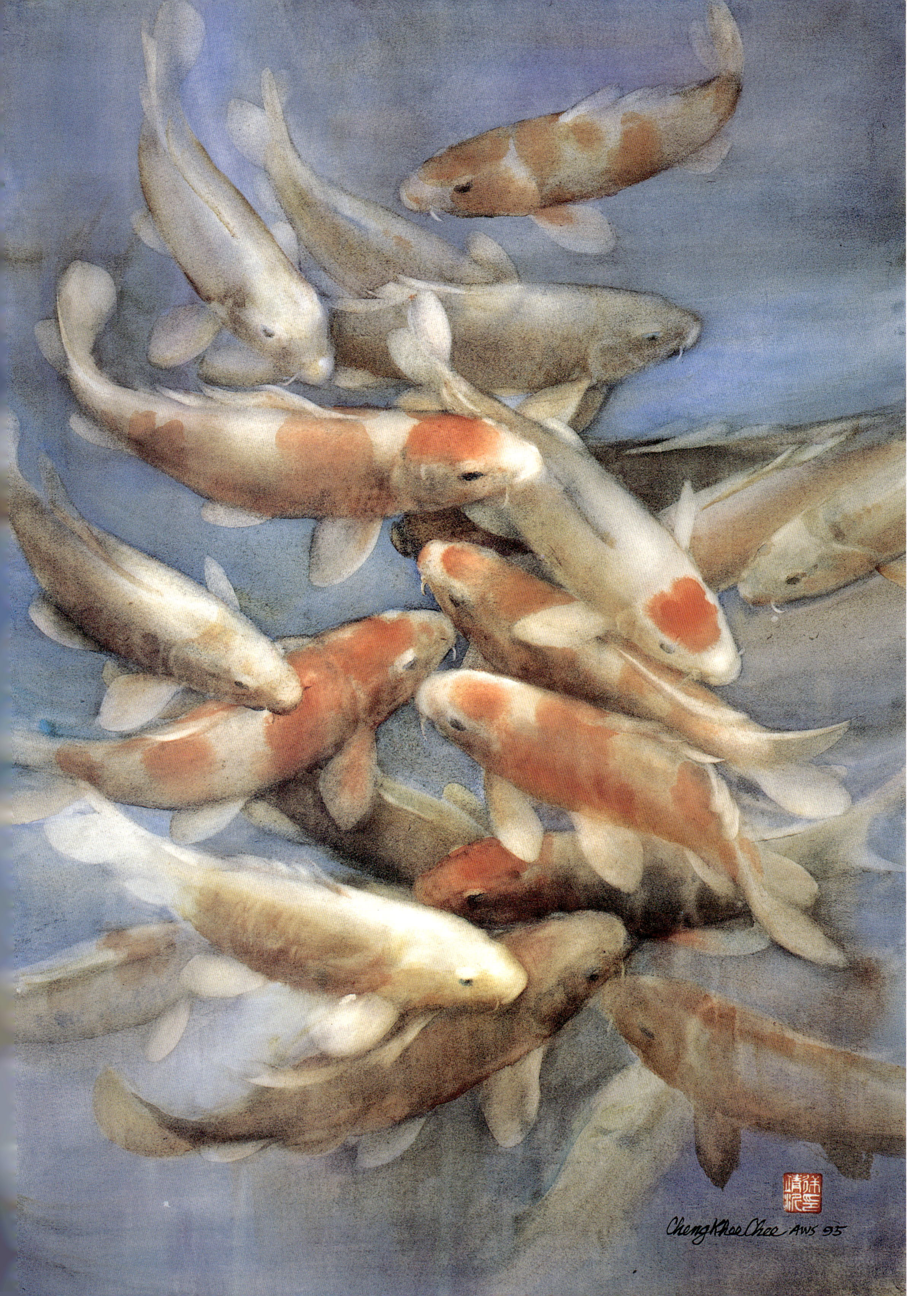
Cheng Khee Chee AWS 95

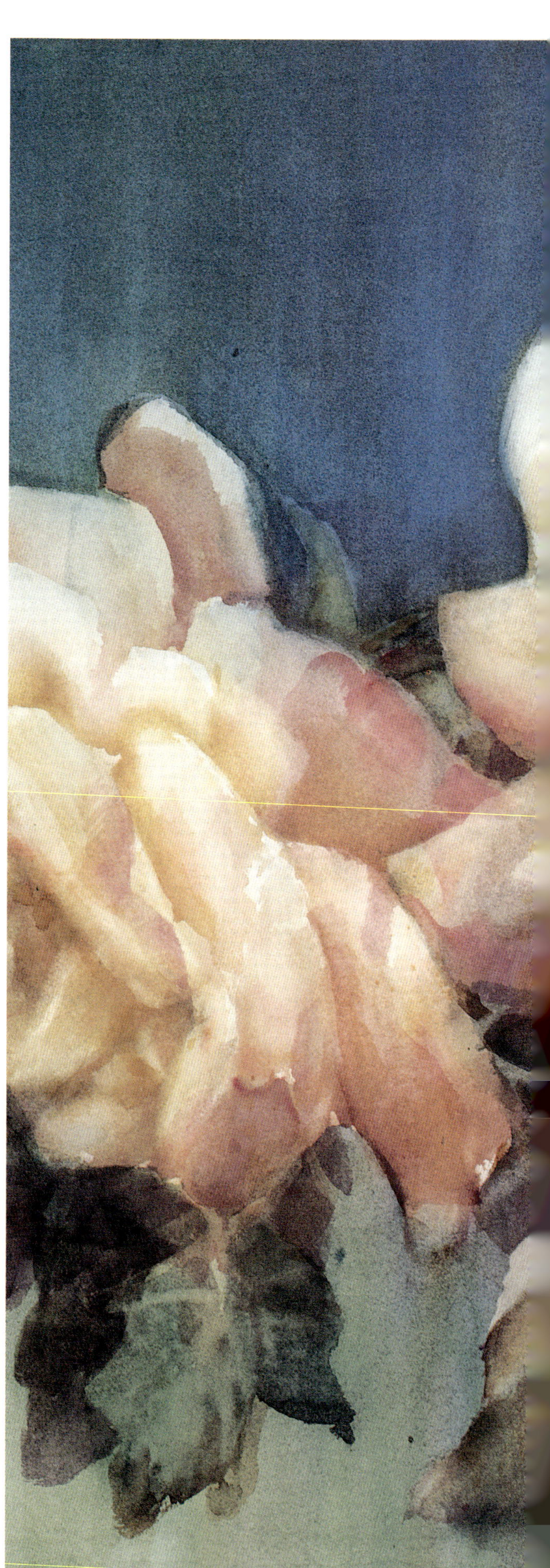

55

ROSES 95 NO. 1

玫瑰95年1号

25" x 40" 63cm x 102cm

1995

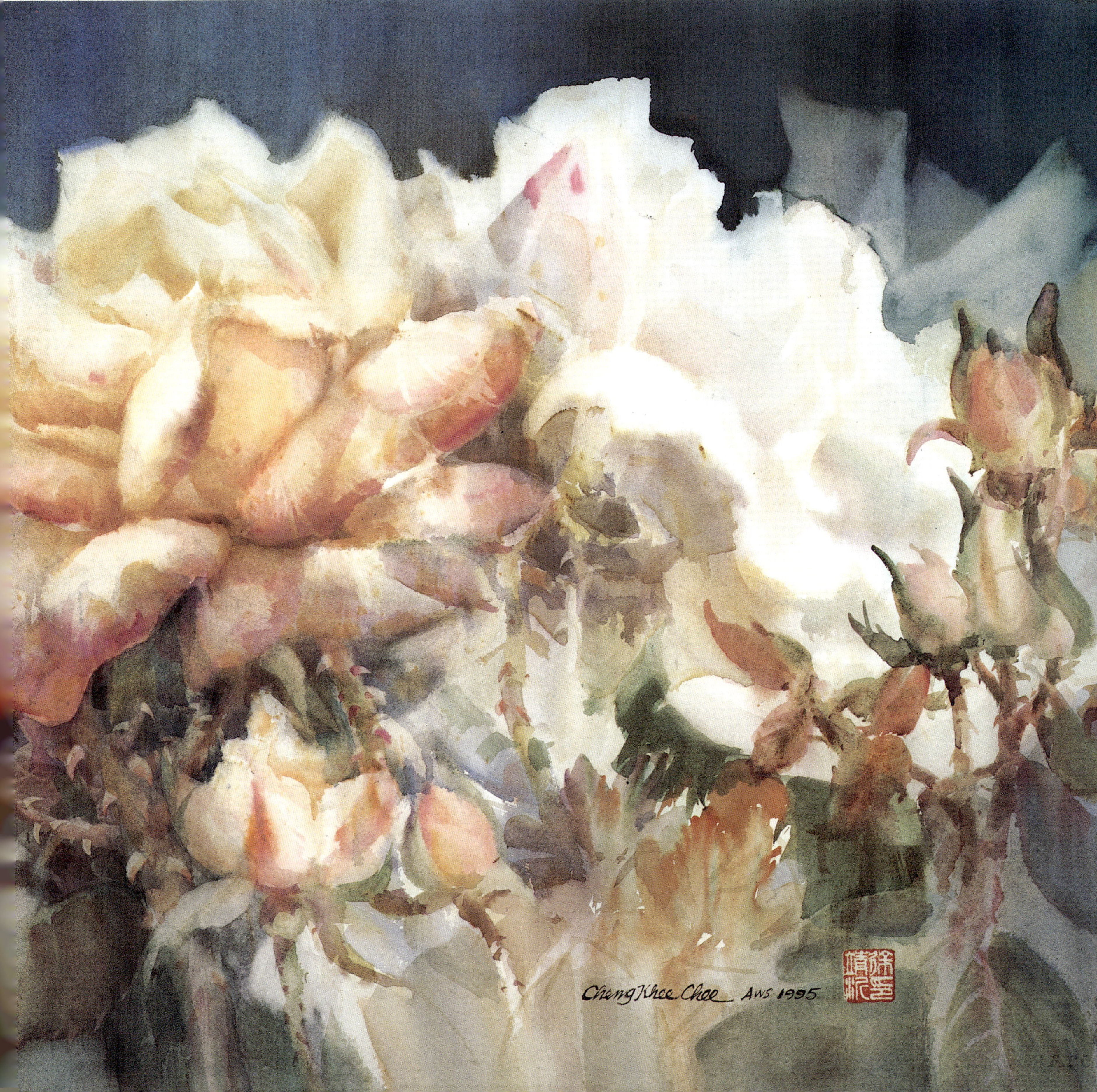
Cheng Khee Chee AWS 1995

56

Koi 95 No. 2

锦鲤96年2号

30" x 40" 76cm x 102cm

1996

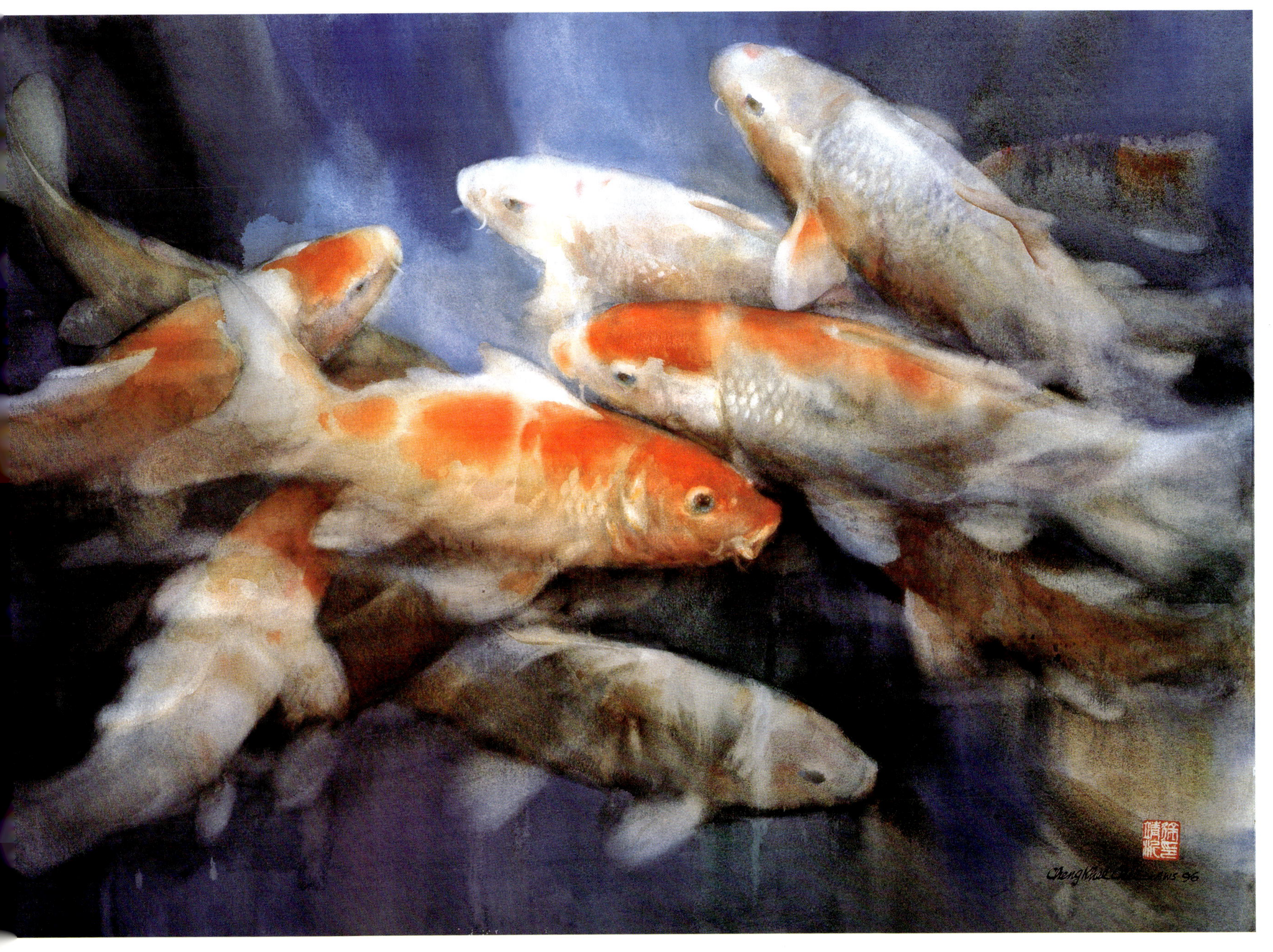

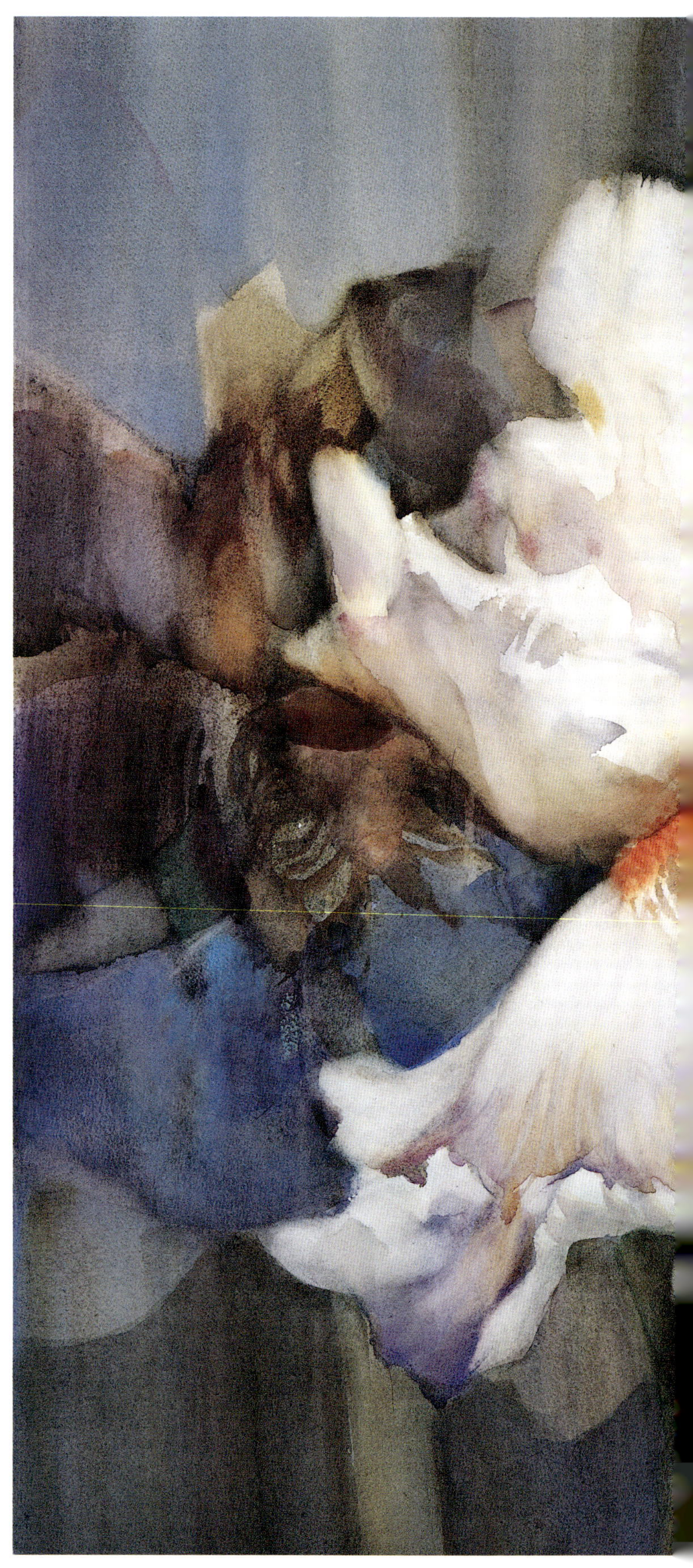

57

White Iris

白蝴蝶兰

30" x 40"   76cm x 102cm

1996

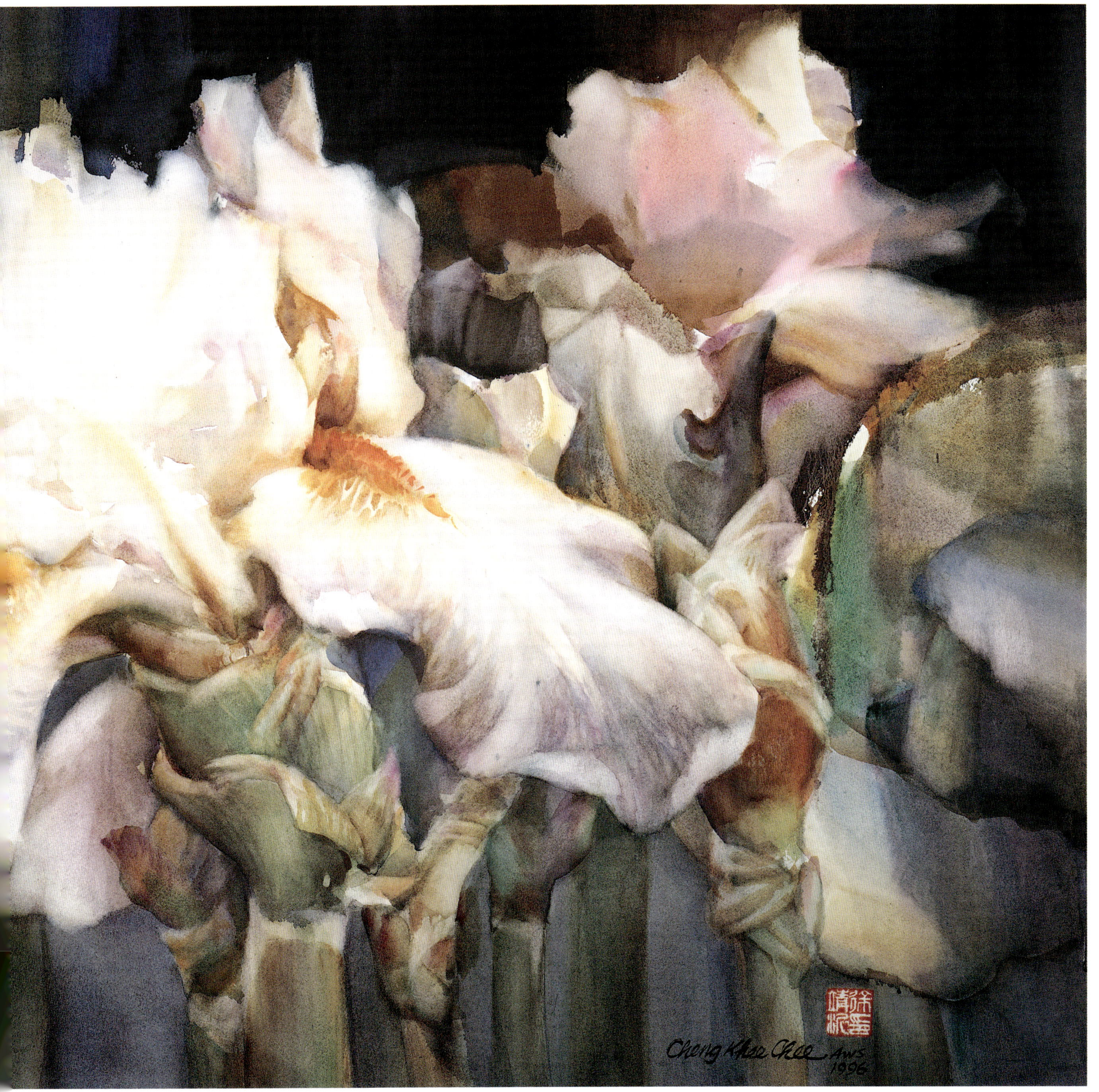
Cheng Khee Chee AWS
1996

58

Orchids

胡姬花

30" x 40" 76cm x 102cm

1996

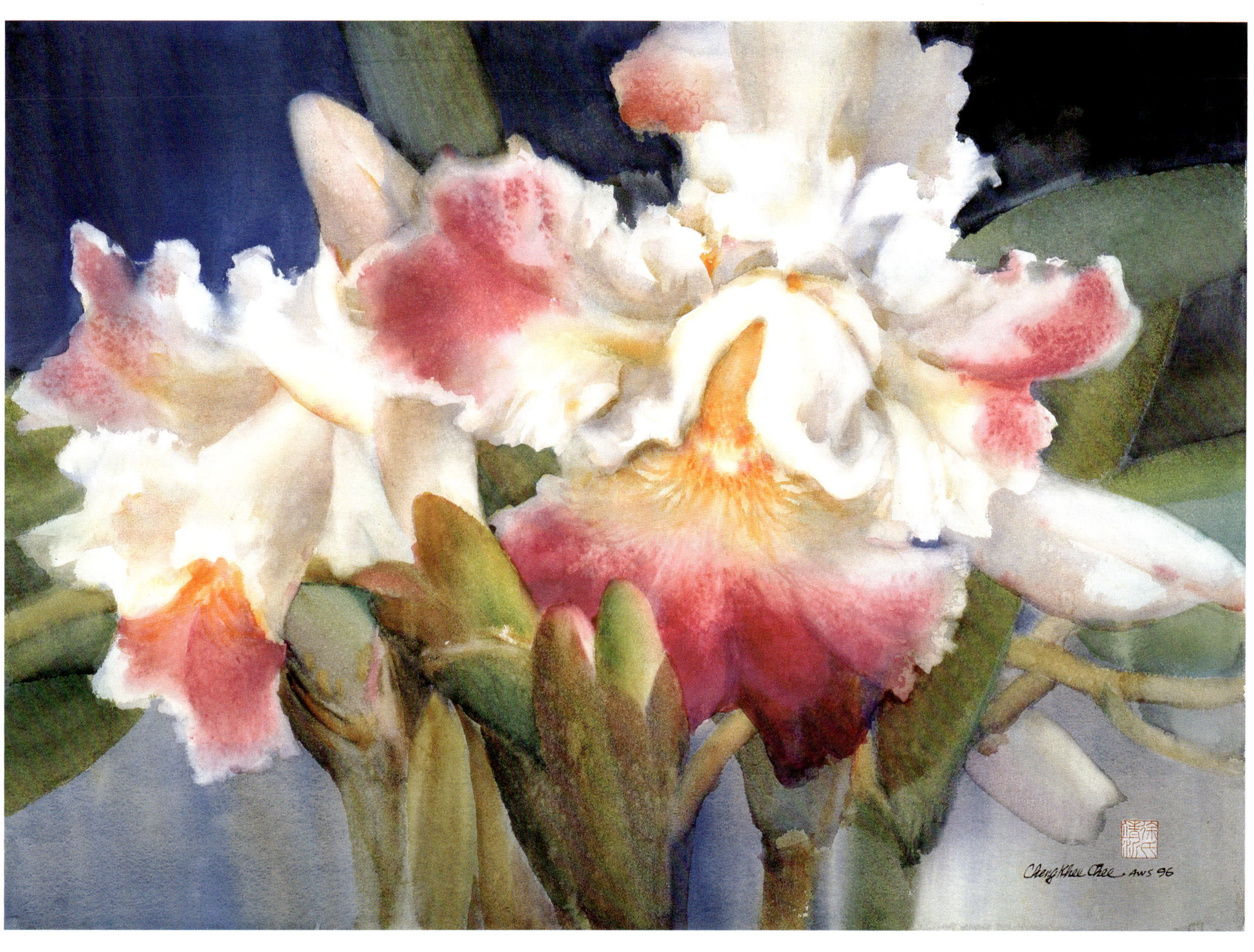

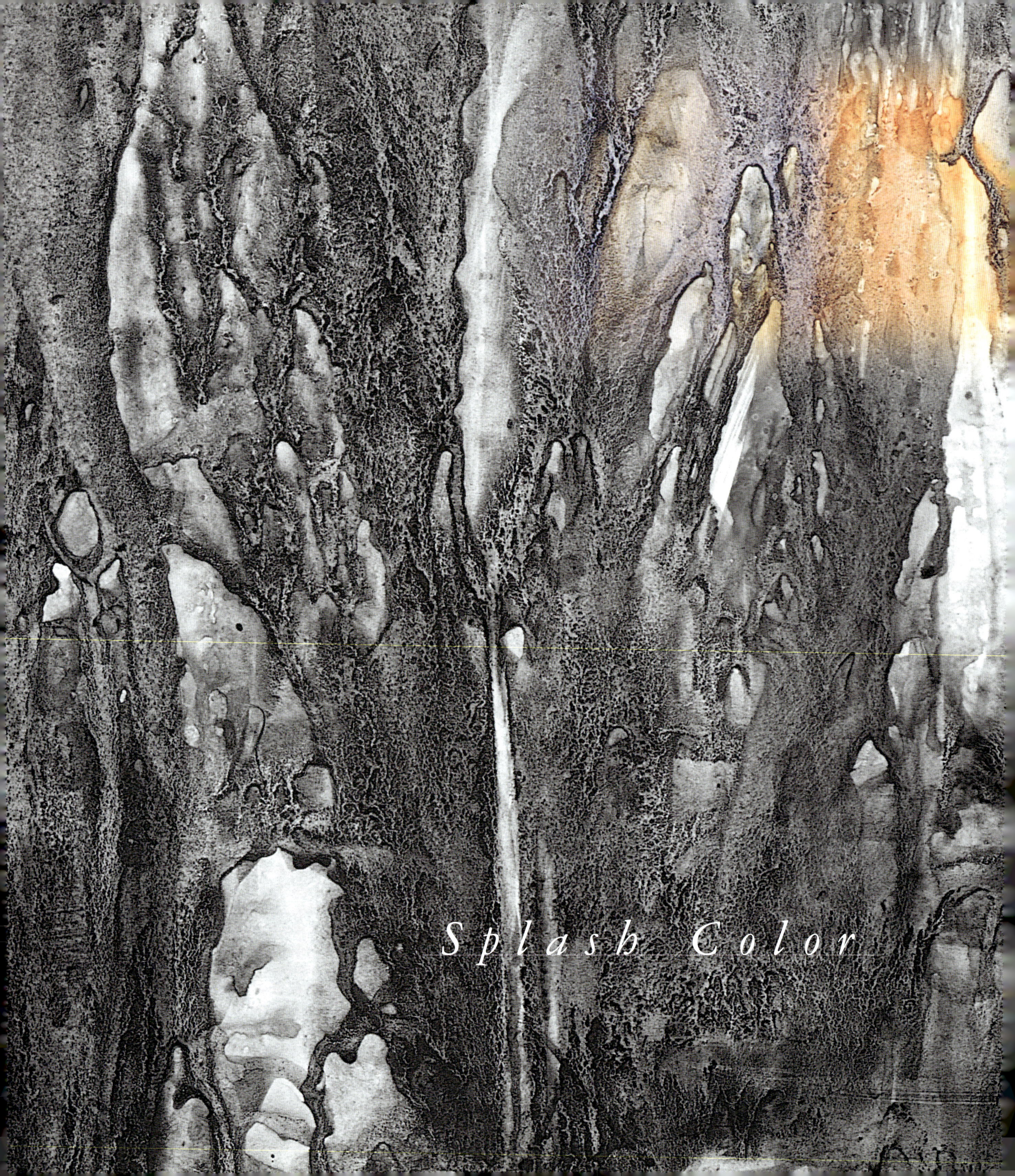

Splash Color

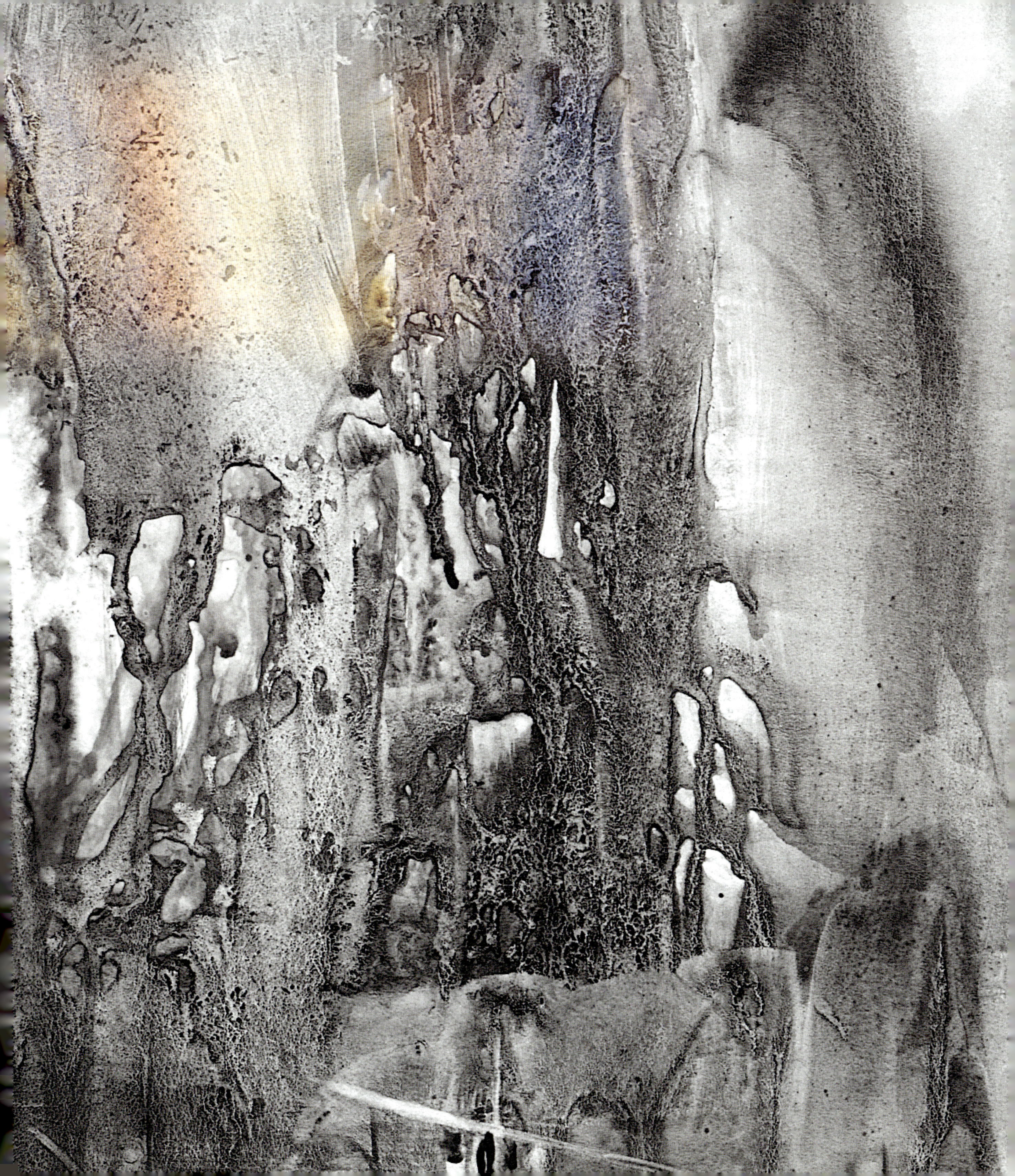

Improvisational Splash Color Technique

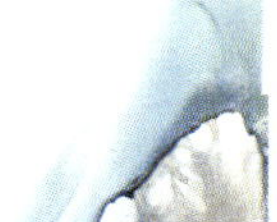

Subject Matter and Esthetic Concept

I use this method for painting rocks (Lake Shore Series) and mountainscapes (Along the Li River Series). I was born by the Pacific Ocean in southern China, I grew up by the Indian Ocean in Malaysia, I attended college on the Island of Singapore, and I now live by Lake Superior in the inland port city of Duluth. Rocks, water, surf, and gulls are a part of my life and, therefore, form an important part of my paintings.

My home in China was surrounded by mountains. Over the years I have made several trips back to see my homeland and to experience the Chinese landscapes beloved and revered by Chinese painters for centuries: the mist-filled and ever-changing Yellow Mountain, the breathtaking gorges along the Yangzi River, and the towering mountains in the valley of Li River near Guilin. Experiencing the unbelievable grandeur, I felt a profound inner identification with the Sung Masters, whose works I have admired since childhood.

In 1980 I acquired my first plastic John Pike palette. After using it for a few painting sessions, I discovered exciting 'paintings' of rocky shores and mountainscapes on the mixing surface of the palette. So I started searching for a painting surface as smooth as plastic that would give me the same results as the plastic surface. I finally found the strathmore 500 series high-surfaced illustration board most satisfactory. I also discovered that applying a diluted acrylic gel medium to the surface of the paper enhances results.

When a broad brush charged with color is swept over the gel-medium-coated surface, the paint is immediately repelled, creating tensions and other unexpected and exciting textural effects resembling rocks and mountains.

Tools and Supplies

1" & 2" squirrel, camel, or other soft-hair brushes
Strathmore 500 Series Illustration Board (240-5)
Tube watercolors premixed in dishes
Acrylic gel medium

Painting Procedure

1. I dilute gel medium with 50% water and stir it to a smooth consistency.
2. I apply the diluted gel medium to the surface of the illustration board where texture is desired, then dry the surface with a hair dryer.
3. I premix tube watercolors in dishes so they can be applied to paper readily.
4. I start the painting with strong emotion and energy, and with great speed. I work at white heat for about twenty minutes, trying to cover the entire surface. This encourages my subconscious to work. I use no preliminary sketches, nor do I have any preconceived plan of composition. I am concerned only with achieving accidental relationships of warm and cool colors, variety of shapes, light and dark value patterns, and texture. Gradually, through the act of painting, I discover the subject matter, which combines dream with reality, emotion with reason, abstraction with realism. At this point I exert more conscious control and guide the painting to its finishing stage. The painting develops in the very process of painting. The finished painting could be abstract, semi-abstract, or representational.

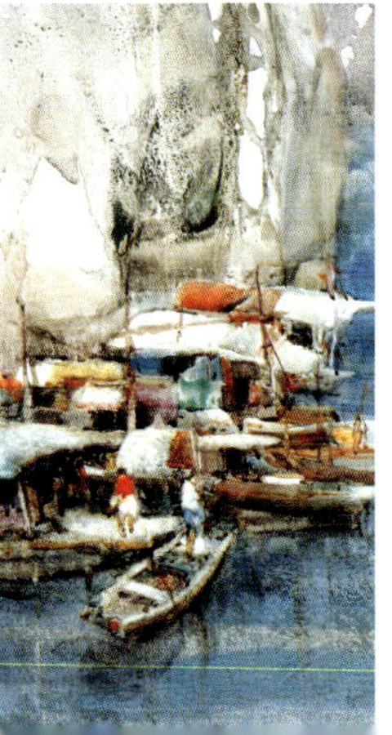

即兴泼彩法

1. 材料：光面卡纸、丙烯调色剂(Acrylic Gel Medium)、水彩颜料
2. 特点：在光面卡纸上刷上一层冲淡了的丙烯调色剂，待乾后用大扁笔刷上颜色，因为纸面有抗御颜色和水分的性能，产生了各种丰富奇特的纹理。
   光面卡纸不会吸收颜色，多数色粒浮在纸面上，显得比较鲜丽。用光面的画纸比较容易修改。
3. 画法：采用这画法的目的是要尽量发挥媒介本身的性能及制造偶然的效果。开始画的时候最好不要胸有成竹，甚至於也不决定题材。鼓起激情勇气，用很快的速度处理画面。起初完全是激情、偶然、抽象、主观。进一步则凭着抽象的设计原理，注意画面冷暖、乾湿、浓淡、虚实、粗糙和光滑、平静和动荡等的对比，并注意某种题材的漾现和章法的发展。最后应用理性、必然、具象、客观去处理画面，采精去芜，初步完成一幅画。
   通常在半个小时内初步完成了约九成的画面，最后的一成则要用冷静的头脑，慢慢地去分析、推敲、斟酌而抵於成。

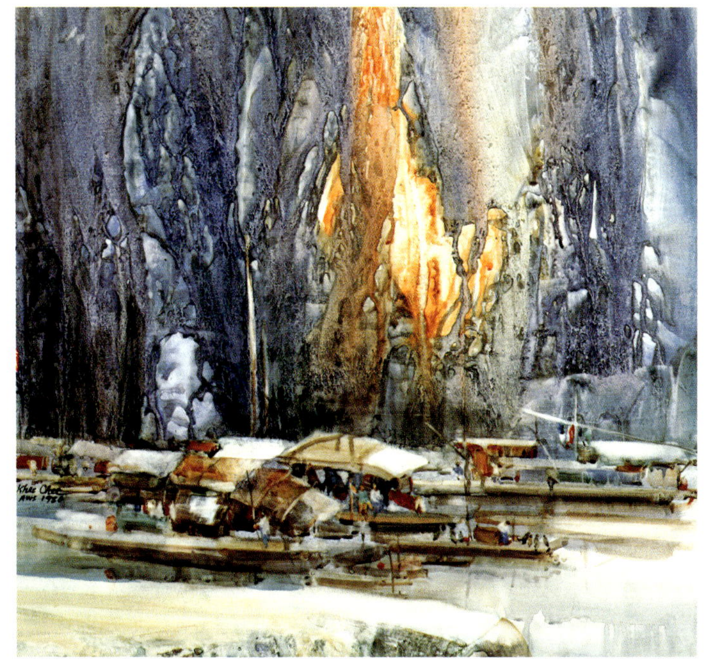

   这种画法最理想是能够从杂乱无绪的开端到顺理成章的结局，一气呵成。这样，画家的心手和媒介的性能充分合作，人性与物性交融，达到天衣无缝，气韵生动的境界。
   这种画法是在画的过程中求画，冒险性大；但是意想不到的效果带来无穷的韵味和兴奋。
4. 画例：湖岸组画，漓江组画、西北组画。

59

Lake Shore 82 No.1

湖岸82年1号

30" x 40" 76cm x 102cm

1982

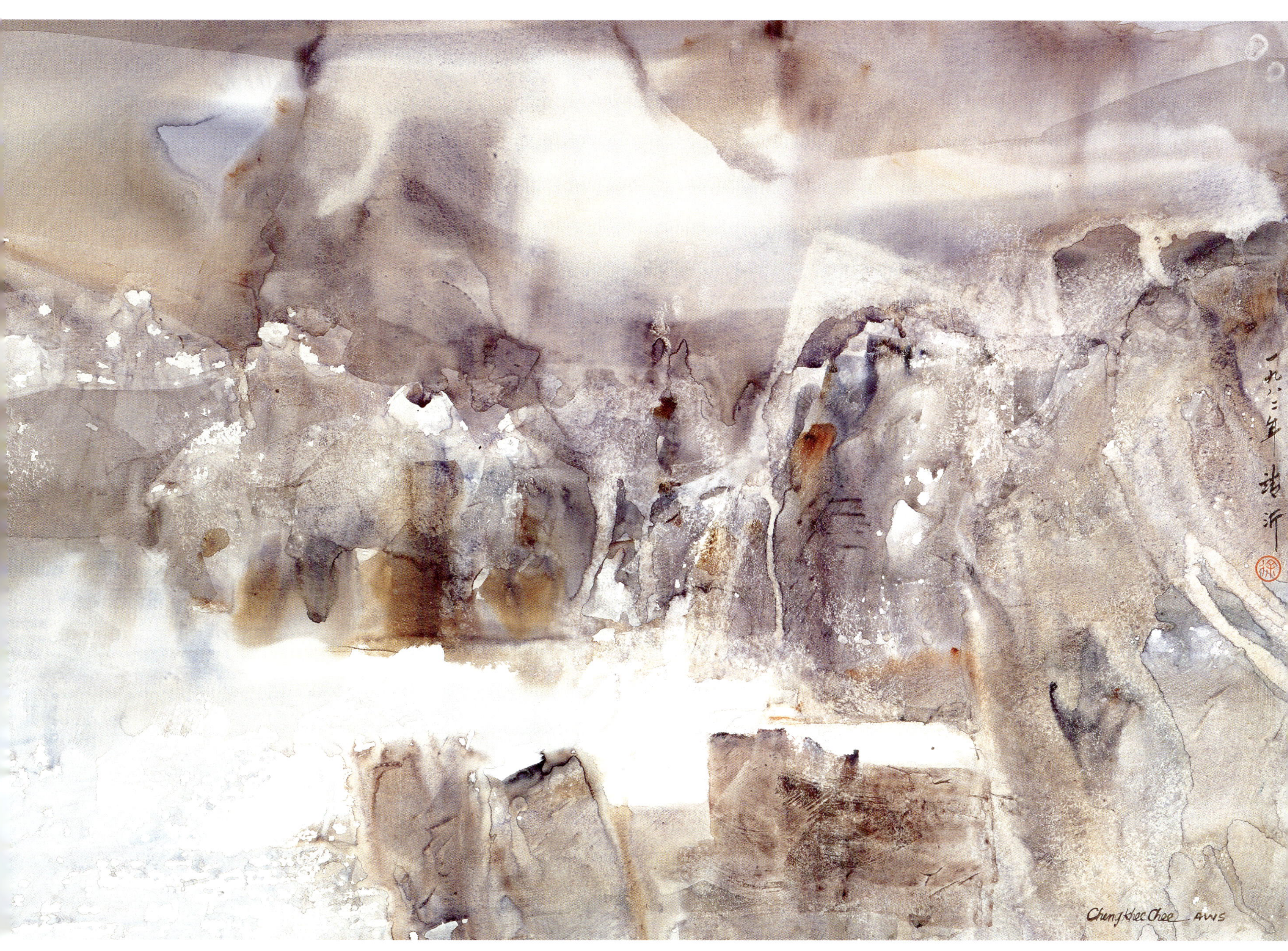
Cheng Khee Chee AWS

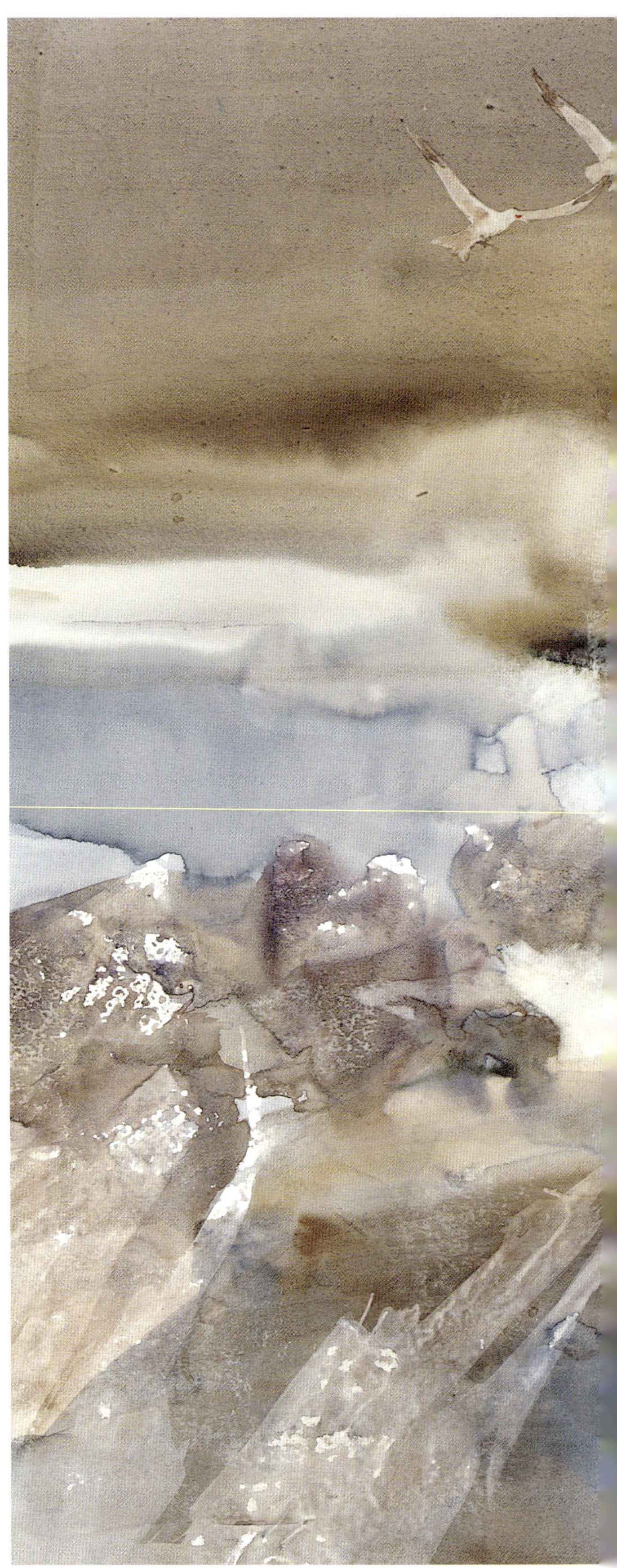

60

Lake Shore 82 No.3

湖岸82年3号

30" x 40" 76cm x 102cm

1982

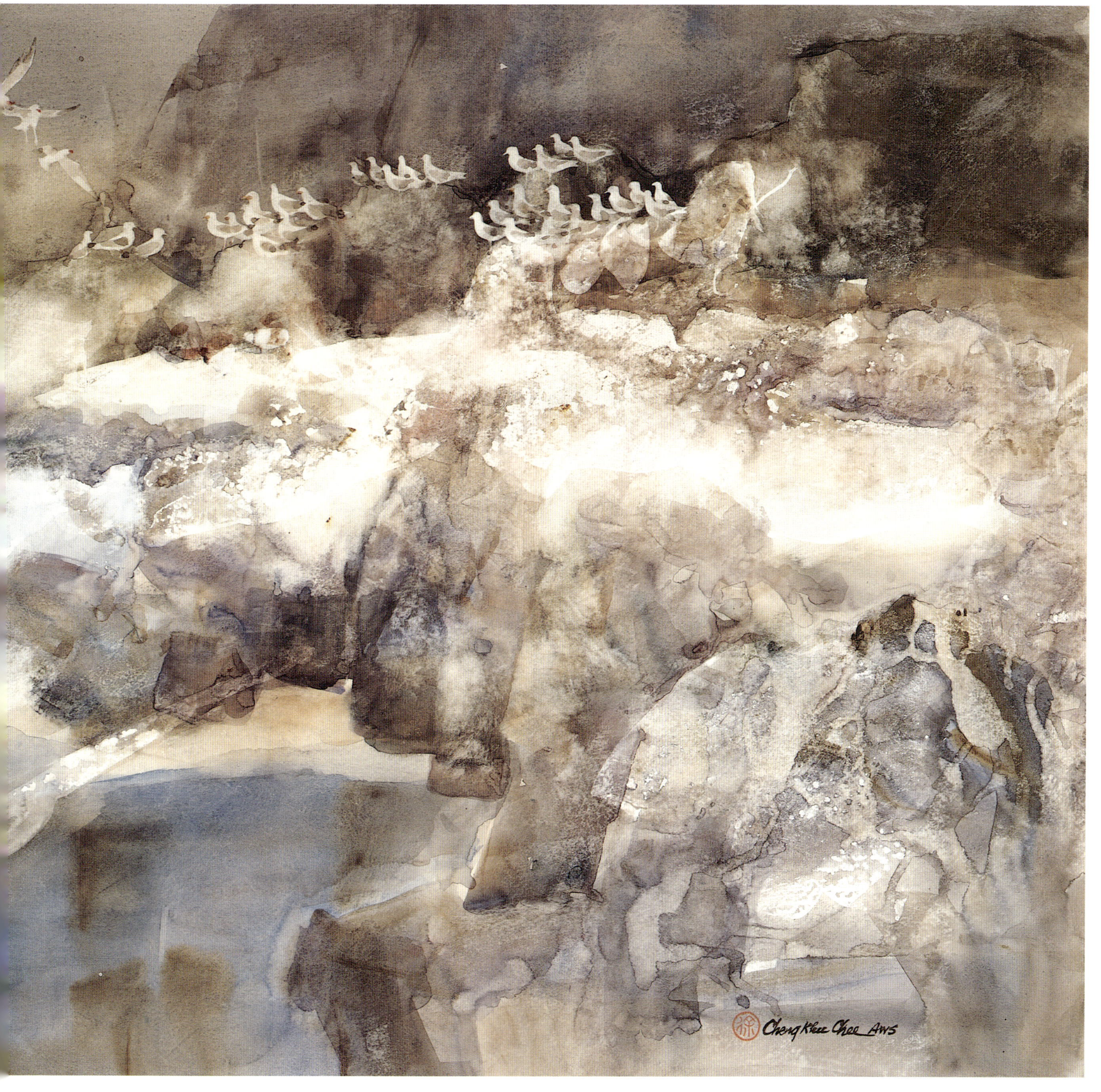
Cheng Khee Chee AWS

61

Li Jiang at Dawn

漓江拂晓

40" x 60"   102cm x 152cm

1982

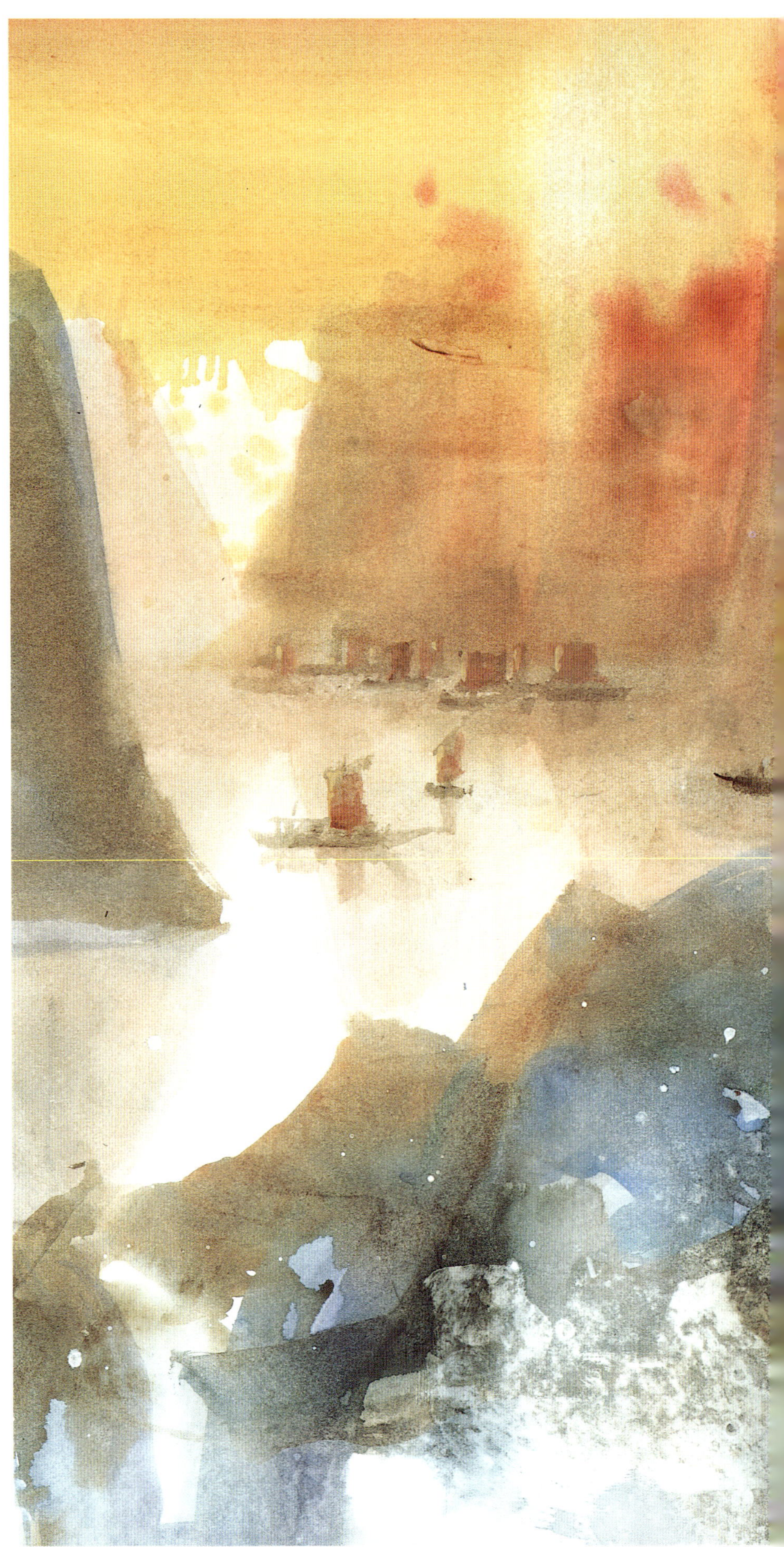

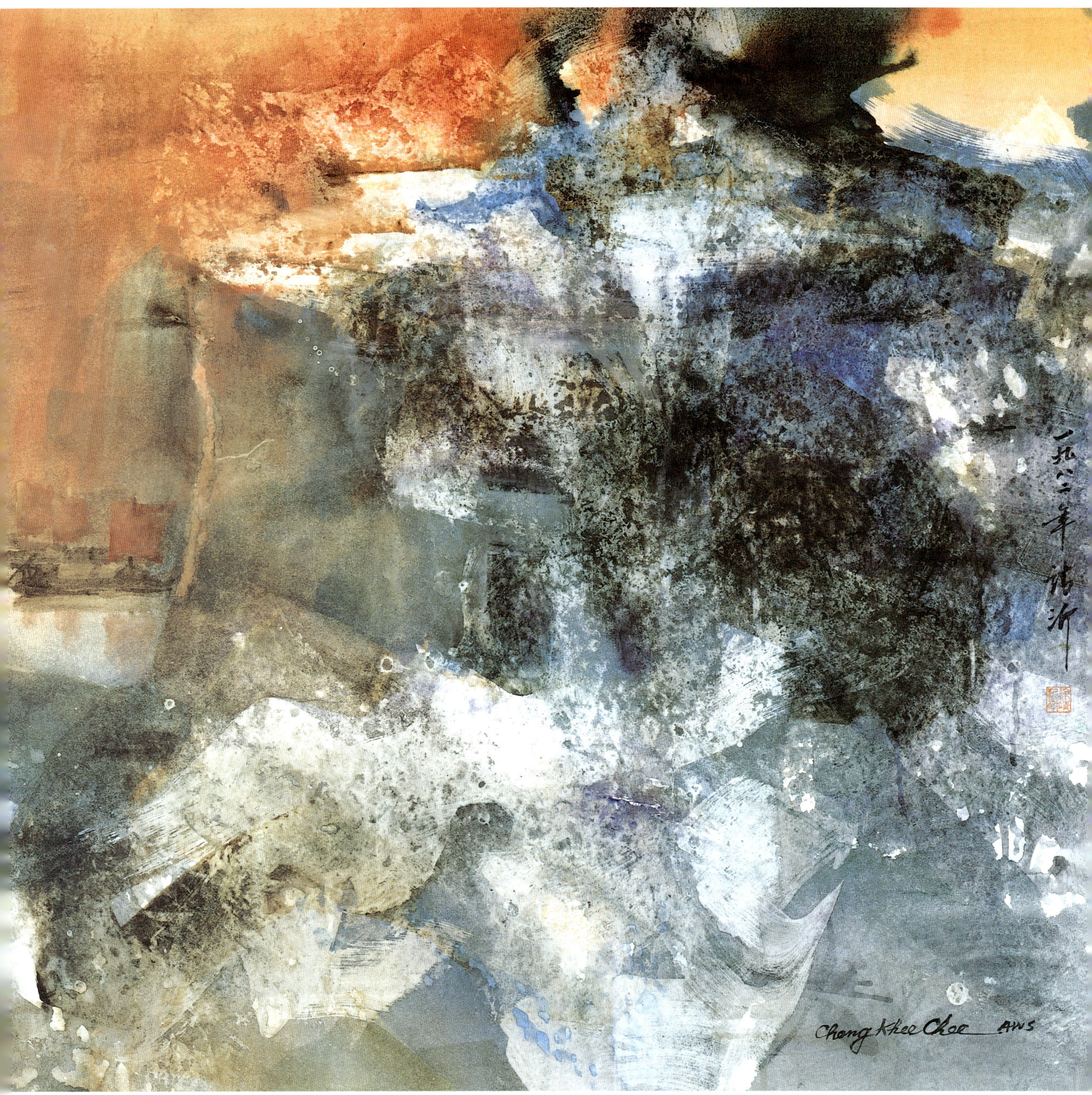

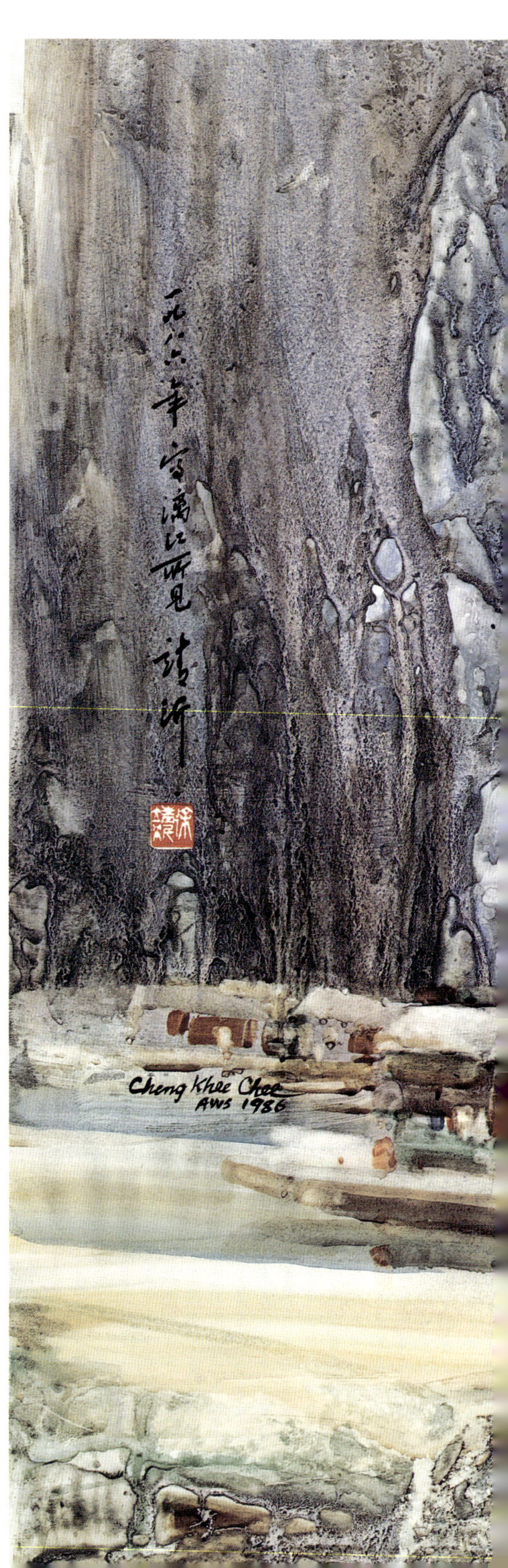

62

Along the Li River 86 No.1

漓江 86 年 1 号

30" x 40"   76cm x 102cm

1986

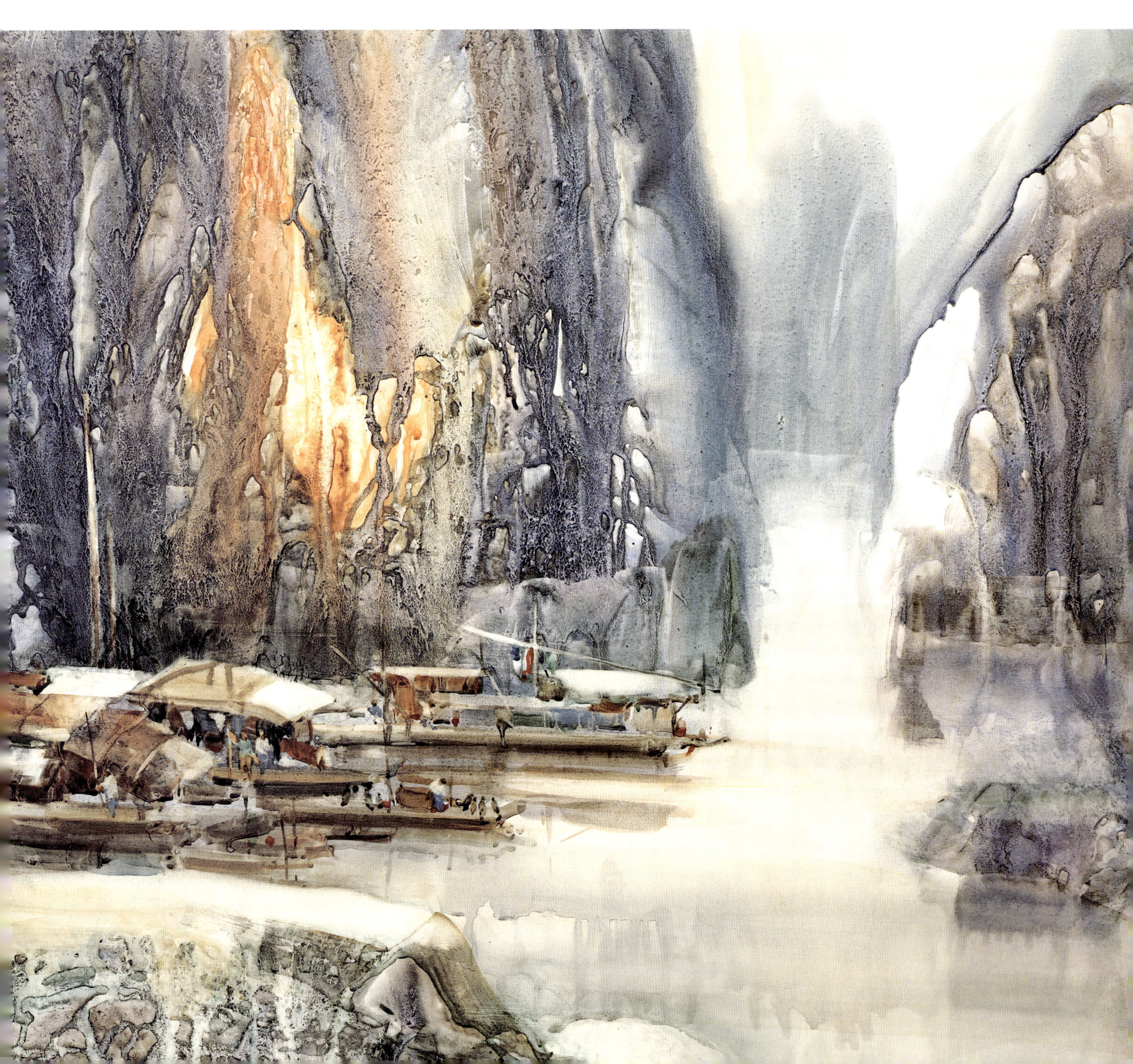

63

HIGH SNOWS

雪山

30" x 40"   76cm x 102cm

1986

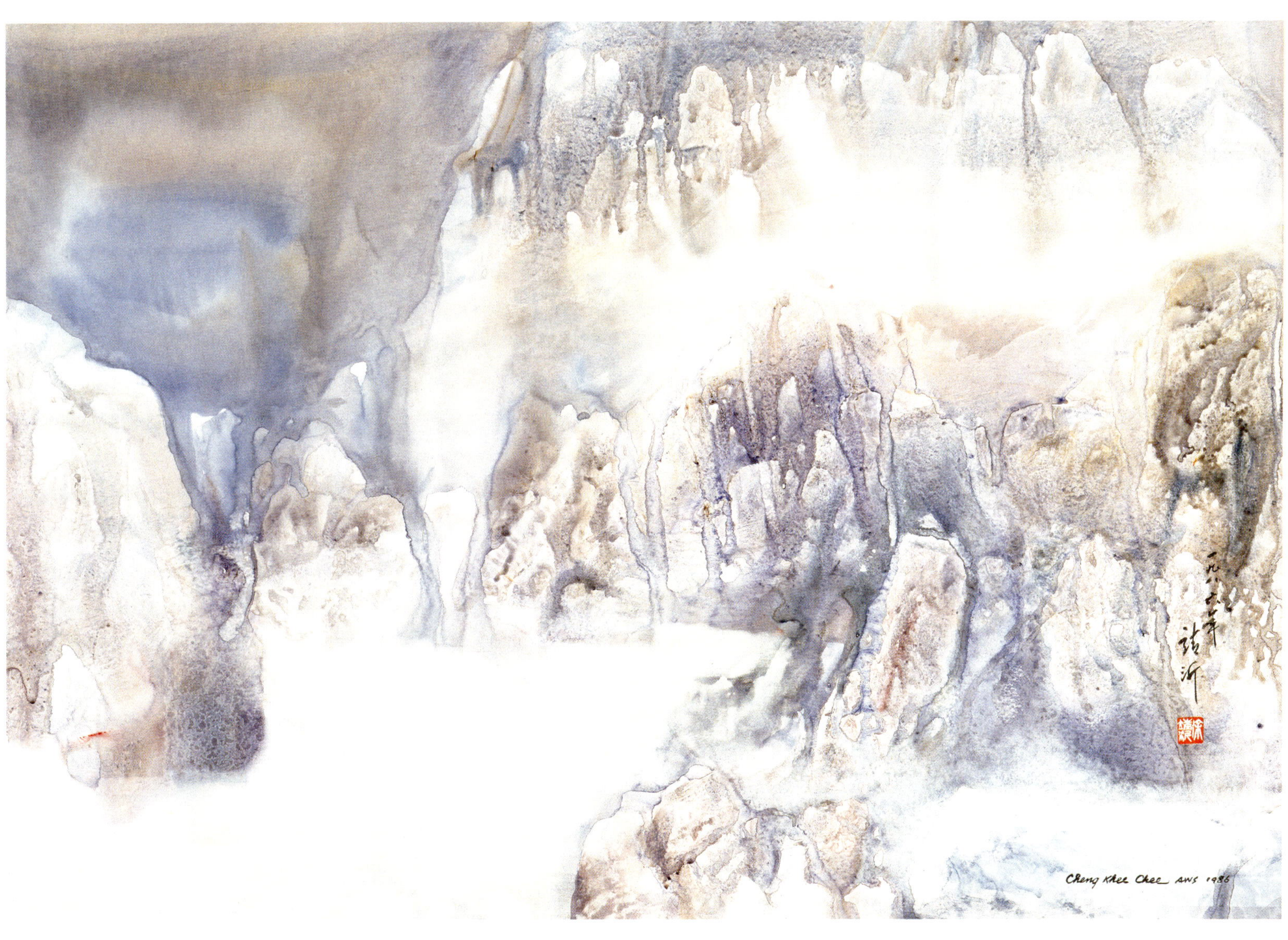
Cheng Khee Chee AWS 1986

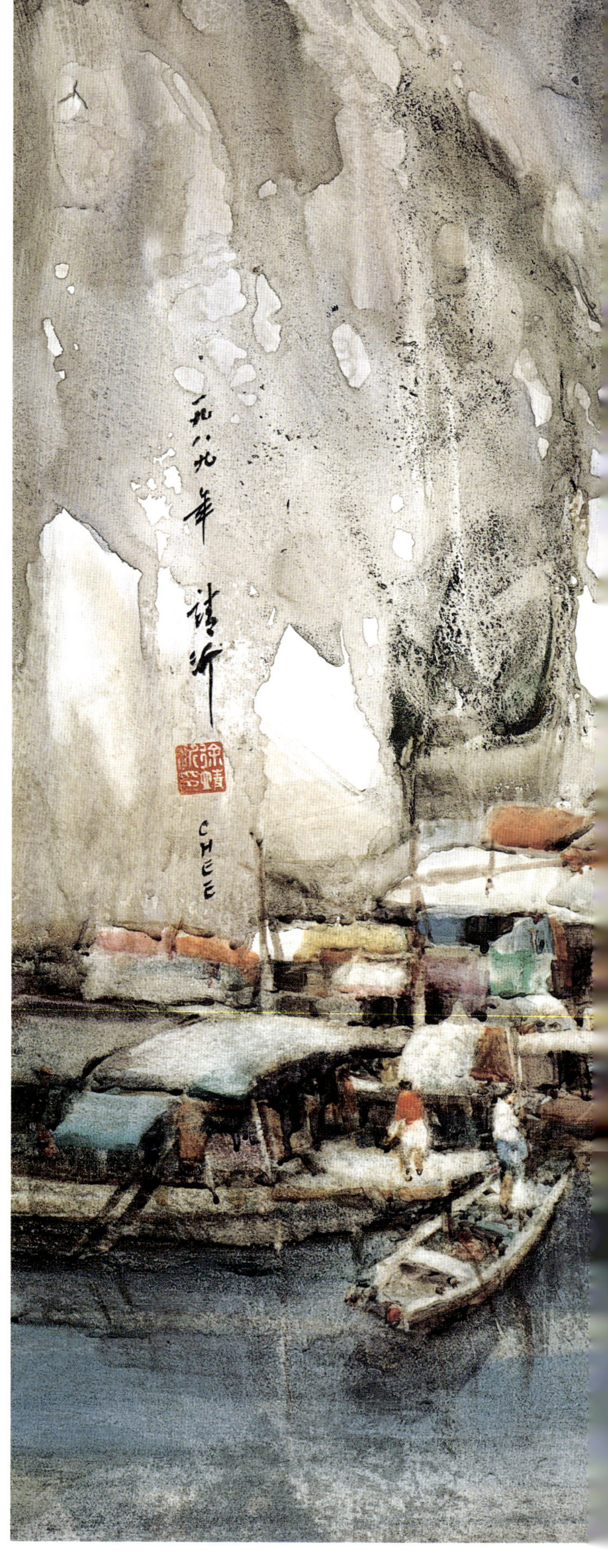

64

Along the Li River 89 No.2

漓江 89 年 2 号

30" x 40"   76cm x 102cm

1989

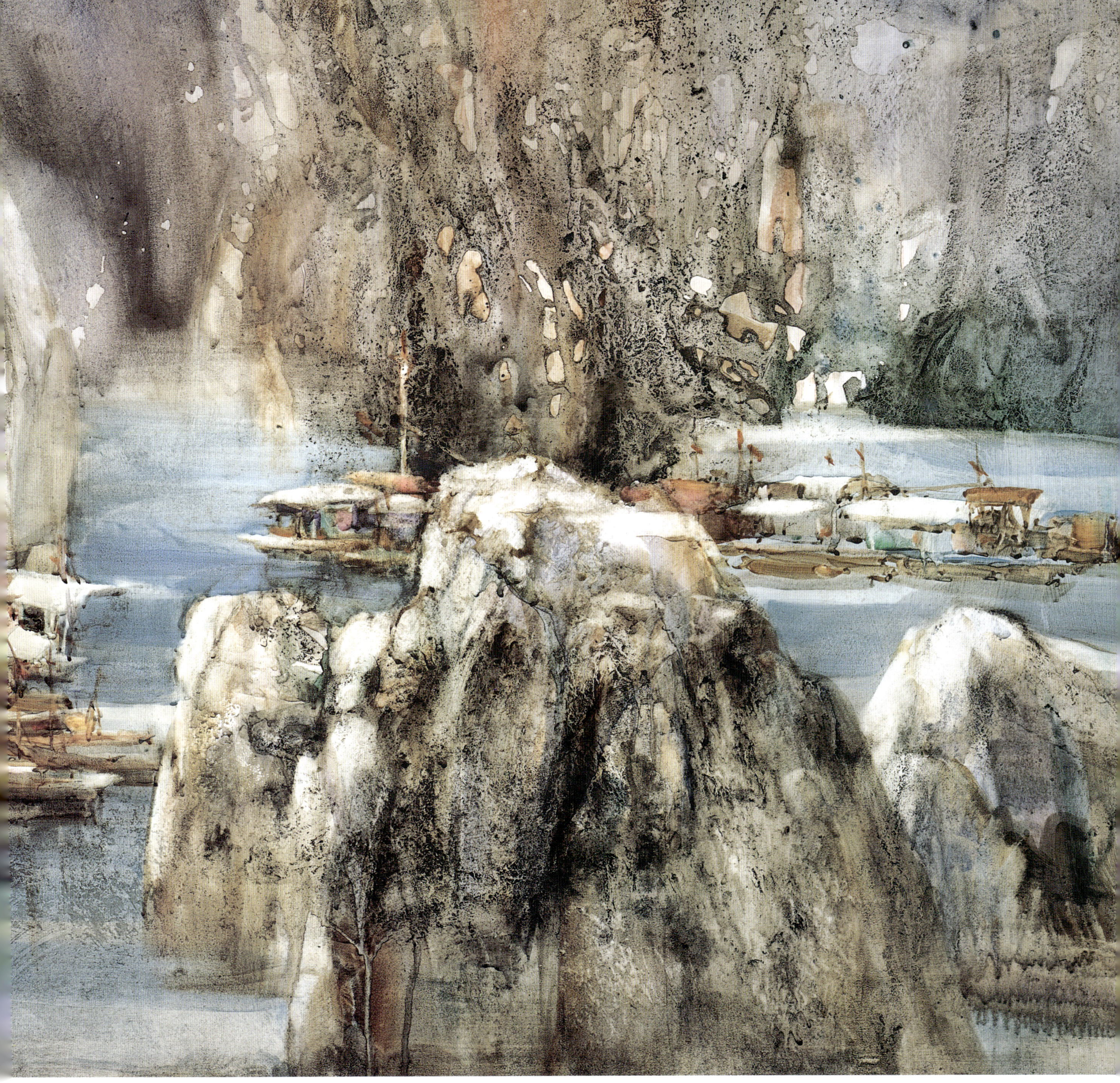

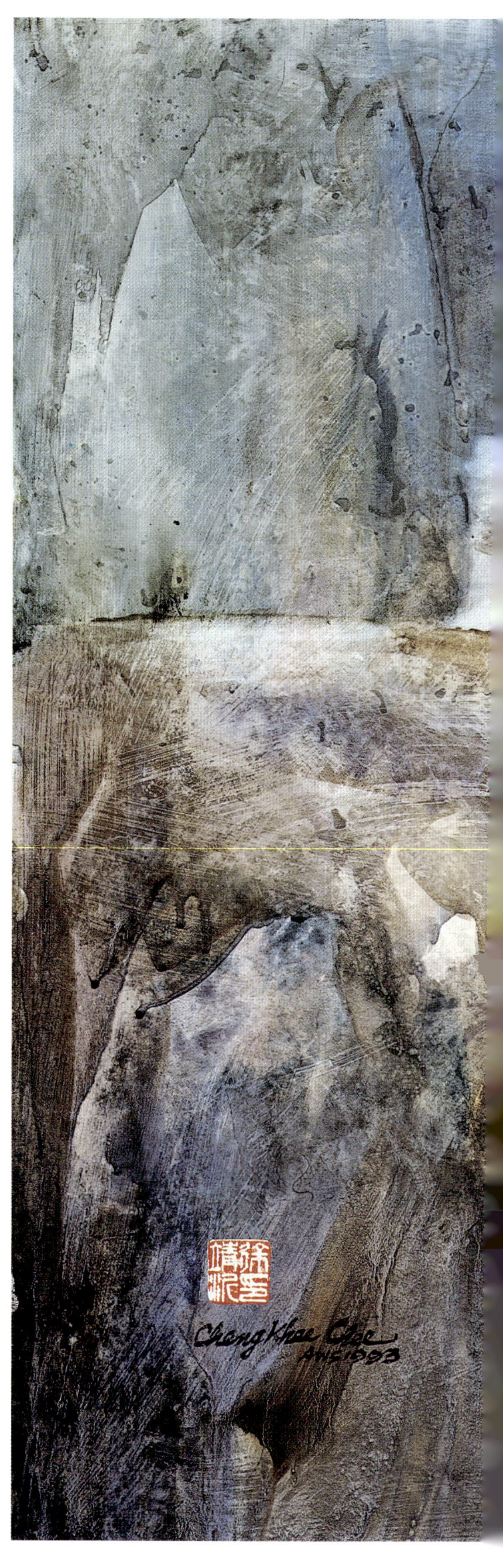

65

Lake Shore 93 No.1

湖岸93年1号

30" x 40"   76cm x 102cm

1993

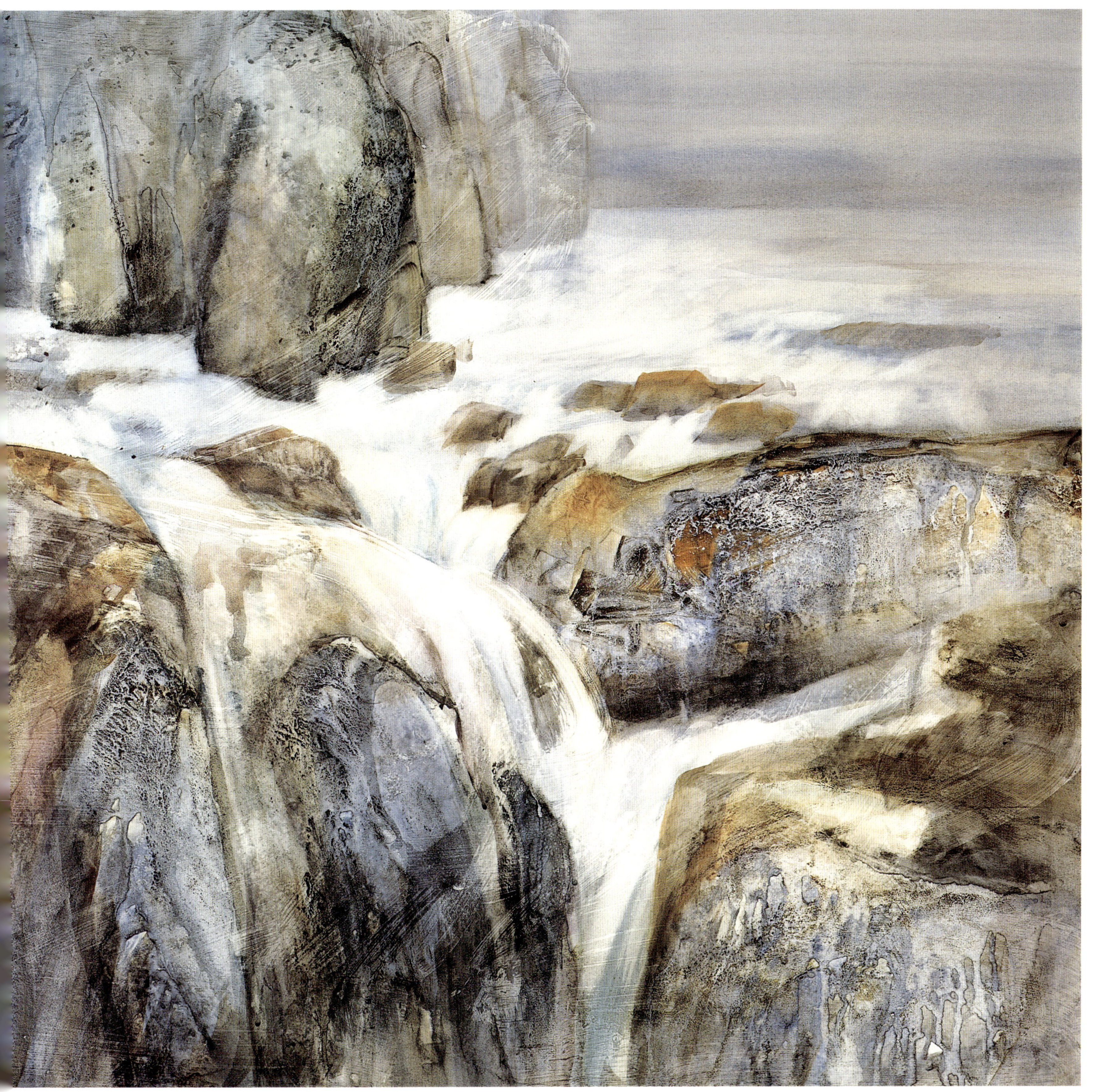

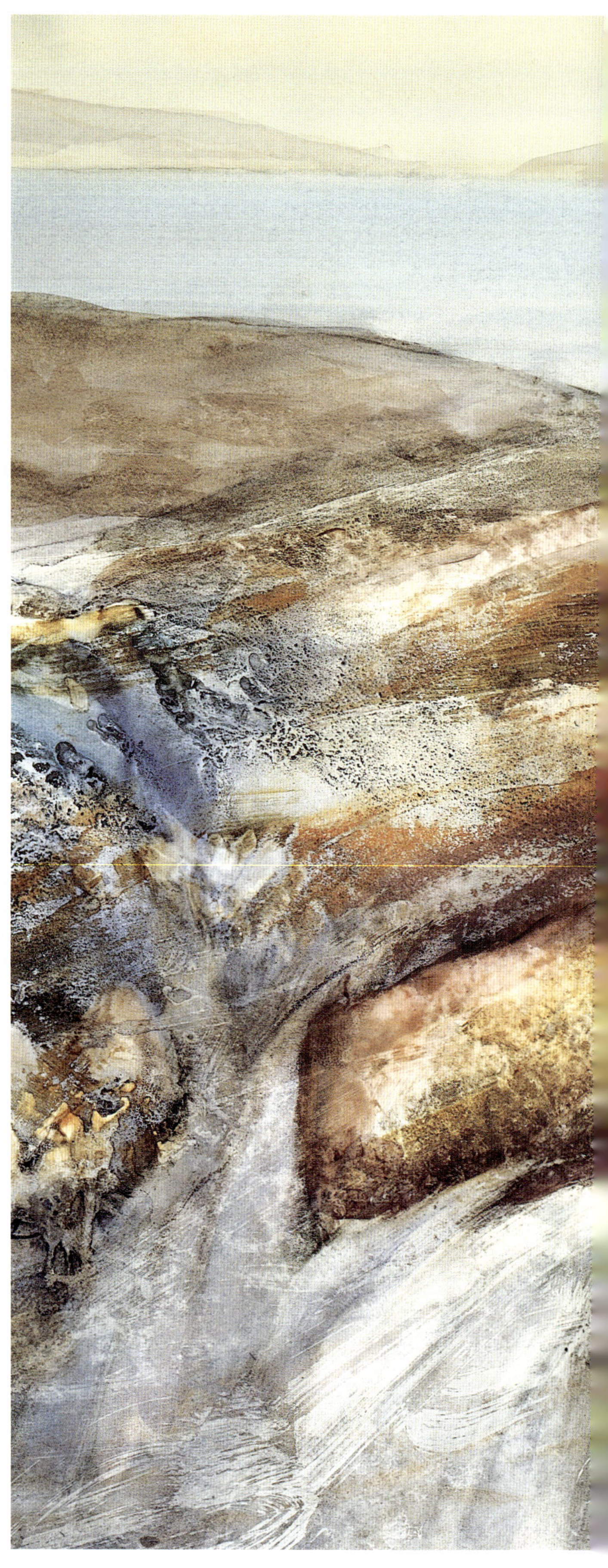

66

LAKE SHORE 93 NO.2

湖岸93年2号

30" x 40"   76cm x 102cm

1993

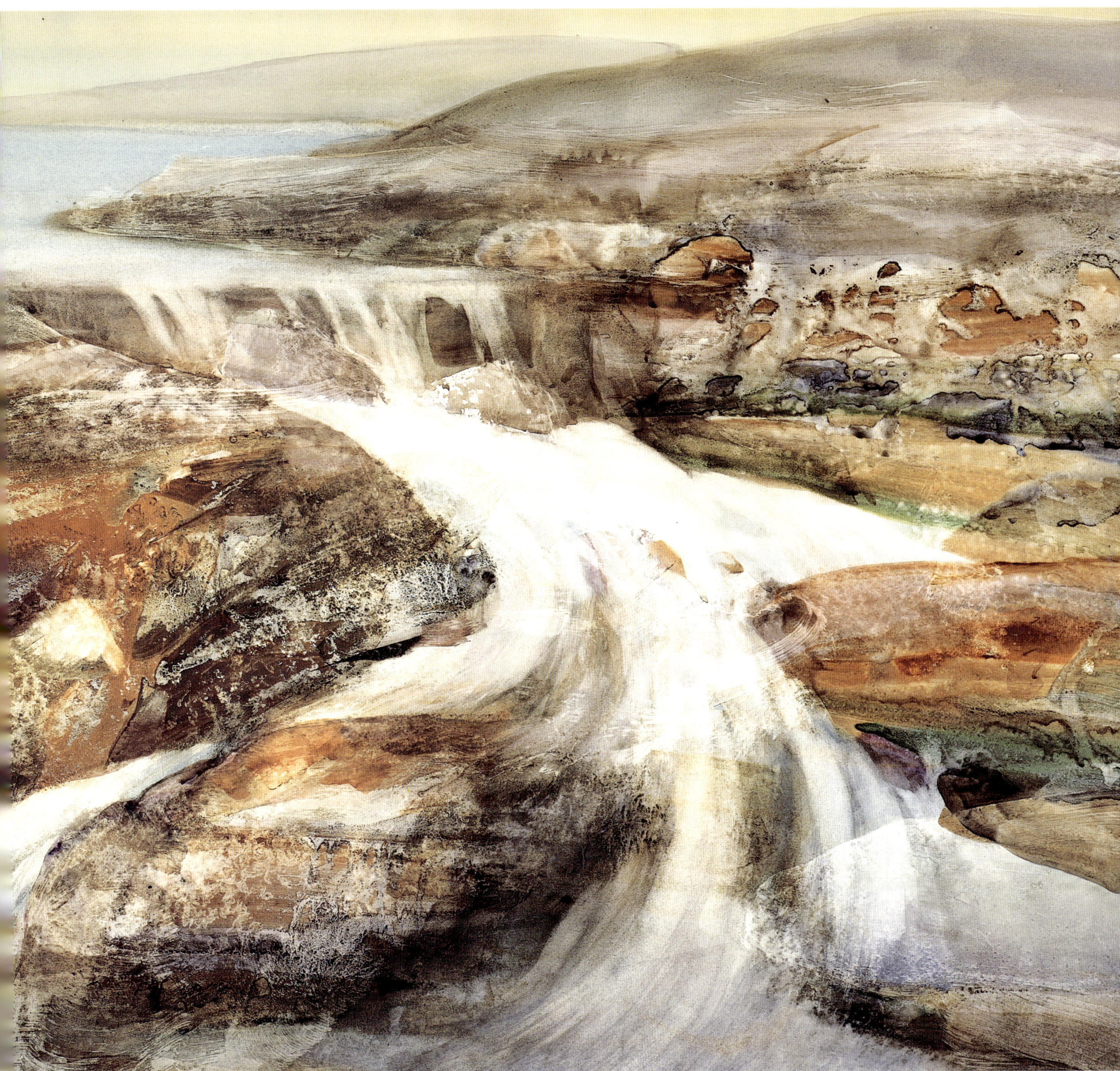

67

Yangzi River 93 No. 1

长江游93年1号

30" x 40"   76cm x 102cm

1993

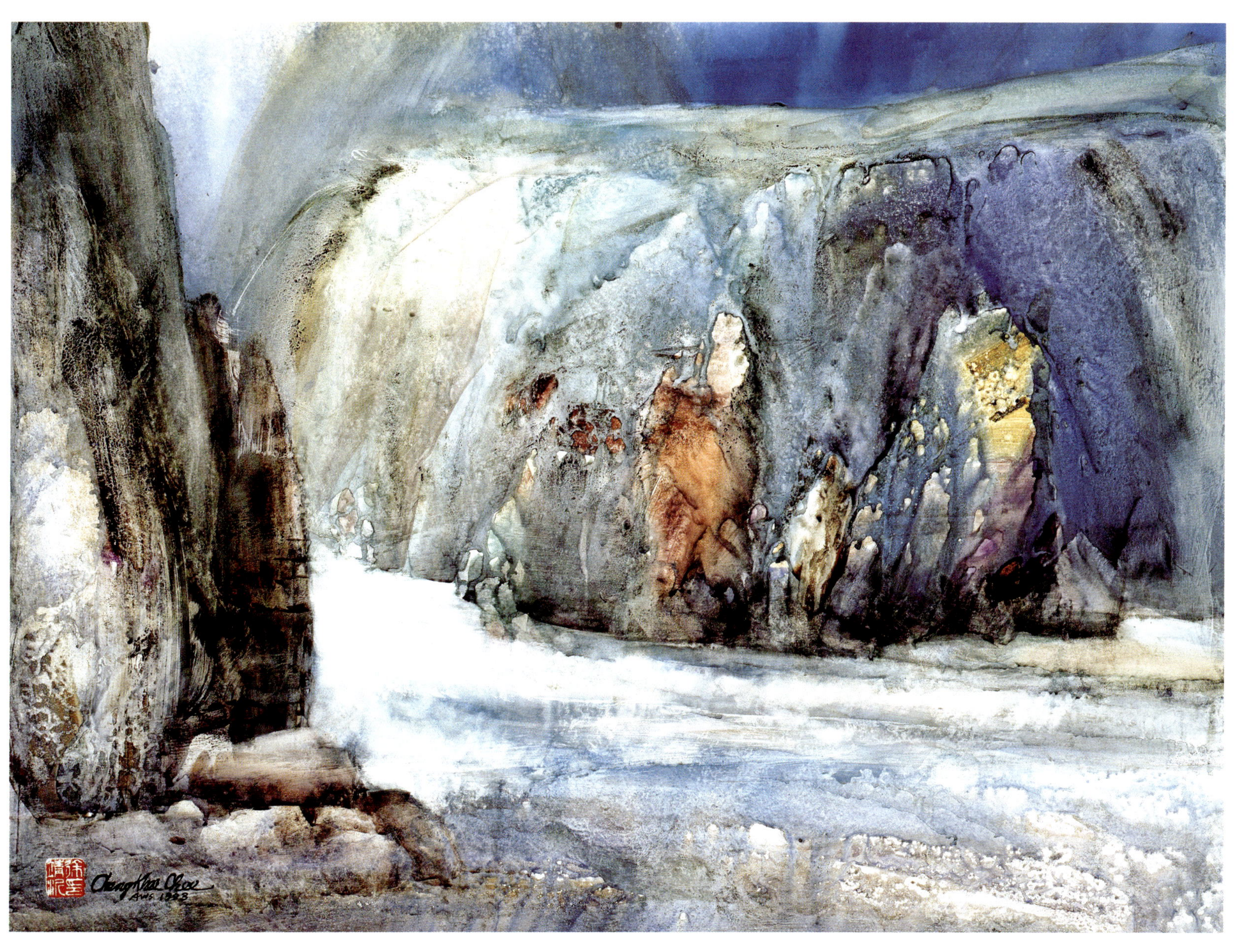

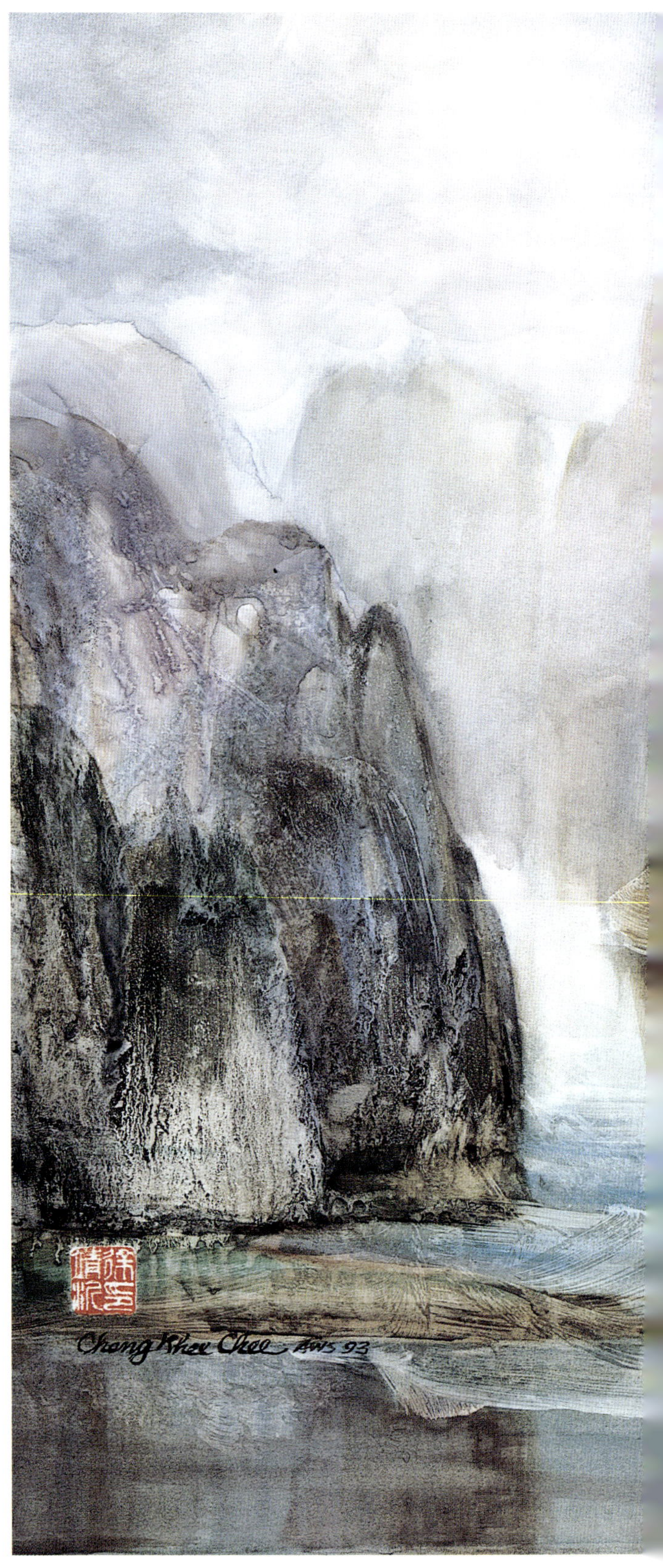

68

YANGZI RIVER 93 NO.3

长江游93年3号

30" x 40"   76cm x 102cm

1993

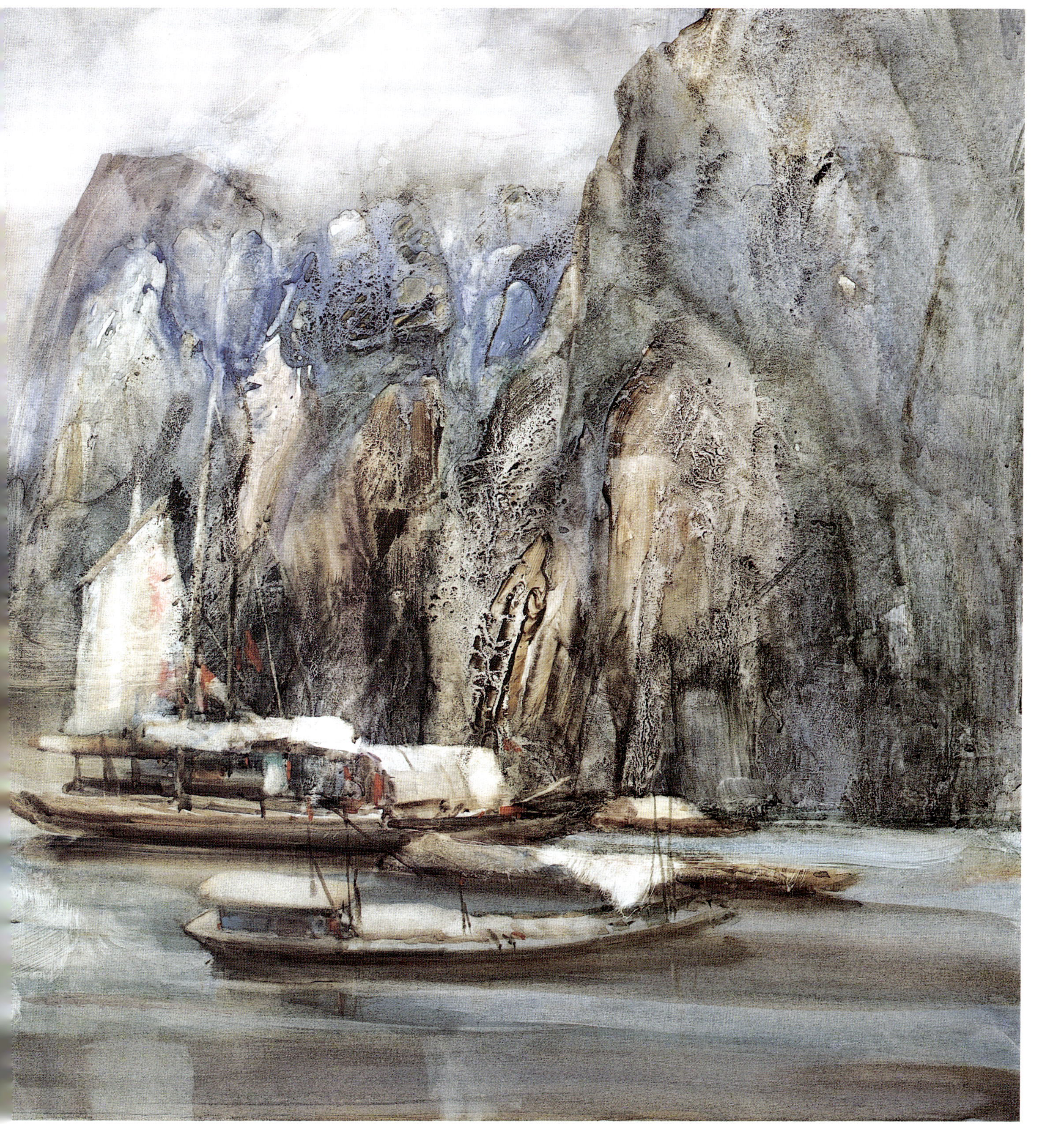

69

SPIRIT OF SOUTHWEST 95 NO.1

西北精神95年1号

30" x 40" 76cm x 102cm

1995

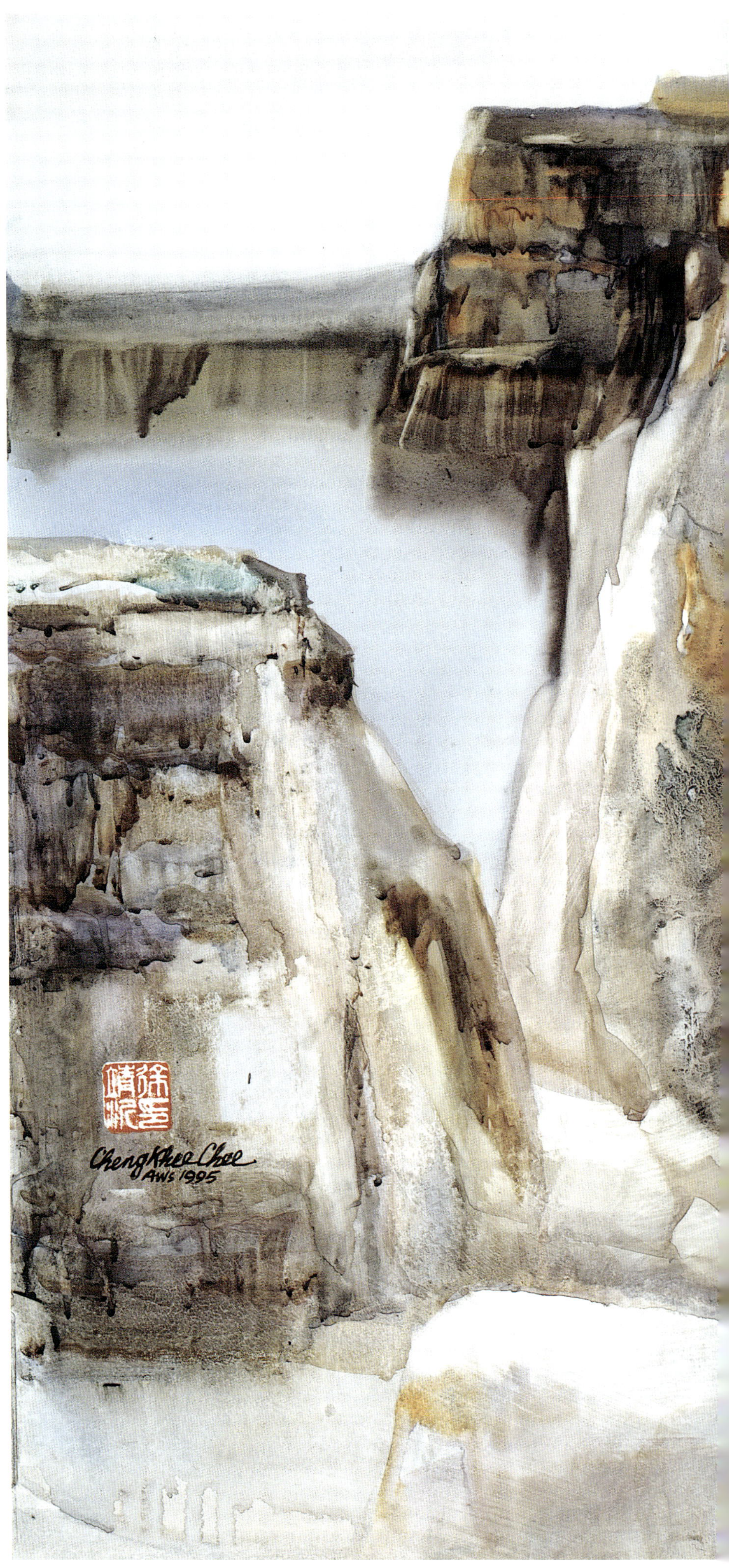

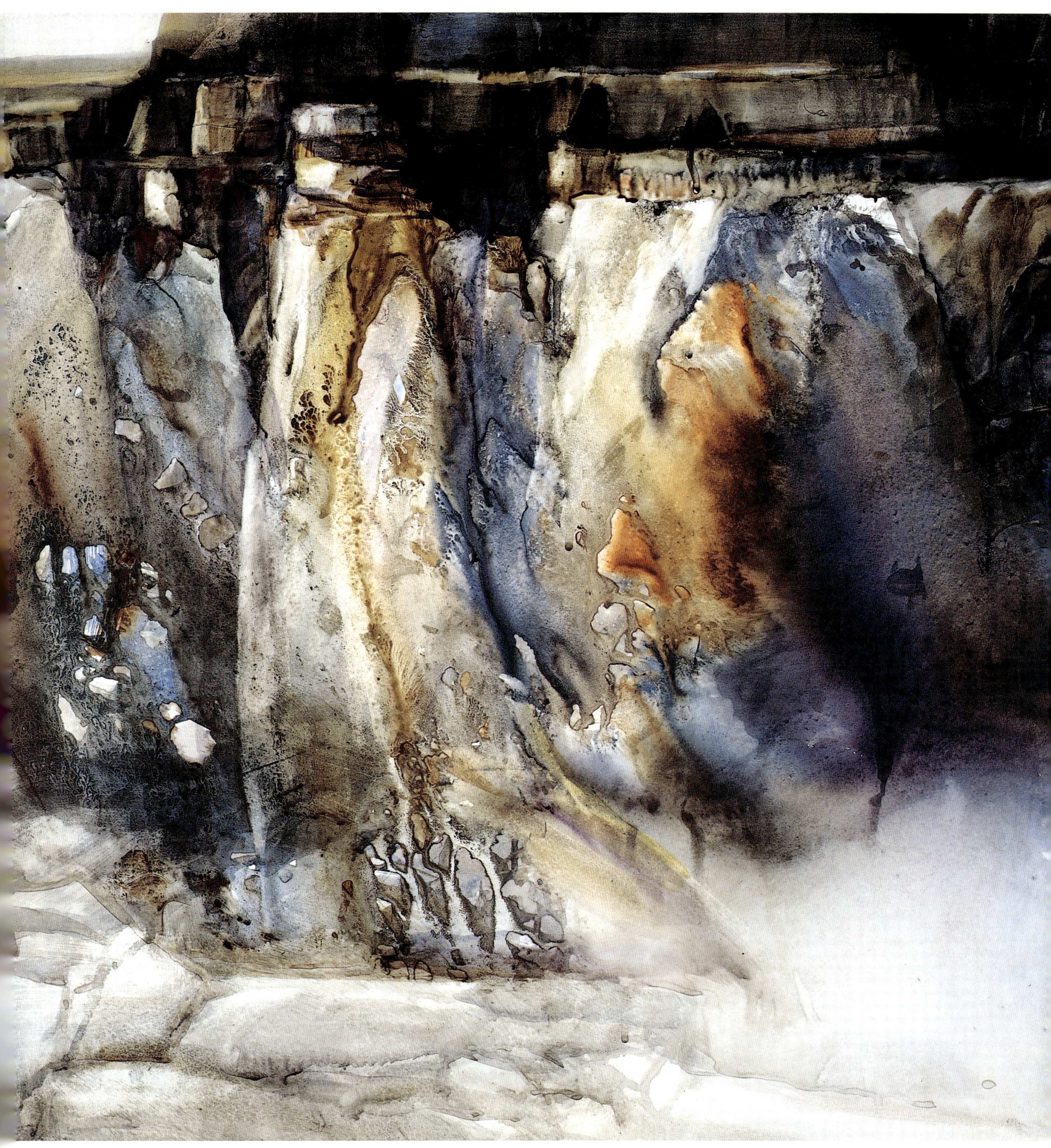

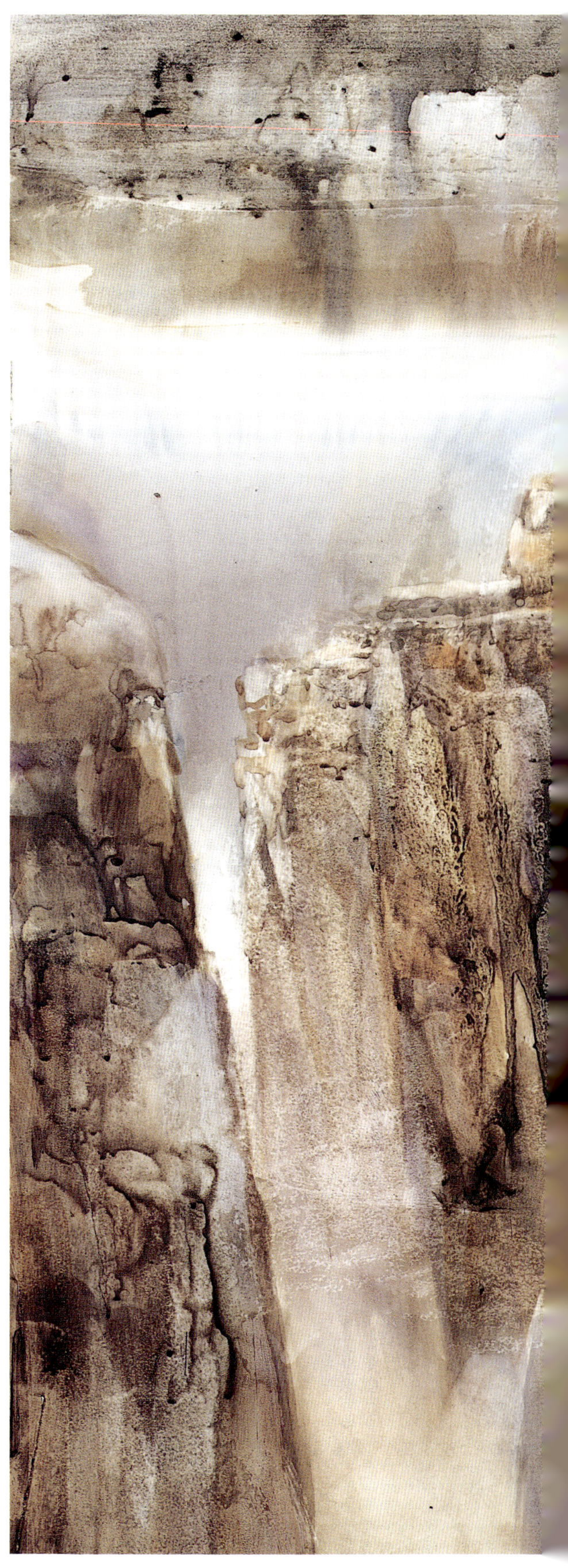

70

Spirit of Southwest 95 No.2

西北精神95年2号

30" x 40"   76cm x 102cm

1995

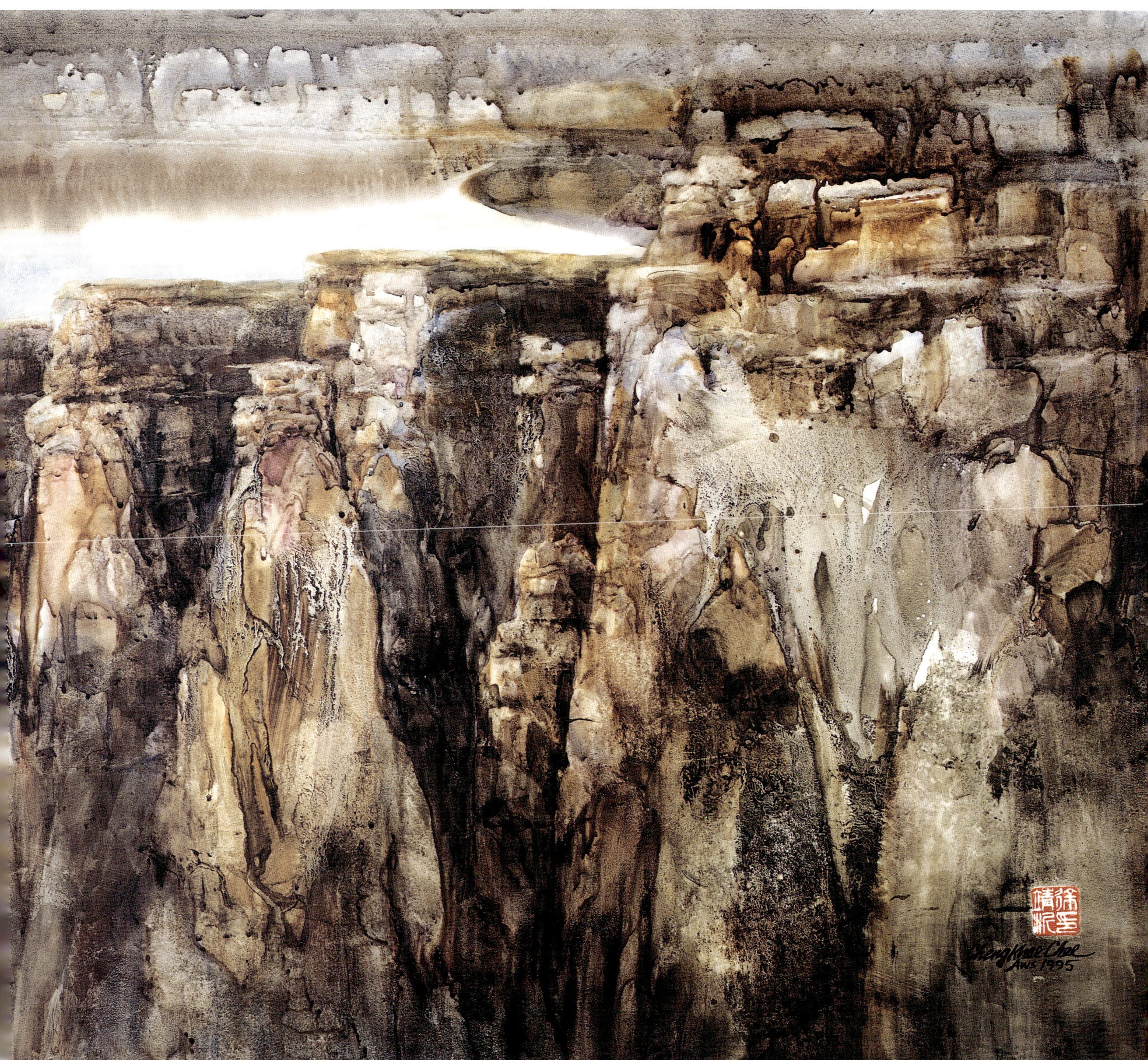
ChengKhee Chee
AWS 1995

71

Along Colorado River 95 No.2

科罗拉多河95年2号

30" x 40"   76cm x 102cm

1995

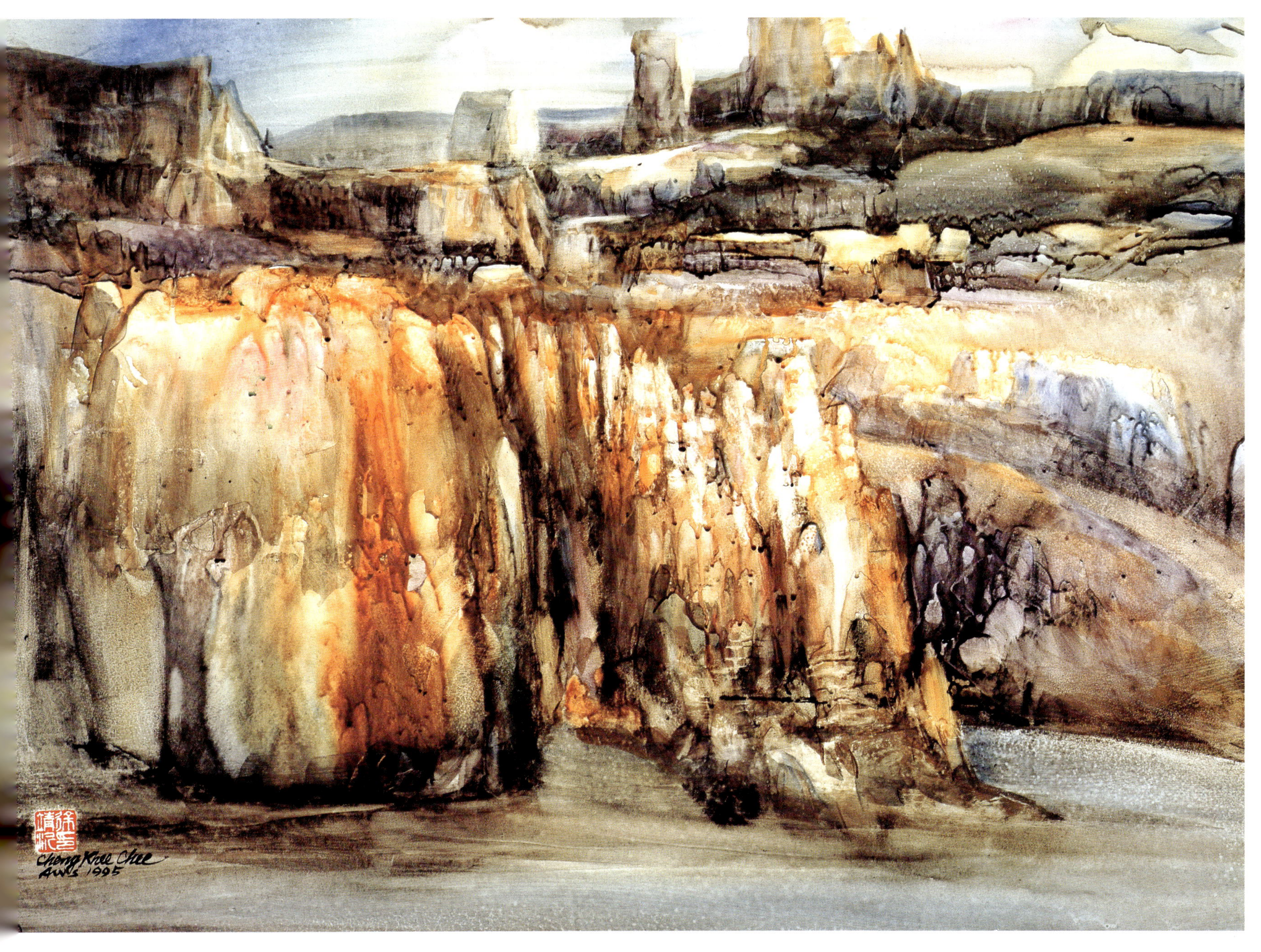
Cheng Khee Chee
AWS 1995

72

Along Colorado River 95 No.3

科罗拉多河 95 年 3 号

30" x 40" 76cm x 102cm

1995

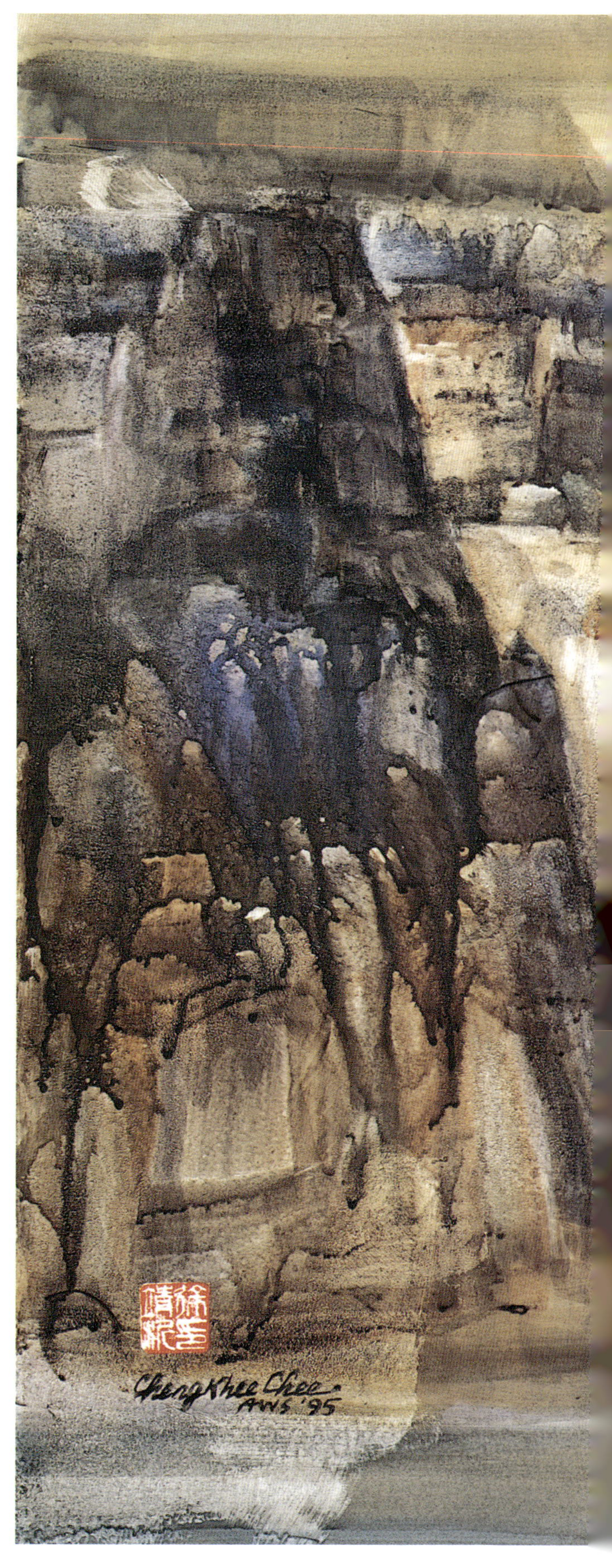

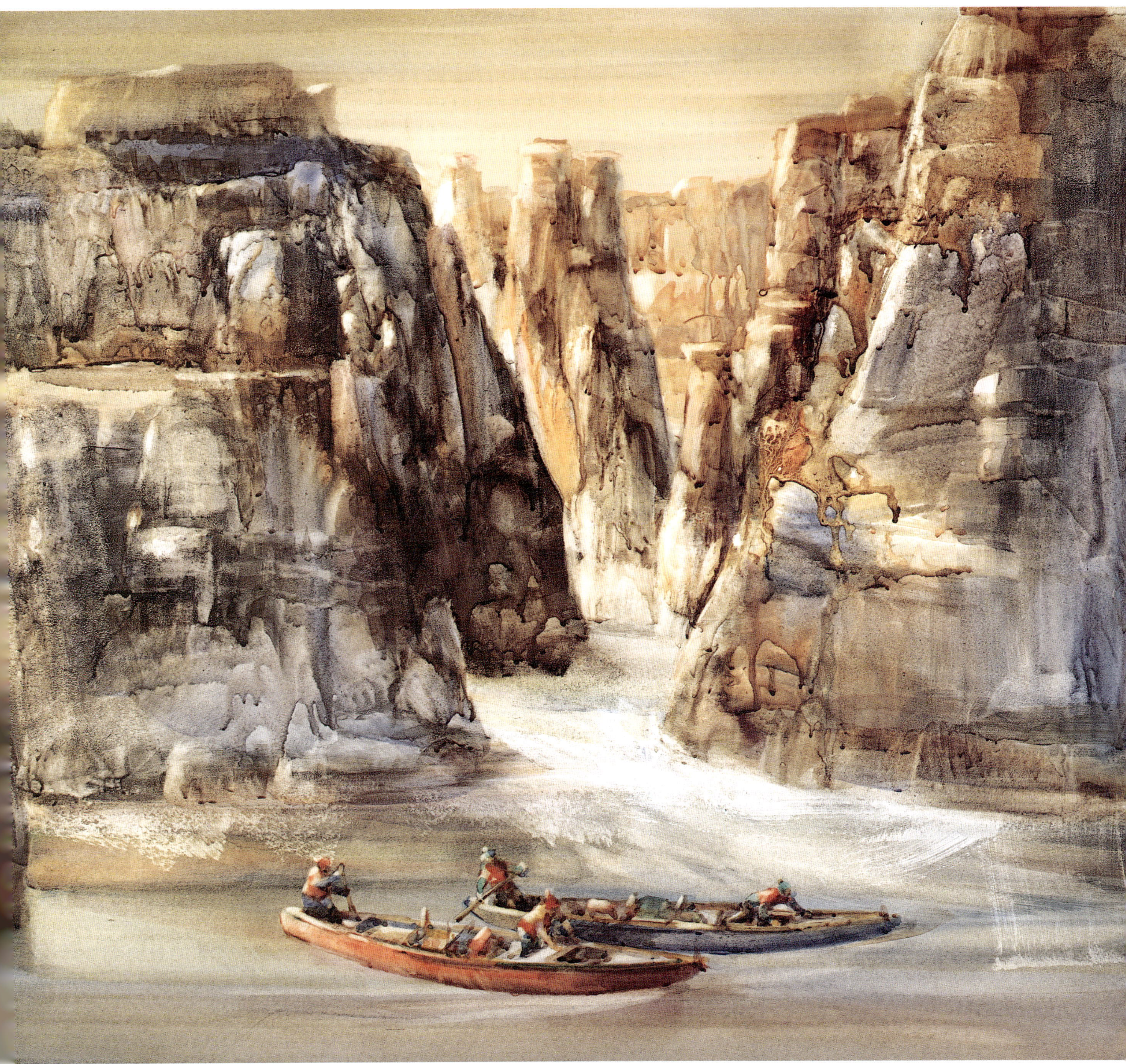

73

CANYON MIST

峡谷积雾

30" x 40"   76cm x 102cm

1995

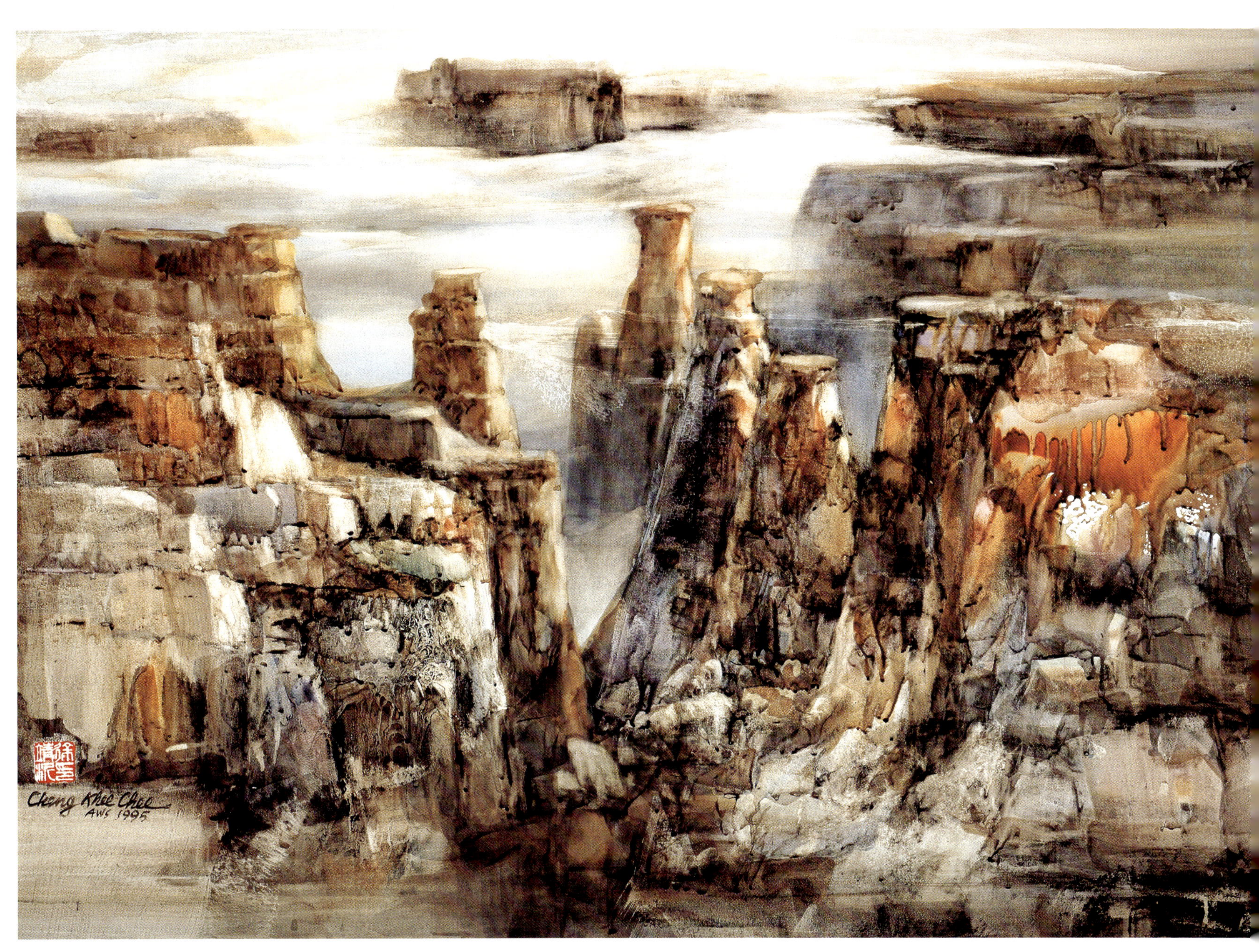
Cheng Khee Chee
AWS 1995

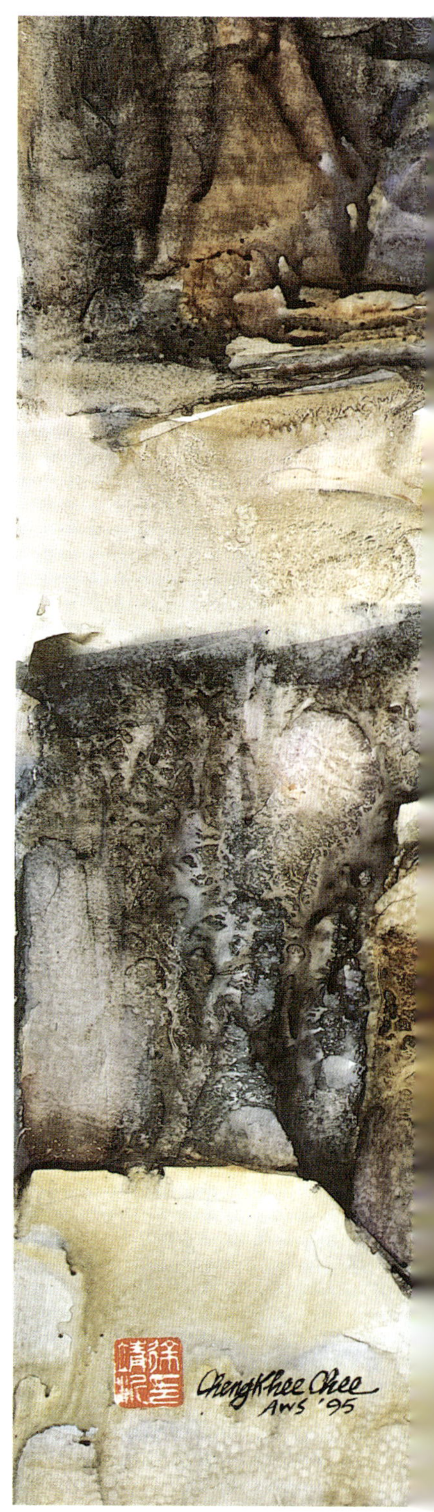

74

Lake Shore 95 No. 1

湖岸 95 年 1 号

30" x 40" 76cm x 102cm

1995

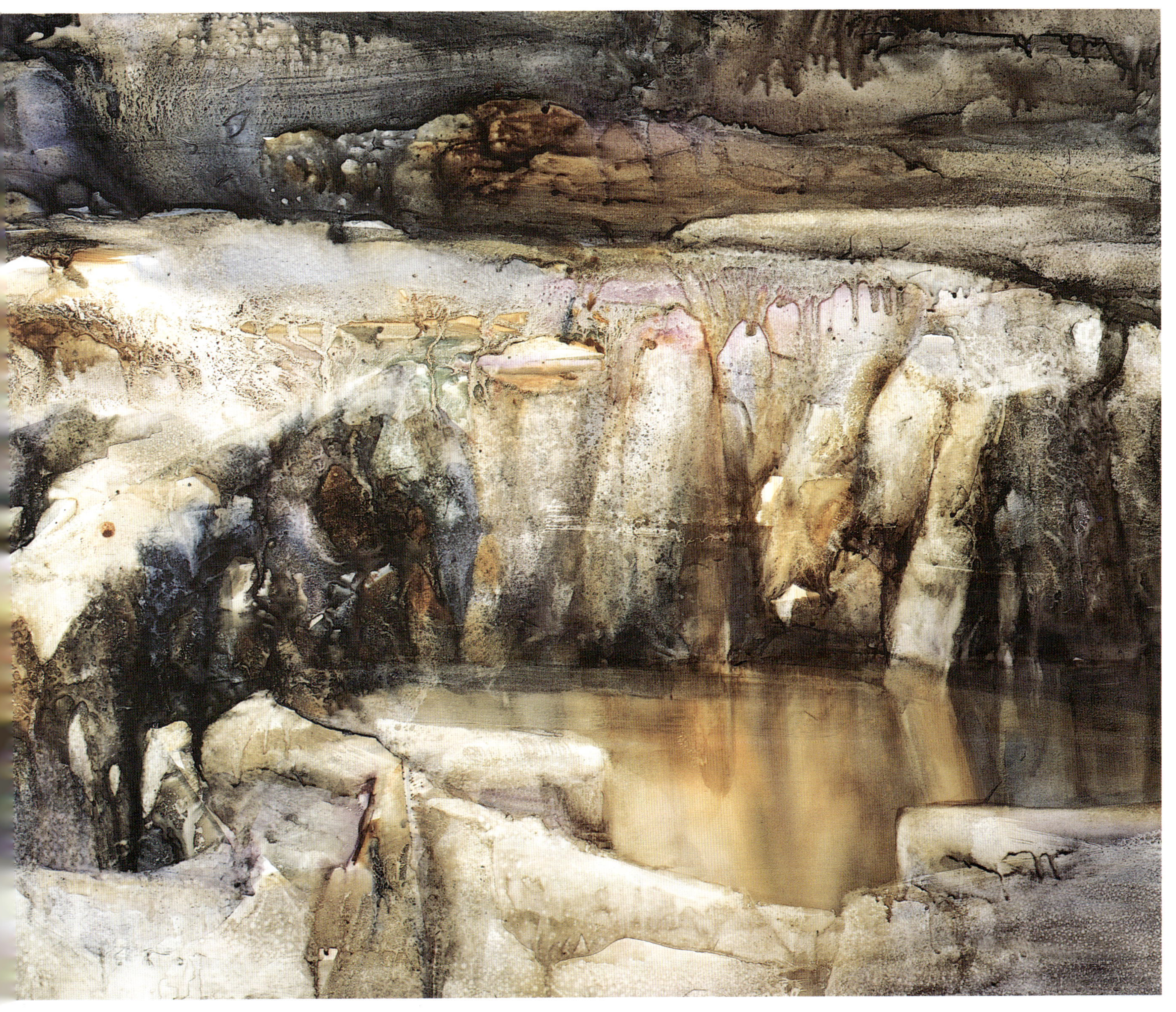

75

Lake Shore 95 No.2

湖岸95年2号

30" x 40"   76cm x 102cm

1995

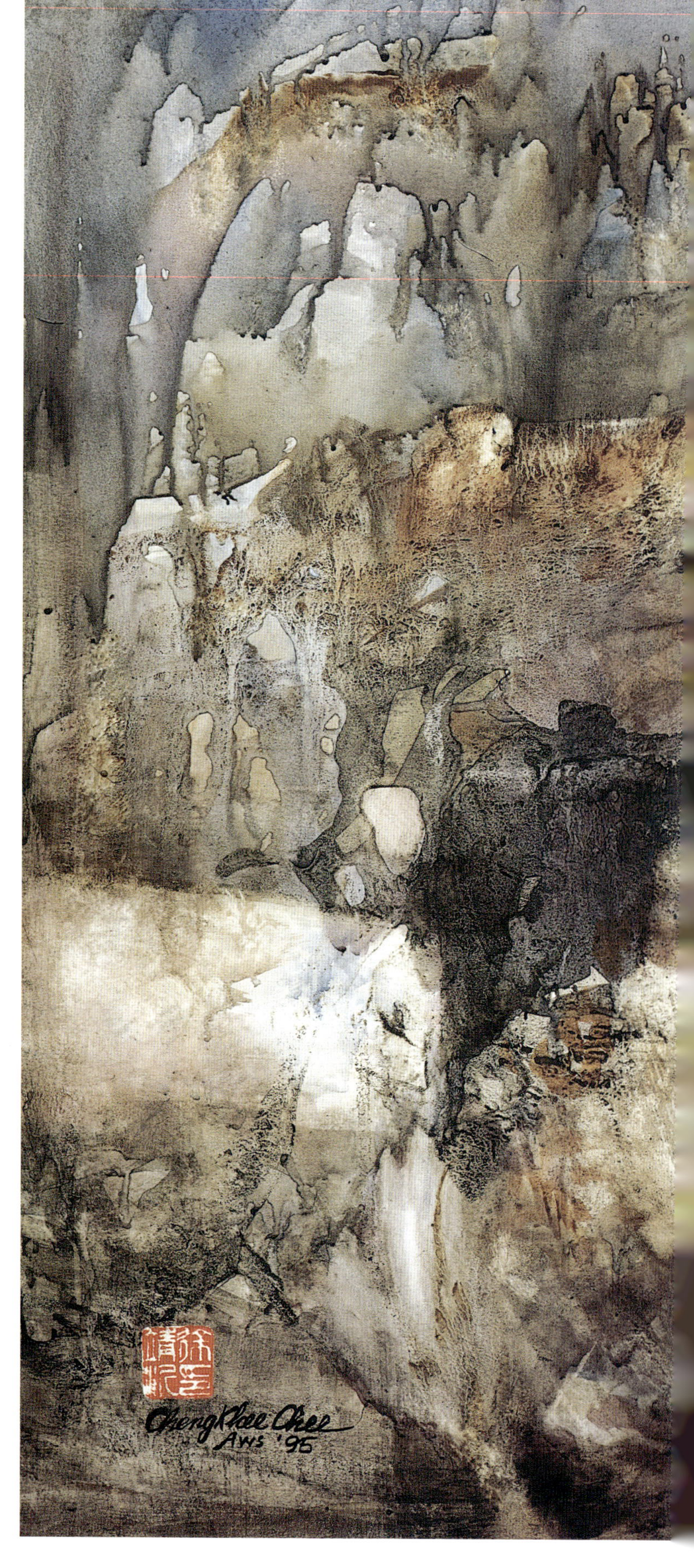

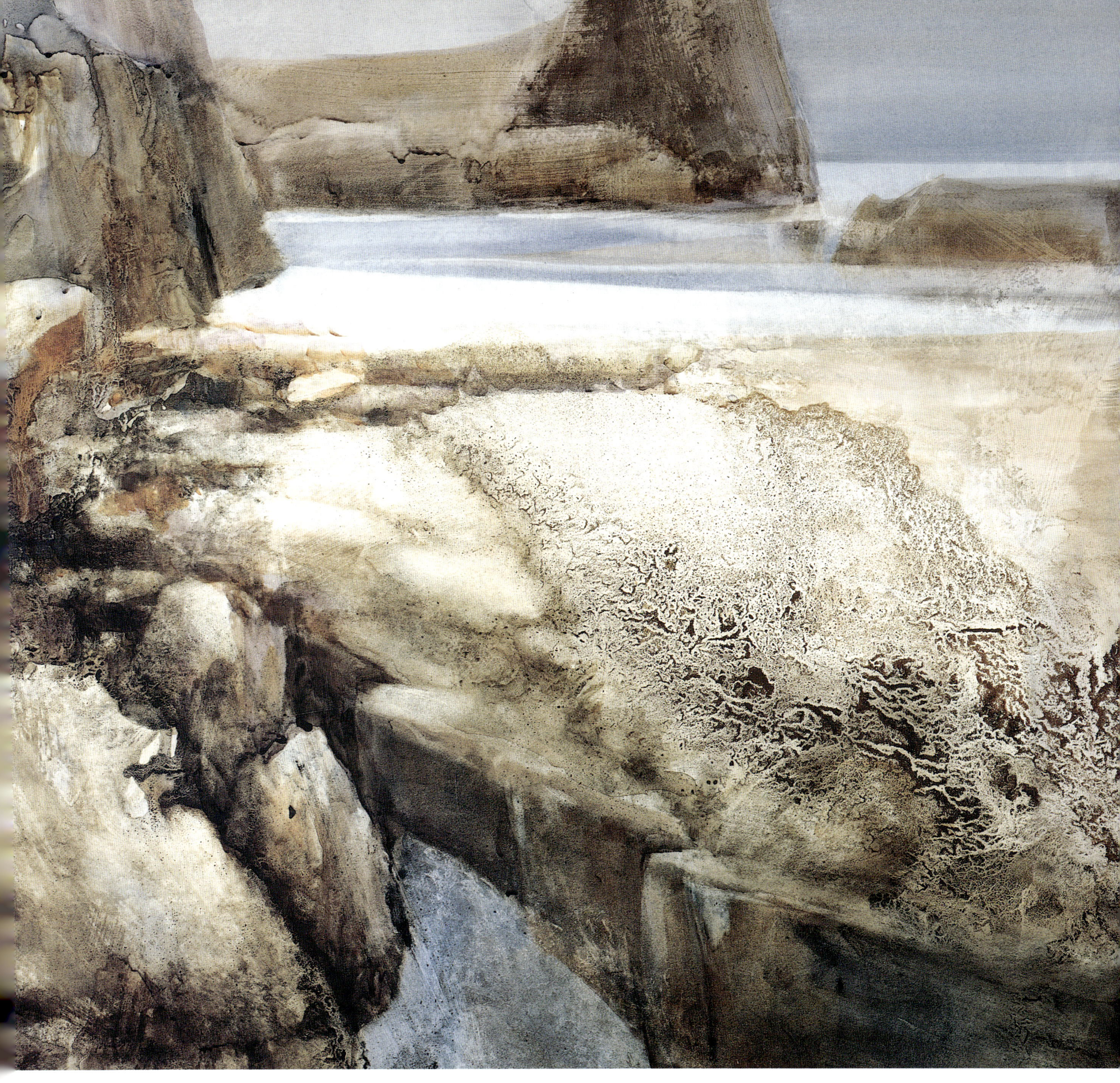

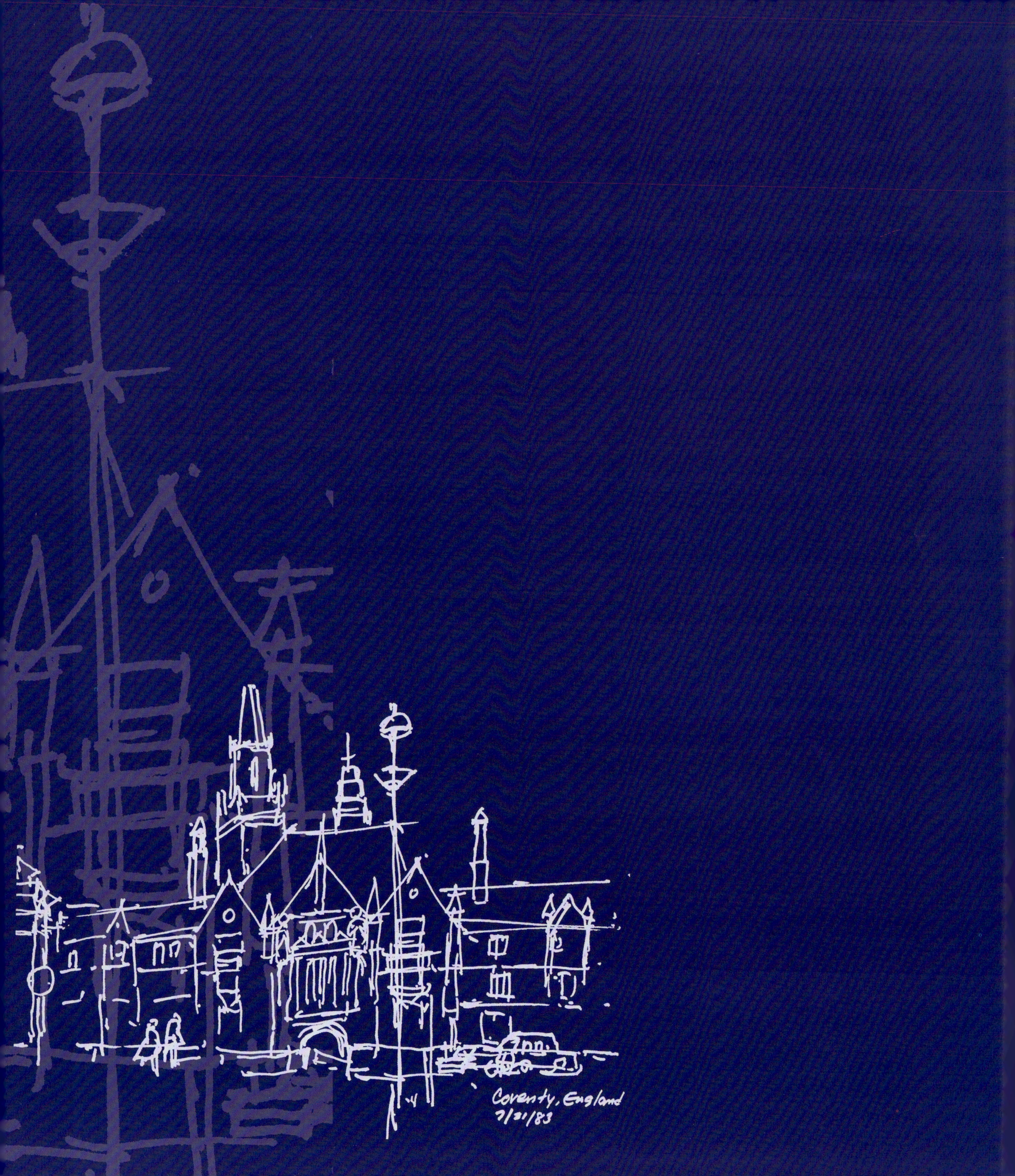
Coventy, England
7/31/83

Art Activities

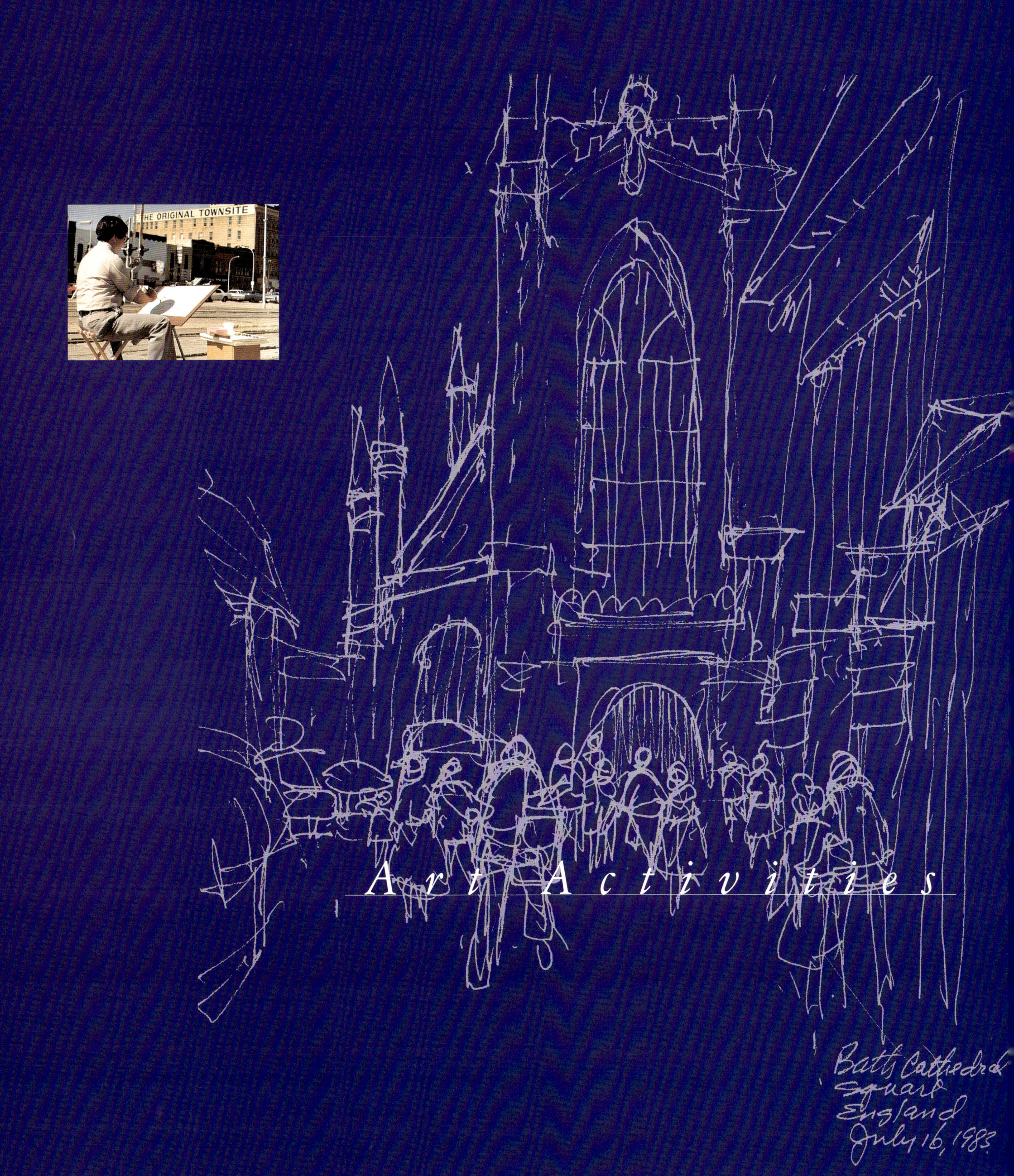

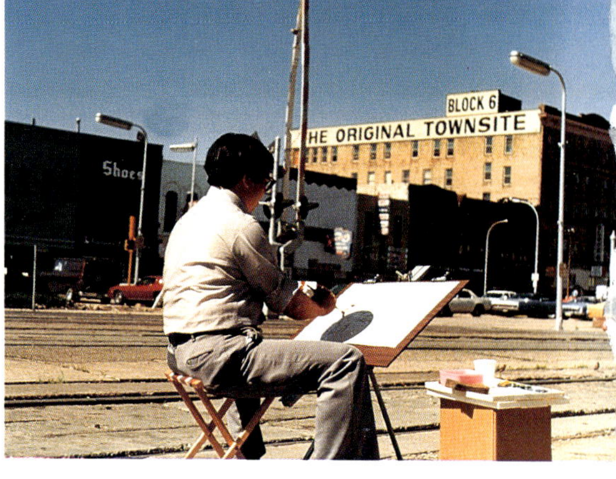

Chee painting on location
户外写生

Cheng-Khee Chee Art Activities 1973 – 1996

1973 Returned to active painting after attending Professor Gaell Lindstrom's Advanced Watercolor Painting Workshop at the University of Minnesota, Duluth

Received 2 Merit Awards in the Northern Minnesota Art Exhibition, Tweed Museum of Art, University of Minnesota, Duluth

Exhibited in the Minnesota State Fair Art Exhibition, St Paul

'Squirrels' received 3rd prize in the 40th Arrowhead Art Exhibition sponsored by the Duluth Art Institute,

1974 Exhibited in the Duluth Art Institute Annual Exhibition

Exhibited in the 41st Arrowhead Art Exhibition sponsored by the Duluth Art Institute

Received 3 Merit Awards in the Northern Minnesota Art Exhibition, Tweed Museum of Art

Team taught Women's Seminar 'Oriental History and Culture', University of Minnesota

'Duluth Harbor 1974' received University of Minnesota Special Programs Purchase Award in the State Fair Fine Art Exhibition

1975 Held one-man exhibition at the North Star Gallery, University of Minnesota, St Paul Campus

Received a grant-in-aid from the National Committee on United States-China Relations to study the Chinese Archaeological Exhibition at the Nelson Gallery-Atkins Museum in Kansas City

'Sometimes the Twain Meet', a biographical article by Roland Lovstad published in *Duluth News-Tribune Sunday Supplement Accent North*, May 25

Travelled, painted and visited relatives and friends in Singapore and Malaysia in August

'The Depot' selected for American Watercolor Society's Annual National Exhibition in New York City and for national tour exhibition for one year

'Rainy Day' selected for exhibition in Watercolor USA, sponsored by the Springfield Art Museum, Springfield, Missouri

'Duluth Winter' received Merit Award in the Minnesota State Fair Fine Art Exhibition

'Duluth Winter' received Special Merit Award in the Northern Minnesota Art Exhibition

1976 Held one-man exhibition 'Malaysia: A Painterly Travelogue' at the University of Minnesota

Held one-man exhibition at the Northwestern Bank of Commerce, Duluth

'St Paul Cathedral' exhibited in the Metamorphose / one-St Paul Official Bicentennial Art Exhibition, Minnesota Museum of Art, St Paul

'Malay Village' received Colorado Centennial Award in Rock Mountain National Watermedia Exhibition, Golden, Colorado

'Malay Village' exhibited in the 42nd Arrowhead Art Exhibition sponsored by the Duluth Art Institute

'St Paul Street Scene' was exhibited in the Minnesota State Fair Fine Art Exhibition, St Paul

'Duluth Harbor' exhibited in the Marine Art Exhibition sponsored by Tweed Museum of Art, University of Duluth

1977 Exhibited in the Duluth Art Institute Invitational Exhibition Celebrating the Grand Opening of the St Louis County Heritage and Arts Centre, Duluth, May 2 – 22

Awarded 1977-78 Outstanding Service Award by the University of Minnesota

Served as Juror of Awards for the North Star Watercolor Society's First Annual Exhibition

'Tugs at Docks' received Honorable Mention and Mesabi Tire Company's Purchase Award in the Midwest Watercolor Society's Annual National Exhibition, Tweed Museum of Art, Duluth

'Winter Boatyard 77 No. 2' received Merit Award in the Northern Lights Art Exhibition, Minnesota

1978 Exhibited in Works on Paper, An Invitational Exhibition of Prints, Watercolors and Drawings by Minnesota Artists, Minneapolis Institute of Arts, Minneapolis, Minnesota

Held one-man exhibition at the Twin Cities Federal Atrium Gallery Minneapolis

Held one-man exhibition at the Lakewood Community College Art Centre, White Bear Lake, Minnesota

Exhibited in the Duluth Art Institute Annual Exhibition,

Participated in the Edgar Whitney Watercolor Workshop, Grand Rapids, Minnesota

'St Paul Cathedral' received Travel Award in the American Watercolor Society's Annual National Exhibition, New York City

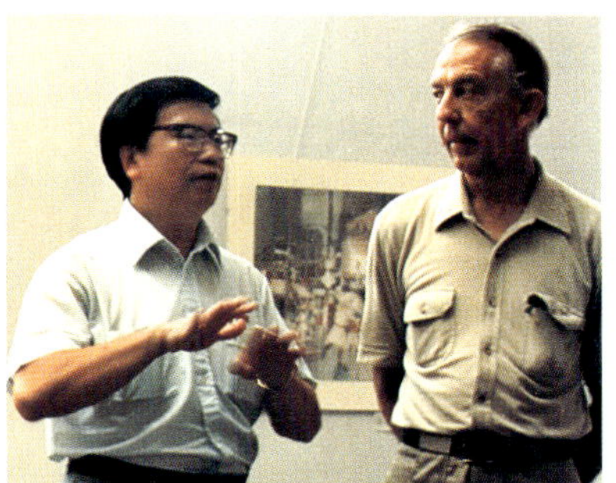
Chee participated in Professor Gaell Lindstrom's Watercolor Workshop in 1973. They met again at the Zhejiang Academy of Fine Arts in 1984
一九七三年夏参加林基教授
水彩研究班
一九八四年在浙江美术
学院重逢

徐靖沂艺术活动年表 *1973 – 1996*

1973 年

参加林基教授水彩研究班，重新致力水彩探索和创作
参加明尼苏达州北区美术展览获荣誉奖
参加明尼苏达州美术展览
“松鼠”获美国中西部五州第四十届美术展览第三奖

1974 年

参加都鲁市美术协会邀靖展览
参加明尼苏达州北区美术展览获荣誉奖
参加美国中西部五州第四十届美术展览
参加明尼苏达州美术展览
参与讲授明尼苏达大学都鲁市学城妇女进修班“东方历史文化”课题
“都鲁市码头”获明尼苏达州美术展览荣誉奖和明尼苏达大学购藏奖

1975 年

在明尼苏达大学圣保罗学城美术馆举行个人画展
都鲁市新闻日报专题报导“徐靖沂的艺术”5.25
获中美友谊协会奖金赴康萨斯市尼尔逊－爱根斯美术博物馆参观研究中国出土文物展览
去新加坡，马来西亚探亲，旅行和写生
“都鲁市车站”第一次参加美国水彩画会全国年展入选并被选送全国巡迴展览
“雨天”入选美国密苏里州春田艺术馆举办全国水彩展览
“都鲁之冬”获明尼苏达州美术展览荣誉奖

1976 年

在明尼苏达大学都鲁市学城举行“马来西亚纪游”个人画展
在明尼苏达都鲁市西北商业银行举行个人画展
“马来乡村”获美国石山区全国水彩年展科洛拉多州百周年纪念奖
“马来乡村”入选美国中西部五州第四十二届美术展览
“圣保罗天主教堂”入选明尼苏达州艺术馆主办美国建国两百周年纪念美术展览
“圣保罗街景”入选明尼苏达州美术展览
“都鲁市码头”入选明尼苏达大学都鲁市学城艺术馆主办海洋美术展览

1977 年

参加明尼苏达州圣路易郡艺术中心落成纪念邀请展览
获明尼苏达大学都鲁市学城杰出服务奖
挡任明尼苏达州北极星水彩画会第一届展览评审
“靠坞拖船”获美国中西部水彩画会全国年展荣誉奖和麦莎比公司购藏奖
“船场之冬 77 年 2 号”获北极光美术展览荣誉奖

1978 年

参加明尼亚玻利斯市美术博物馆举办明尼苏达州版画，水彩，素描邀请展览
在明尼亚玻利斯市双城联邦银行举行个人画展
在明尼苏达白熊湖湖林学院举行个人画展
参加都鲁市美术协会年展
参加艾格威尼水彩研究班
“圣保罗教堂”获美国水彩画会全国年展巡迴展览奖
“马六甲市场”获美国中西部水彩画会全国年展优胜奖
“溪涧之冬”获美国中西部五州第四十三届美术展览荣誉奖
“船场之冬 77 年 1 号”获北极光美术展览优胜奖
“码头之冬”获明尼苏达州美术展览第二奖
“船场之冬 78 年”入选美国石山区全国水彩年展

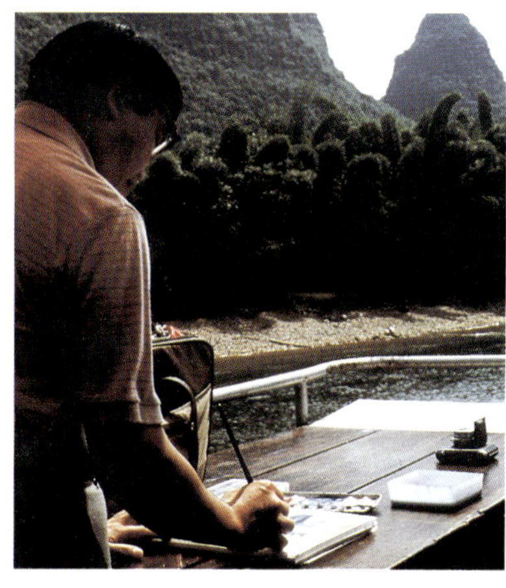

Sketching on the boat along the Li River
在漓江游艇上写生

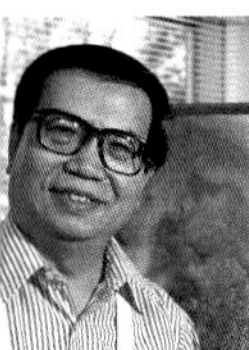

'Malacca Market Place' received Midwest Watercolor Society Award in the Midwest Watercolor Society's Annual National Exhibition, Tweed Museum of Art, Duluth

'Chester Creek' received Merit Award in the 43rd Arrowhead Art Exhibition sponsored by the Duluth Art Institute

'Winter Boatyard 77 No. 1' received Award of Excellence in the North Lights Art Exhibition, Minnesota

'Winter Harbor' received Second Premium in the Minnesota State Fair Fine Art Exhibition, St Paul

'Winter Boatyard 78' exhibited in the Rocky Mountain National Watermedia Exhibition, Golden, Colorado

1979

Began teaching watercolor painting at the University of Minnesota

Held one-man exhibition at the University of Minnesota, Duluth, Tweed Museum and presented a lecture on 'The Art of Watercolor Painting' in conjunction with 'An Evening with a Professor program'

Held one-man exhibition at the Northwestern Bank of Commerce, Duluth

Participated in the Dong Kingman Watercolor Workshop, Fargo, North Dakota

'St Paul Boat Club' received Travel Award in the American Watercolor Society's Annual National Exhibition, New York City

'Foggy Harbor' received Award of Excellence in the Northern Lights Art Exhibition, Minnesota

'Spring Thaw' was one of 30 prize winners in the 1979 National Artists in Watercolor Competition sponsored by TH Saunders and Bockingford Papers

'Grain Elevators' exhibited in the Midwest Watercolor Society's Annual National Exhibition

'Minnesota Winter' exhibited in the Sumi-e Society of America Annual National Exhibition

1980

Elected Signature Member of the Midwest Watercolor Society

Exhibited in the Minnesota State Fair Fine Art Exhibition, St Paul

'The Ore Carriers' received Gold Medal of Honor in the Allied Artists of America's Annual National Exhibition, New York

'Duluth Alley' received Pauline G West Award in the Knickerbocker Artists' Annual National Exhibition, New York

'Rainy Day Toronto' received Midwest Watercolor Society Vice-President's Award in the Midwest Watercolor Society's Annual National Exhibition

'The Harbor' received Award of Merit and William J Rutledge Purchase Award in the Kentucky Watercolor Society's Annual National Exhibition

'Happy Family' received Merit Award in the 44th Arrowhead Art Exhibition sponsored by the Duluth Art Institute

'Grain Terminals' exhibited in the Rocky Mountain National Watermedia Exhibition, Golden, Colorado

'Winter Woods' exhibited in Audubon Artists' National Exhibition, National Art Club, New York

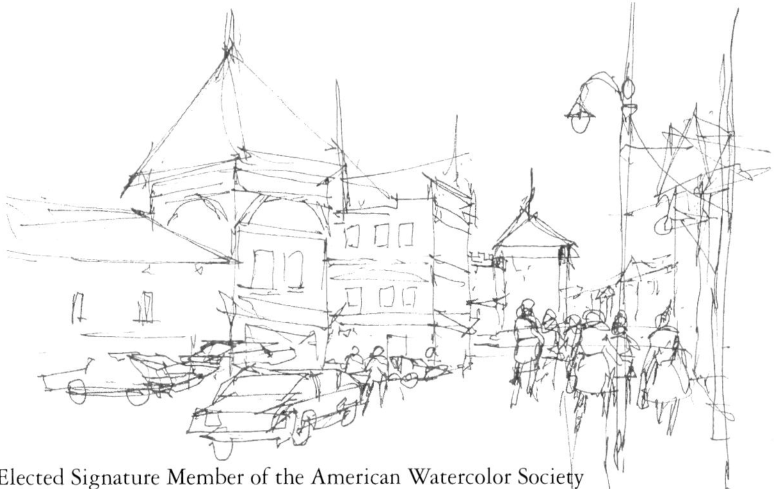

1981

Elected Signature Member of the American Watercolor Society

Promoted to Assistant Professor of the University of Minnesota

Held one-man exhibition at the Itasca Community College, Grand Rapids, Minnesota

'For Watercolorist Chee, the Work Has Just Begun', a feature article by Robert Ashenmacher published in *Duluth News-Tribune Sunday Supplement Accent North*, March 29

'Cheng-Khee Chee – Artist', a TV program produced by Robert Pietrs and Lee Wall of WDIO TV Duluth

'Rainy Day – New York' received Travel Award in the Kentucky Watercolor Society's Annual National Exhibition

'Grain Terminals' received Travel Award in the American Watercolor Society's Annual National Exhibition

'Happy Family' received Rebecca Coleman Memorial Award in the Georgia Watercolor Society's Annual National Exhibition

'Goldfish 81 No. 2' received Grumbacher Bronze Medallion Award in the Knickerbocker Artists' Annual National Exhibition

'The Blizzard' exhibited in the Salmagundi Club Non-member National Juried Exhibition, New York

'The Ore Carriers' exhibited in the Northern Lights Art Exhibition, White Bear Lake, Minnesota

1982

Held *Cheng-Khee Chee Retrospective Exhibition, 1973 – 1982* at Tweed Museum of Art, University of Minnesota, Duluth, Dec 5 1982 – Jan 16, 1983

Published *Cheng-Khee Chee Retrospective Exhibition* Catalogue

Established the Lake Superior Watercolor Society and held the first Annual Membership Exhibition at Tweed Museum of Art, University of Minnesota, Duluth

Elected Signature Member of the Georgia Watercolor Society

Listed in *Who's Who in American Art*, 15th ed. RR Bowker, New Providence, New Jersey, 1982

Served as Juror of Awards, Northern Wisconsin Art Exhibition, Ashland, Wisconsin

Organised and co-led (with Terry Anderson) the University of Minnesota Art and Craft Tour of China, Aug 1 – 22. The itinerary included Hong Kong, Guangzhou, Beijing, Tianjin, Xian, Nanjing, Suzhou, Shanghai and Hangzhou

Visited the Zhejiang Academy of Fine Arts and met with academic leaders to discuss the possibility of establishing an exchange program with the University of Minnesota

Visited hometown Fenting, Sianyou, Fujian

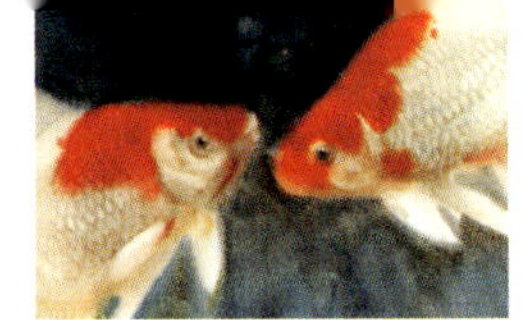

1979 年

应邀在明尼苏达都鲁市西北商业银行举行个人画展
应邀在明尼苏达大学都鲁市学城举行个人画展并作“水彩艺术”专题演讲
参加曾景文水彩研究班
开始在明尼苏达大学都鲁市学城讲授水彩课程
“圣保罗游艇俱乐部”获美国水彩画会全国年展巡迴展览奖
“雾中码头”获北极光美术展览优胜奖
“初春解冻”获白金福特纸厂水彩比赛荣誉奖
“谷仓码头”入选美国中西部水彩画会全国年展
“明尼苏达冬天”入选美国墨画会全国年展

1980 年

获选美国中西部水彩画会署名会员
参加明尼苏达州美术展览
“铁矿船”获美国美术家联盟全国年展金牌奖
“都鲁市后巷”获美国尼葛巴葛美术家协会全国年展波琳韦斯特奖
“多伦多雨天”获美国中西部水彩画会全国年展副主席奖和普度大学购藏奖

1980 年

“码头”获美国肯塔基水彩画会全国年展优胜奖和购藏奖
“快乐的家庭”获美国中西部五州第四十四届展览荣誉奖
“谷仓码头”入选美国石山区全国水彩展览
“树林之冬”入选纽约奥都棒美术协会全国年展

1981 年

获选美国水彩画会署名会员
升任明尼苏达大学助理教授
应邀在明尼苏达州艾塔斯卡学院举行个人画展
都鲁市《新闻报》专题报导“水彩画家徐靖沂的工作才开始”3.29
都鲁市 WDIOTV 电视台播送专题节目“水彩画家徐靖沂”
“纽约雨天”获美国肯塔基水彩画会全国年展巡回展览奖
“谷仓码头”获美国水彩画会全国年展巡回展览奖
“快乐的家庭”获美国佐治亚州水彩画会全国年展丽贝卡科尔曼纪念奖
“金鱼组画 81 年 2 号”获美国尼葛巴葛美术家协会全国年展古兰芭葛铜牌奖
“暴风雪”入选纽约沙马甘地艺术协会全国非会员年展
“铁矿船”入选北极光美术展览

1982 年

在明尼苏达大学都鲁市学城艺术馆举行 1973–1982 个人回顾展
出版徐靖沂水彩画回顾展览目录
创立苏必烈湖水彩画会并在明尼苏达大学都鲁市学城艺术馆举行第一届会员展览
获选美国佐治亚洲水彩画会署名会员
列入《美国美术家名人录》
挡任威斯康辛州北部美术展览评审
组织并带领明尼苏达大学中国工艺美术参观团去中国。行程包括香港、广州、北京、天津、西安、南京、苏州、上海和杭州
参观浙江美术学院并与院领导商谈和明尼苏达大学建立学术关系的办法。到久别的福建仙游枫亭家乡探亲
访问汕头，在韩江江畔写生并凭吊韩愈
去桂林漓江游览写生
“湖岸组画 82 年 1 号”获美国中西部水彩画会全国年展优胜奖
“湖岸组画 82 年 3 号”获爱地兰特美国水彩全国展览北区美术家协会奖
“石、浪、鸥”获美国大湖区域美术展览水彩组第二奖和购藏奖
“铁矿船”获美国佐治亚州水彩画会全国年展中部信用银行奖
“金鱼组画 81 年 1 号”获美国墨画会全国年展亚司多摩奖

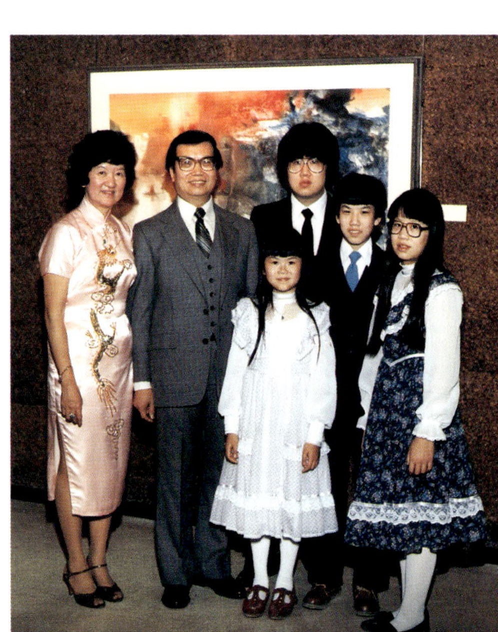

Family portrait taken at show opening of One-Man retrospective exhibition at Tweed Museum of Art, University of Minnesota, Duluth, 1982

一九八二年在明尼苏达大学举行十年回顾展

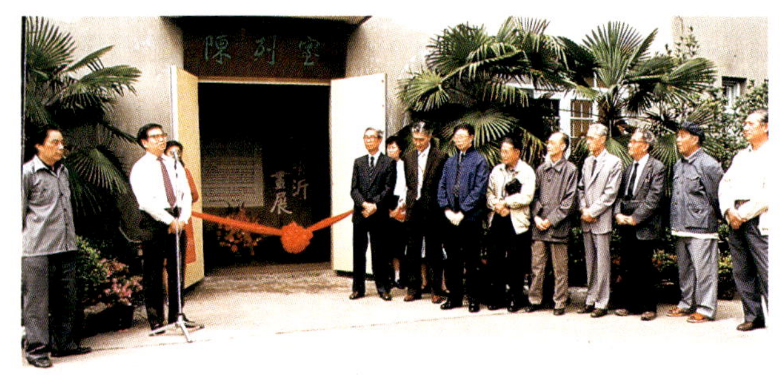

Opening ceremony of the Shanghai University Academy of Fine Arts Art Gallery
上海大学美术学院
展览馆开幕典礼

Travelled to Guilin to sketch & paint

'Lake Shore 82 No. 1' received Western Reserve Award in the Midwest Watercolor Society's Annual National Exhibition

'Lake Shore 82 No. 3' received North Country Artists Guild Award in the Adirondacks National Exhibition of American Watercolors, Old Forge, New York

'Rocks, Surf, Gulls' received 2nd Prize in Watercolor and Women's Federal Purchase Award in the Great Lakes Regional Art Exhibition, Chagrin Falls, Ohio

'The Ore Carriers' received Trust Bank of Georgia Award in Georgia Watercolor Society's Annual National Exhibition

'Goldfish 81 No. 1' received Yasutomo Award in the Sumi-e Society of America's National Exhibition

1983 Held one-man exhibition at the Itasca Community College, Grand Rapid, Minnesota

Exhibited 'Watercolor Paintings by 15 American Watercolor Society members from the East Coast and Midwest', Mitchell Museum, Mount Vernon, Illinois, Jan 8 – Feb 6

Exhibited in Sumi-e Society of America's '20th Anniversary Invitational Exhibition', Meridian House International, Washington DC, March 23 – April 30

Elected Signature Member of the National Watercolor Society

Co-led the 'Watercolor and Culture Adventures in England Tour' July 7 – 25 to paint & study British watercolor and culture

Featured in WDSE TV 'Venture North Program', Duluth, Feb 3 and 6

Featured in the 'University of Minnesota Matrix Program', Jan 30 & Feb 20

Served as Juror of Awards, Fargo Regional Art Exhibition, North Dakota

Served as Juror of Awards, *Duluth News-Tribune* Press Award, Fine Arts Category

'The Forbidden City' received MWS Award & Robert Simon Award in the Midwest Watercolor Society's Annual National Exhibition

'Fenting – My Hometown' received Atlanta Artists' Club Award in the Georgia Watercolor Society's Annual National Exhibition

'Rainy Day – Duluth' published in a limited ed. of 125 prints, the Depot Foundation, Duluth

1984 Established the University of Minnesota Duluth 'Chinese Landscape Painting and Watercolor Painting Program' at the Zhejiang (China) Academy of Fine Arts in Hangzhou. Led the first group of American artists to China, May 20 – July 14

Travelled to Hong Kong, Hangzhou, Shaoxin, Guilin, Huangshan, Wuxi, Shanghai, Nanjing and Beijing

Held one-man exhibition at the Zhejiang (China) Academy of Fine Arts in Hangzhou, China

Elected Signature Member of the Rocky Mountain National Watermedia Society

Published *Cheng-Khee Chee Watercolor Portfolio*

'Autumn 83 No. 1' received Best in Show Award in the Sumi-e Society of America's National Exhibition

'Shanghai Morning' received Grumbacher Gold Medallion Award in the Midwest Watercolor Society's Annual National Exhibition

'The Lost Horizon 84 No. 1' received 2nd Prize in the 'Patrons Watercolor Gala' sponsored by the Oklahoma Christian College

1985 For second time led American artists to the Zhejiang (China) Academy of Fine Arts in Hangzhou to study Chinese painting and calligraphy

Travelled to Dong Hu, Shaoxin, Wuxi, Guilin, Shanghai, Nanjing and Beijing

Held one-man exhibition at J-Michael Galleries, Edina, Minnesota

Exhibited in Blandin Foundation's Inaugural Exhibition at its new headquarters, Grand Rapids, Minnesota

Exhibited in Oriental Brush Painting Society of America's Second Annual Exhibition, 'Landscape in All Seasons', Oklahoma Centre of Science and Arts, Oklahoma

Hong Shi-Qing's article 'The Watercolor Paintings of Cheng-Khee Chee' published in *Fujian Pictorial*, Sep 1985

'Goldfish 85 No. 1' received Grumbacher Gold Medallion Award (First Prize) in the Midwest Watercolor Society's Annual National Exhibition

'Autumn 83 No. 1' received Gold Award in the Georgia Watercolor Society's Annual National Exhibition

'Winter Landscape' received Richard Beueley Memorial Award in the Oklahoma Watercolor Association's Annual National Exhibition

'Watertown 85 No. 2' received Second Prize in the 'Patrons Watercolor Gala' sponsored by the Oklahoma Christian College

'Lake Shore 82 No. 3' published in limited editions of 550 prints by Artists' Impressions, Minneapolis

'Winter Pleasure' published in limited editions of 550 prints by Artists' Impressions, Minneapolis

'The Basilica' published in limited editions of 300 prints, Courage Center, Minneapolis

'The Duluth Marina' published in limited editions of 250 prints by the Duluth Convention and Visitors Bureau, Duluth

1986 Listed in *Who's Who in the Midwest*, Marquis Who's Who, New Providence, New Jersey

Lok Tok 'Professor Cheng-Khee Chee's World of Watercolor' published in Kong Wah Daily Sunday Supplement (Penang, Malaysia), Oct 12 and 19, 1986

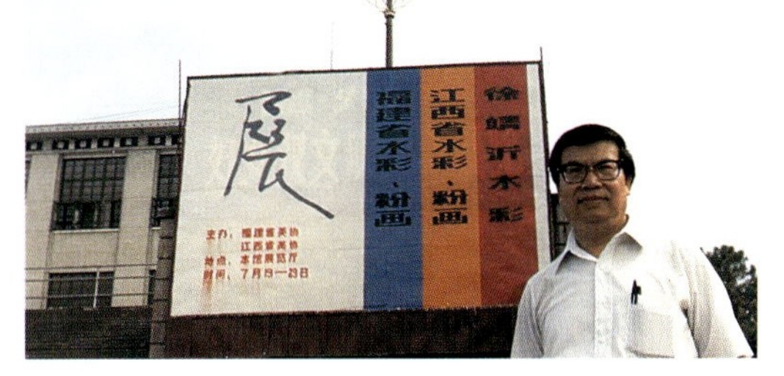

May First Square Exhibition Hall in Fuzhou

福州五一广场展览馆

1983 年

获选美国全国水彩画会署名会员
应邀在明尼苏达爱德思卡学院举行个人画展
参加伊利诺州米切尔博物馆举办美国水彩画会东部和西部十五名会员邀请展览
参加美国墨画会二十周年纪念邀请展览
挡任美国北达科达美术展览评审
带领明尼苏达大学绘画班去英国考察美术和写生
都鲁市教育电视台播送专题节目“水彩画家徐靖沂”
“紫禁城”获美国中西部水彩画会全国年展特优奖
“枫亭－我的家乡”获美国佐治亚州水彩画会全国年展阿兰大美术家协会奖

1984 年

在杭州浙江美术学院举行个人画展
获选美国石山区水彩画会署名会员
出版活页《徐靖沂水彩画辑》
组织明尼苏达大学中国绘画学习班并带领学员去杭州浙江美术学院学习中国绘画和书法。结业后在中国游览写生。行程包括黄山、桂林、无锡、绍兴、上海、南京和北京。
“秋组画 83 年 1 号”获美国墨画会全国年展第一奖
“上海之晨”获美国中西部水彩画会全国年展古兰芭葛金牌奖
“缥缈组画84年1号”获美国奥克拉荷马基督教大学全国年展第二奖

1985 年

第二次带领明尼苏达大学中国绘画学习班学员去杭州浙江美术学院学习中国绘画和书法。
结业后在中国游览写生
在明尼亚玻利斯市杰麦各画廊举行个人画展
参加明尼苏达州布兰丁基金会大厦落成美术展览
洪世清文章”徐靖沂的水彩画“在《福建画报》1985.9 发表，转载《人民日报》海外版 1985.11.26
“金鱼组画85年1号”获中西部水彩画会全国年展古兰芭葛金牌奖（第一奖）
“秋组画83年1号”获美国佐治亚州水彩画会全国年展金牌奖
“冬的大地”获奥克拉荷马水彩画会全国年展理查标利纪念奖
“水乡组画85年2号”获美国奥克拉荷马基督教大学全国年展第二奖
“湖岸组画 82 年 3 号”出版限数复印画 500 幅
“冬天乐”出版限数复印画 500 幅
“都鲁游艇坞”由旅游局出版限数复印画 250 幅
“明尼亚玻利斯天主教堂”出版限数复印画 300 幅

1986 年

列入《美国中西部名人录》
骆拓文章“徐靖沂教授的水彩世界”在光华日报星期刊 1986.10.12 & 19 发表
第三次带领明尼苏达大学中国绘画学习班学员去杭州浙江美术学院学习中国绘画与书法结业候在中国游览写生
“水乡组画85年2号”获美国中西部水彩画会全国年展芝加哥美术联盟奖
“松鼠组画 85 年 1 号”获美国墨画会全国年展第一奖
“冬天乐”获美国纽奥良美术协会全国年展第一奖
“水乡组画 85 年 1 号”获爱地兰德美国水彩全国展览第二奖
”杭州后巷”获佐治亚州水彩画会全国年展温莎牛顿奖
“漓江组画86年1号”获纽约沙马甘地艺术协会全国非会员年展水彩第一奖

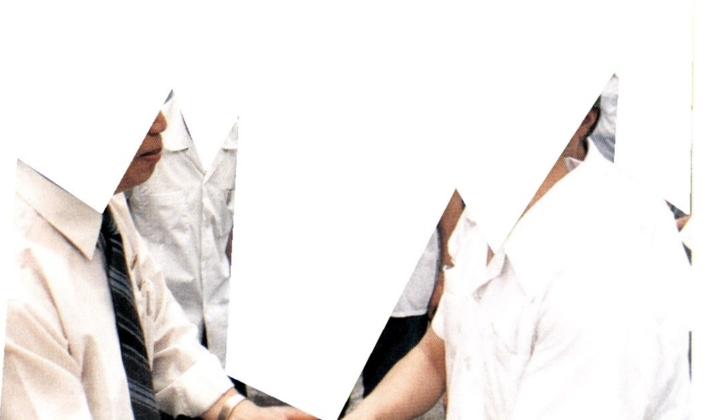

President Xiao Feng and Vice President Wang De Wei welcomed Prof. Chee and the American students at the Zhejiang Academy of Fine Arts

肖峰院长和王德威副院长
欢迎徐靖教授及学员

For the third time led American artists to the Zhejiang (China) Academy of Fine Arts in Hangzhou

Travelled to Ningbo, Shaoxin, Guilin, Shanghai, Nanjing, Beijing

'Watertown 85 No. 2' received Municipal Art League of Chicago Award in the Midwest Watercolor Society's Annual National Exhibition

'Squirrels 85 No. 1' received Best in Show Award in the Sumi-e Society of America's National Exhibition

'Winter Pleasure' received First Place Award in the New Orleans Art Association's National Art Exhibition

'Watertown 85 No. 1' received Old Forge Hardware Prize (2nd Place Award) in the Adirondacks National Exhibition of American Watercolors

'Hangzhou Alley 85 No. 1' received Winsor & Newton Award on the Georgia Watercolor Society's Annual National Exhibition

'Along the Li River 86 No. 1' received Elliot Liskin Award in the Salmagundi Club's Non-member National Art Exhibition, New York

1987 Held one-man watercolor touring exhibition & lectured in China at the invitation of the Zhejiang (China) Academy of Fine Arts and the Chinese Artists Association's Provincial Branches. Exhibiting cities, dates, and sponsors:

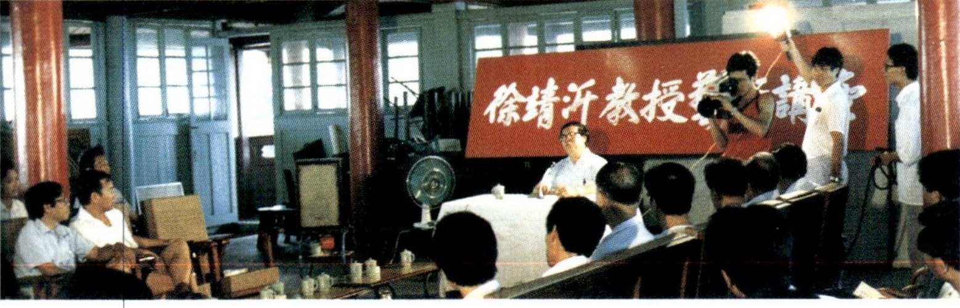

Lecture sponsored by the Chinese Artists Association Fujian branch, Fuzhou Art Academy and the Fujian watercolor

中国美协福建公会，福州画院，福建水彩协会
联合举办讲座

Zhejiang (China) Academy of Fine Arts, Hangzhou, June 1 – 12

Shanghai University college of Fine Arts, Shanghai, June 17 – 26

Nanjing Normal University, Nanjing, July 3 – 10

May First Square Exhibition Hall, Fuzhou, July 19 – 29

Shangdong Province Art Museum, Jinan, Aug 13 – 18

Guangzhou Academy of Fine Arts, Guangzhou, Sep 1 – 14

Hunan University, Changsa, Oct 19 – 30

Jiang Xi Normal University, Nanchang, Nov 19 – 29

Tianjin Academy of Fine Arts, Tianjin, Dec

Published *Cheng-Khee Chee Watercolor Exhibition Catalogue*

Published *Cheng-Khee Chee Watercolor Exhibition Portfolio*

Articles about Cheng-Khee Chee published this year:

Han Shan-Yi. 'Appreciation of Cheng-Khee Chee's Watercolors', *Wen Hui Bao* (Wen Hui Daily, Shanghai), June 22 1987

Hong Zai-Xin. 'The Watercolor Paintings of Cheng-Khee Chee', *Mei Shu* (Art, Beijing), Sep 1987

King, Shannon. 'Cheng-Khee Chee: East meets West', *Midwest Art US Art*, Nov/Dec 1987

Vileta, Jean. 'Cheng-Khee Chee: Closing the Gap between East and West', *Zenith City Arts* (Duluth), Sep 1987

Zhou Lu-Man. 'An Eastern Artist Marches Toward the World: An Interview with Chinese American Artist Cheng-Khee Chee', *Hua Shen Bao* (Voice of Overseas Chinese, Beijing), Aug 14 1987

Zhou Shi-Cheng. 'On Cheng-Khee Chee's Watercolors', *Xin Mei Shu* (New Art, Journal of the Zhejiang Academy of Fine Arts), June 1987

Zhu Jin-Lou. 'From Abstraction to Realism: Watercolorist Cheng-Khee Chee's Theory & Practice', *Xin Mei Shu* (New Art, Journal of the Zhejiang Academy of Fine Arts), June 1987

Travelled to Qingdao and lectured at the Qingdao Art Association
Travelled to Jinan and lectured at the Shandong Academy of Fine Arts
Travelled to Taishan and Qifu, paid respect to Confucius
Travelled to Chongqin, took a boat ride from Chongqin to Wuhan
Travelled to Ningbo and Puto Shan

Honored as Advisor of the Shanghai Watercolor Society

Honored as Advisor of the Fujian Watercolor Society

Honored as Zhejiang Watercolor Society's Honorary Member

Exhibited in 'Research and Exploration, A Combined Studio Arts Faculty Exhibition from all campuses of the University of Minnesota', Tweed Museum, Duluth

'Winter Harbor' received MWS Skyledge Award (First Place Award) in the Midwest Watercolor Society's Annual National Exhibition

'Springtime Lake View' published in a limited edition of 500 prints

'St Paul Cathedral' published in a limited edition of 750 prints

1988 Promoted to Associate Professor of Art of the University of Minnesota

Received Distinguished Artist-Teachers Award from the Sumi-e Society of America

Exhibited in the Tweed Museum of Art's 30th Anniversary Commemorative Exhibition, Duluth

Exhibited in the Sumi-e Society of America's 25th Anniversary Invitational Exhibition

Served as Juror of Awards for the Montana Watercolor Society's Annual National Exhibition

Served as Juror of Awards for the Idaho Watercolor Society's Annual Exhibition

Minneapolis Star Tribune featured Michelle Miller's article 'East Meet West in Studio of Duluth Watercolorist Chee', July 7

City of Duluth presented the painting 'Lake Shore Surf' to its sister city Petrozvosk of Russia

'Chongqing No. 1' received Award of Excellence in the Midwest Watercolor Society's National Exhibition

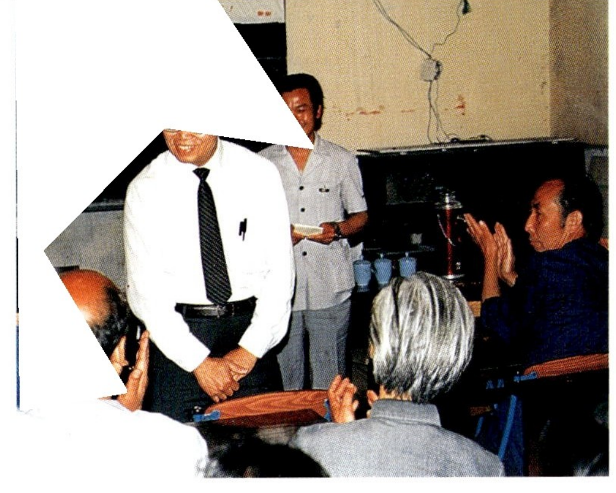

Qing Dao Artists Association
青岛美术协会

1987 年

应浙江美术学院及中国美术家协会各省分会之邀请，在中国举办个人水彩画巡回展览和讲学。展出城市、地点、日期、及举办机构如下：

杭州浙江美术学院，六月一日至十二日

上海大学美术学院，六月十七日至二十六日

南京师范大学美术馆，七月三日至十日

福建福州五一广场展览馆，七月十九日至二十九日

济南山东省美术馆，八月十三日至十八日

广州美术学院，九月一日至十四日

长沙湖南大学岳麓书院，十月十九日至三十日

南昌江西师范大学美术馆，十一月十九日至二十九日

天津美术学院，十二月

出版《徐靖沂水彩画展目录》

长沙湖南大学岳麓书院，十月十九日至三十日

南昌江西师范大学美术馆，十一月十九日至二十九日

天津美术学院，十二月

出版《徐靖沂水彩画展目录》

出版活页《徐靖沂水彩画辑》

朱金楼文章“抽象的开始具象的结束：水彩画家徐靖沂的理论与实践”在《新美术》107.2 发表

周诗诚文章“徐靖沂先生的水彩画”在《新美术》107.2 发表

周鲁闽文章“走向世界的东方画家，记美藉华人画家徐靖沂教授”在《华声报》1987.8.14 发表

洪再兴文章“徐靖沂的水彩画”在《美术》1987.9 发表

韩尚义文章“欣赏徐靖沂的水彩画”在《文汇报》1987.6.22 发表

金善能文章“徐靖沂：东西相逢”（英文）在《中西部美术》(Midwest Art) 1987.11/12 p.60–65 发表

维烈大文章“徐靖沂：缩短东西的距离”（英文）在《天顶美术》(Zenith Art, Duluth) 1987.9 发表

游青岛，在青岛美术协会讲学

游济南，在山东美术学院讲学

游泰山，曲阜，瞻仰孔庙孔林

游重庆，从重庆下长江到武汉。在杭州时顺道游宁波和普陀山

上海水彩画研究会聘请为该会顾问

福建水彩画研究会聘请为该会顾问

浙江水彩画研究会聘请为该会荣誉会员

参加明尼苏达大学美术系教授作品联合展览

“码头之冬”获美国中西部水彩画会全国年展第一奖

“湖岸春光”出版限数复印画 500 幅

“圣保罗教堂”出版限数复印画 750 幅

1988 年

升任明尼苏达大学副教授

获美国墨画会杰出画家／教师奖

参加明尼苏达大学都鲁市学城艺术馆建立 30 周年纪念展览

参加美国墨画会 25 周年纪念展览

挡任美国蒙天那州水彩画会全国年展评审

挡任美国爱大候州水彩画会全国年展评审

《明尼亚波利斯市星报》介绍徐靖沂及其作品 7.7B 版

都鲁市以“湖浪拍岸”一画赠送俄国姐妹城

“重庆组画 1 号”获美国中西部水彩画会全国年展优胜奖

1989 年

获选美国尼葛巴葛美术家协会署名会员

都鲁市总商会杂志《都鲁人》介绍徐靖沂及其作品 1989.3/4

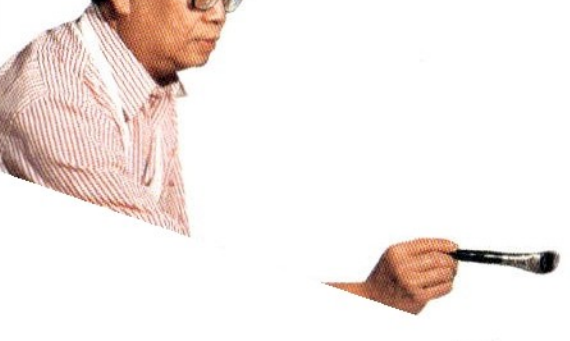

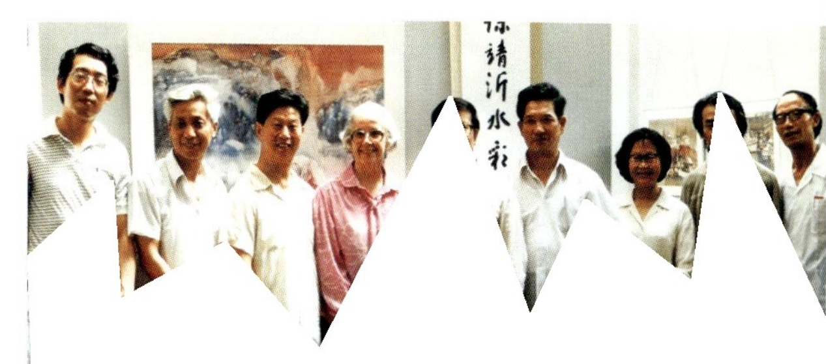

Zhejiang Academy of Fine Arts Exhibition Hall
浙江美术学院展览馆

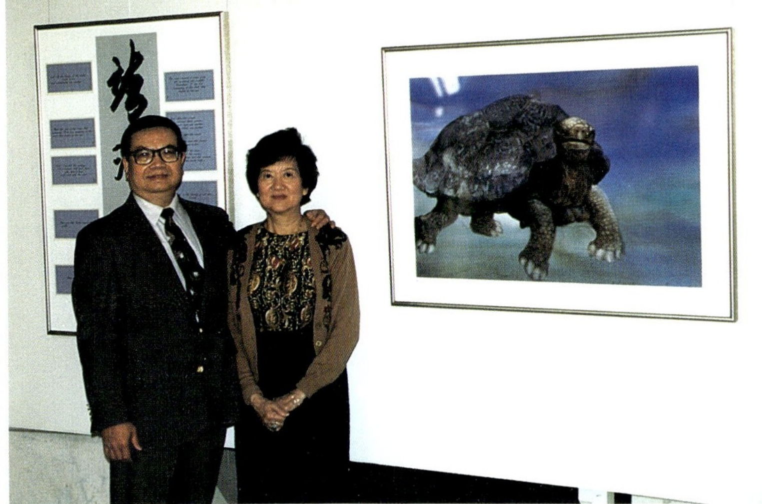

Paintings for the children's book Old Turtle were exhibited at the Cannon House Office Building, Rotunda Gallery, Washington DC, Nov 1993
一九九三年十一月童话《老乌龟》
水彩插图在美国国会圆堂展出

1989 Elected Signature Member of the Knickerbocker Artists USA

Featured in *The Duluthian* 'A Man of All Seasons' by Jane Bissett, March/April

Served as Juror of Selection and Awards for the Iowa Watercolor Society's Annual Exhibition

Interviewed by Roy Flynn, WDSE TV Venture North, Jan 19 and 22, Duluth

Interviewed by Patty Craig, KBJR TV, Channel 6, Apr 28, Duluth

'Koi 89 No. 1' received Gold Medal of Honor in the Knickerbocker Artists' Annual National Exhibition

'Ningbo Harbor' received Special Merit Award in the Midwest Watercolor Society's National Exhibition

'Along the Li River 86 No. 1' received Grumbacher Gold Medallion Award in the Georgia Watercolor Society's Annual National Exhibition

'Along the Li River 89 No. 1' received Travel Award in Adirondacks Exhibition of American Watercolors

'Along the Li River 86 No. 2' received the Winifred Morse Award for a Watercolor in the Salmagundi Club's Annual National Exhibition for Non-members, New York

'Summer at the Bay' published in a limited edition of 950 prints

1990 Held one-man exhibition at the Bloomington Art Center, Bloomington, Minnesota

Held one-man exhibition at the Owatonna Art Center, Owatonna, Minnesota

Exhibited in 'Metaphorical Fish', University of Minnesota Art Museum Invitational Exhibition, Minneapolis, Minnesota

Exhibited in the 'University of Minnesota Faculty Artists and Writers Exhibition', Paul Whitney Larson Gallery, St Paul

Served as Juror of Selection for the Midwest Watercolor Society's Annual National Exhibition

City of Duluth presented the painting 'Springtime Lake View' to sister city Ohara, Japan

Painted watercolors to illustrate the children's book *Old Turtle*

Featured in *Watercolor 90, an American Artist Publication*, Spring Issue

'Koi 90 No. 1' received President's Award in the Montana Watercolor Society's National Exhibition

'Autumn 89 No. 1' received the North East Watercolor Society Award in its Annual National Exhibition

'Koi 90 No. 3' received Winsor & Newton Award in the Oklahoma Watercolor Association's Annual National Exhibition

1991 *Old Turtle*, text by Douglas Wood, watercolors by Cheng-Khee Chee, published by Pfeifer-Hamilton of Duluth

Exhibited in 'Diversity of Influence, Works by University of Minnesota Studio Art Faculty', Tweed Museum of Art, University of Minnesota, Duluth

Held one-man exhibition at Phipps Center for the Arts, Hudson, Wisconsin

Paintings from the Old Turtle were exhibited at the Tweed Museum of Art, University of Minnesota, Duluth, Nov 15 1991 – Jan 5 1992

'Koi 90 No. 9' received Silver Medal of Honor in American Watercolor Society's International Exhibition

'Koi 90 No. 4' received Humana Foundation Award (First Prize) in the Kentucky Watercolor Society's Annual National Exhibition

'Hangzhou Alley' received Transparent Watercolor Award in Knickerbocker Artists' National Exhibition

'Hangzhou Alley' received the Ballantyne Memorial Award in the Allied Artists of America's Annual National Exhibition, New York

'Koi 90 No. 2' received Special Merit Award in the Midwest Watercolor Society's Annual Exhibition

'Koi 90 No. 10' received Bitterroot Award in the Montana Watercolor Society's National Exhibition

'Watertown 90 No. 1' received Grumbacher Gold Medallion Award (First Prize) in the North East Watercolor Society's Annual National Exhibition

'Watertown 89 No. 1' received Adam Group Award in the Georgia Watercolor Society's Annual National Exhibition

'Autumn 89 No. 1' received Albert Gordon Memorial Award in the Adirondacks National Exhibition of American Watercolors

'Iris 90 No. 1' published in a limited edition of 950 prints

1992 Elected Signature Member of the Allied Artists of America

Served as Juror of Selection for the Adirondacks National Exhibition of American Watercolors

Exhibited in the 'Asian-American Renaissance Conference's Visual Art Invitational Exhibition', College of St Catherine, St Paul, Minnesota

Old Turtle received the Minnesota Young Adult Book Award and the Midwest Best Children's Book Award

Paintings from 'Old Turtle' selected for exhibition in 'Picture This! Contemporary Children's Book Illustration from Minnesota', Minneapolis College of Art and Design

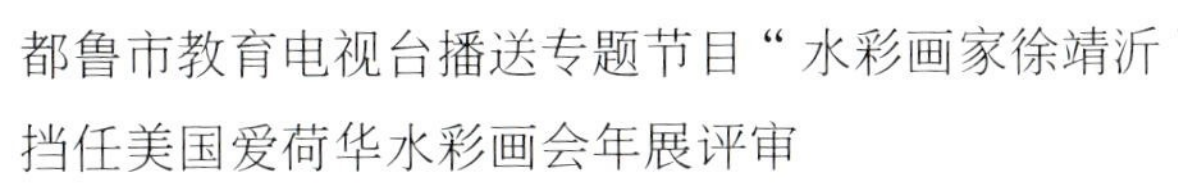

都鲁市教育电视台播送专题节目“水彩画家徐靖沂”
挡任美国爱荷华水彩画会年展评审
“锦鲤组画89年1号”获美国尼葛巴葛美术家协会全国年展金牌奖
“宁波码头”获美国中西部水彩画会全国年展特优奖
“漓江组画89年1号”获美国佐治亚州水彩画会全国年展古兰巴葛金牌奖
“漓江组画89年1号”获爱地兰德美国水彩全国展览巡回展览奖
“漓江组画89年2号”获纽约沙马甘地艺术协会全国非会员年展威尼夫列莫斯奖
“港湾之夏”出版限数复印画950幅

1990年

挡任美国中西部水彩画会全国年展评审
应邀在明尼苏达州布鲁明顿艺术中心举行个人画展
应邀在明尼苏达州奥华多那艺术中心举行个人画展
应邀参加明尼苏达大学艺术博物馆举办“鱼的艺术”作品展览
应邀参加明尼苏达大学美术和作家作品展览
都鲁市以“湖岸春光”一画赠送日本大原姐妹城
为童话《老乌龟》一书绘制插图
《美国美术家》杂志90年水彩特集介绍徐靖沂作品
“锦鲤组画90年1号”获美国蒙天那州水彩画会全国年展会长奖
“秋组画89年1号”获美国东北部水彩画会全国年展东北部水彩画会奖
“锦鲤组画90年3号”获美国奥克拉荷马水彩画会全国年展温莎牛顿奖

1991年

出版活页《徐靖沂水彩画辑》
应邀在威斯康辛州菲必斯艺术中心举行个人画展
童话《老乌龟》一书出版，吴达作文，徐靖沂绘制水彩插图
参加明尼苏达大学美术系教授作品展览
“锦鲤组画90年9号”获美国水彩画会国际年展银牌奖
“锦鲤组画90年4号”获美国肯塔基水彩画会全国年展第一奖
“杭州后巷89年1号”获美国尼葛巴葛美术家协会全国年展透明水彩奖
“杭州后巷89年1号”获美国美术家联盟全国年展波兰亭纪念奖
“锦鲤组画90年2号”获美国中西部水彩画会全国年展特优奖
“锦鲤组画90年10号”获美国蒙天那州水彩画会全国年展必得录奖
“水乡组画90年1号”获美国东北部水彩画会全国年展古兰芭葛金牌奖
“水乡组画89年1号”获美国佐治亚州水彩画会全国年展亚旦集团奖
“秋组画89年1号”获爱地兰德美国水彩全国展览歌顿纪念奖
“蝴蝶兰组画90年1号”出版限数复印画950幅

1992年

获选美国美术家联盟署名会员
明尼苏达大学都鲁市学城艺术馆展出《老乌龟》水彩插图
挡任爱地兰德美国水彩画展评审
参加美国美藉亚洲人复兴会议美术邀请展览
童话《老乌龟》获1992年度明尼苏达州少年图书奖和1992年度美国中西部最佳儿童图书奖
童话《老乌龟》的插图参加明尼亚波利斯美术学院举办的明尼苏达州现代儿童图书插画展览
“金鱼组画92年1号”获美国全国水彩画会全国年展透明水彩奖
荷塘锦鲤”获美国中西部水彩画会全国年展特优奖
“锦鲤组画90年3号”获美国佐治亚州水彩画会全国年展银牌奖
“锦鲤组画90年3号”获美国尼葛巴葛美术家协会全国年展透明水彩奖

1993年

列入《美国名人录》
列入《北美华裔美术家名人录》

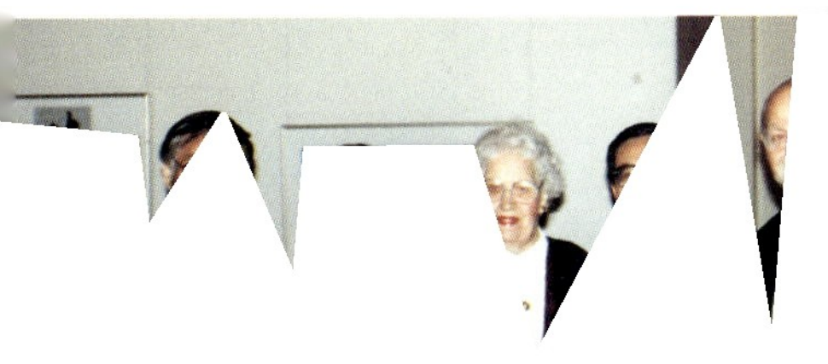

Rotunda Gallery and guests
国会圆堂展厅一瞥

'Goldfish 92 No. 1' received Transparent Watercolor Award in the National Watercolor Society Annual National Exhibition

'Lily Pond with Koi' received Special Merit Award in the Midwest Watercolor Society's National Exhibition

'Koi 90 No. 3' received Silver Award in the Georgia Watercolor Society's Annual National Exhibition

'Koi 90 No. 2' received Transparent Watercolor Award in Knickerbocker Artists' National Exhibition

1993 Listed in *Who's Who in America* 48th ed., Marquis Who's Who, New Providence, New Jersey, 1994

Listed in *Artists of Chinese Origin in North America*, Point Fine Arts Inc., Westmont, Illinois, 1993

Old Turtle received the 1993 American Booksellers Association's Children's Book of the Year Award (ABBY) and the International Reading Association's Children's Book Award. The book became a bestseller

Penang *Kwong Wah Yit Poh* featured the book *Old Turtle* in full color, July 9

Paintings from *Old Turtle* were exhibited in the US Congress House-Office Building's Cannon Rotunda Gallery in November

Exhibited in '(Un)titled', University of Minnesota Studio Art Faculty Exhibition, Duluth

Served as Juror of Selection and Awards for the Georgia Watercolor Society's 1993 National Exhibition & conducted a one-week watercolor workshop

Received the City of Duluth Medal of Honor, presented by Mayor Gary Doty

Interviewed by Julie Kellner, WDSE TV Album Program, Duluth, 2 parts, Apr 15 and 22

Interviewed by Voice of America's Chinese Program, Washington DC, Nov 13

Interviewed by Michael Baker of WNVC TV, Washington DC, Nov 12

'Koi 92 No. 1' received the Knickerbocker Artist' Grand Prize Gold Medal & Purchase Award of $10,000 for Excellence. The Painting became the first work in the Society's permanent collection

'Goldfish 92 No. 1' received Silver Medal of Honor in the Allied Artists of America's National Exhibition

'Goldfish 92 No. 1' received Special Merit Award in the Midwest Watercolor Society's National Exhibition

'Along the Yangzi River 93 No. 1' received First Prize in the Western Colorado Watercolor Society's Annual National Exhibition

'Lake Shore 93 No. 1' received Member's Award in the Montana Watercolor Society's Watermedia 93 National Exhibition

'Koi 90 No. 2' received Grumbacher Gold Medallion Award in the North East Watercolor Society's Annual National Exhibition

'City in Bloom' published in a limited edition of 950 prints

'Sleigh Ride' published in a limited edition of 950 prints

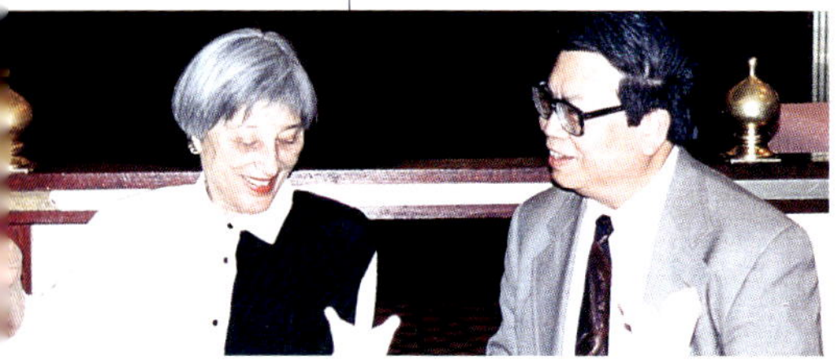

Discussing the book Old Turtle with Dr Han Su Yin at the Nanyang University Global Alumni Reunion in Toronto
一九九二年在多伦多参加南洋大学全球校友联观会与韩素音老师交谈童话《老乌龟》一书

1994 Listed in *Who's Who Among Asian Americans* 1st ed., 1994

Listed in *Something About the Author: Biographical and Bibliographical Guide to Writers and Illustrators of Children's Books*, Gale Research Inc., Detroit, Michigan

Elected Dolphin Fellow of the American Watercolor Society

Served as Juror of Selection for the American Watercolor Society's Annual International Exhibition

Served as Juror of Selection and Awards for the Western Colorado Watercolor Society's National Exhibition

Co-curated American paintings for the 'Watercolor Exhibition by the Artists of ROC, USA and Australia', Taipei, Taiwan

Received the University of Minnesota, Duluth Campus, Chancellor's Distinguished Service Award

Received the University of Minnesota Continuing Education and Extension, Distinguished Teaching Award

Honored as Duluth's Cultural Ambassador to the World by Mayor Gary Doty

Awarded Signature Member of Excellence by the Georgia Watercolor Society

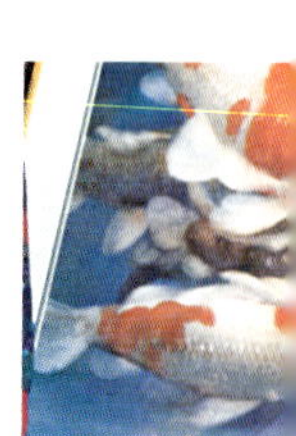

Held one-man exhibition at Waldorf College, Forest City, Iowa

Published *Cheng-Khee Chee Watercolor Portfolio*

Visited Singapore, Malaysia and Fujian to see relatives, friends & to paint & make arrangements for the 1997 Southeast Asia Touring Exhibition

Visited the Singapore Watercolor Society and gave a lecture

Attended opening of the 9th Annual Exhibition of the Asian Watercolor Confederation in Kuala Lumpur

'Lake Shore 93 No. 2' received High Winds Medal in the American Watercolor Society's Annual International Exhibition

'Goldfish 92 No. 1' received Grand Award from the Akron Society of Art's National Grand Exhibition

'Koi 90 No. 4' received Gold Award in the Red River Watercolor Society's National Exhibition

'Koi 94 No. 1' received Edgar Whitney Memorial Award in the Midwest Watercolor Society's Annual National Exhibition

'Lake Shore 94 No. 2' received Piermont Fine Arts Gallery Award in the North East Watercolor Society's Annual National Exhibition

Contributed a chapter on Cheng-Khee Chee watercolor techniques and 10 paintings in color reproductions to the book *Learn Watercolor the Edgar Whitney Way*, North Light Publications, Cincinnati, Ohio

'Koi 90 No. 4' & 'Lake Shore 93 No. 2' selected for publication in *Splash 3: Ideas and Inspirations*, North Light Publications, Cincinnati

'Roses 94 No. 1' published in a limited edition of 950 prints

参加明尼苏达大学美术系教授作品展览
挡任佐治亚州水彩画会1993年度全国展览评审并主持一星期水彩训练班
都鲁市长授于荣誉奖牌
去新加坡、马来西亚和福建省访问、探亲、写生并安排97年东南亚巡回展览事宜
都鲁市教育电视台播送节目“水彩画家徐靖沂”
华盛顿美国之音中文部专题访问
华盛顿教育电视台童话《老乌龟》一书专题访问
吴凤美特写“徐靖沂教授为《老乌龟》插图赋生命力”在槟榔屿《光华日报》发表 1993.7.9
《老乌龟》童话获美国书业公会 1993 年度儿童图书奖和国际读书会1993年度最佳儿童图书奖而成为美国今年度最畅销的儿童图书
《老乌龟》的大型水彩插图在华盛顿美国国会众议院圆堂展出
《老乌龟》的插图应邀参加明尼亚波利斯美术学院举办的明尼苏达州现代儿童图书插画展览
“锦鲤组画 92 年 1 号”获美国尼葛巴葛美术家协会综合媒介作品年展全场金牌奖和万元购藏奖
“金鱼组画 92 年 1 号”获美国美术家联盟全国年展银牌奖
“金鱼组画 92 年 1 号”获美国中西部水彩画会全国年展特优奖
“长江组画 93 年 1 号”获美国科洛拉多西部水彩画会全国年展第一奖
“湖岸组画 92 年 1 号”获美国蒙天那州水彩画会全国年展会员奖
“锦鲤组画 90 年 2 号”获美国东北部水彩画会全国年展古兰芭葛金牌奖
“满城春花”出版限数复印画 950 幅
“雪橇郊游”出版限数复印画 950 幅

1994 年

列入《美国亚裔名人录》
列入《儿童图书作家和插图家传录》
美国水彩画会授于海豚会士衔

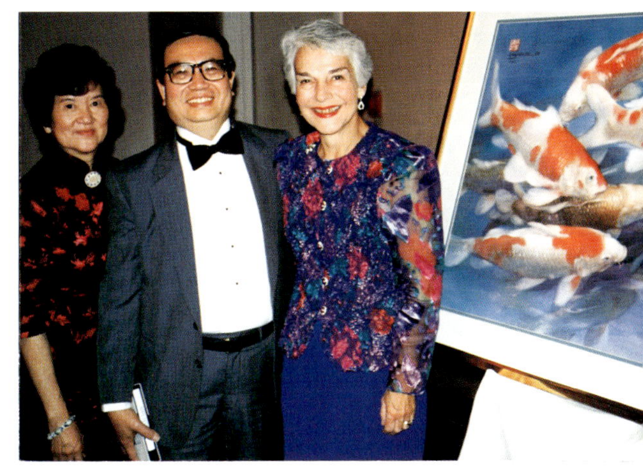

'Koi 92 No. 1' received Gold Medal and Purchase Prize for Excellence in the Knickerbocker Artists 1993 Annual International Exhibition

与锦鲤作品合影

挡任美国水彩画会国际年展评审委员
挡任科洛拉多州西部水彩画会全国年展评审
挡任台北“中美澳三国水彩画联展”美国部分作品评审
明尼达大学都鲁市学城校长授于杰出服务奖
明尼达大学进修部授于杰出教学奖
明尼达都鲁市市长授于都鲁市世界文化大使荣衔
佐治亚州水彩画会授于杰出署名会员奖
应邀在爱荷华州武多夫学院举行个人画展
出版活页《徐靖沂水彩画辑》
去新加坡、马来西亚和福建省访问、探亲、写生并安排97年东南亚巡回展览事宜
访问新加坡水彩画会并举行讲座
参加亚洲水彩联盟在吉隆坡举行第 9 届展览的开幕典礼
《学习爱格威尼水彩法》一书出版，附徐靖沂水彩技法及彩色作品十幅
“湖岸组画 93 年 2 号”获美国水彩画会国际年展高风奖牌
“金鱼组画 92 年 1 号”获美国亚克戎美术协会全国年展冠军奖
“锦鲤组画 94 年 1 号”获美国中西部水彩画会全国年展爱格威尼纪念奖
“湖岸组画 94 年 2 号”获美国东北部水彩画会全国年展比尔门画廊奖
“锦鲤组画90年4号”和“湖岸组画93年2号”被选入《泼彩三：意念与灵感》一书发表
“玫瑰组画 94 年 1 号”出版限数复印画 950 幅

1995 年

列入《华人艺术家成就博览大典》
挡任红河水彩画会全国年展评审

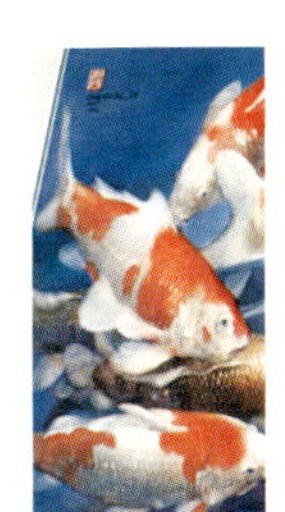

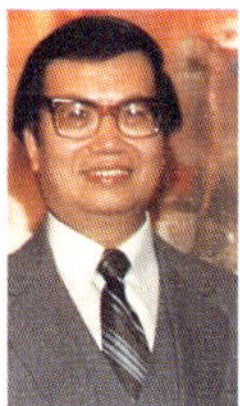

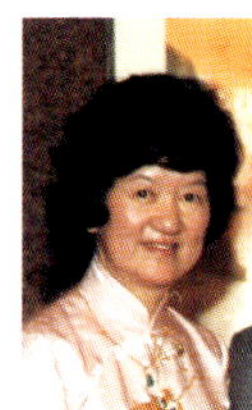

1995 Listed in the *Dictionary of World Chinese Artists Achievements*, Great World Publishing Co., Hong Kong

Lake Superior Magazine featured the article 'Chee Pursuing Excellence – Portrait of the Artist', by Hugh Bishop, May/June 1995

Served as Juror of Selection and Awards for the Red River Watercolor Society's Annual National Exhibition

Lake Superior Paper Industries commissioned the 'Winter Lake View' and published in a limited edition of 950 prints to commemorate its 10th Anniversary

'Goldfish 92 No. 1' received Emily Lowe Memorial Award in the American Watercolor Society's Annual International Exhibition

'Lake Shore 95 No. 1' received Strathmore Paper Company Award in the Kentucky Watercolor Society's Annual National Exhibition

'Lake Shore 95 No. 1' received Creative Watercolor Award in the Allied Artists of America's Annual National Exhibition

Martin Parsons commented, 'Cheng-Khee Chee, on the other hand, demonstrates utmost fluidity in a large, misty atmospheric watercolor that combines the impact of Western abstraction with the poetic delicacy of traditional Chinese landscape painting.' *Artspeak* v. 18 no. 3, Dec 1995/Jan 1996

'Lake Shore 95 No. 3' received Anne Martinez Award in the Western Colorado Watercolor Society's Annual National Exhibition

'Lake Shore 93 No. 2' received Artworks Gallery Award in Montana Watercolor Society's Watermedia 93 Annual National Exhibition

'Koi 94 No. 1' received D'Arches Award in the Georgia Watercolor Society's Annual National Exhibition

'Roses 95 No. 2' received Juror's Award of Excellence in the Oklahoma Art Workshop's National Exhibition

'Goldfish 92 No. 1' selected for publication in the *Best of Watercolor*, Rockport Publishers, Massachusetts

1996 Elected Board Director of the American Watercolor Society to serve 1996-1998 term

Listed in *World Famous Chinese Artists Almanac*, Hong Kong, 1996

Listed in the *Index of Asian American Artists*, Point Fine Arts Inc. Westmont, Illinois, 1996

Visited Singapore and Malaysia to see relatives, friends and to travel and paint

Named as Honorary Member of the Singapore Watercolor Society

Honored with Key to the City of Cloquet by Mayor Fred Little, Minnesota, 1996

'Morning Harbor' selected for publication in *Splash 4: the Splendor of Light*, North Light Publications, Cincinnati

'Iris 90 No. 1' selected for publication in *The Best of Flower Painting*, Rockport Publishers, Rockport, Massachusetts

'The White Iris' published in a limited edition of 950 prints

'The Yacht Club' published in a limited edition of 950 prints

'Lake Shore 95 No. 2' received First Place Award in the Louisiana Watercolor Society's Annual International Exhibition

'The Spirit of Southwest 95 No. 1' received Forest Runes Award in honor of Lloyd Schafer in the Adirondacks National Exhibition of American Watercolors

'The Spirit of Southwest 95 No. 2' received Honorable Mention in New England Watercolor Society's Annual National Exhibition

'Roses 95 No. 1' received Winifred E Morse Award for Best Watercolor in the Salmagundi Club's Annual Non-member National Juried Exhibition, New York

'Goldfish 86 No. 1' received Winsor & Newton Award in the Midwest Watercolor Society's Annual National Exhibition

'The Yacht Club' received 4th Award with Medal in the Pennsylvania Watercolor Society's 17th Juried National Exhibition

'The Koi Pond' received the Mississippi Watercolor Society Award (2nd Prize) in the Mississippi Watercolor Society's Annual National Exhibition

'Roses 95 No. 1' received Leo Smith Memorial Award in the Southwestern Watercolor Society Annual National Exhibition

'Xiamen Harbor 95 No. 2' received the Bernadine Fox Memorial Award in the Montana Watercolor Society's Annual National Exhibition

'Koi 96 No. 1' received Key Bank Award in the Northeast Watercolor Society Annual National Exhibition

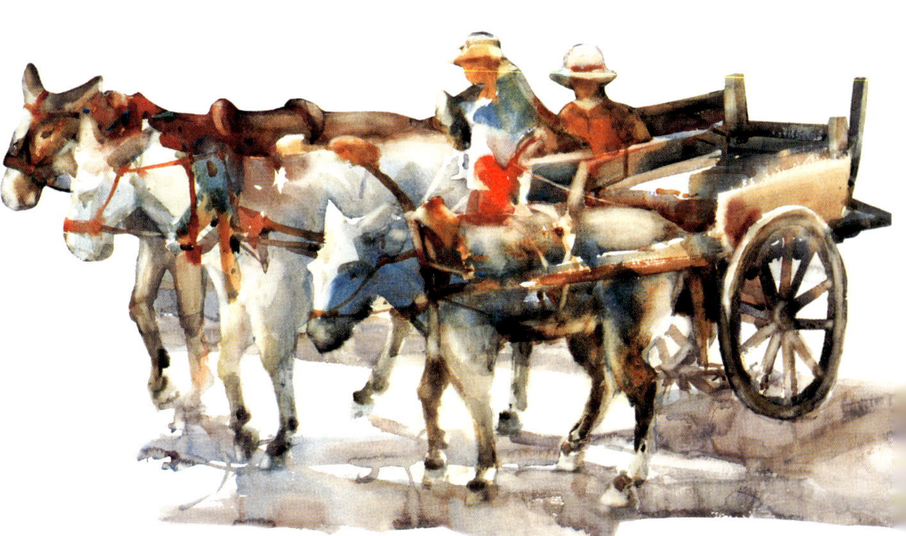

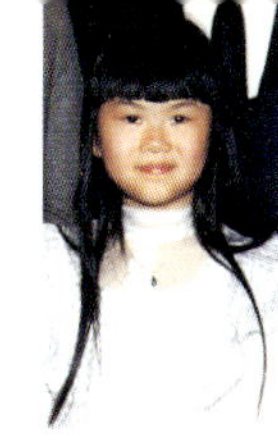

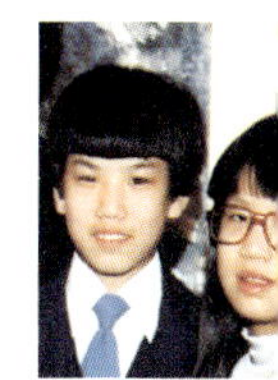

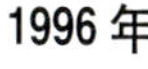

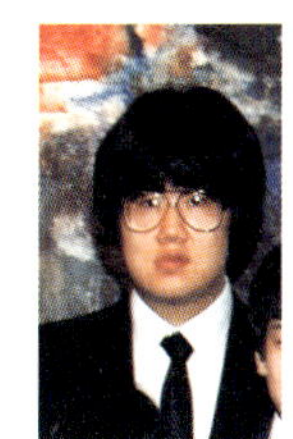

苏必烈湖纸厂出版"冬天的湖景"复印画950幅以庆祝建厂十周年纪念

《苏必烈湖杂志》发表介绍文章"徐靖沂——一位追求至善画家的写照"

"金鱼组画92年1号"获美国水彩画会国际年展艾茉莉罗纪念奖

"湖岸组画95年1号"获美国肯塔基水彩画会全国年展司德司末纸厂奖

"湖岸组画95年2号，获美国美术家联盟全国年展创新水彩奖

纽约艺评家马丁帕尔森在《谈艺术》杂志中评此画说：「徐靖沂的画超然地表现水彩的流动性和气氛的朦胧感。他巧妙地结合西方抽象性的冲击力和传统中国山水画的优美诗意。」

"湖岸组画95年1号"获美国科洛拉多西部水彩画会全国年展安马丁尼芝奖

"湖岸组画93年2号"获美国蒙天那州水彩画会全国年展艾沃克画廊奖

"锦鲤组画94年1号"获美国佐治亚州水彩画会全国年展亚其斯纸厂奖

"玫瑰组画95年2号"获美国奥克拉荷马州美术培训中心全国年展评审优秀作品奖

"金鱼组画92年1号"被选入《最优秀水彩画集》一书

1996年

获选美国水彩画会1996-1998年度理事

列入《世界华人美术名家年鉴》(1996)

列入《北美亚裔美术家名录》

明尼苏达州科洛开市市长李特尔授予荣誉市民钥匙

应邀在明尼苏达州圣克老大学美术馆举行个人画展

去新加坡和马来西亚访问、探亲、写生并为97年东南亚巡回展览作最后安排

新加坡水彩画会授予荣誉会员衔

"渡头之晨"被选入《泼彩四：光的华丽》一书

"蝴蝶兰组画90年1号"被选入《最优秀花卉画集》一书

"白蝴蝶兰"出版限数复印画950幅

"游艇俱乐部"出版限数复印画950幅

"西北精神95年1号"获爱地兰德美国水彩全国展罗会西法荣誉奖

"西北精神95年2号"获新英格兰水彩画会全国年展荣誉奖

"湖岸组画95年2号"获路易斯安那州水彩画会全国年展第一奖

"玫瑰组画95年1号"获纽约沙马甘地艺术协会全国非会员年度威尼夫列莫斯最佳水彩奖

"金鱼组画96年1号"获美国中西部水彩画会全国年展温莎牛顿奖

"游艇俱乐部"获美国宾夕法尼亚州水彩画会全国年展第四奖

"锦鲤荷塘"获美国密西西比州水彩画会全国年展第二奖

"玫瑰组画95年1号"获美国西南部水彩画会全国年展李欧史密斯纪念奖

"厦门码头95年2号"获美国蒙天那州水彩画会全国年展贝娜丁，福克斯纪念奖

"锦鲤组画96年1号"获美国东北部水彩画会全国年展开业银行奖

List of Paintings 作品目录

TRADITIONAL WATERCOLOR 传统水彩

No.	Title	Year	Size (in)	Size (cm)
1	Ore Carriers 铁矿船	1980	25" x 40"	63cm x 102cm
2	The Blizzard 暴风雪	1980	25" x 40"	63cm x 102cm
3	Grain Terminals 谷仓码头	1980	30" x 40"	76cm x 102cm
4	Farm at Twig 农场	1980	25" x 40"	63cm x 102cm
5	Rainy Day – New York 纽约雨天	1981	25" x 40"	63cm x 102cm
6	Fenting – My Hometown 枫亭一我的家乡	1982	25" x 40"	63cm x 102cm
7	Beast of Burden, Xian 西安骡车	1983	25" x 40"	63cm x 102cm
8	Forbidden City 紫禁城	1983	25" x 40"	63cm x 102cm
9	English Fishing Town 英国渔镇	1984	25" x 40"	63cm x 102cm
10	Duluth Harbor 都鲁码头	1984	25" x 40"	63cm x 102cm
11	Watertown 85 No.1 水乡 85 年 1 号	1985	25" x 40"	63cm x 102cm
12	Watertown 85 No.2 水乡 85 年 2 号	1985	25" x 40"	63cm x 102cm
13	Hangzhou Alley 85 No.1 杭州后巷 85 年 1 号	1985	25" x 40"	63cm x 102cm
14	Hangzhou Alley 85 No.2 杭州后巷 85 年 2 号	1985	25" x 40"	63cm x 102cm
15	Winter Harbor 码头之冬	1986	25" x 40"	63cm x 102cm
16	Hangzhou Alley 89 No.1 杭州后巷 89 年 1 号	1989	30" x 40"	76cm x 102cm
17	Watertown 90 No.1 水乡 90 年 1 号	1990	30" x 40"	76cm x 102cm
18	Duluth Winter 92 No.1 都鲁之冬 92 年 1 号	1992	30" x 40"	76cm x 102cm
19	Penang Fishing Boats 槟城渔舟	1993	22" x 30"	56cm x 76cm
20	Fenting Morning 枫亭之晨	1993	22" x 30"	56cm x 76cm
21	Morning Harbor 湄洲之晨	1995	30" x 40"	76cm x 102cm
22	Xiamen Harbor 95 No.1 厦门渡头 95 年 1 号	1995	30" x 40"	76cm x 102cm
23	Xiamen Harbor 95 No.2 厦门渡头 95 年 2 号	1995	30" x 40"	76cm x 102cm
24	Yacht Club 游艇俱乐部	1996	30" x 40"	76cm x 102cm
25	Penang Fishing Village 96 No.1 槟城渔村 96 年 1 号	1996	30" x 40"	76cm x 102cm
26	Malacca Impression 马六甲印象	1996	30" x 40"	76cm x 102cm
27	Singapore Impression 新加坡印象	1996	30" x 40"	76cm x 102cm
28	Kuala Lumpur Impression 吉隆坡印象	1996	30" x 40"	76cm x 102cm

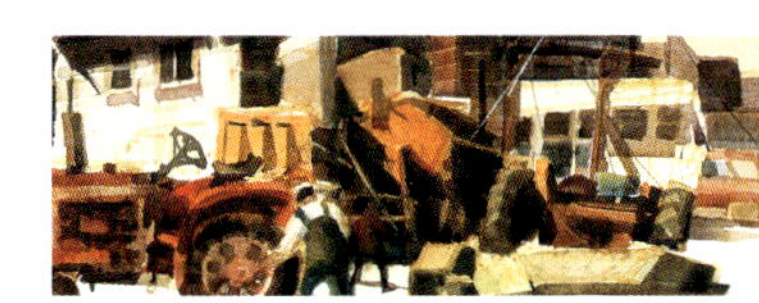

CRINKLING TECHNIQUE 揉纸法

No.	Title	Year	Size (in)	Size (cm)
29	St Paul's Cathedral 圣保罗教堂	1978	21" x 31"	54cm x 79cm
30	Goldfish 81 No.1 金鱼 81 年 1 号	1981	25" x 40"	63cm x 102cm
31	Autumn 83 No.1 秋 83 年 1 号	1983	25" x 40"	63cm x 102cm
32	Winter Pleasure 冬天乐	1984	25" x 40"	63cm x 102cm
33	Duluth Winter 86 No.1 都鲁之冬 86 年 1 号	1986	25" x 40"	63cm x 102cm
34	Springtime Lake View 湖岸春光	1987	25" x 40"	63cm x 102cm
35	Spring 96 No. 1 春 96 年 1 号	1996	30" x 40"	76cm x 102cm
36	Autumn 89 No. 1 秋 89 年 1 号	1989	24" x 36"	61cm x 91cm
37	Winter 96 No. 1 冬 96 年 1 号	1996	25" x 40"	76cm x 102cm

MARBLING 拓印法

No.	Title	Year	Size (in)	Size (cm)
38	Lost Horizon 83 No.1 缥缈 83 年 1 号	1983	24" x 36"	61cm x 91cm
39	Lost Horizon 83 No.2 缥缈 83 年 2 号	1983	24" x 36"	61cm x 91cm
40	Clouds, Earth, Water 云、地、水	1983	24" x 36"	61cm x 91cm
41	Rhythm of the Shore 岸边旋律	1996	30" x 40"	76cm x 102cm
42	Koi Pond 锦鲤荷塘	1996	30" x 40"	76cm x 102cm
43	Canyon with Junipers 古柏幽谷	1996	30" x 40"	76cm x 102cm

SATURATED WET 纯湿法

No.	Title	Year	Size (in)	Size (cm)
44	Goldfish 85 No.1 金鱼 85 年 1 号	1985	25" x 40"	63cm x 102cm
45	Koi 90 No.4 锦鲤 90 年 4 号	1990	25" x 40"	63cm x 102cm
46	Iris 90 No.1 蝴蝶兰 90 年 1 号	1990	25" x 40"	63cm x 102cm
47	Goldfish 90 No.1 金鱼 90 年 1 号	1990	25" x 40"	63cm x 102cm
48	Koi 90 No.2 锦鲤 90 年 2 号	1990	25" x 40"	63cm x 102cm
49	Koi 90 No.9 锦鲤 90 年 9 号	1990	35" x 43"	89cm x 110cm
50	Koi 92 No.1 锦鲤 92 年 1 号	1992	30" x 40"	76cm x 102cm
51	Goldfish 92 No.1 金鱼 92 年 1 号	1992	30" x 40"	76cm x 102cm
52	Lily Pond with Koi 荷塘锦鲤	1992	25" x 40"	63cm x 102cm
53	Goldfish 89 No.1 金鱼 89 年 1 号	1989	30" x 40"	76cm x 102cm
54	Koi 95 No.1 锦鲤 95 年 1 号	1995	30" x 40"	76cm x 102cm
55	Roses 95 No.1 玫瑰 95 年 1 号	1995	25" x 40"	63cm x 102cm
56	Koi 96 No.2 锦鲤 96 年 2 号	1996	30" x 40"	76cm x 102cm
57	White Iris 白蝴蝶兰	1996	30" x 40"	76cm x 102cm
58	Orchids 胡姬花	1996	30" x 40"	76cm x 102cm

Splash Color 泼彩法

59	Lake Shore 82 No.1 湖岸 82 年 1 号	1982	30" x 40"	76cm x 102cm
60	Lake Shore 82 No.3 湖岸 82 年 3 号	1982	30" x 40"	76cm x 102cm
61	Li Jiang at Dawn 漓江拂晓	1982	40" x 60"	102cm x 152cm
62	Along the Li River 86 No.1 漓江 86 年 1 号	1986	30" x 40"	76cm x 102cm
63	High Snows 雪山	1986	30" x 40"	76cm x 102cm
64	Along the Li River 89 No.2 漓江 89 年 2 号	1989	30" x 40"	76cm x 102cm
65	Lake Shore 93 No.1 湖岸 93 年 1 号	1993	30" x 40"	76cm x 102cm
66	Lake Shore 93 No.2 湖岸 93 年 2 号	1993	30" x 40"	76cm x 102cm
67	Yangzi River 93 No.1 长江游 93 年 1 号	1993	30" x 40"	76cm x 102cm
68	Yangzi River 93 No.3 长江游 93 年 3 号	1993	30" x 40"	76cm x 102cm
69	Spirit of Southwest 95 No.1 西北精神 95 年 1 号	1995	30" x 40"	76cm x 102cm
70	Spirit of Southwest 95 No.2 西北精神 95 年 2 号	1995	30" x 40"	76cm x 102cm
71	Along Colorado River 95 No.2 科罗拉多河 95 年 2 号	1995	30" x 40"	76cm x 102cm
72	Along Colorado River 95 No.3 科罗拉多河 95 年 3 号	1995	30" x 40"	76cm x 102cm
73	Canyon Mist 峡谷积雾	1995	30" x 40"	76cm x 102cm
74	Lake Shore 95 No.1 湖岸 95 年 1 号	1995	30" x 40"	76cm x 102cm
75	Lake Shore 95 No.2 湖岸 95 年 2 号	1995	30" x 40"	76cm x 102cm

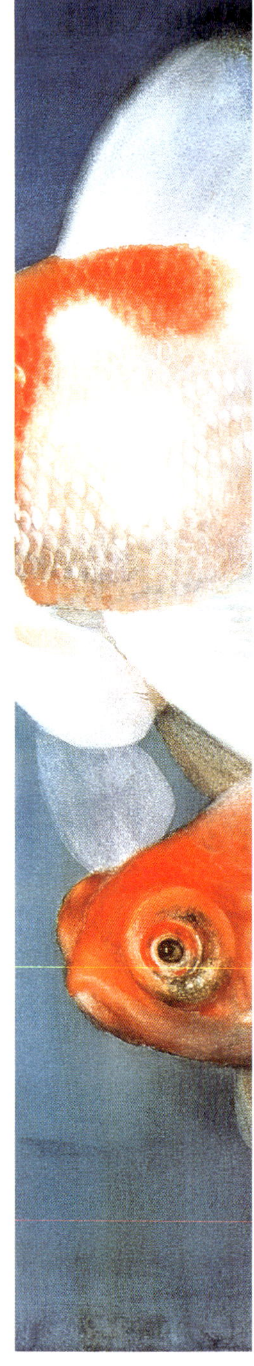

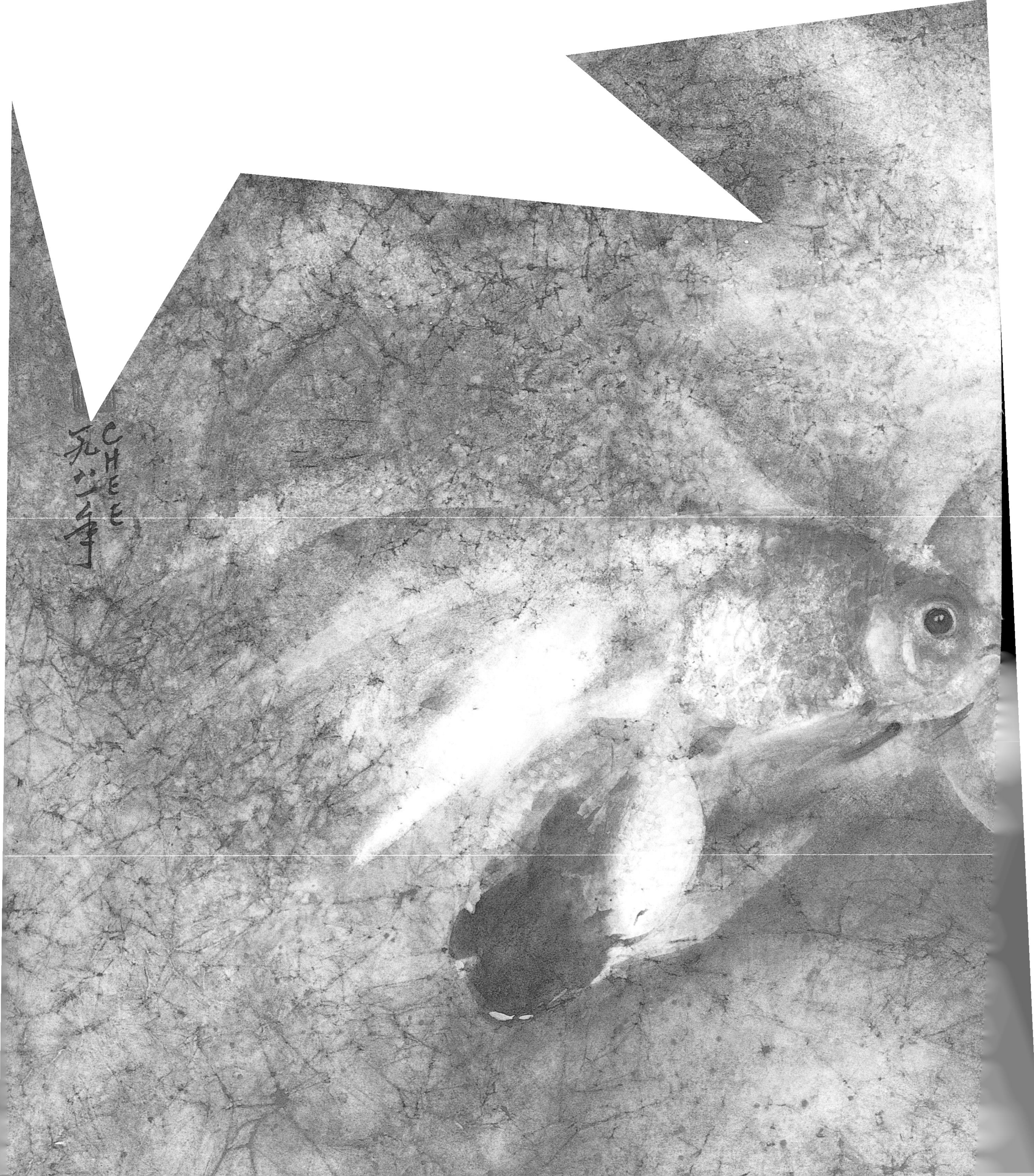
CHEE